The Law Comes To Texas

Major John B. Jones, Commander of The Frontier Battalion and Adjutant General of Texas. Courtesy The Texas State Library, Archives Division.

The Law Comes To Texas

The Texas Rangers
1870-1901

by

Frederick Wilkins

STATE HOUSE PRESS

Austin, Texas

1999

Library of Congress Cataloging-in-Publication Data

Wilkins, Frederick, 1916-
The law comes to Texas : the Texas Rangers, 1870-1901 /
by Frederick Wilkins.
p. cm.
Includes bibliographical references and index.
ISBN 1-880510-60-X (alk. paper)
ISBN 1-880510-61-8 (pbk. : alk. paper)
1. Texas Rangers—History—19th century.
2. Texas—History—1846-1950. 3. Frontier and
pioneer life—Texas. I. Title.

F391.W67 1999
976.4'061—dc21   98-40940

Printed in the United States of America

cover design by David Timmons

STATE HOUSE PRESS
P.O. Box 15247
Austin, Texas 78761

Table of Contents

*This book is dedicated to the memory of
John B. Jones,
commander of the Frontier Battalion,
Adjutant General of the State of Texas,
and truly a man
who made a difference.*

Acknowledgments

The author wishes to thank the members of the Archives, Texas State Library, for their many services during the research on this history. Donley Brice was especially helpful, as always, sharing his own studies on N.O. Reynolds as well as his vast knowledge of the archives. Every member of the department, by phone, mail or in person, assisted in some way in the task of screening the Ranger Papers.

Appreciation is also due to the library personnel of Trinity University, San Antonio, the Main Library of San Antonio, and the University of Texas at San Antonio.

Albert McNeel kindly allowed the author to read and use his grandfather's memoirs and other documents covering the Garza Trouble.

Ralph Elder at The Center for American History, University of Texas at Austin, photocopied numerous documents from the Center's Leander McNelly Papers, saving a no-longer-young writer many trips to Austin.

Preface

The nineteenth-century history of the Texas Rangers during the three decades from 1870-1901 is probably the best known in the Ranger story, certainly the most popular. The "Wild West" gave a certain legendary twist, not just to Texas lore but to all of American history. As I have often stated, separating myth and legend from actual events is not a simple task; it does not help that actual events were sometimes more startling than the myths.

In 1870 the Texas frontier was little different from earlier days, still a lawless territory raided by Indians and renegade Mexican bands but now harassed by a considerable number of white outlaws. Expansion to the west was complete, but warring gangs dominated entire interior counties. Once again, Texas turned to the Rangers.

The Rangers of the 1870s and following decades were little changed from the men of the 1840s and 1850s. Their weapons continued to improve as cartridge arms replaced muzzle loaders. The men still furnished their horses and equipment. In one basic improvement, for the first time a Ranger force was permanently established. This prospect of permanency corrected a defect in all of the earlier Ranger units; an experienced cadre of Rangers was maintained in service, despite mandatory reductions during times of financial crisis.

Starting as a military battalion's patrolling the western border areas, the Rangers soon became a police force trying to suppress outlaw bands along the rapidly developing areas of the disappearing frontier. Additional Ranger companies were formed solely to fight white criminal gangs. In these exciting final decades of the century, the Texas frontier vanished, railways crossed the state, the last Indian fight took place early in 1881, telegraph and telephone became normal means of communication, and the typewriter began

to be used in Ranger correspondence. The Rangers adapted
to all of these changing conditions, shifting from paramilitary duties to police actions and even to individual detective
work. Their important role within a changing Texas has been
overlooked and overshadowed by gunfire and gore.

My only agenda in this tale is to tell an accurate story
without apology, glorification, or revisionism. In recent years
there has been a tendency to tear at the Ranger legend and
confuse the exaggerated events which occurred during World
War I with *all* of the Ranger deeds before and after. It has
been almost a matter of glee to point out that Leander H.
McNelly was not even a Ranger but a member of the "Washington County Volunteers;" McNelly, a hard commander in
a harsh time, must be judged in terms of his era. One of the
Rangers, Bass Outlaw (his true name), has been cited to
exemplify that *all* Rangers were drunken killers; but Outlaw
served well, and when he strayed he was kicked out of the
Rangers—as were others, enlisted and commissioned, who
failed to maintain the strict standards of conduct set for the
Rangers. Their standards are examined in this book, as well
as the status of McNelly and the Washington County Volunteers—Rangers all!

What emerges from thousands of pages of muster and
pay rolls, reports, memoirs, newspaper accounts and diaries
is not always the fluff of romantic writers. When it is all
examined, the Rangers appear as neither the villains nor the
supermen which some writers have chosen to depict. By and
large they did an outstanding job, especially considering the
small number of men in the force. This is the story of the
Rangers, both the famous and the almost forgotten. It is
history, not romance, and the tale unfolds as the records
and their memories indicate it happened.

This is the way the Rangers would have wanted it.

— 1—

Reconstruction in Texas
1865-1873

The last land battle of the Civil War was fought in south Texas on May 13, 1865, not far from the old battlefield of Palo Alto. It was a month, more or less, after Appomattox, and the Confederate victory changed nothing—not even in Texas. By an ironic coincidence, Colonel John S. Ford, the Texas commander in this last battle, had also played a key role in the Mexican War's last battle which also took place after a formal peace had been signed.[1]

Despite a meaningless victory the fighting was over, but another war of sorts was developing. Like the rest of the defeated South, Texas was facing Reconstruction; unlike her fellow ex-rebels, Texas was a frontier state with vast areas not only unsettled but largely unknown. Of the states now under military rule, only Texas was faced with the threat and reality of Indian raids, and while lawlessness was not uncommon in the Old South following the Civil War, Texas had a problem of major proportions.

Geography accounted for much of the problem. State maps of the era show an outline very similar to today's but do not reveal the reality on the ground. The Panhandle was uninhabited, a blank area on the maps. Buffalo hunters crossed the region from time to time, but major terrain features were largely unknown. A major division of the Comanche people roamed the region in complete freedom.

The Trans Pecos area of far West Texas was crossed by a few stage and military roads. Below the small settlement of El Paso del Norte on the Rio Grande, several tiny settlements and old missions marked the limits of settlement to the southwest. Abandoned army posts along the stage road were the only sign of civilization from Castroville, a few miles west of San Antonio, to El Paso, an area the Mescalero Indians claimed as their land. The old Comanche War Trail cut through the area from the northern plains to northern Mexico.

While the southern part of the state, from the Nueces River to the Rio Grande, was officially the United States, it really belonged to whomever was on the land at the time, and then only if they were well armed. A number of settlements had developed or expanded following the Mexican War, joining the old town of Laredo, and several army forts had been located along the Rio Grande, but they had never been able to control the Indian and Mexican raiders. Abandoned for some time following the Civil War, these forts did little more than provide shelter for the homeless.

During the war years ranchers and rustlers had slipped down into the Strip, gathering up cattle and land not protected by other armed riders. Rustlers from south of the Rio Grande continued their time-honored custom of rounding up Texas cattle. The usually lawless border had been further aggravated by conditions in Mexico during the U.S. Civil War, when Mexico had been forced to accept a foreign ruler, Maximilian, and the U.S. had been too-otherwise-occupied to protest the establishment of a monarchy there. The Republican forces led by Benito Juarez never fully submitted and waged a guerrilla campaign that was still going on at the end of the American Civil War. The Imperialists favored the Confederacy, the *Juaristas* supported the U.S. Federal Government, and there was an active trade, legal and otherwise, between Texas agents and foreign brokers in Mexico. Deserters from both armies in the United States, and Mexicans fleeing from the fighting in Mexico's interior, ended up along the Rio Grande; when the Civil War ended there were several thousand men, out of work or on the run, scattered along the lower Rio Grande. Cattle rustling advanced from grabbing a few head in Texas to an organized business.

There was little popular support for law enforcement agencies even within the settled areas of Texas. As federal troops assumed control of the state, they briefly tolerated and then removed elected officials, replacing them with men who were considered Union supporters. In 1867 District Judge Richard Coke, an ex-rebel, was removed from office by General Philip Sheridan, who merely stated Coke was "an impediment to reconstruction;"[2] the phrase was all that was required to oust any former Confederate from office. Over time most of the officials in Texas, from the governor to county clerks, were removed and replaced. The average Texan looked on their new officials with feelings ranging from distrust to disgust.

Texas, however, suffered less from the "carpetbagger" than did other southern states. Her carpetbaggers were more often Texans who had sided with the Union or who had fought in Texas units in the federal army. These men usually expected some reward for their loyalty to the Union, but for each man thus rewarded there was an ousted official, with his family and friends, who turned against the new government. Many Texans began to believe the law was weighed against them and that if justice were to be obtained, it had to be by a gun.

John Wesley Hardin, who would play a notorious role in this era, wrote down his impression of Reconstruction justice following his initial brush with the law.

> This was the first man I ever killed, and it nearly distracted my mother and father when I told them. All the courts were then conducted by bureau agents and renegades, who were the inveterate enemies of the South and administered a code of justice to suit every case that came before them and which invariably ended in gross injustice to Southern people, especially to those who still openly held on to the principles of the South.[3]

Hardin had just killed a black man under conditions that seemed justifiable to him. He would kill many more men, usually under conditions he considered good cause. In fairness, some of these killings were self-defense or allowable under the rules of the day, but nevertheless he completely disdained the law when administered by a black policeman, militiaman or soldier. In his memoirs he describes how he and "about 25 men good and true" reacted when they thought a mob of black police in Gonzales were going to "depopulate the entire country." They sent word to the blacks to come along, but there would not be enough of them left alive to tell the tale. The mob dispersed. Hardin also mentions the attempt of a black posse sent from Austin to arrest him in September 1871. He killed three of them and sent the survivors home "sadder and wiser."[4] It is a small step from disregard for *one* form of law to complete disregard for *all* law, and the use of black policemen had an inflammatory effect on many Texans. They quickly assumed the right to shoot a black policeman; in time it became acceptable to kill *any* policeman.

It was a time of extended families, which sometimes led to family feuds with distant cousins and in-laws' actively supporting their kin. Wes Hardin became involved in the most famous of these struggles, the bitter Sutton-Taylor feud, which started with a simple disagreement over a cattle drive. One of the Taylors accused Bill Sutton of moving stolen horses in a herd they were sending to market; words led to gunfire. Hardin, a Taylor in-law, became involved in the fight, which soon turned DeWitt and Clinton counties into a battleground and cost numerous lives as relatives and friends rallied to support their side. The feud was actually misnamed, since it involved only one Sutton, but what law there was in the region supported him and soon became the Sutton faction, a situation which caused Hardin much bitterness and led him to further violence.[5]

The Texas Hill Country, with its large German population, was another potential trouble spot. Fredericksburg, Comfort and Boerne had been settled in the 1840s by German immigrants who, for the most part, remained loyal to the Union during the Civil War. Some suffered bitterly for their loyalty; their neighbors' distrust for German-speaking people carried over into Reconstruction and would eventually break out into open conflict for years.

Texas remained under military occupation for approximately four years after the war. President Ulysses S. Grant's order for elections to be held on November 30, 1869, to return Texas to civilian control, did not signal the end of Reconstruction for the majority of Texans. Major General John J. Reynolds, the Reconstruction military commander and a friend of President Grant's, took a firm hand in the approaching election, favoring Edmund J. Davis in an election which was actually no more than a contest between two factions of the Republican Party. Reynolds did everything possible to insure a win for Davis, even changing voting days to favor his man. The black citizenry, a significant bloc, was believed to have voted almost entirely for Davis. Few former

Confederates could vote; the voter list seemed to consist only of blacks or former Union men.[6]

There was never any official count of the votes; Reynolds simply announced Davis had won, and Davis was sworn in as provisional governor on the day his election was announced. He began to sign papers as governor even before his official swearing in on April 28, 1870,[7] which seemed an act of no consequence at the time but which would result in a major conflict at the end of his term of office.

The new governor would become one of the most controversial chief executives in Texas history. In all fairness, Davis was faced with monumental problems. The breakdown of respect for the law has been cited, but the recurring and unending threat of Indian raids presented a more immediate danger along the entire Texas frontier and even into more settled areas. Many Texans took a tolerant view of gunfighters and outlaws, but they were deadly afraid of the Indians. Control of the Indians was the responsibility of the U.S. Army, and the federal government had begun sending garrisons to some of the abandoned army forts as early as 1866. Unfortunately, there were never enough soldiers for this task. The huge army at the end of the war in 1865 was demobilized as rapidly as possible, and there were fewer and fewer soldiers available to meet the continuing Indian threat in Texas.

There was yet another difficulty in defending the frontier. Initially the federal government would not allow state troops—which would have been composed largely of ex-rebels—to protect the Texas frontier under the reasonable belief these units might be used to coerce freedmen. Federal officials a long way from danger refused to believe there was any major Indian threat and considered the constant Kiowa-Comanche depredations nothing more than horse-stealing raids which posed no threat to white settlers. General Reynolds reported that wholesale murders in the interior counties presented a more urgent need for troops than did the isolated Indian raids.

People in the frontier counties saw matters in a different light. As early as July 1866, residents of six counties petitioned for relief from Indian attacks. In Jack County, one of the hardest-hit areas, surviving residents abandoned their farms on the frontier and sought shelter around the small settlement of Jacksboro. Several years later, when the army was still considering the raids to be a matter of a few lost horses, they compiled a list of 129 known dead for the years 1859 to 1871. There was no way to count the missing and injured. Stock losses were in the thousands.

During the post-Civil War years, the U.S. Army did not believe there was an Indian problem in north and west Texas except for some horse stealing by individuals and small bands which could be controlled if the Texans were to exercise more care. When General W.T. Sherman and a small escort narrowly escaped a war party that would later massacre a wagon train, the army position began to change. Construction of a major post near Jacksboro and the assignment of a cavalry regiment did not solve the problem. Some relief occurred when the humanitarian policies under Quaker control of the Indian reservations were changed to allow the arrest and trial of suspected renegade Indians. Within a few years the administration was to remove the Quakers from control of the reservations,[8] but in the meantime the Texas government had to look to the defense of its own territories.

Governor Davis began his administration on a positive note, addressing the need for protection of the exposed Texas frontier. Davis briefly traced the evolution of Indian troubles in Texas, both in Spanish-Mexican times and during the Anglo settlement, and disputed the belief that the Indians were merely trying to right old wrongs. He iterated the national government's responsibility for defense of the borders, but he stated that Texas must look to her own protection, despite the financial burden, if the federal government failed in its mission.[9]

The Twelfth Texas Legislature, looking back to historical precedent, authorized the governor to form a Frontier Force of twenty companies to protect the northern and western frontiers. Each company was to consist of a captain, a lieutenant, a medical officer, three sergeants, four corporals, a bugler, a farrier and fifty privates.

Lawmakers allowed for adequate pay of $100 a month for the company commander and $80 for each lieutenant. Enlisted pay was set at $54 for sergeants, $52 for corporals and farriers, and $50 for privates.

Ranger traditions were continued; the men had to furnish their own horses, equipment and arms. To provide for more uniform weapons, however, the state intended to obtain the most effective breech-loading cavalry long arms and ammunition; the cost of his weapon was to be paid from the first money due each man. Each man was required to have a six-shooter of army size and a good horse, both to be inspected prior to enlistment. The governor was authorized to contract for fifteen hundred arms and necessary ammunition. The state was also to furnish provisions, and forage for the mounts when practicable.

The act establishing this Frontier Force—in effect reestablishing the Rangers—required recruitment from frontier counties where possible. The governor was to divide the frontier counties into districts, each with a district commander who could form the various companies in his area into whatever force was required to meet an emergency. Enlistments were for twelve months. Rangers were to be governed by the same laws and regulations as were army units; other provisions provided for paymaster and special agents to arrange for contracting supplies. The act was to be effective after June 13, 1870.[10]

In such manner Rangers, by whatever name, returned to Texas.

Passing a law, however, did not automatically translate into frontier defense, and several factors not addressed in the act would arise later to hamper the new Rangers. The agreement between General Reynolds and the governor to allow the Rangers to draw supplies from army depots would cause future problems. Although the legislators stipulated proper pay, they never did appropriate enough money; an adequate force was authorized but not funded, and it would not be long before finances would undercut Ranger numbers. The Ranger companies were also formed in the frontier counties where there was a limited pool of available recruits. Throughout, there was confusion between the provisions of the act forming the Frontier Force and certain Special Orders implementing the act.

It also took time to select the various company commanders. In late June, John R. Kelso wrote the adjutant general, noting that he had seen his name announced as one of the new captains and asking for specifics on mustering his men.[11] H.R. Biberstin received his commission on August 10 and immediately wrote asking for instructions.[12] J.P. Swisher, trying to form a company in early August 1870, had twenty-five men ready in Lampasas County but was confused by a letter, from one of the assistant adjutant generals, which seemed to suspend the entire process of forming the Frontier Force.[13]

Kelso evidently had some of his questions answered; on August 11 he wrote about reporting to San Antonio but asked where to report and to whom. He was also curious about the pay of his medical officer because the amount of compensation would largely determine the qualifications of the doctor. Despite his problems, he optimistically expected to be able to report to San Antonio with his men on or before August 27.[14] In actuality, Kelso did not muster-in until September 10, 1870.[15]

Suitable recruits were scarce in some counties. In early August Franklin Jones, the commander of Company A recruiting in Mason, his designated station, wrote the adjutant general complaining that a Jim Hunter, "supposed to be a Captain of the Rangers," was discouraging men in the county from joining Jones' unit by telling them Jones had no authority to form a company and that, if they joined, they would be paid in script. Jones claimed that Hunter's actions had delayed him in filling his unit, and also that a Mr. Biberstin of Fredericksburg in Gillespie County

> has made application for a Commission [. He] also has been telling the men who were anxious to join my company that they would be as the old Rangers by being paid in script at a discount, causing them to sell their horses and return to their homes. I can only say such men as the aforesaid are not fit for a private in any company.[16]

Despite the not-always-gentlemanly competition for recruits, the companies began to take shape. Captain Gregorio Garcia was first on line, taking station in El Paso County in the western tip of the state on August 21, 1870. Captain Jones and Captain John W. Sansom had their men mustered four days later.[17]

The composition of the companies reflected the population of the counties where recruited. Garcia, in El Paso County, had a largely Hispanic company, as did Captain C.G. Falcon based in Starr County. Company H in Zapata County also contained many Hispanic recruits.[18] Captains occasionally recruited men about whom they had reservations to fill their ranks; Captain Jones reported to the adjutant general that he had a fine company except for several men who had developed into troublemakers. He wanted authority to discharge them.[19] A few Rangers either brought old grudges into the ranks or developed new hatreds after enlisting. On November 3, 1870, Private Frank Holmes shot Private J.S. Singleton four times in the back, killing him instantly.[20] Fortunately, such extreme cases were rare, and the vast majority of the new Rangers expended their energy chasing Indians.

By the end of August 1870 only five companies had been mustered into service, and recruiting continued until November 15 when the final unit was officially formed [see list at Appendix A]. Although the authorized twenty companies were never mustered in—lack of recruits and funds held the number to fourteen[21]—it was still the largest group of Rangers in service since the Mexican War. After the companies were formed and mustered in, however, many still faced long marches to reach their assigned districts. In some cases, a month or more was required before they were able to begin active scouting.

Financial realities continued to hamper commencement of Ranger activities. It became clear during the formative weeks of enlistment that there would not be enough money to pay even the fourteen companies that were forming. General Order No.8, from the adjutant general, directed reduction of each unit to a total of only fifty officers and men, solving the problem of the few undesirables but also cutting most companies by twelve men, a considerable reduction. Because the number of privates varied in each company, the reduction was not uniform; Captain A.H. Cox lost only six men while Captain Sansom listed the full twelve.[22]

In some ways the loss of manpower was not as troublesome as the decision of the Secretary of War to overrule General Reynolds and refuse to allow the Rangers to be supplied from army stores. This action in October 1870 forced Ranger captains to contract for their own supplies and forage, a task not always easy on the frontier. Each captain did the best he could, but suddenly having to provide their own supplies hampered operations and cut into already meager operating funds.[23]

In spite of all obstacles, the Ranger companies gradually took their posts and began scouting. Captain Sansom's

Company C was at work in October, patrolling Kerr County. They encountered one Indian band and recaptured six horses and two mules. This minor success was offset by the forced mustering-out of Company A on November 12, 1870.[24]

Although the primary mission of the Frontier Force was to defend the northern and western borders, Captain H.J. Richarz' Company E was dispatched to Fort Inge, below Uvalde and recently abandoned by the army, with the mission of countering raids from Mexico. In early December 1870 one of his patrols chased a raiding party from below the Rio Grande and recaptured five horses in their initial contact.[25]

At first glance, Captain Richarz seems an unlikely prospect for a Ranger company commander. Born near Cologne at a town on the Rhine where his father was second *burgomeister*, young Richarz grew up in a military tradition and entered the rifle legion in which his father had fought during the Napoleonic Wars. He was promoted several times but resigned to take a position with one of the new railroads. During the widespread revolutionary outbreaks in Europe in 1848, Richarz sided with the losers and decided he had to leave Germany for his personal safety. After considerable hardship, he and his wife and family finally reached San Antonio. Despite shipwreck and harsh overland travel, he managed to save some Saxon merino rams and went into partnership with a friend in the first sheep-raising enterprise to use merino stock.

Richarz moved to Medina County in 1853 and settled into a new life on the frontier where the former infantryman, schooled in the rigid tactics of European warfare, was tossed into the middle of Indian combat. The German adapted as if born on the frontier. In the 1850s he served as a leader of civilian scouts, and he served as a major commanding mounted home guards during the Civil War. He remained in unofficial, volunteer service until 1870.[26]

His experiences had taught Richarz the necessity of constant patrolling, and he kept his men out as much as possible. Departing Fort Inge with fourteen Rangers and three civilian volunteers on December 5, 1870, Richarz began scouring the extensive area between the San Marcos and the Rio Grande in search of a raiding party that had stolen horses about a hundred miles from his post. The first day out they met couriers from Fort Duncan and learned that an estimated three hundred Comanche and Kiowa warriors were down from the north and that another two hundred Lipan and Kickapoo raiders were up from Mexico, all well-equipped with firearms as well as their traditional weapons. About twenty-five miles above the Rio Grande, Richarz met another messenger and learned his second scouting party had been in a hard fight with one of these bands.

This second Ranger scouting party was led by Doctor J.E. Woodbridge, who had volunteered to suspend his medical practice and serve as an officer, assisted by Corporal Eckhart. Their patrol, also fourteen strong but with three of the men on a side scout, met an estimated seventy Comanches about twelve miles north of the Rio Grande. The Indians formed two lines on a slight rise and soon flanked the eleven Rangers, who made a stubborn resistance using their repeating Winchesters to wound several of the Indians. In the rush and circle of a typical Indian fight, Woodbridge was hit in the head by an Indian and unhorsed in a hand-to-hand encounter. Several of the Rangers broke through to him and drove back his attackers. In this early stage of the fight, Ranger Lorenzo Biediger was killed.

The three absent Rangers heard the sounds of heavy firing and returned at a run, striking the flank of the surprised Comanches, killing a chief and breaking the circle for the time being. After some heavy firing, the Comanches fell back about three hundred yards, reformed and left the field. The Rangers remained in the vicinity to rest their horses.

Reports of war parties in every part of the sector were no exaggeration. One band killed two Rangers within sixteen miles of the fort, but from the tracks and empty cartridge cases the two young men, Private Walter Richarz, son of the captain, and Private Joseph Riff, had made a gallant fight. By the time Captain Richarz returned to Inge, Lieutenant Xaver Wanz had departed with the reserve force to track the party that had slain the two Rangers.

A report of a war party near Uvalde caused no panic; as soon as they had rested their horses, most of the men started out after the lieutenant, either to help him or to cut off any Indian retreat to the north. Taking his last three men, Richarz started south to find Doctor Woodbridge and must have been relieved to meet the doctor and other Rangers just outside the post. Woodbridge had recovered and was carrying a chief's shield as a trophy. The several days of scouting and fighting in this series of engagements had cost three Ranger lives, but eight Indians had been killed and possibly another fifteen wounded.

In his report of these events, Captain Richarz asked for men to replace the losses brought about by General Order No.8, pointing out that he could not field two strong patrols with only thirty-eight privates. The tribes based in Mexico were operating in complete safety and freedom and had notified him they were going to drive him out and sweep the country north to Bexar. Richarz told the adjutant general that he would do his best, despite his small command. He was neither the first nor the last Ranger to feel that if it were not for the restrictions of international law, he would know how to handle the problem.[27]

A Ranger scout that resulted in serious fighting was the exception; most of the patrols—and there were many—did not lead to combat. Such reports as remain in the archives have a sameness: days of scouting, infrequent fresh Indian sign, now and then spotting a few Indians driving stolen horses. A typical occurrence was reported by Company L on January 3, 1871; the Rangers chased three Indians on foot into dense brush and recovered several horses.[28]

First-person accounts of Ranger activities in this period are rare. The only detailed version was written in his later life by Ranger A.J. Sowell, a private in Captain David P. Baker's Company F. Young Sowell, desiring to see something of Texas besides his home town, enlisted on November 5, 1870, the day the unit was mustered into service. His experiences give contemporary readers some idea of what Ranger service was like in 1870-1871.

What would become Sowell's Company F formed on the Salado near San Antonio, at a location Sowell believed to be near the 1842 battlefield. From the Salado, fifty-two officers and men began a long winter ride north to their patrol area in the Wichita Mountains. In bitter cold December weather they reached Captain J.P. Swisher's camp in central Texas, men and horses' suffering from constant sleet storms. They had a supply wagon, but provisions were low and the Rangers began to suffer from hunger. Obtaining some supplies at Fort Griffin, they headed for Jacksboro and Fort

Richardson, near which newspapers blowing across the open country were grim reminders of a recent stagecoach ambush on the stage road between the two army posts. They had left Jacksboro on December 20, 1870, after having been on the road one month, and supplies there must have been limited because Sowell recalled they had only parched corn and salt for Christmas Day. The snow-covered ground and low temperatures limited hunting for fresh meat.

Snow melted as the weather moderated somewhat in January 1871. The Ranger company was now in its assigned patrol area, and Captain Baker started sending out scouting parties. The Indians, taking advantage of the slightly warmer weather, began to come down from the reservations. In mid-January, Sergeant E.H. Cobb and eighteen men were sent to an advance camp twenty-five miles above the main base. A subsequent move to a location twenty-five miles south of the Red River placed them very close to the Indian routes into the Texas settlements.

In early February, Sergeant Cobb and twelve Rangers found and began to follow the trail of a war party of raiders. On February 7, when the Rangers finally came in sight of the Indians and discovered they had been trailing over forty braves, about half on horseback, they were none too pleased at facing such odds. Cobb dispatched one Ranger, who managed to depart without attracting pursuit, to the nearest ranch to bring settler help. After the long chase, the Rangers' horses were tired; Cobb realized they would be unable to run if attacked or to pursue if the Indians fled. None of the Rangers had ever been in an Indian fight, and only Cobb and one other ex-Confederate had ever been in battle. The sergeant was a good soldier, passing out what extra ammunition he had and cautioning his young followers not to fire at long range.

Late in the day, with an estimated two and a half hours of sunlight remaining, a chief rode out from the Indian ranks and began the classic Comanche riding feats designed to draw enemy fire. At three hundred yards he galloped about, dropping to the side of his horse, raising and lowering his shield, dashing towards the Ranger line for a short distance then galloping back. None of the Rangers fired at such a range and Cobb ignored the rider. Shifting his men to one side and discovering a second Indian group in the high grass, Cobb moved the Rangers to a ravine, still without drawing an attack. At this point, Sergeant Cobb decided to attack, explaining his plan to his men.

The Rangers advanced slowly towards the two Kiowa and Comanche raiding parties, and Cobb had them dismount about eight yards from the nearest Indians. Firing from under their horses, the Rangers took advantage of the high grass. Believing they were facing settlers with single-shot rifles, the Indians charged after the Rangers' first volley. When the Rangers continued to fire with their repeating Winchester carbines, however, the Indians broke and ran or hid in the grass, using their shields to protect their backs. As far as the Rangers could see, however, little damage was done by either side.

Cobb did not like his position and had his men move towards a slight hill. Believing the Rangers were trying to escape, the Indians charged again and easily caught up with the tired Ranger horses. Hand-to-hand fighting ensued; an Indian chief was killed and Private Billy Sorrell was seriously wounded. Private William Caruthers was hit by a spent ball. Fully armed with lance, bow and arrows, many Indians also had firearms, and the Rangers faced a barrage of arrows, rifle balls and lance thrusts. Unable to overrun the Rangers, the Indians fell back.

Just before sundown the Kiowa chief gathered his men and made a final charge against the Rangers, who had regrouped around the gravely injured Sorrell. Waiting to fire until the Indians were within pointblank range, they killed the Kiowa chief and another brave at twenty paces, wounding several others. The Indians retreated with the body of their dead chief but, largely out of ammunition and with broken-down horses, the Rangers entertained no thought of following the scattering Indians. Supporting Sorrell on a horse, they rode slowly to a ranch where the gravely wounded Ranger was able to get medical attention.[29]

Accustomed to fiction and Western movies, readers may be puzzled why the hundreds of rounds fired by the Rangers caused so few casualties among the Indians. Never still, an Indian on horseback made a poor target, and an Indian's hiding in tall grass was neither easy to see nor to shoot. The large, circular shields carried by the Kiowa and Comanche warriors, constructed of double-thickness buffalo hide covered with deerskin and often with padding between the layers of hide, were undoubtedly able to stop many of the bullets fired at them, even at close range. In the early 1870s the Rangers were still using percussion-cap revolvers with low muzzle velocity. Although the new Winchesters were repeaters, they fired an earlier rim-fire case with low muzzle velocity and limited range. In order for the rim-fire's copper case to be detonated by a blow from the hammer or striker, it had to be thin and therefore could not withstand high gas pressure. Powder charges were therefore light; the cartridge used in the Winchester held only twenty-eight grains of black powder.[30]

Sowell often describes how the Indians, charging and retreating, used their shields to cover their bodies. The shields were slung on a thong, allowing the brave to use both hands for bow or gun when necessary. Sowell notes that few Rangers escaped Indian battles without numerous bullet holes in their saddles, clothing or equipment. Life on the Texas frontier was not a Western romance in which horses could gallop forever; men in combat were sensibly frightened, jittery, and fired many rounds without striking their targets, which were some of the best horsemen in the world.

The few records which remain, in the archives or in print, reveal few positive Ranger accomplishments in return for the money, time and lives spent in 1871. In addition to the events described, the following actions are listed in reports of the adjutant general:

> Captain Falcon's Company G caught up with Mexican cattle thieves on April 21, 1871, and recovered 130 head of stock, wounding one rustler;

> Captain [B.] Chamberlain of Company H arrested several rustlers on February 25, 1871;

> Sergeant R.V. Parker and eleven Rangers from Company B caught a band of Indians in Palo Pinto County, killed ten of them and recaptured forty horses. Four Rangers were wounded in this fight on May 4, 1871;

> Captain Swisher of Company P had a skirmish

with Indians on January 23, 1871, killing one and wounding several others. Thirty-eight horses were retaken.[31]

Considerably more, however, was accomplished than is indicated by these few incidents. Indians tended to avoid regions in which they observed the tracks of shod horses, and there is little doubt that Indian raids decreased in the districts patrolled by the Rangers. The settlers certainly observed a difference; when Captain Kelso's company was scheduled for mustering out in January 1871, the settlers in the Uvalde region sent a strong letter of protest to the adjutant general, noting the work done by the Rangers.[32]

The safety of the frontier settlers, however, was outweighed by the state's shortage of funds. Kelso's unit was disbanded January 20, 1871, and one by one the other companies were also mustered out. By mid-June 1871, the Frontier Force was no more.[33]

In an effort to furnish some protection against continuing Indian raids, twenty-four Minute Companies were authorized November 25, 1871 [see list at Appendix B]. These so-called companies were nineteen-man detachments much like the county detachments of the late 1850s. Considered Rangers, the Minute Men furnished everything except their arms, ammunition and accoutrements, which were supplied by the state and which remained state property. There were enough Winchester carbines in store to supply the detachments, but the state's treasury was still depleted and the Minute Men were paid at a set rate of two dollars a day for only ten days a month, and then only when Indians were actually in the county.

Even with the limitations on their service, Minute Men reports list six Indian engagements in 1872 with twenty-three raiders killed and sixty-five horses recovered. One Ranger was killed and three wounded during the year the Minute Men were in service.[34]

Many of these detachments were reorganized at various dates in 1873 [see list at Appendix C]. Seventeen of the units saw some service on a pay status; an additional five detachments were formed to meet emergencies and served without pay. The 1873 Minute Men/Rangers saw some action and engaged Indians on nine occasions, killing four raiders and recovering 117 horses. One Ranger was killed. Money set aside from the sale of bonds was not enough to pay everyone in the force, and it was some years before the legislature passed a deficiency appropriation to pay them for their service.[35]

Governor Davis made a final effort to bring the Indians under control on November 1, 1873, when he called out eleven Ranger companies, each to serve for four months [see list at Appendix D]. There was no money to pay these men, and they were formed subject to future legislative appropriations. Events in Texas were moving in other directions, however, and these Rangers played little part in slowing Indian attacks. Only a report of recaptured horses indicates that at least eight of these units were ever formed. In this report, for the first time these companies were designated "Rangers."[36]

These 1873 Ranger companies nevertheless possessed one important feature. Based on the experiences of the fifty-man companies of 1870-1871, the 1873 companies were expanded with an additional lieutenant, four new corporals, and twenty-five privates for a total of seventy-five officers and men.[37] It was a change that would influence the legislators when they reestablished the Rangers in 1874.

The return of the Rangers in 1870 to combat Indian raids along the frontier was matched by the creation of a second force to handle the widespread breakdown of law in the interior counties. Traditionally Rangers had been employed to defend against Indian and Mexican incursions, and this was still considered their proper role, but a strictly police force was also deemed necessary to support law enforcement in the interior. On July 1, 1870, the State Police came into being as a police force which could operate anywhere in Texas without regard to county boundaries. Efforts *were* required to match the growing lawlessness in Texas, but unfortunately the work of the State Police never matched that of the Rangers. Far from solving the problem of lawlessness, they came to be perceived *as* the problem.

The controversial story of the State Police is an interesting one,[38] but it is important to Ranger history only for the impact the State Police would have on the further breakdown of law and the determination of legislators in Texas to maintain a tight rein on future law enforcement entities. There are two, often widely different, documentary versions of the State Police. Most contemporary accounts depict the

Police as a reactionary, repressive body more intent on raising money by fines than on administering justice, but the official documents of the Davis administration report the State Police to be a positive force for good with an impressive arrest record. For example: from July 1 to December 31, 1870, there were 978 arrests listed by the Police, of which 130 were on murder charges and another 130 for assault to kill. Based on incomplete county records, there were 2,790 persons wanted for various crimes in the state. Governor Davis pointed out that this arrest record had been achieved with a reduced State Police force and urged the legislature to increase it,[39] but what might have been a cause for support for Governor Davis eventually turned out to be one of the most unpopular acts of his administration.

As originally organized, the State Police consisted of four captains, eight lieutenants, twenty sergeants and 125 privates. Every other police officer in Texas was also a member and subject to the call of the adjutant general. Of the original captains, only Leander H. McNelly made a name for himself as a peace officer, but only *after* he left the force.

The Police wasted little time in beginning what was perceived as a deliberate pattern of abuse and extortion. Early in 1870 a Police posse searched the house of one Colonel James Gathing who, angered by the illegal act, gathered some friends and "arrested" the Police! The citizen posse took the prisoners into Hillsboro, where the justice of the peace bound them over to a date when there was no court in session, thus insuring no trial would be held. A few days later, Adjutant General James Davidson and one hundred armed men rode into town and told the sheriff they had come to arrest the mob that had captured the State Police.

Trying to avoid a blood bath, the sheriff first talked Davidson into keeping his men in town, then he went out and talked the colonel and his friends into surrendering. Believing they had done nothing wrong, the unsuspecting men rode into town and were thrown into jail. The true purpose of Davidson's visit was made clear when he demanded $5,000 in gold, or else he would place the county under martial law and quarter his men on Colonel Gathing. The sheriff bluntly told Davidson he would never have persuaded the men to surrender if he had known the result.

Texas was a poor state and $5,000 in gold was an impossible demand, but the threat of martial law was grave enough for many of the county leaders to bargain with Davidson. One lawyer brought in $1,500; the sheriff and the lawyer canvassed the county and raised another $2,000; Colonel Gathing signed a note for the balance. There is some question about the amount Davidson finally accepted; the newspaper accounts mentioned $2,765.[40] As one editor lamented, "Here we have the melancholy and humiliating spectacle of an officer engaged in plundering a citizen of his property by aid of military power...."[41]

Unfortunately this was not an isolated incident. An altercation with State Police in Groesbeck on September 30, 1870, resulted in a civilian's being shot by the State Police. Attempts to arrest the Police were futile; they fled to shelter and were protected by a large party of armed blacks. Local officials made every effort to avoid a situation that would lead to martial law. Citizens petitioned the governor not to declare a state of emergency, but Davis placed Limestone and Freestone counties under martial law and assessed a penalty of $50,000 to be paid by a three percent tax.[42]

As respect for law decreased, especially as displayed by the Police, even the threat of martial law was not always enough to preserve the peace. When a black man was murdered in Walker County, Captain L.H. McNelly and a detachment of State Police were sent to investigate the killing, quickly arrested four men suspected of the murder, and brought them in for trial. After a preliminary investigation lasting three days, one of the men was released and the other three were held for the next regular court session. When this decision was announced, there was a loud cry of protest from the packed court room. The three accused men rose and opened fire on the judge and the prosecuting attorney; the sheriff and his deputies had conveniently neglected to search the prisoners. McNelly and one of his men rushed forward and were wounded; the other State Police fled the scene. In the confusion the prisoners escaped, and when the sheriff tried to form a posse only two men in town volunteered to help.[43]

After Governor Davis declared martial law in Walker County on February 15, 1871, Adjutant General Davidson formed a military commission to try twenty people accused of complicity in allowing the prisoners to escape. One man was sent to the penitentiary for five years; others were fined. The so-called expenses of the commission were paid by a twenty-five cent fine for each one hundred dollars of taxable property in the county.[44]

There was one positive result from this episode; McNelly, while recovering from his wound, had time to reflect on his service with the State Police. It was more than a man of his character could stomach. In an interview at the time, McNelly stated he did not believe martial law was necessary and was little more than an excuse to raise money.[45] Neither McNelly's frankness nor his service in the State Police had any negative influence on his later career, and within a few years he would return and become one of the Ranger legends.

While there was never any formal, organized resistance to the State Police, certain individuals and families were in open war with them. No town or county wanted to risk being put under martial law with its attendant financial burdens, but some individuals simply shot their way clear when confronted by the Police. It is not surprising that Davidson could compile a list of several thousand wanted men.

John Wesley Hardin headed Davidson's list, and Hardin's notoriety attracted even more attention to the Sutton-Taylor battle that had started as a disagreement between two men over stock and then had become a bloody struggle between two factions for supremacy in DeWitt and Clinton counties. Jack Helm, a former State Police captain, was now sheriff of DeWitt County and leader of the faction opposed to the Taylors. His chief deputies and co-leaders in the gang were Joe Tumlinson and Jim Cox. Bill Sutton, another of Helm's deputies,[46] was the man who had been involved in the original altercation and was the only Sutton family member involved.[47]

Since Hardin was an in-law rather than a blood relative, Helm seems to have believed he could persuade the young man to change sides and offered the gunfighter the choice of being with them or against them. It was a simple decision for Hardin, who remained loyal to his in-laws. In late April 1873, Helm and fifty men attempted to capture or kill Hardin and his friends. In May they were unlucky enough to run into Hardin; in the shootout two of Helm's men were killed.

Helm, retreating from the use of force to diplomacy, met Hardin and Jim Taylor to arrange a truce in a small settlement in Wilson County, but the meeting ended in another gunfight in which Helm was killed. According to Hardin,

Taylor was the one who shot Helm, but Hardin was blamed. Hardin said that most law abiding people thanked him.[48]

There were no more shootings until December 1873 when one of the Taylor supporters was killed. Jim Taylor tracked Bill Sutton to Indianola where his old foe, whom he had made previous efforts to kill, was preparing for a cattle drive north. There was a face-off and Sutton was killed.[49] Taylor escaped; he and Hardin remained at liberty by hiding with friends and evidently had little trouble in evading what passed for the law.

Charles Webb, a deputy from Brown County, was the next lawman to take a part in the fighting. It was never clear if Webb was a secret partisan of Tumlinson's, now the leader of the anti-Taylor forces, or merely trying to make a reputation as the man to bring down Hardin, but he was killed when he attempted the arrest. Young Hardin surrendered to the sheriff of Comanche County where the fight took place, but it soon was apparent that the dead deputy had not come alone when a gang tried to take Hardin and Taylor from the sheriff. The disgusted prisoners "unsurrendered," regained their horses and arms and fled.[50]

There was nothing to set apart Webb's death from a score of other shootings credited to Hardin, but it would be this killing that would be the cause for his later arrest. The "feud" in DeWitt and Clinton counties was the largest and most bitterly fought struggle to challenge the Rangers and would provide continuing work for them in later years.

By 1873 direct challenges to the authority of the State Police had become more frequent. One of the more famous encounters took place in the settlement of Lampasas, where it was common for the more enlightened members of the community to meet in a local saloon, play cards, drink some whiskey and discuss the matters of the day. These philosophical musings must have become rather loud at times, because some of the quieter members of the community petitioned the governor for help in keeping the peace. Davis, always eager to keep the peace, as he saw it, sent a detachment of the State Police to Lampasas.

A family of six brothers had a great deal to do with the Police's being summoned. The Horrells, ranchers, hunters and skilled marksmen raised on the frontier and not inclined to accept restraint in any form, had a considerable reputation as troublemakers and were evidently mentioned by name when the complaint was sent to Austin. Asking for directions on the way to Lampasas, a Captain Thomas Williams commanding the Police detachment mentioned he was going to Lampasas to "clean up the dammed Horrell boys."

In Lampasas the Police tied their horses and left them under the guard of the black member of the patrol while the three white members, with a civilian volunteer from town, entered the saloon. Williams walked to the bar and asked for a drink. Seeing a man to one side with a pistol belt and weapon, Williams stupidly told him he was under arrest. Mart Horrell got up from a table and told the officer the man had done nothing and should not be arrested. Williams turned and shot at Horrell, wounding him.

The saloon turned into a battlefield as the other Horrells started firing, joined by most of the men in the room. Williams was slain instantly; a Doctor Daniels who had joined the Police was shot down at the bar. One of the state policemen managed to get through the saloon door before being killed. The third officer died out in the street. Hearing the firing, the black officer mounted his horse and fled.

Davis sent a larger militia force to Lampasas but did not invoke the punitive measures of earlier days. Mart Horrell and his friend Jerry Scott were later arrested and taken inland to Georgetown, where it was thought they were far enough from relatives and friends to be secure. On the frontier, however, friendship and family often triumphed over geography; a strong party made the long ride from Lampasas, broke into the jail, and released Horrell and Scott.

The Horrells and some friends gathered their cattle and started on a leisurely ride to New Mexico. They notified the sheriff of when and where they would pass a prominent landmark, but the law wanted nothing more to do with this family. The brothers settled in New Mexico for a time, getting into trouble with anyone who crossed their path. In time they returned to Texas[51] where, along with other problems like Hardin, Mexican raiders and the German-American frictions, they would provide much deadly work for the Rangers in the coming years.

As the election of 1873 approached, people in Texas turned to politics. Unlike the election of 1870, there seemed to be a chance for ex-Confederates to have a vote that would make a difference. Evidence from newspapers, diaries, memoirs and oral tradition indicate that most Texans of the day did not favor Governor Davis, although recent historians have tended to be kinder to Davis than his contemporaries.

Support for Davis declined, even among Republicans, as he continued to preside over a growing disaster of lawlessness. A cultured and personally honest man, he headed a corrupt administration; poor men entered the legislature and became rich. State Treasurer George Honey neglected to keep records, for good reason, and the state was approaching bankruptcy as Davis' term came to close. Amidst all this corruption, Davis was nevertheless responsible for the passage of laws establishing free schools and improving education to the extent that frontier Texas was decades ahead of most of the nation in this respect. Tragically, money for many improvements was squandered on other things.

The Davis empire was collapsing when the Thirteenth Legislature assembled and abolished the State Police. The people of Texas had suffered enough, and Republicans joined Democratic foes to abolish the hated body. Adjutant General Davidson had a keen eye for timing as well as extortion; collecting over $37,000 from the state treasury, he fled the country.[52]

Davis was opposed by Richard Coke, the Democratic nominee, in an election marred by considerable fraud on each side. No soldiers were assigned to control the voting on December 2, 1873, and Davis lost by almost a two-to-one margin. At first Davis refused to accept the results, although he admitted he had been outvoted, and clung to a technical interpretation of the law by claiming he should be governor until April 28, 1874, four years from the date he was officially sworn in. The Democrats pointed out he had in fact assumed office earlier as provisional governor, and in a move that surprised no one the Texas Supreme Court declared the election void. The old Thirteenth Legislature refused to acknowledge the new Fourteenth, and Austin became an armed camp. The capitol became a fortified area with each faction's defending part of the building.

It is incredible that the dispute did not end in a gun fight. To Davis and his supporters it became clear that they did not have enough support to win a street battle, so they put their faith in presidential action and telegraphed Washington for help. Coke, however, was very careful to avoid anything that would give the federal government an excuse to declare martial law; he and his supporters had worked too hard to lose everything by a rash act. On January 12, 1874, President Grant sent a telegram saying the election results had been examined and there was no reason to interfere. Grant concluded, "would it not be prudent, as well as right, to yield to the verdict of the people as expressed by their ballots?"[53]

The same day the new legislature met and organized while armed men patrolled the streets of Austin. The Travis Rifles, the local militia company, gradually brought order to the town, but for several more days Davis and his chief officials refused to surrender vital seals and records. In a last desperate move to stay in office, Davis wired for aid from the Attorney General of the United States. The answer, much the same as before, was the last hope for the Republicans; the federal government had examined the election and saw no cause to interfere. There were still some delays, but a new administration was in power and reconstruction in Texas was over.

— 2 —

The Frontier Battalion
1874

Texas' new Democratic administration faced severe challenges in the opening months of 1874. The frontier counties, under threat of Indian attack and with little or no local law, were in a state of chaos. In the settled counties, the constant replacement of officials at the pleasure of Austin had turned even law-abiding persons against the justice system. The State Police had been abolished, but the organization had lasted long enough to give all lawmen a bad reputation. The state was in debt, and the nation's economic Panic of 1873 was being felt. Governor Coke and the legislature could envision solutions to some of the problems, but the funds required to put then into practice would be slow in coming. Once again, the need to protect the frontier was a high priority, and by April 10, 1874, the legislature had completed work on a General Act, to provide for the defense of the frontier, which would be the basis for restoring law to Texas. Despite the shaky financial status of the state, the legislature allocated $300,000 to pay the costs of implementing the act.

The legislature realized that the state required defensive forces to meet the threats they faced, but at the same time the legislators did not want another police force that would dominate civilian life. Some members must also have remembered the perennial problem of short-enlistment Ranger companies. The 1874 act was clearly an attempt to address the potential problems of frontier and interior defense with both short-term companies to meet a specific, localized emergency, and a larger, *permanent* force to protect the frontier.

To meet the first need, the governor was authorized to

John B. Jones, Major of the Frontier Battalion. Photo courtesy of the Texas Ranger Hall of Fame and Museum, Waco, Texas.

raise twenty-five to seventy-five man companies in any county needing special protection. If necessary, these companies could cooperate with similar units in adjoining counties. The companies, military forces of the state, would be governed by the rules and regulations of the U.S. Army and would be paid the same as other state forces raised under the act. The members of these companies were to be enlisted for an emergency and would revert to civilian life when the emergency was over or when the governor so decreed.

In Section 19 of the act, the legislature addressed the second need, for a permanent force.

> That in addition to the force herein provided for, the Governor be and is hereby authorized to organize a battalion of mounted men, to consist of six companies, of seventy-five men each. The commissioned be one major, who shall command the battalion, and one captain and two lieutenants for each company, and one Quartermaster. The battalion and company officers shall be appointed by the Governor, and shall be removed at his pleasure.

Other sections stated the battalion was not to be a standing force but could be moved, assembled or disbanded as the governor's judgment and "exigencies of the frontier may demand." Earlier military forces had usually been raised to meet a specific emergency or for a stated period of time, but these new units were to remain in the field as part of an over-all defensive plan to be paid for from regular funds of the state. The soldiers volunteered for a period not to exceed four years. Each soldier would furnish his own horse and be reimbursed if the animal was lost in service. The state would furnish arms and ammunition at cost, the amount to be deducted from the first pay of each soldier.[1]

In drafting the new law, the legislature was clearly establishing a paramilitary force, an Indian-fighting unit, and the men are everywhere described as "soldiers." The organization was patterned on the U.S. Army. At no point in the act is the term "Ranger" used, although the legislature had reverted to the earlier Ranger custom of having each man furnish his own mount and weapons. They also, however, evidently considered the conditions in Texas and decided the soldiers might have to serve as police; Section 28 stated, "Each officer of the battalion and of the companies herein provided for, shall have all the powers of a peace officer. . . ." The detested State Police had nevertheless possessed one good feature—they could cross county lines and operate anywhere in the state; the obvious intent of the drafters of the act was to enable the soon-to-be-raised battalion members also to be able to act as police as well as to fight Indians. At the time, no one gave any thought to possibilities of later and special interpretations of the act, and it would be a quarter-century before a matter of the phraseology would destroy the battalion.

Laws passed are, after all, only words on paper. It takes actions to make the laws work or fail, and Texas was fortunate in having a governor determined to make his new laws effective. Richard Coke was a man worthy of the challenges that faced him. Physically impressive, a man who had been a soldier and officer in the Confederate Army, he fitted the popular concept of a frontier fighter. Coke had already appointed William Steele to be adjutant general, a key position in bringing back law and order, and on May 2, 1874, he designated John B. Jones of Corsicana to be the major in command of the new battalion.[2]

The selection did not meet with widespread approval. Jones was not well known across Texas, and many people believed a man with frontier experience should have been chosen. The doubts about Jones would die hard; as late as August, friends of Jones and the governor would be defending the appointment.[3] There had been numerous other candidates for the job, of which William Jeff Maltby, an experienced Indian fighter, was the best known. When the news of the formation of the battalion was announced, James W. Taylor, a friend of Maltby's, organized two petitions in Burnet County. One went to Maltby, asking him to take command; the other went to Governor Coke asking him to select Maltby. Taylor took the petition to Austin and actively campaigned for his man. Coke listened, but his mind was made up. He replied politely that he didn't know Maltby, but he did know Jones, had served with him, and knew what he could do.[4]

Maltby traveled to Austin to plead his case personally. Coke did not change his mind, but he did offer Maltby command of one of the companies. The frontiersman did not think he could accept a lesser position, but events on the frontier changed his mind. For at least eight years Maltby had been trying to catch or kill a Kiowa chief named Big Foot, but for some time there had been no sign of the raider and Maltby had hoped the Indian was dead. While still in Austin, however, he heard that Big Foot was very much alive, again raiding, and had killed several people near Maltby's home; Maltby returned to Coke and accepted the command of a company, providing he could have James G. Cornell as his first lieutenant. Coke, after conferring briefly with his adjutant general, accepted the terms. Maltby, not noted for his modesty, was given Company E and said his lieutenant was the only officer not selected in Austin.[5]

Maltby's appointment and that of Cornell are among the few officer appointments that can be explained; how Coke selected the other five captains and numerous lieutenants is guesswork. G.W. Stevens had commanded Ranger detachments in 1870-1872 and one of the companies in 1873; while little is known as to his accomplishments, he evidently impressed the governor. Another designated captain, C. Rufus Perry, was an old Ranger who had served with the legendary Jack Hays in the days of the Texas Republic. However selected, the new Ranger commanders were soon well known in Texas. Adjutant General Steele published General Order No. 1, forming the Frontier Battalion. General Order No. 2 was published the same day, outlining the battalion.[6] Major commanders were:

Commander	Major John B. Jones
Company A	Captain John R. Waller
Company B	Captain G.W. Stevens
Company C	Captain E.F. Ikard
Company D	Captain C.R. Perry
Company E	Captain W.J. Maltby
Company F	Captain Neal Coldwell[7]

The general orders also contained instructions for the new captains, who were to call their lieutenants and proceed to form their units as quickly as possible. The period of service would be twelve months, unless sooner discharged. Since it was expected the force would be actively employed, the captains were to enlist young men in good physical condition, without families, who owned good horses. Drunk-

Captain Neal Coldwell. Coldwell had a lengthy service as a Ranger, first as a company commander, then as the Battalion Quartermaster.

ards and persons under indictment or with known bad character were not to be accepted for service. The captains were to make temporary arrangements to supply necessary foodstuffs—beef, bread, coffee, sugar and salt—and present receipts to the battalion quartermaster who, however, had not yet been selected.

Considering that the captains were meeting lieutenants they did not know and were going out to a frontier that was sparsely settled to recruit men not known, the formation of the Frontier Battalion proceeded at remarkable speed. The only detailed account of these first days is Maltby's description of the organization of Company E. In Austin, the adjutant general gave him two mules and a hack filled with arms and ammunition and told him to go recruit. Maltby sent Lieutenant Cornell to Brownwood to recruit twenty-five privates, the orderly sergeant, and one duty sergeant. When this was accomplished, Cornell was to go to Camp Colorado and instruct Lieutenant B.F. Best to raise twenty-five men, a duty sergeant and two corporals. Maltby remained in Burnet County to recruit another twenty-five privates, the commissary sergeant, two duty sergeants and two corporals. All detachments were to assemble in Brownwood in two weeks. The three officers found their men, and the new company assembled in Brownwood to take the oath and be sworn into service. By the time muster rolls were prepared and Company E ready for duty on May 30, 1874,[8] Maltby and a few of his men had already been busy returning two stolen horses and bridles to their owner.[9]

Major Jones played a quiet but key role in the early days of the battalion. He remained in Corsicana during much of May, watching each detail of organization and issuing Special Orders to distinguish them from the General Orders of the adjutant general. Jones was concerned about arming the new men, many of whom did not have personal weapons, and on May 15 he ordered two of the companies to await instructions from Austin on arming their men. He decided at an early date not to waste time assembling the entire battalion in one location; instead the companies were ordered to assemble in the counties they were assigned to protect.[10] The stationing of the companies determined to a large degree what type of activity and how much trouble each unit would face. Location would give some companies an opportunity to make outstanding records while others, just as capable, simply did not encounter much opposition.

Five of the companies were organized and on line during the last half of May. Company F was slower, not filled until June 4,[11] but activities were not delayed. Captain E.F. Ikard of Company C had a fight with raiding Indians on May 7 before his unit was officially formed and sworn in. Ikard and six men chased a band of Indians who had stolen a herd of cattle, engaging them in a running fight for fifteen miles. They wounded one Indian, captured a horse and killed another, and recovered $1,500 worth of stock.[12]

Captain Waller, commanding Company A, was among the first, if not the first, to have his entire company on line and in action, but they were to fight white desperados rather than Indians. Stationed in Comanche County, his company found itself in the midst of the Sutton-Taylor trouble and the chase after John Wesley Hardin. Sixty years later J.H. Taylor, who with his brother joined Waller's company in Comanche on May 23, 1874, wrote down—with a great deal of original spelling and punctuation—his memories of his first days in the unit.

> Write from the start the County was overr Run with lawless characters & among them was that notorious killer John Westley Hardin the evening before Capt waller arrived Hardin & two of his men killed Charley Webb a Deputy Sheriff from Brownwood rite on the street of & defied arrest & rode out of town with Pistols poppin our work commenced at once & continued for three weeks we had at one time seventeen Prisoners at one time in a rock building some of them was turned loose some went to the Pen & three was mobbed it took just three weeks to clean out that part of Texas but we done a finished job. . . .[13]

Waller's official reports show Taylor had a good memory.

> I commenced scouting at Comanche, Comanche County, the 28th day of May,...three fourths of my Command was kept in constant service until the 12th of June, during that time I made over twenty two arrests. Seven of the Parties arrested I sent to

Dewitt County, supposed to belong to John Wesley Hardin's gang of outlaws, the other Parties arrested I turned over to Sheriffs of different Counties. . . .[14]

Waller mentions his men killed two outlaws, supposedly part of the Hardin gang. He stated he exchanged shots with Hardin, perhaps wounding him, but the outlaw escaped on good horses.

It was not all white desperados for Company A. Lieutenant J.W. Millican and a large party scouted out to Eastland County without finding any Indian sign, and the company remained in Comanche throughout June, scouting and working with sheriffs in Comanche, Brown and Coleman counties. Official reports seldom give more than the bare facts. Fortunately, Taylor wrote down a few of the events during June in Comanche, but he was careful to describe only the events in which he took part.

Comanche was a small town whose citizens lived in fear that the lawless element would burn their settlement. During their early days in Comanche the Rangers camped five miles west of town and were alerted one night by a frantic rider who was certain that outlaws were burning the town. Sergeant Halstead and forty men galloped into town ready for a battle, but the fire was accidental, not arson. Afraid for the safety of the town, however, Waller moved the company into the main square.

Taylor describes several scouts after outlaws. In one the Rangers were after horse thieves. Early one morning before most of the men had eaten breakfast, a man remembered by Taylor only as Mr. Hesley rode into camp and said some thieves had stolen horses from his father-in-law and that he could show them where the trail started. Despite the hour, one of the sergeants took out his notebook and wrote down the names of the nearest ten men, who saddled up and were led by Hesley to where the thieves had broken down a rock fence and stolen five horses.

A little-used trail beside the corral had not been used by the thieves. Scouting around, the Rangers picked up a trail, in the tall grass that covered the countryside, which the outlaws evidently believed would cover their tracks. Having trouble keeping the horses together, they rode slowly, and by afternoon the Rangers had caught up with the men, who were still working to control their stolen animals. Seeing the Rangers, they let the animals go and tried to reach a small hill. Cut off by a wide circle of some of the pursuers, they halted, dismounted, formed their horses into a circle and waited, rifles across their saddles.

The leader began cursing the Rangers, but the sergeant refused to become excited and pointed out their hopeless situation to the surrounded men, who surrendered after a half hour of shouting back and forth. Taking their prisoners, the hungry Rangers rode back a few miles to a water hole and spent the night. They were up and riding before daylight, arriving back in camp about three in the afternoon. Taylor estimates they had ridden 65-70 miles without food for the two days. They reached camp "tired out but Mr. Campbell had his horses & law had the thieves such was part of the life of the Texas rangers 68 [years] ago We indeavered to make life & Property saffe regardless of the hardships that we had to under go. . . ."[15]

By and large, fugitives had a chance to surrender to the Rangers and, if they gave up, were brought in alive. During the three weeks Company A was in Comanche, they arrested twenty-two men and brought all in alive. They did, however, kill two who did not surrender, in an incident also described by Taylor.

According to Taylor, the countryside was split into two factions, outlaws and others, with spies from one faction watching the other. Taylor never mentions the Sutton-Taylor troubles, but he does indicate the Rangers considered Hardin the leader of the outlaws; during this period, almost any wanted man was considered part of the Hardin gang. Taylor does not date this scout, but from the official reports it must have occurred in June 1874, the only month in which the Rangers reported killing anyone during their stay in Comanche.

Two wanted men were known to have relatives in Comanche County, and the Rangers began watching for them. They had an extra inducement; the widow of a slain man had offered $1,500 for the arrest of the two men. Taylor did not remember any names, but the only men killed during this time were identified only as Barkman and Anderson, murderers of Colonel Love of Navarro County.[16]

The eastern half of the county was an area of dense thicket with few streams. A few settlers lived in the regions near water, but the area was basically a hideout for every degree of outlaw. Not infrequently, out of fear or sympathy, the settlers sheltered the fugitives. The Rangers had "run" the area twice, exchanging shots with fleeing men but making no arrests. It was believed one of the settlers twelve miles east of town, who came into town for supplies upon occasion, was sheltering the two murderers, but nothing could be proved.

To their surprise, one day the settler came into town and reported the general location and movements of the men to the Rangers. In short order, Sergeant C.Y. Pool had a nine-man detail ready to ride. Taylor's horse was lame, but his brother was one of the detail and later told him the story. Sergeant Pool and his men took all the cold food they could stuff into their saddle pockets, reached the home of the repentant settler, and found a log cabin and a small out-building about eighty feet from the larger structure. The sergeant and four of the Rangers hid in the cabin while the other five with all the horses remained in the woods. One of the wanted men arrived soon after the Rangers were in place, but Pool wanted both of them and made no move. When the man rode off again, Pool sent a messenger back to camp with his location.

Lieutenant Millican, back in camp and preparing for a night sweep through the southwest part of the county, changed his plans and rode to help Pool, arriving about midnight. Taylor does not mention the fact, but Millican may have had civilian reinforcements.

The combined Ranger forces divided into two groups; Pool spread twenty men in a skirmish line, and Millican scattered ten men along the edges of the thicket covering two sides of a rough triangle. Pool and his men, the third side of the triangle, slowly rode in the dark through the trees and brush trying to flush out the fugitives toward Millican, but they found neither men nor horses and, disgusted, reassembled. One of the Rangers who had remained on guard rode up and told Millican he had found some tracks leading into the woods but none leaving, so the men must still be in the trees.

Millican placed all but three of the men in line for a slow, quiet move through the woods. The other three Rangers were to ride along the creek bank edging the thicket in case the men attempted to escape toward that direction. Everyone was to ride toward any sound of firing.

The three men on the creek bank heard movement and the neigh of a horse and, according to Taylor,

> the two outlaws jumped up from their Pallets & shot they were asleep & the horse woke them they shot two shots the Rangers but they was shot to death immediately by the boys they made their word good They said they would not be taken alive.[17]

The activities of Company A during this period are also mentioned in Hardin's autobiography. He describes hiding out while Waller's men searched for him, and he specifically mentions actions during June when the Rangers were scouting six miles west of Comanche. Hardin's accounts generally correspond with Waller's reports, but some of Hardin's allegations and claims cannot be proved. According to Hardin, the sheriff wanted Waller to help arrest him, but the Ranger refused because he himself was part of a vigilante gang! Hardin's father told Captain Waller that his son would surrender if the Ranger would guarantee his safety, but Waller refused and roused five hundred men to search for Hardin.

Nevertheless Hardin decided to leave the country; the Rangers were making life uncomfortable for him in Comanche. He even claims Waller told him that if he stayed, the Rangers would kill his father and son "and wind up on the women and children." On his way out of the county he exchanged shots with Waller and some Rangers but escaped.[18] Shortly after his escape, a mob lynched Hardin's brother and Tom and Bud Dixon; two other friends of Hardin's were shot at their home.[19]

With about twenty allies, Hardin hid in Gonzales County where, according to him, he received a letter from Waller on June 20 with news that the Rangers were moving some prisoners to Gonzales. If any attempt was made to release them, Waller "would kill my father and little brother, and probably my wife and child, whom he now held as hostages." Hardin describes how the Rangers brought the prisoners to Gonzales and put them in jail, even though there were no charges against any of the men. On the night of June 30 the Rangers turned over the prisoners to the Tumlinson-led mob, who hanged three of the men. Two days later, eighteen Rangers attacked Hardin's camp but were beaten off and one Ranger was killed.[20]

Hardin's are the most serious allegations ever made against a Ranger officer but have little to back them. Before Hardin wrote his book in the 1890s, it seems no one noticed his charges or took them seriously. It is even likely that Hardin confused the Rangers with civilian groups, vigilante bands or his enemies with the Tumlinson faction. Waller *was* a Ranger captain for a short time, but little is known about him. From his documented actions, it appears likely he would have welcomed an attempt by Hardin to free any prisoners and thus give the Rangers an opportunity to capture the outlaw. In his monthly report for June, Waller mentioned one fight with Hardin but does not report losing any of his men, and his prisoners were turned over to the sheriff rather than to a mob. Unfortunately, some of them *were* lynched, and sixty-eight years later Taylor remembered the three unfortunates who were "mobbed."[21] Examining what evidence is available, it appears Hardin was writing about his feelings rather than facts in this part of his autobiography.

There is no dispute about Hardin's next move; Texas had become too dangerous and he left the state. Undoubtedly the actions of Company A were responsible, because the gunfighter still had a gang of twenty men who would have been more than able to hold their own against only the Tumlinson gang. He had his way in Comanche until the Rangers appeared, then he slipped away to New Orleans and even further east. He was not through with Texas, however, and the Rangers were not through with him.

The activities of Company A have been described in some detail because this unit, despite being the first to engage whites rather than Indians, has been neglected. All the companies were on line and generally active; no commander had any problem in recruiting men. By the end of June, all companies reported the authorized seventy-five men; Company A even had seventy-six, and E and C each had seventy-eight. Company C even carried a bugler on the rolls![22]

All of the officers shown on General Order No.2 reported for duty except for a few lieutenants. The most important change was in Company D where, when he lost one officer, Captain Perry offered a commission to his old friend Dan W.

Roberts who reported to his new company at the organizing camp on the San Saba River about twenty miles below Fort McKavett.[23] Perry's choice of Roberts was fortunate; Roberts would become one of the great Ranger leaders.

Company B, organized in Young County, was not as active as Company A during June. Company C was posted in Archer County, Company D in Menard, and Maltby's Company E in Brown County. Company F, near the headwaters of the Guadalupe River where it was responsible for the area between the Nueces and the Llano rivers, was commanded by Neal Coldwell and organized on June 11, the last company to be formed.[24] Although he was later than the others in arriving on line, Coldwell had one of the busiest records during the initial month of the new Rangers, exceeded only by Waller in Company A. The list of the scouts for Company F shows:

> Lieutenant Nelson   72 miles
> Captain Coldwell   150 miles
> Lieutenant Dolan   312 miles
> Lieutenant Nelson   114 miles
> Lieutenant Dolan   178 miles, and still
> out on a third scout when the monthly report
> was made.[25]

None of these extensive sweeps encountered Indians, as was true with the majority of scouts, but they served an important purpose by alarming raiding parties. Company E was also active, logging 1,095 miles on scouts during June 1874.[26]

June remained a time for organization after the rush to recruit and move to a camp. Few of the new Rangers, the generally accepted term for the unit's members, had much experience as Indian fighters. A considerable number of the men did not yet have weapons, and Major Jones spent a great deal of time seeing they were supplied with arms and ammunition. Like earlier Rangers, the men were responsible for their horses and weapons, but the state supplied them with pistols and rifles, deducting the cost from their first pay.

The files in the adjutant general's office began to fill with requests for weapons and ammunition. Captain Perry needed fifty-seven Colt revolvers, sixty-four Sharps rifles, and the full authorization of pistol cartridges for his company;[27] Company C had to wait until July for an issue of forty-one Colt revolvers.[28] Fifty-two officers and men of Company E signed a petition asking Captain Maltby "to procure for us Colts improved Breech loading pistols of the latest and best improved quality, For which we will pay cost price out of the first money we draw from the State for our services." Maltby's trip to Austin to see about delivery of the weapons displeased Major Jones, who thought Maltby should have stayed with his company and let the pistols be delivered.[29]

The Frontier Battalion was a more formal command than earlier Ranger units. The state had specified the strength and composition of the companies, and it had also officially decided how the Rangers would be armed by controlling the type of ammunition supplied—.45 caliber for pistols and .50 caliber for rifles or carbines. Although a Ranger could use any other weapon he owned or liked, he did not get free ammunition for it.

The state's choice of pistols was easy; there were thousands of percussion revolvers left over from the Civil War, many modified to fire cartridges. The new Colt revolver was another logical choice. In 1871 the Colt factory had developed a new, center-fire cartridge revolver which was an improved version of the famous percussion weapon, stronger, more reliable, firing a .45 caliber ball weighing 235 grams with a propellant charge of forty grains of black powder. Barrel lengths varied from 4 3/4 inches to 7 1/2 inches. Tested and adopted by the U.S. Army in 1873 and officially called the New Model Army Metallic Cartridge Revolving Pistol, in short order the long-barrel Colt became "The Peacemaker," favored arm of the West.[30]

The state's choice of rifles does not make as much sense, and today the decision to use the single-shot Sharps seems absurd. At the time it made more sense, even though there were a number of repeating shoulder arms such as the Spencer and Henry rifles on the market. Additionally, Winchester had opened a new factory and introduced a new, improved repeater, the Winchester 66, using the old Henry as a model.

Any of these weapons seemed superior to the large-caliber, heavy Sharps, a weapon favored by buffalo hunters, which was selected by the state. The decision to abandon the Winchester 66 was influenced by what seemed poor performance in Indian fights in 1870-1871. Army tests in 1873 eliminated the Winchester from military consideration when fine sand jammed the mechanism. Texas officials were also probably influenced in their decision by contemporary military belief that soldiers with repeaters would carelessly discharge ammunition rather than taking careful aim at their targets.

In 1873 all the repeating rifles fired rim-fire ammunition with copper-cased cartridges that limited the amount of powder that could be used for the charge. As a result the weapons had relatively short ranges and striking power with a high percentage of misfires.[31] Winchester solved this shortcoming in 1873 by designing a new, center-fire round with a brass case.

Proving again that the type of cartridge determines the type of rifle, the Winchester designers introduced a new rifle to use their new .44 caliber round, the "New Model of 1873" soon known as the "Winchester 73." By using iron instead of brass, and gun metal in many parts, Winchester's new firearm was much stronger and lighter. A special cover protected the formerly exposed loading mechanism, eliminating much of the possibility of stoppage from dirt and moisture.[32] Had this rifle been introduced a year earlier, it probably would have been the choice for the Rangers, but in Texas in 1874 it was still new, not proven, and the decision-makers in Austin stuck with a known rifle which was also much cheaper.

Although the language of the act creating the Frontier Battalion mentions "soldiers," from the first day the men were known as Rangers, a name which was already part of Texas lore even in 1874. People still lived who remembered the legendary Jack Hays and his Rangers of the 1840s. Many Rangers recalled with pride how they had become nationally known during the Mexican War, and the Rangers of the 1850s had fought Indians and Mexican bandits. When the legislature passed the act to defend the frontier, everyone believed the Rangers had returned, and the new men assumed the honored name with pride.

The commander selected by Governor Coke to direct the activities of the battalion, Major John B. Jones, was a new type of Ranger commander who provided direct supervision of his battalion in the field rather than from Austin. He made regular marches up and down the frontier, visiting each company several times a year. He was the first Ranger to control a full battalion, but he soon served in another capacity as an administrator in a role almost as important as his function as the commander.

It was a new era, and the old Ranger tradition of making do with what was at hand was unsuitable for contemporary conditions. The new state government was run like a business, and the more businesslike procedures had an impact on Ranger operations. In earlier days Ranger commanders had only to fill out a muster roll, which often also served as a pay record. Now the commanders had a variety of printed forms and records to keep current and accurate, showing money spent and the status of equipment as well as personnel in the company. The most important of these forms was the monthly return, a large, printed sheet showing the number of men in the company and the status of each. There was a section in which to list the state's property, and the condition of equipment such as tents, wagons, mules and ammunition. Another section provided for a brief account of the scouts made during the month of the report. Men recruited or lost during the month were listed in another section. The back of the monthly return was generally used to show arrests. Running out of forms was no excuse for non-submission; the orderly sergeant simply ruled off a piece of blank paper and filled it in. Quite often the remarks sections contain a plea for more blank forms. Filling in these returns and the various other records required by Austin must have been tedious and time-consuming, but today they are a treasure house for historians.

Early on, Major Jones realized he had a problem funding his command. For the first time a Ranger force was taking the field with a stated amount of money to cover its operations; $300,000 was an immense sum in comparison to earlier days but nevertheless only a fraction of the money needed to keep the full battalion in the field for a year. The appointment of Martin M. Kenney as quartermaster and pay master relieved Jones of many of his administrative duties, and either Jones or Kenney developed a plan for buying supplies. Rather than using certified accounts or script, their plan was to pay cash for supplies, principally food-stuffs. The adjutant general borrowed $70,500 from the National Bank of Austin, eventually paying $988.43 in interest, but the old method with its careless bookkeeping and payment on certificates charged against the appropriation would have been much more expensive. Adjutant General Steele estimated they saved enough money just on coffee to more than pay the full interest charge.[33] Careful bookkeeping enabled the battalion to operate a little longer.

Jones insisted his commanders keep records of every purchase made in the field, and often they had to obtain food when the regular issue of rations could not be forwarded by the quartermaster. Purchase records were forwarded to the quartermaster, where they were examined before being paid, in cash rather than script. Over the years, the records of the quartermaster became almost as expansive as records of the scouts, battles and arrests. To insure there would be no guesswork or fraud about the value of lost horses, for example, Jones had each horse appraised by three disinterested civilians and the value put in writing. Jones made no exceptions; his horse was appraised with all the rest.[34]

During this early period Jones added Doctor S.G. Nicholson to his staff as the battalion surgeon. Although his position was not authorized in the legislative act, and how he was paid remains a mystery, Doctor Nicholson served with elan, riding with Jones from camp to camp and suffering all the trail hardships of the Rangers. He was always a welcome visitor, as much for his personality as for his medical skills which, according to one observer, were seldom required because the young Rangers were a healthy lot.[35]

Jones gave his company commanders a free hand but also put his personal stamp on the battalion by riding from company to company, checking on operations and getting to know the officers and men. He had acquired a command of unknown men and had been given little say in the selection of officers, and he had to evaluate them and the senior sergeants. Jones usually rode in an ambulance, a form of light wagon, with his horse tied behind; Dr. Nicholson usually rode horseback. By July 1874 Jones had selected five men from each company to form his escort, a force sufficiently large to locate Indian trails, reinforce troubled areas, and sweep the unsettled and lawless regions that were the domain of the Frontier Battalion. Only one or two guards would have been of little use and dangerously vulnerable to being attacked by Indians. The escort never kept to roads, even where roads existed, and Jones never returned the same way from a trip so his movements kept both Indians and white outlaws guessing. He explored a great deal of unfamiliar country, checking on water sources, stream crossings, and possibilities for new roads.

His visits to the various company camps in July were the first time most of the men had ever seen him. First impressions were probably disappointing; Jones was neither a large man nor a commanding figure. At five feet and seven inches and about one hundred and twenty pounds[36] he was smaller than his captains. A neat man always well dressed who did not smoke or drink or curse, very religious and completely lacking a sense of humor, especially where his dignity was concerned, he nevertheless escaped being stuffy. The Rangers soon learned he had definite plans and expectations for the battalion, and that he never told a man to do anything he was unwilling to do himself. He had definite standards and expected officers and men to measure up to them. He had no sympathy for inept leaders or cowardly or lazy privates and removed them when found. After his first swing up and down the line of Ranger camps, the Rangers knew who was in command and what was expected of them.

In early July, Jones and his escort reached the camp of Captain Stevens near Fort Belknap. After some discussion, Jones had Stevens relocate his camp about twelve miles east of and two miles above Graham. While Jones was becoming acquainted with this last company and resting for his return down the line of camps, events were developing that would give him a chance to show how he operated in combat.

The entire area was turning into a battlefield as the Plains Indians became increasingly aware that white hunters were destroying the buffalo herds to extinction. The Indians could raise horses, or steal them from the Texans, but the buffalo provided food, clothing, and almost everything else they needed for their way of life. After 1872, white hunters began butchering the animals by the millions solely for their hides, leaving the skinned carcasses to rot on the prairie. All the Comanche and Kiowas could do was lash out in fury.

In June 1874 a large war party of Comanche, Kiowa and some Cheyenne attempted to destroy a party of hunters at Adobe Walls, a fortified camp on the Staked Plains. Although they killed three hunters outside the camp, the Indians could not break through the building walls. The hunters' buffalo guns caused great loss among the circling Indians and they finally broke off, scattered, and began a series of devastating raids along the frontier. One Kiowa chief, Lone Wolf, whose son and nephew had been killed by soldiers when they returned from a raid into Mexico, may have been at Adobe Walls, but he also began a series of revenge raids.

On July 10 a party of Kiowa braves led by the medicine man Maman-ti started south from the North Fork of the Red River in Indian Territory. The same day Comanche braves raided the Oliver Loving ranch, killing John Heath and stealing a large number of horses.[37] Two days later Loving and three of his hands were almost caught by Indians but managed to outrun them. He rode in and reported the incident to Fort Richardson authorities. The same day, Lieutenant J.T. Wilson of Company A, commanding Jones' escort, found Indian tracks along Salt Creek and reported to his commander. He was assigned the escort and some men from Stevens' company, thirty-seven in all, and sent to follow the trail.

Close to noon, the Indians who had chased Loving spotted another party of whites led by Major Jones riding up from the southwest. The original party of fifty Kiowa braves had been joined by an equally large group including some Comanches, and before the day was over an estimated 150 Indians were engaged in battle.[38] Although this may have been a high estimate, the Indians did possess superiority in numbers as they watched the whites ride up. The Indians sent out two decoys but hid most of their force along the sides of Lost Valley.

Jones and another party of Rangers had been riding hard all morning after having discovered a wide Indian trail early in the day. They followed the tracks towards Lost Valley, where their advance guard saw the two Indian decoys. The Rangers, for the most part not familiar with Indian tactics, began chasing after the two braves. Despite warnings from the main Ranger force, most of the advance guard galloped into the valley after the braves, who retreated just enough to keep the Texans advancing. The Rangers rode right into the trap.

The hidden Indians possessed many rifles, and Ranger Lee Corn was shot from his horse in the first volley. Another

Ranger dismounted and dragged Corn into some brush along a stream where, cut off by the movement of the fighting, they remained hidden the rest of the day.

When the advance guard charged headlong into the valley, Jones and the rest of his force remained out on the level valley floor but were in range of rifle fire coming from two sides. They returned the fire, though with little more for targets than smoke puffs. It was Jones' first Indian fight, the first time his men had an opportunity to see him handle himself in battle, and he maintained control of his somewhat rattled men. Retreating back along the valley to a draw, he had his Rangers dismount and prepare for the real battle.

During a pause in the fighting, the Rangers found they had two wounded men, Roger Moore and William A. Glass. Several other Rangers were missing, and several horses had been hit. Jones spread out the men in good defensive positions, using the banks of the draw for breastworks; trees along the banks provided extra protection. The Indians positioned themselves in three groups, one party circling in front of the Rangers, the other two on the flanks. There was no effort to charge the sheltered Texans; instead, with feints they tried to draw the Rangers into the open. Later there was talk of the Rangers' being surrounded, but this was never the case. From their defensive position the Texans used their heavy Sharps rifles to advantage. The big guns outranged the lighter Indian rifles, and the odds began to shift.

The leader of the war party evidently had no intention of attacking the Rangers in force after Jones' main body had refused to charge into the valley where they would have been exposed to fire. At about four in the afternoon after some long-range shooting with the Indians at a disadvantage, the Rangers heard a yell from the hillside and the Indians began riding away towards the west, taking their wounded or dead with them.

Jones decided to try sending a courier to Fort Richardson on Corn's horse, a fast animal. The Ranger was able to get through to the fort with a message from Jones who, with his men, continued to watch for Indians in the valley. Despite their orders to remain in position until it was certain all Indians had gone, a few of the men decided it was safe to go for some water. Mel Porter and David Bailey took all the canteens they could carry and rode to a water hole, unaware that a few Kiowa braves had been left in ambush near the water hole on Cameron Creek.

Porter dismounted to fill the canteens while Bailey stood guard. When the Indians attacked, Porter managed to mount his horse and run, but Bailey was cut off, surrounded, lanced and felled to the ground. Porter was also knocked from his horse and fell into the creek where the water was quite deep. The Ranger swam underwater as long as he could and finally came up for air near to where Corn and the other Ranger had been hiding all day. The three remained hidden in the brush and cane, but the Indians made no further effort to look for Porter.

Bailey was not as fortunate. Lone Wolf hacked his head into pieces and disemboweled his body. Their mission complete, the ambush party hurried after the other Indians.

By five, Jones was satisfied the Indians had gone and decided to leave. With a third of the men on foot and several missing, the dispirited Rangers began moving towards Loving's ranch where they had water and food for the first time that day. William Glass, a member of Stevens' company, had been wounded and had died, his body recovered; they were uncertain about the other missing men. About three in the morning two companies of the 10th Cavalry arrived at the ranch. When it was light, Jones and the Rangers who still had mounts joined the cavalry in a sweep through Lost Valley. They found several trails but no Indians. The previous day Lieutenant Wilson and the detached escort of thirty-seven men had, however, located the reserve camp of the war party on the Big Wichita and captured forty-three horses, many blankets, packsaddles and other camp gear. Two days later, Ranger scouts picked up a trail and followed it to a crossing on the Wichita. The main body escaped.

The Rangers found Bailey's mutilated body and took his corpse with Glass' for burial to Jacksboro where the two wounded men were left for treatment; both recovered. Jones collected his escort and returned to Stevens' camp on Flat Top Mountain. On July 14 his report of the incident included three Indians killed, three wounded, and the capture of one Indian horse and a large collection of lances, shields, arrows and other gear.[39]

It was a costly experience, but the Rangers had learned a great deal about fighting Indians. Although the honors went to the Kiowa, a major war party had been turned back with the loss of two Rangers and a ranchhand at Loving's ranch. No cattle were lost. The Indians had also lost a considerable number of horses when their reserve camp was overrun. Another result of the aborted raid was of far more significance; the U.S. Army was finally convinced that the pacific supervision of the reservations was a mistake and began a strict policy of control and all-out war on the Plains Indians.[40]

The fight was widely publicized, and the commander of the Frontier Battalion became well known in Texas. Ranger Z.T. Wattles wrote in a newspaper account of Lost Valley:

> In conclusion, I must say a word or two concerning our Major's management of the affair. His cool conduct, and at the same time his unmistakable determined courage elicited, though not uncalled for, many remarks from both experienced and unexperienced frontiersmen, as to his capacity as an officer, and carried conviction to the hearts of many not knowing him personally, that we in truth had an officer in whom we could put the utmost confidence in all cases of emergency.[41]

Jones did not tarry long with Stevens after the fight in Lost Valley. A week later he was with Captain Ikard in Archer County, where he decided to shift the company to the southwest part of Clay County not far from Stevens at Flat Top Mountain,[42] probably in order to have adequate strength in case another large war party hit the area. This done, he started south.

The Lost Valley fight was the largest of the Indian fights during this period and the largest battle the Rangers were ever to fight against the Plains Indians. The Indians never again attacked by the hundreds, but they continued to raid and July was an active month for all six of the Ranger companies. Signs of Indian were found all across the frontier. Monthly returns for the month are filled with lists of scouts; many returns have additional pages attached in order to list all of them. These extensive scouts covered thousands of miles, but few led to actual contact. Nevertheless, for the first time in decades the Indian war parties were likely to run into an armed, determined group of men who had no other purpose than chasing and killing them.

Fortunately, some of the Rangers who served in the early days of the Frontier Battalion later wrote memoirs which today provide a firsthand look at Ranger life and activities. One of the few experienced frontiersmen in the battalion, Jeff Maltby who had enlisted to find his old enemy Big Foot, left an interesting account of the first seven months of his company. He prided himself on his skill and experience but admitted the Kiowa and Comanche braves got the best of him now and then. On one scout he had his horses stampeded by Indians who had slipped into the Ranger camp. They even stole his horse, a fine animal named Solum, but Maltby did not worry too much about the loss; he knew no man could long control the wily Solum. He took one of the remaining horses and rode back to the main camp, returning with sixteen fresh horses for his dismounted Rangers, and within three days they had recaptured all the lost mounts. The sly Solum made his way back to the base camp on his own, as expected, and nothing was lost save a little pride.[43]

A man learned quickly on the frontier, or he died. Maltby remembered one terrible night during the first few months of operations when the company area was devastated by a flash flood. Carelessly camping near a stream, although the weather seemed clear when they went to bed, the Rangers were awakened by a wall of water surging over the camp. Men ran about, half dressed but with weapons and cartridge belts, trying to save the horses and wagon. The supply wagon vanished in the flood; horses floundered trying to swim to safety. When the deluge was over, one man was missing and a horse was lost. Next day the wagon was found far downstream, wedged in some trees.[44]

For a time it was difficult, if not impossible, to cross the streams in the area, but the rain and mud made tracking easy. Some of the Rangers followed Indian tracks they found near a stream in Coleman County and spotted an Indian raiding party near an isolated house. The Rangers surprised the Indians, killed one and wounded two. One of the Indians turned and began shooting at the Rangers with his bow until a shot hit his hand, breaking the bow. The brave drew a knife and rushed at Sergeant Mather who twisted to one side, avoiding the blade which drove into his horse. Several other Rangers shot the Indian and the others scattered. Collecting the weapons and gear left on the ground, the

Rangers rode into nearby Brownwood from where they started out early the next morning, even though their horses were still tired from the long scout in the deep mud. They followed the main trail of the Indians for a time, but the Indians again separated and the Rangers returned to camp.[45]

Maltby finally ended his long chase for Big Foot when the Kiowa was finally slain, justifying Maltby's primary motive for joining the Rangers. Shortly after this scout the Kiowa, who left huge moccasin prints, was riding with a Comanche band when the Rangers from Maltby's company caught them; Maltby claimed he killed the legendary leader. Another Indian, wounded and captured, told the Texas they had come from the Sill Reservation. Although they still carried and used their traditional bows and arrows, many of the Indians had modern weapons; Big Foot had been using a Spenser repeating rifle and a Remington pistol. The Rangers took a considerable pile of bows, arrows, shields, lances, saddles and moccasins as trophies back to camp.[46]

By October Maltby began thinking about winter quarters and took twenty men on a combined buffalo hunt and scout. They were fortunate enough to find a small herd, about ten miles from present-day Ballinger, and while Maltby stood guard the men began killing the animals for skins to keep their tents warm during the cold months ahead. The captain became so carried away by the excitement of the hunt that he left his post to join the buffalo chase. He was ashamed of breaking his own rules and sentenced himself to stand extra spy duty as punishment.[47]

There is little doubt Maltby was a popular commander, certainly one of the most experienced captains with a long history of Indian fighting. Despite his individual skills and high standards, he may have been somewhat too lenient in enforcing discipline, and he was definitely lax in allowing his men to have furloughs. Major Jones complained about excessive furloughs as early as July and again in August, when he countermanded some leaves in Maltby's unit.[48] Interestingly enough, Maltby seems to have borne Jones no ill will, and he praised Jones in the latter part of his account.[49]

Major Jones continued his trips along the frontier, moving from company to company learning which of his captains and lieutenants were doing their job and checking on sergeants and corporals. He wrote the adjutant general in mid-September that he was with Neal Coldwell and had approved several disciplinary actions the captain had taken. Coldwell had discharged a private and a sergeant for insubordination, a move that met with Jones' full approval. Jones also eased a lieutenant out of the battalion, convinced the man could not do a satisfactory job.[50]

Not all of Jones' problems were with Indians and white outlaws. A lot of people along the frontier, convinced the battalion was not another State Police unit, welcomed the Rangers, but they also believed the new force was sent just to protect them. Jones received requests for special placing of every unit; petitions and even demands were common, some supported by political influence. Jones, however, maintained his men where he thought they were most needed rather than where friendships or politics dictated.[51]

By October, aware that the appropriation for frontier defense would not cover an entire year, Jones was forced to make some difficult decisions. Late in the month he was again in Jacksboro where he issued instructions, and a warning reminding his commanders that the rations issued by the state were for the Rangers and not for loafers hanging about the camps on the pretext of enlisting. Another warning of things to come was ominous, "In view of the fact that it may be necessary to disband a portion of the command before a great while, no more recruits will be received until further orders." He also reminded his officers and men that they were in the employment of the government, being paid for their time and service, and consequently they should be busy all the time either on scouting between companies or on extended scouts after Indians.[52]

The monthly returns and the memoirs of men who served during this period indicate the Rangers continued to work long hours under difficult and often dangerous conditions. A partial listing of the scouts that actually engaged Indians reveals something of the battalion's actions. On July 25 Sergeant M.T. Israel of Company E engaged six Indians near the head of the Clear Fork of the Brazos. In November Lieutenant B.F. Best, also from Company E, had a running fight with Indians near Brownwood, killing three and wounding one. In this fight, two Rangers were wounded, one horse killed and another injured. The day before, Lieutenant J.W. Millican of Company A had a running skirmish in the mountains of Shackelford County, capturing two horses and two mules. Lieutenant Dan W. Roberts of Company D chased eleven Comanches in Menard County, killing five in the initial encounter.[53]

Lieutenant Roberts' fight is worth examining in more detail because Roberts wrote a full account of the scout. Major Jones was in the area visiting Company D and planning to leave when two Rangers galloped into the company's camp and said they had been attacked by Indians about five miles away. Captain Perry was with Jones over at the escort camp, leaving Lieutenant Roberts in command at the company camp, and he immediately sent men to bring the horses closer to the tents where they would be secure from any Indian threat. He then selected nine men to accompany him on the chase after the Indians. An armed civilian, John Staggs, was in the camp and volunteered to go with the Rangers.

Jones' escort had already departed their camp when Roberts and his patrol started out with men on the flanks so as not to miss any Indian tracks. About eight miles from camp they overtook the escort. Roberts said he found the escort officer, identified by him as Lieutenant Best, also following the trail with two scouts well ahead, but Roberts thought they were moving too slowly and diplomatically asked the escort officer if he might assist. Roberts, junior to the escort commander, did not want any protocol problems with the possibility looming of an Indian fight, so he and his Company D Rangers did not gallop ahead until the officer accepted his help.

The Indians had come down along the streams, raiding near the settlements, and were returning the same way. Roberts tracked them along the Saline, up a tributary, and then out onto the open prairie. They finally spotted the Indians riding slowly, and the braves halted to fight. The numbers of men on each side were roughly even.

Roberts slowed his men, cautioning them to shoot low to hit horses rather than miss a shot; the accurate Sharps were deadly but slow to reload, and Roberts did not wish to waste rounds. Roberts advanced, keeping him men in check until they were within pistol range, then the leader of the war band charged, firing as he approached, and shot Roberts' horse in the shoulder. Fearing the animal might fall and pin him, Roberts dismounted and killed the Indian.

Corporal Thurlough Weed rode up and shot another Indian who had moved to a spot where he could shoot at Roberts with a rifle. When the Indians fled, Roberts remounted, not sure his horse could run. Ranger George Bryant's sorry-looking horse, an object of jokes, easily kept up with Robert's wounded horse. They overtook two Indians riding one horse, and Bryant's shot struck the rear rider through the head. The other rider kept on for a few paces until the horse, exhausted from carrying a double load, slowed and stopped. In an expected turn of events, the rider threw up his hands and surrendered! Equally unexpected, the two Rangers allowed him to live.

Weed rode up again, and they took the Indian's weapons, tied him and left Weed to guard him. As quickly as possible they rejoined the chase, catching and killing two more Indians until Roberts' horse was too tired and too hurt to continue. The chase was halted until the escort commander galloped up with two Rangers and saw that the fleeing Indians were still in sight. They passed the worn-out Company D riders and chased the distant braves.

Roberts' men could do no more. He mounted behind one of the Rangers and they rode slowly back to camp. Two Rangers managed to get Roberts' wounded horse back late that night; much to Roberts' joy, the horse survived and gave valiant service for many more years. Weed had reached camp with his prisoner before the others and had the Indian seated before a fire. Roberts recalled the poor man looked miserable and scared, certain the fire was for him. They finally convinced him he was in no danger.

During this time, the officer Roberts thought was Lieutenant Best continued chasing the Indians, once nearing close enough to exchange shots. He may have wounded one, but the survivors reached a large creek, evidently a place they knew, with a huge rock overhang, almost a cave, that sheltered horses and Indians. The three Rangers believed they finally had the Indians cornered and fired into the darkness of the shelter. It was becoming dark, and the lieutenant sent one of his men to Menard, the nearest town. He stayed with the other Ranger to guard the cave. Help reached them by daylight, but by then the Indians had gone.[54]

The man Roberts identified as Best was actually Lieutenant L.P. Beavert of Company B, the escort commander, who killed one Indian at the cave and wounded another. During the entire chase, six Indians were killed, one wounded and one captured. Five Indian horses were captured and two killed. The Rangers had three wounded mounts.[55]

There is little doubt the Frontier Battalion was organized primarily to fight Indians, and during the first months of operations that was what they did, except for Waller and Company A. The Rangers were also available, however, to help civil authorities. Sergeant N.H. Murray arrested one "Thos. Hopper, desperado," the day after Felix Mann and accomplices were brought to justice. Company E brought in a suspected horse thief and turned him over to the Brown County sheriff. A few days later, the real Lieutenant Best arrested another thief and presented him to the sheriff. Best was a good officer, very active, who caught two more wanted men in Comanche County in July. Neal Coldwell arrested "Wm. Hobbs, burglar and thief, from Wood county," and turned him over to the sheriff in Kerr County.[56] During the first seven months in the field, the Rangers provided assistance to civil authorities fourteen times, arresting and delivering forty-four wanted men to civil authorities. They recovered $9,850 worth of cattle and horses stolen by white thieves.[57]

On October 8, Jones left Jacksboro with his escort and a force of one hundred Rangers drawn from the northern companies. The size of the scout suggested he expected to encounter a major Indian raiding party, but they marched to the Pease River and back without any sign of hostiles. When he returned, Jones reported his movements to the adjutant general and expressed his confidence in the way the battalion had developed.[58] In a matter of four months, he had made four swings up and down the frontier, taking a different route each time and covering an estimated twenty-five hundred miles.[59]

By October it was clear something drastic had to be done to keep the Frontier Battalion in the field. The $300,000 appropriation, seemingly so large at first, had shrunk at an alarming rate. The battalion was not the only command drawing on the fund; the act had authorized special units within the counties for emergencies, and several had been organized.

Under the terms of the act, two 25-man detachments,

commanded by lieutenants, were formed and held elections to elect officers and noncommissioned officers. These elections were supervised by the senior justice in the county, who swore the men into the state's service. The mustering-in papers clearly state the detachments were formed under the authority of the act of April 10, 1874. Lieutenant Refugio Benavides' command in Webb County with Laredo as a base was sworn in on June 13, 1874. On October 13 it was sworn in again for a two-month term and was disbanded December 13, 1874. Telesfero Montes commanded the El Paso County unit stationed in San Elizario. Mustered on May 27, 1874, this unit served until November 27, 1876, and had at least one fight with Apaches in September 1874. The rangers killed two Indians and captured several horses, saddles and bows and arrows. A small boy, taken eight months earlier by the Apaches, was recovered and returned to his family.[60]

A third county unit based in Corpus Christi was organized in Nueces County on June 29, 1874. Captain William Wallace led this fifty-man company, known as the Nueces & Rio Grande Frontier Men. The unit was controversial and served for about three months before being discharged on September 29, 1874. Wallace seemed to have had some success in quieting his extensive area from the Nueces to the Rio Grande, but there were a number of complaints against him and his men, mostly from Mexican citizens. These cases were referred to the courts. Wallace's troubles were a forerunner of what was ahead in the Nueces Strip; his rough headcount in part of the area listed approximately eighteen hundred people, only thirty of whom claimed American citizenship![61]

While clearly formed under the authority of the Act of 1874, these county units have not always been considered Rangers, largely because of the way some muster and pay rolls were filled in. An examination of the few surviving records of the units clearly shows they often used old Frontier Force printed forms, making pen and ink changes to the printed forms as necessary. They could not, for example, fill in the blank for company designation and instead substituted entries such as El Paso County or Webb County. Sometimes the Frontier Force heading was not changed; in other examples Frontier Men was inked in. Rarely, the term Minute Men was used. All three of the areas in which these companies were formed had been areas where either a Frontier Force or a Minute Men company had been based during 1870-1872, and it was logical to fall back on familiar terminology. Montes had been in the El Paso Company of the Frontier Forces and probably used the old forms in his Frontier Men company. In cases where printed forms were not used, all three companies submitted hand-written rolls with designations such as "El Paso County Company." There is no question these companies were Rangers and so considered themselves. On at least one roll, July 31, 1874, Wallace signed as commanding "Ranger Company."

These various commands all drew against the frontier defense fund, as did several militia companies called to duty to support civil authorities, and it was clear the money would run out long before the end of a full year. Jones had some hard recommendations to make: remain at full strength for three more months and then see the entire battalion disbanded, or greatly reduce the command but still have an active Frontier Battalion. Just how he arrived at his figures and recommendations is not officially documented. It is clear the adjutant general accepted his plan to reduce from 470 men to nearly 200, maintaining a viable force capable of expansion when money was again available. The reduction was the first of many juggling efforts and financial crises that would plague Jones during the next few years. If he had done nothing else, Jones' efforts to keep the battalion in the field would have earned him a place in Texas history.

As December approached, with the reduction a month away, Jones began summarizing what his men had accomplished in a half year. Writing from Kerr County, he told the adjutant general:

> Although the force is too small, and the appropria-
> tion insufficient, to give anything like adequate
> protection to so large a territory, the people seem
> to think we have rendered valuable service to
> them, and there is a degree of security felt in the
> frontier counties that has not been experienced
> for years before. Many on the extreme border are
> moving further out, while others in the interior are
> taking their places, and many more coming with
> them. The citizens in several unorganized coun-

ties think they will have population sufficient for organization very soon, and one county, the organization of which was broken up several years ago, and at one time since then had only one family within its borders, has recently re-organized, and is filling up very rapidly with an industrious and thriving community of farmers.[62]

Jones had reason to be proud of what his Rangers had accomplished. In the field for seven months, the men of the Frontier Battalion had made a major contribution towards restoring law and order on the frontier. At no time had the Rangers acted in a lawless or arbitrary manner; Texans were beginning to forget the excesses of the State Police and display some respect for the law. The battalion had provided a shield against the raids of the Indians, and settlers were beginning to feel secure enough to begin again to move west. It was not a full restoration of the law, but it was a strong and encouraging start.

However much the Rangers had accomplished, there was no way to overcome the money crisis. Reduction of the battalion was scheduled for December but did not take place on a specific date. Scouting and local conditions undoubtedly played a role in how many and how soon men were discharged in each company. By the end of December, Companies A and C had finished their cutbacks to thirty men in each company, commanded by a lieutenant. Companies B and D each showed thirty-one on the rolls in January; for some reason, Company F still had forty-six men in January.[63]

Not much is known about how men were selected either to stay or leave. The decision to replace all the captains with lieutenants was purely financial. Rufus Perry had been in service before and was much older than the others; leaving for him was probably easy. Maltby had accomplished his mission of killing Big Foot and evidently returned to civilian life with no difficulty. He took the fifty men discharged from Company E to Austin to be mustered out of service. There they bought him a fine suit of clothes as a going-away present and paraded up the main street.[64]

Neal Coldwell reverted to the rank of lieutenant, at least for a time, and remained on duty. Perry recommended Dan Roberts as his replacement, and Major Jones appointed

Roberts to be the Company D commander. Robert's appointment so disgusted the incumbent first lieutenant that he resigned.[65]

The less-than-half of the battalion remaining faced a formidable task. They were, however, either the best of the original crew or ones who were willing to stay and fight. They had all gone through a hard seven months in the field, and the green men of June 1874 were well-trained Rangers in January 1875.

Before leaving the events of 1874, more than passing mention must be made of another county company, as it marked the start of the Ranger career of one of the legends of the service. During the summer of 1874, conditions in DeWitt and Clinton counties deteriorated to such an extent that it became clear some outside force had to be sent into the region to restore a semblance of law and order. The old Sutton-Taylor feud—the Tumlinson faction's fighting the Taylor adherents for control of the area—was again the cause. A special company from Washington County was authorized for six months and recruited within the county under the command of Captain Leander H. McNelly. It was believed these men were far enough from the fighting to be neutral in their actions.[66]

McNelly had been a captain in the State Police, an assignment that would have eliminated any other man from serving in the Rangers. What undoubtedly made the difference in his case was his Civil War record. Although the majority of Ranger officers during this period had also fought for the Confederacy, McNelly had special talents and experience that made him particularly suited for certain police work.

Born in Virginia, he moved to Washington County, Texas, with his family in the fall of 1860. When war broke out, sixteen-year-old McNelly went to San Antonio and enlisted in the 5th Regiment, Texas Mounted Volunteers. He served throughout the campaign of Sibley's Brigade in the failed attempt to establish a Confederate base in the West. During the battle of Valverde, McNelly was cited for valor and made an enlisted aide to his regimental commander.

Young McNelly survived the long march back through New Mexico and Texas and went with his regiment to the

fighting in Louisiana. It was soon apparent the young soldier
had a talent for scouting and spy duties. His work was well
known, and on December 19, 1863, he was promoted from
private to captain and sent back to Washington County to
recruit a special spy company.[67] He continued to distinguish himself and was wounded in April 1864. In the late
months of the war, McNelly was sent back into Washington
County to apprehend deserters, work which involved the
development of an extensive net of spies. His scout company
was one of the last Confederate units in Texas to disband.

McNelly went back to farming near Burton, married and
had his first child in 1866. It was a tame life for a twenty-two
year-old man who had spent five violent years in combat.
McNelly was probably one of the most experienced scouts
and intelligence officers in the South; his papers contain
numerous commendations for bravery and skill. He was well
known and admired, despite his youth, and it was no
accident he was selected for this assignment.

The specific cause for organizing McNelly's command
was the trial of Jim Taylor in Indianola. Adjutant General
Steele raised a special militia force to guard the court, but
it was widely believed trouble would break out when this
force was disbanded.[68] The new company was ordered to
Clinton, the county seat of DeWitt, and arrived about August
1, 1874. McNelly described conditions in the area.

> On arrival here about the 1st of Augt, a perfect
> reign of terror existed in this and adjoining coun-
> ties; armed bands of men were making predatory
> excursions through the country, overawing the
> law-abiding citizens, while the civil authorities
> were unable, or unwilling to enforce the law
> framed for their protection. The lives of peaceful
> citizens who had given no cause of offense to
> either party were in jeopardy, as neutrals were
> considered obnoxious to both factions.[69]

The Rangers had an almost impossible mission in bringing law to the area. Civil authorities were either afraid to
help or actively supported the Tumlinson faction. Each side
of the fight could field one hundred or more armed men; the
strength of McNelly's company, from the few muster rolls
that survive, varied from twenty-seven to thirty-two.[70] It was

a challenging assignment, and McNelly used every trick he had learned in the war.

> A system of espionage kept upon the leading spirits in this feud becomes the means of my having a knowledge of their plans and they can make no plot of which I will be ignorant, and the scouting parties which are kept continually on the move prevent any gathering of these people for unlawful purposes.[71]

McNelly was under no illusions about completely restoring law and order, but he made a considerable beginning. The Rangers, unlike other peace officers, were completely impartial, and offered the cowed neutrals some hope for peace. Intimidation stopped, and there were none of the violent incidents that had plagued the region before the arrival of the Rangers. Despite the temporary calm that existed at the end of November 1874, McNelly knew the peace would last only as long as his men were in place unless an honest and fearless group of county officials could be installed. The year ended and the Washington County Volunteer Militia—Rangers by whatever name—were disbanded. The troubles were not over, and McNelly and other Rangers would return.

Sergeant James B. Gillett. This picture, taken in 1879, gives a good idea of Ranger gear of the period. Originally a tin-type, N.H. Rose reversed the image to show Gillett with his holster and knife on his right hip, where he carried them.

A Smaller Frontier Battalion
1875-1876

During the winter of 1874-1875 the United States Army mounted a major campaign against the Southern Plains Indians. The objective was to force all bands and tribes onto reservations and curtail their ability to raid into Texas. The Red River Campaign was a success and a clear demonstration of the difference between Ranger and soldier. The Rangers never possessed the numbers, logistical support or staff for large campaigns for which the army was equipped and trained. Much of the Red River Campaign took place outside of Texas and employed troops not stationed in Texas, but one part of the effort took place in the Panhandle and involved Colonel Ranald Mackenzie and the 4th Cavalry.

One of the premier commanders of the day, Mackenzie caught up with the last large Comanche band still off the reservation, captured and destroyed the Indian horse herd, and scattered the Indians into a harsh winter. By spring of 1875 the remnants began to trickle into the reservation at Fort Sill, still led by their last chief Quanah Parker. It was the end of major tribal raids in north and central Texas, but no one in Texas was yet aware of this; nor did it mean smaller Indian parties would not slip away from the Sill reservation to raid for some years to come. The army was not trained or organized for small-scale tracking of raiding Indian parties; the Rangers, with their good horses, mule pack animals, and personnel experienced in tracking and close combat, were specifically formed for this purpose.

The beginning of the year 1875 must have been a depressing time for Major John B. Jones and his reduced battalion of Rangers, even though he had seen his new command take the field, go through the usual shakedown period and perform with distinction, win public praise and show great promise for the future. It was the first time Texas had put a permanent frontier defense command in the field, and expectations had been high. The dream had lasted seven months, but by early January 1875 Jones reported that the Frontier Battalion had been reduced and reorganized as directed by General Order No. 8.[1]

The companies in the battalion were now less than half the size of the original units, and were now commanded by a lieutenant rather than a captain. This reduced strength had one advantage: the remaining men were experienced men with names that, as they began to appear regularly on scout reports and monthly returns, would make Ranger history in the following years.

Company A was based in Stevens County with 2nd Lieutenant J.T. Wilson in command. Evidently Wilson believed his men were becoming a trifle lax, because he issued several company special orders to bring discipline back to expected levels. On February 8, 1875, he ordered that no Ranger would leave the camp or go hunting without permission. Earlier he had directed that cartridges would not be issued unless the men were going on a scout, and would be collected upon return, undoubtedly an economy measure. Another order stated that any Ranger on guard without his horse saddled and ready would receive extra duty; a second offense would mean dismissal from the service.[2] It was a rough life, and even a small lapse in timing or judgment could mean death.

The other companies were based in or near their previous 1874 locations, except for Company F. Now led by Neal Coldwell, back as a lieutenant, Company F had been moved by the adjutant general to Hidalgo County, arriving February 18.[3] The next few months scouting the border counties and patrolling the Rio Grande was a new experience for them, frustrating and eventually without definitive results. During March Coldwell scouted down to Brownsville, and in April he had reports of ranch burnings by white vigilantes.[4] The situation in the lower valley, and indeed within the entire Nueces Strip, was completely out of hand, and another special Ranger company would eventually be brought in to deal with the crisis. Company F was recalled and brought back to its old station at Concepcion in May.[5]

Luck and location played a considerable part in how active a Ranger company would be. The requirement to maintain scouts in the field kept them all busy, but most patrols did not result in actual contact, gunfire or casualties. Throughout the entire period Company D was the unit's drawing the most blood, primarily due to its location where it was more likely to discover Indian trails coming into or withdrawing from the settlements. Company D also had a considerable number of outstanding men in the ranks, six of whom would become Ranger captains, a record shared by no other unit.

On March 17, 1875, Captain Martin M. Kenney resigned as the battalion quartermaster and Jones was designated quartermaster until further orders.[6] His administrative load increased drastically, but he made no complaint and assumed this task as he did all the others. The decision saved a captain's pay of one hundred dollars a month, a considerable sum during a period of limited funds. Kenney's resignation and the requirement to balance and clear his books also led to increased work for all the company commanders. With all his other problems, Jones received more bad news on March 17 when the adjutant general directed him to reduce the battalion even further. By the end of March Jones had disbanded Company A and reduced the other companies by one sergeant and nine privates.[7]

The next few months were the most critical in the history of the battalion. Had he done nothing else, Jones deserves a place in Texas history for managing to maintain the Frontier Battalion in the field by convincing the men to stay in service without pay! The only written account of his action is a sentence in the Report of the Adjutant General for 1876. In March of that year Jones wrote, "I induced the men to serve without pay and take chances of the next Legislature making an appropriation to pay them."[8] There were many critical periods in the history of the Frontier Battalion, but the months during which the Rangers served without pay has to be one of the most spectacular. There is almost no official documentation as to the number of months, but a sizable number of Rangers were serving on faith alone during the spring and summer, until the legislature provided funds in September.

Despite his administrative problems, Jones never curtailed his active supervision of the frontier; his trips up and down the line never stopped. In mid-April he was in Mason, having just visited Company D and found it in good shape. A scout had just returned from the Guadalupe and upper Llano without finding Indian sign nor the expected gathering of outlaws, although a group of men, supposedly cow thieves, had been camped near the junction of the North and South Forks of the Llano but had scattered, probably hearing of the Ranger patrol. The Rangers found the settlers they visited were encouraged by the visits and welcomed them.

Jones continued his report with the news that Dan Roberts wanted to resign on May 25, the day his enlistment was up. The major talked him into staying until at least September 1 in the hope that the legislature would find new money for the battalion. Roberts agreed to stay "under the arrangement for pay of which we spoke before I left Austin" and would enlist as many of his men as would agree to serve until there was money to pay them, up to half the company. He would keep the weapons of those who did not want to continue as Rangers, as well as the arms of the men released under Special Order No. 14; Jones was looking ahead and wanted these weapons to arm new recruits if the legislature allowed him to recruit back up to forty-man companies. He did not deprive ex-Rangers of their personal arms and directed that the men be given certified accounts for their Sharps and Colts.

Evidently Jones had been discussing a new pay arrangement with his men as he rode north; Adjutant General Steele had suggested paying the men by check, rather than cash, and depositing the funds to their account in a bank nearest their camp. Since there was nothing much to buy on the frontier, most of the Rangers were in favor of the new scheme because it reduced the danger of loss in transporting cash from Austin. It also reduced serious gambling among the men.

Jones concluded his long report by scribbling he was leaving within the hour to visit Company E in Coleman County. On the way he would pass through the settlement in McCulloch County were two men had been killed by Indians and where he had instructed Roberts to make a scout during the "moon," a term for "month" commonly used in reports and correspondence. There had been reports of Indians' stealing below Fort Concho, but the raiding party must have turned back north because the Rangers found no tracks to the south. Jones signed off on the report hastily written on three pages of paper with the letterhead of "David Doole, Dealer in Dry Goods, Groceries, Hardware." Jones had probably been in the store buying supplies for the rest of the trip and had taken the opportunity—and the paper— to report to the adjutant general.

Along his route Jones had talked enough Rangers into staying to form four companies of forty men. It was a small battalion, but the force was still in the field.[9]

One of the four companies, Company D, was fortunate in having an officer and his wife, Captain and Mrs. Dan Roberts, as well as one of its enlisted men, write memoirs in later years which would supplement the bare-bones descriptions in the official records. The enlisted man, James B. Gillett, was a young cowboy when he decided to join the Rangers in May 1875. With his friend Norman Rodgers, he rode to Company D's camp near Menardville and asked to become a Ranger. Lieutenant Roberts talked to the young men, but neither had suitable horses and Roberts told them to come back when they had proper mounts. They later returned with ponies good enough to enlist, and on June 1 the recruits took the oath to Texas, became Rangers, went through the usual hazing, and became accustomed to the more ordered camp life of the Rangers.[10]

Gillett's first fight with Indians occurred in mid-August when Roberts' camp was at Las Moras.[11] Ranger L.P. Sieker, in Mason on business, learned of an Indian raid and rode all night covering the fifty miles back to camp. He arrived about sun-up, and Roberts was in action almost before Sieker had finished his verbal report. A messenger was sent to bring in the horses; other men began to gather supplies for a ten-day ride. Roberts decided to lead the scout himself and ordered Sergeant Jim Hawkins to select men for the ride. Gillett was one of the men, as was Ed Sieker, brother of the man who brought the news of the Indian attack.

Roberts' considerable experience with Indians before he joined the Rangers made him one of the best Indian fighters in the battalion. He moved fast, but without haste or wasted motion; the Indian party had a good lead and the Rangers would have to "walk them down." The scout found a trail, within ten or twelve miles of camp, that indicated the Indians had a large horse herd which would slow them, and

Roberts settled down on the trail. They discovered an abandoned pony from whose condition Roberts estimated they were a half day behind the raiders.

He had a good idea of the country from their earlier patrolling, and they covered about sixty miles the first day, settling at dusk at a campsite with water. Roberts' horse needed shoeing, and one of the Rangers did a passable job by the light of a campfire. They were actually north of the Indian trail because Roberts believed they could be detected by Indians on high ground if they followed directly behind the war party.

Next morning the Rangers rode parallel to the trail. Some of the men were convinced they had lost the tracks, but the lead tracker finally located the trail and they again settled down for another long day. They took a break at noon to rest the horses and eat a little.

When it was time to start again, the Rangers discovered they had been near a snake den and two horses had been injured. Roberts' mount had a bite above the knee, and Ranger Jim Day's mount had been bitten on the head as it grazed. Neither animal could walk, but Roberts was not about to stop and had one of the two pack mules unloaded and all the supplies placed on the other. He then saddled the mule and prepared to start again. Since Ranger Day could not be left alone, Private Dave Cupps was ordered to stay with him. They were to remain with the injured horses until the animals got well or died. If they died, both men could ride Cupps' horse back to camp. Leaving them supplies, the patrol started along the trail.

That night they reached a camp, on the South Concho, maintained by an old man Roberts called "Wash" DeLong. Shot and crippled by Indians, DeLong refused to be intimidated and lived where he pleased. Gillett remembered that some of the men were becoming a little tired by now and that two of the older Rangers were saddle sore. They all pulled their share of guard duty, however, and were up and on the trail at an early hour.

The mule Roberts was riding did not step out as briskly as his fine horse, but the animal was dependable and could keep going after horses had given up. In the afternoon the trackers halted, and Roberts rode up to see where the Indians had stopped to kill a wild horse for food using a .50 caliber buffalo gun—the casing was found off to one side.

Roberts was elated, certain the Indians felt confident that there was no pursuit and would stop to cook the large cuts of raw meat.

By now the Rangers were traversing the land between the South Concho and the Pecos at the beginning of the Staked Plains. They discovered water holes, where the Indians had halted long enough to cook and eat the meat, then the trail turned north. About dark they found where the raiding party had halted again to cook more meat; the ashes were fresh and Roberts promised his men a fight on the next day.

After a restless night without fires or hot food, the Rangers were up and moving as soon as the trackers could see enough to follow the trail. By sunrise they had covered five miles and had the Indians in sight. Roberts had his men dismount, to tighten their cinches and see to their gear, and gave them a short talk. He and Sergeant Hawkins were the only ones who had ever before been in a fight, and he cautioned his men not to draw a weapon or fire until he gave the order and to ride only where he commanded. They remounted and started out in single file, reducing the chance of being seen and making it more difficult to estimate their number. This far from the settlements, the Indians had grown careless and were riding along with no particular order. Two Indians, trailing the others and the horse herd, gave the alarm when they finally spotted the Rangers. The rest of the Indians changed to fresh mounts when the two braves started yelling, and the leader scattered his men along a slight rise where they dismounted and took shelter behind their horses.

Roberts was delighted. He led his men to within a hundred yards and dismounted. Both sides opened fire, but the Rangers were better marksmen with superior rifles for more accurate work. The Sharps were slow firers but deadly. After one Indian was shot through the leg and a number of the Indian horses killed or wounded, the leader yelled and the Indians scattered. The Rangers remounted and took out after the running Indians, cutting free the pack mule.

Gillett and Ed Sieker started after the closest Indian, who had picked up another of the Indians who had lost his horse. The two Rangers figured no grass-fed animal carrying two men could outrun a grain-fed horse with just one rider, and for a time they loped across the prairie. The rear Indian

fired at Gillett with a Winchester, and from time to time
Gillett managed to get off a shot with his Sharps despite the
difficulty of reloading. Riding ahead of Sieker and refusing
to stop for a rifle dropped as bait, he began to overtake the
Indians. A rawhide rope was also tossed away, but the chase
continued. When Gillett was at close range, the Indian
began turning to shoot arrows then swerved his horse into
some brush and grass. Gillett fired again and killed the
horse, which fell and pinned one of the riders. As he rode
by, Gillett saw the Indian was actually a white boy about
fifteen or sixteen!

Believing the pinned boy was helpless, Gillett continued
through the brush towards some trees, trying to hit the
other Indian now on foot. Ed Sieker, who had been following
Gillett, rode up, dismounted, and shot the second rider
between the shoulders, killing him instantly. The two Rangers went back to capture the white boy, but he was gone.
After a search, Sieker went back and scalped the dead
Indian, then the two men rode back to rejoin the others.

When the Indians had scattered along the rise, Roberts,
Sergeant Hawkins, Paul Durham and Nick Donnaly [vari-
ously spelled Donley or Donnelly] started after a group of
seven Indians. They pursued the men for several miles until
the rear Indian jerked his horse about and rode towards the
Rangers, shouting in Spanish. Roberts, who understood
Spanish, yelled to his men not the shoot; the man was a
friend!

He told Donnaly to guard the prisoner while they kept
on, but their horses were worn out and they watched the
Indians shrink to specks on the horizon. Roberts called off
the chase, and they found Donnaly and his captive back at
the site of the first fight on the hill. Sieker and Gillett soon
rode up bringing a Winchester, a rope, some moccasins and
a lance as trophies. The Rangers searched for some time
trying to find the pack mule, but the animal had vanished.

Loss of the mule left them without supplies other than
some strips of cooked meat the Indians had dropped. They
rode slowly during the long ride back to let the horses
recover. Two days later they finally obtained decent food at
DeLong's camp, where the delighted man fed them all they
wanted at no cost. It took another two days to return to their
base camp at Las Moras where, to their delight, they found
the two Rangers and the recovered horses.

Roberts was back in camp on August 26 when he reported to his commander. He said they left on August 20, "travelled 150 miles from here—northwest [,] had a round with them, killed one—wounded another[,] and captured a Mexican boy about 13 or 14 years old...." He reported they brought back twenty-three captured horses and apologized after a fashion for not killing more, but his horses had broken down and "they changed horses on me." The boy had given valuable information concerning water holes and trails that they did not know about. Roberts concluded, "I am very tired & hope this brief report will be satisfactory.[12]

Jones was quite interested in any information which the boy, captured several years earlier from a ranch near Fort Clark, might give them about the Plains, a largely unknown region. His release from his Indian captors was reported in a number of newspapers, attracting the attention of his parents who took him back home.

The other white boy who had escaped from Gillett and Sieker in the high grass managed to cross the prairie on foot and return to his Indian captor-friends. Taken prisoner as a child, he had been raised by Comanche and Apache tribes, soon forgetting his name and language. Some years after the fight with the Rangers he was identified as F.H. Lehman and purchased back from the Indians. In his later years he wrote and rewrote his memoirs, describing this fight and a host of other adventures. Surprisingly enough, his version agrees very closely with the recollections of Roberts and Gillett, even to mentioning how surprised the Indians were when they found the Rangers had been tracking them for days. It is the only Indian fight with accounts from both sides.[13] Lehman and Gillett even met forty-nine years later in San Antonio during a reunion of the Old Time Trail Drivers.

This chase and fight demonstrate why and how the Rangers were successful in small-scale Indian warfare. First, they responded immediately. The Comanche and Kiowa warriors hit and escaped quickly with their booty; if they were allowed too much head start, they simply vanished out on the prairie. Once on the trail, the Rangers "walked them down" until they either caught the Indians or until their own horses gave out, remaining on the trail until the Indians thought they were safe and became careless and slowed down. Lehman, who had ample opportunity to observe the Texans, said the Indians hated the Rangers, "We dreaded them....[They were] sleepless and restless. . . ."[14]

Part of the success of the Rangers was due to their animals, the best horses they could afford and fed on grain rather than grass. On long scouts the men carried forage on their pack mules and thus were not wholly dependent on the condition of the countryside. A patrol carried enough water, food, ammunition and other supplies to enable them to remain for days on the trail.

The tough little mules could keep up with the horses and were a vital part of every Ranger company, contributing as much, in their way, as the more handsome horses. Company D's Rangers, therefore, hated to lose one of their mules and searched long and hard trying to find their animal missing after the Indian fight. The mystery of the vanished pack mule was solved several months later when the U.S. Army asked Roberts to provide a guide to help them lay out a military road between Fort McKavett and Fort Stockton. At the time there was no direct road between the two installations, and army officers had heard of the scout by Company D within the area between the posts. Ed Sieker was assigned to guide the army party.

The Ranger had a marvelous sense of direction, using the stars and remembering landmarks from his earlier scouts to guide his party on a straightforward march west, taking care to hit the Pecos near the Horsehead Crossing. According to Roberts' memoirs, Sieker had a good sense of humor and was amused at the respect shown him by his soldier companions, who considered Sieker to be another Kit Carson. This flattered the Ranger, but he was also somewhat amazed that men in their profession were so dependent on an outsider for such basic support.

They passed near the location of the Indian fight, where Sieker stumbled upon the skeleton of the lost mule. The poor animal had a bullet hole in the head, and Sieker surmised it had been struck by a random shot and had died in the high grass. The food in the mule's packs had been eaten by wild animals, but the five hundred rounds of ammunition in a carrier was undisturbed. Other mules were lost in service, but this Jennie was the only one killed in combat.

Sieker continued to travel west, now through unknown terrain, scouting well ahead of his party. While following antelope tracks he discovered several deep springs and plenty of fresh water. The rest of the trip was easy, and the water supply made the route he had taken a good one. Sieker returned to camp an army hero, an example of the varied tasks that were becoming part of Ranger life. The springs he discovered continued to be important in the westward movement along the new road, but army map-makers instead named them after the army colonel commanding the area; "Grierson's Spr." was a prominent feature on maps well into the 1880s.[15]

The commander of Company D, Lieutenant Dan Roberts, was a handsome man, tall with dark auburn hair and beard, always well dressed, appearing more like a college dean than a hunter of felons.[16] In 1875 he was thirty-five and beginning to think he had spent too much time on the frontier. When Major Jones visited Company D after the fight, he found Roberts ready to resign and get married, but Jones could not afford to lose an experienced commander. He told the lieutenant to take off all the time he needed, get married, then bring his wife back to camp.[17]

Roberts did just that; he married Luvenia Conway in Columbus on September 13, 1875, then traveled by train to Austin where they met some of the "boys" from Company D who were in town to escort their officer and his lady out to camp.[18] After a combined tour and honeymoon, Roberts left his bride in Mason and hurried to camp.

Much had happened while he was gone, not only in Company D but all along the frontier. Early in August, Major Jones had alerted the company commanders to expect another reorganization on September 1. Each company was to be discharged, then reformed with one officer, three sergeants, three corporals and thirty-four privates. The original recruiting standards still applied: good, sober men with one horse.[19] Company F, which had recently been serving in the Nueces Strip, had been somewhat larger than the other units; now an additional order placed Company F on the same footing as the other Frontier Battalion companies.[20]

Jones had also announced a new system for his tours up and down the line. The company commanders had never liked his original plan of taking a detachment from each company for his escort. Jones now decided to make one company his permanent escort and selected Company A, to be led by Lieutenant Ira Long. In a letter announcing the new plan, Jones also told Lieutenant Roberts to provide a special twenty-man detail under Sergeant N.O. Reynolds for an extended scout in September out to the Devil's River and the Pecos.[21]

The reorganization caused several changes in officers. Ira Long was moved to Company A, and G.W. Stevens assumed the post at Company B. Jones himself brought twenty-three recruits to Company A, giving the unit a total strength of forty-four men, somewhat over the authorized strength.[22]

As part of the realignment and reorganization, Jones was forced to disband Company C, but he still had a good battalion, with fewer units but each with as many men as before. Planning to join his new escort in Wise County, while still near Roberts' camp he heard of a killing in Mason County and ordered his escort company to join him immediately. He also called on Roberts for additional men to be commanded by Sergeant Reynolds.[23]

Jones was wise to bring all the force he could spare. The Rangers were facing their first county-wide fight since the Sutton-Taylor troubles, in what was to be the beginning of a gradual shift from fighting Indians to chasing white outlaws. Even though there were peace officers in all counties, the sheriffs and deputies often actively supported one side or the other rather than impartially enforcing the law. It was a brewing fight of this nature that brought Jones and his Rangers into Mason County.

The county, settled largely by German immigrants, was the scene of a thriving cattle business. Old animosities between the German loyalists and the ex-Confederates still simmered and were to play a part in the troubles that followed, but the immediate cause was a dispute over cattle.[24] One of the ranchers had an employee, Tim Williamson, who handled his herds and was active in driving cattle to Kansas. There was considerable bitterness over cattle's being stolen and suspicions they were being added to Williamson's cattle drives. Although the offense was never proved, Williamson was arrested on suspicion of theft by Deputy Sheriff John Worley.

On the way toward Mason, the two men were overtaken by a mob. Williamson pleaded with Worley to release him, but the deputy instead shot his prisoner's horse and made it simple for the mob to kill the dismounted prisoner. Worley and the members of the mob disappeared. Although details vary, depending upon which party told the story, there was no disputing the fact Williamson was murdered while in the custody of the law.

Dan Roberts, in town to buy supplies, became embroiled in the trouble when Sheriff John Clark requested his aid to help halt a mob that was going after some other suspected cattle thieves in the local jail. Roberts, the sheriff and another man tried to reason with the armed mob of forty men without success; the men in the mob said they were going to get the prisoners even if they had to hurt the sheriff. Sheriff Clark went for more help, but during the temporary lull the mob broke into the jail, rode off with the prisoners and killed most of them before Roberts and Sheriff Clark and a posse caught up with them.

The murdered cattleman, Williamson, had friends who began to even the score. A former member of Company D named Scott Cooley, who had driven cattle to Kansas with Williamson, was farming near Menardville when he learned of the death of his old friend. Cooley rode to Mason, to avenge his companion, and soon learned the identity of many of the mob who had murdered Williamson.

Cooley rode out to Deputy Sheriff Worley's farm, shot him to death and scalped him, then crossed the county and killed Pete Border, another member of the mob. The killings caused an uproar in Mason, and people began sleeping with locked doors. Cooley, joined by John and Mose Beard, George Gladden, John Ringgold and a considerable number of others, rode into Mason and exchanged shots with a posse of citizens, killing another man.

Mrs. Roberts, new to the frontier and staying in Mason while waiting for her husband to finish suitable quarters out at the Ranger camp, watched the townspeople react to the news Scott Cooley was in town. She wanted to hide under a bed on one shooting occasion, and another time a large party of armed Germans came looking for one of the Cooley gang and searched the boarding house to which she had moved believing it was more protected. When her husband returned she told him she wanted to move to camp. "We were going into a country where Indians raided, but we were leaving a country where white men raided."[25]

Major Jones and his reinforced escort rode as fast as possible to contain this growing violence. On September 28 they reached Keller's on the Llano and were riding along a road when about twenty men hiding behind a stone fence stood and threatened them. Fortunately the accosters saw that Jones and his escort were not enemies and explained they had heard that some of the Gladden gang from Cold Springs, and John and Mose Beard from Burnet, were coming to burn out the "Dutch," a commonly used corruption referring to the German [*Deutsch*] settlers.

The Rangers continued on to Cold Springs where Jones, planning to talk to all factions in the growing war, spent the night. Next day he went into Mason and discovered that members of the American [*i.e.*, "American" vs. ""Dutch"] faction had killed Dan Hoester in town and ridden about firing into the hotel before galloping away. Sheriff Clark had gathered a posse and chased them without result until they caught Mose Beard on the Llano and shot him to death.

Jones split his men into patrols and sent the Rangers out on a continual search for Cooley and his known supporters. He had little luck and reported to the adjutant general that it was difficult to elicit either side's interest in bringing in fugitives; all the wanted men knew the rugged countryside and had plenty of friends to hide them.

There is more to this story than appears in the official reports. Cooley had been a Ranger under Rufe Perry in the early days of Company D, and it became clear to Jones that some, maybe most, of his Rangers were not trying too hard to find the ex-Ranger. According to Gillett, the major reminded the command's members of their oath to Texas; while he understood and respected their friendship with Cooley, they were obligated to serve with undivided loyalties. Any man who could not continue under these conditions would be given an honorable discharge. Gillett recalled that about fifteen men stepped forward and were allowed to resign, but his memory must have played him false because monthly returns for A and D companies show no such reductions. Nor does Roberts, who would have commented if there had been such a drastic cut in personnel, mention any such reduction.[26]

Gillett also relates that one of the Company D Rangers was in a cow camp to exchange his horse and was asked by a stranger in the camp if he knew "Maje" Reynolds, who was the sergeant leading the contingent from Company D. When the Ranger said he did, the man identified himself as Scott

Cooley and gave him a scalp, saying it belonged to Worley but not to mention it to anyone other than Reynolds.[27] This story is probably true, as Cooley must have known Reynolds.

Battalion Special Order No.47 undoubtedly has some bearing on this subject.

> At their own request, approved by the Company Commander, Sergt. N.O. Reynolds and private Jas. P. Day of Co "D" are hereby honorably discharged from the Service of the State for the reason that they say they cannot conscientiously discharge the duty to which they have been assigned.

Their request for discharge certainly indicates Reynolds and Day knew Cooley and had a motivational problem chasing him. Fortunately, Reynolds' resignation was not permanent.

The number of other Rangers who resigned, if any, is uncertain and not important, but Jones' talk evidently had a considerable impact because the Rangers settled down to intense scouting. They swept the county and made twenty-two arrests, twelve of them in Mason. On two occasions parties showed resistance, with a man wounded in each fight. The scouting and the arrests significantly reduced further formal resistance to the law. "Peace in Mason county having been restored," Jones started north again with part of his escort, leaving Lieutenant Ira Long and a detachment in case there was another outbreak.[28]

Cooley vanished, and the "Mason County War" ended when others in his faction were sentenced to the penitentiary. Sheriff Clark realized his life was still in danger and also disappeared, further contributing to a peaceful solution. Roberts summed up one of the problems which had faced the Rangers—they were supposed to support and to operate with the county peace officers and could not arrest anyone not wanted by the sheriff unless a county was under martial law. In Mason, where the sheriff and the justice of the peace were on opposite sides, any writs issued were for men of the opposing faction.[29] In many of the county fights, victory involved getting rid of elected officials.

Jones ran into another problem in Mason County. Besides chasing known killers and preventing the two factions from engaging in battle, he had to endure constant criticism from both sides, each claiming he favored the other. The governor received at least one complaint asking that Attorney General Steele investigate. Hurt by the unjust accusation, Jones replied politely, yet forcefully, to the charge.[30] This is the only suggestion in the records that Jones was biased, and is the only time that any governmental official questioned the major's motivations.

The so-called "war" in Mason County was a major event but not the only activity for the battalion during 1875. Company A remained in Mason until January 1876, maintaining order during an election in November and capturing several cattle thieves the same month.[31] Company records show that N.O. Reynolds joined Company A in October;[32] his short-lived resignation was fortunate for Texas. Company B went on an extended scout to the Pease River from October 16-30 and found an Indian camp that had been abandoned some two weeks earlier.

After the September expansion, a reduction to take place by November 30 must have been frustrating. Each company was reduced to a captain commanding, two sergeants, one corporal and seventeen privates.[33] Reductions, as usual, did not take place uniformly nor on the same date. Company E scouted 1,360 miles during November and twenty men were discharged by November 30 when all the men were back, leaving twenty-one on the rolls. Company D had cut back to twenty-one by November 3; Company A, however, did not cut back until December, when they showed thirty Rangers on the Monthly Return.

Company F under Neal Coldwell was very active during the last three months of 1875. He spent twenty-one days in October on an extended scout to the Devils River and over to the Pecos, covering 428 miles but without any major Indian sightings. At this time he had thirty-nine men in the company. In mid-November Jones directed Coldwell to check on rumors that a strong outlaw band was operating near the headwaters of the Llano River, and a strong patrol left November 16 to scour the area thoroughly for eleven days, covering 205 miles. The rumor was false. For some reason, Coldwell did not reduce his company and maintained forty-one men on the rolls through December.[34]

One other personnel action affected everyone in the

battalion; on December 9 the adjutant general announced that Surgeon S.G. Nicholson had been mustered out of the service effective November 30.[35]

Shortly after Company D settled into winter camp, Gillett and several of his friends decided they wanted to replace their Sharps with the new Winchester carbines. Although they would have to pay forty dollars and furnish their own ammunition, ten men decided it was worth the money for the new repeaters. Charles L. Nevill, one of the Siekers, and a Ranger named Bell obtained Roberts' permission to pick up a case of the new weapons in Austin.[36] This was one of the earliest changeovers to the new Winchesters, and probably the largest conversion within a single company. Texas continued to furnish .50 caliber ammunition for the Sharps for a considerable time, but the Rangers began a gradual changeover to the Winchesters either in rifle or carbine models.

Commanding the Frontier Battalion involved more than riding up and down the line several times a year. Major Jones had to juggle a number of roles and keep abreast of constantly changing conditions. He was tactical commander, administrative officer, supply officer and, at times, a public relations officer, although he probably never thought of his role in that light. He was very much aware of the need to keep the governor and the legislators aware of what the battalion was doing and the need to continue the service. The chases and arrests are the stuff of romance; and endless paper shuffling and administrative details are boring history for the most part but kept the Rangers in the field.

Studying several weeks of Jones' correspondence with just one company gives some idea of the details he had to handle. In mid-October he was in Mason and wrote Dan Roberts that he had sent him the name of Moses[37] Hughes, charged with horse stealing and wanted in San Saba. He was thought to be heading for the forks of the Llano. Jones had another report that Gladden and Cooley were making loud threats in Menardville and suggested Roberts check; Cooley might be near "old Jacksons and I think it would be well for you to hunt him there. There will be no quiet in the community while he is at large."

Roberts answered Jones' letter, saying he had already

checked out the rumors about Cooley and Gladden and doubted either man would show at Jackson's, where they were unwelcome and would be turned in if they appeared. Roberts needed hay for his animals and could find only one man who could supply him, at twelve dollars a ton. Should he have it shipped? He was planning a change of location to Fort Mason and could have the hay shipped to him there. His horses were recovering, and he would resume scouting soon. Roberts also reported he had recruited men to fill the vacancies in his company and needed two pistols and a needle gun.[38] He inquired about Paul Durham's guns. There was no special news.

Four days later, still in Mason, Jones wrote Roberts again, telling him to stay near Menardville because he expected Indian raids the next month. He instructed Roberts to bring the company wagon back to camp and to furnish him ten, well-mounted men with the necessary pack mules for an extended scout of twenty-five to thirty days. Jones told Roberts supplies were on the way from Austin—the hay would be shipped as soon as Jones could obtain transportation—and required a list from Roberts of all supplies on hand. He told Roberts to perform as many scouts as possible because he had to make a special report to the governor at the end of December and wanted to make a good showing. He was going up country the following week and expected to be back about the first of November.

Courier service was prompt; Roberts received this letter the following day. He replied immediately that he had two scouts out and expected them to return soon. The men the major wanted would be sent. Roberts promised to "use all diligence in scouting—hope to furnish you a good record of my Companys work."

He informed the major he was moving his wife near or into the camp so he could spend all his time with his men. Roberts thought he might accompany the ten-man detail to Mason, because he needed some personal articles which were cheaper in town. He reported the mule collars were worn out and he needed new ones. As a last item, he requested the major "to please tell Dr. Nicholson [who was still on the rolls during this October correspondence] to send some Epsoms Salt—or some other kind of purgative Medicine—if he has it—& much oblige me by so doing."

Jones next sent Roberts two pistols and a Sharps carbine, telling him to charge sixteen dollars to whomever received the weapons and send him a certified account for the amount, because he had been personally required to advance the money for the weapons. Jones was sending seven thousand pounds of corn, enough to last Company D until the beginning of December, with more due to arrive about the end of November.

Jones, who had also been corresponding with a man in Fredericksburg about supplying the Rangers, could promise Roberts forage. He had given the merchant instructions on preparing proper vouchers, and where to send them to his agent in Austin. Jones was careful to adjust all the required paperwork so that his supplier did not lose money on the corn;[39] the major may have had to bargain to keep his unit in operation, but he was not going to take advantage of anyone.

These examples of the major's correspondence for a part of one month with just one company do not include his contacts with the adjutant general, the governor, or private citizens. Scouting and fighting were easier. The only things that really bothered Jones were the Texas weather and the Texas legislature; he did the best he could with both and bore with grace what he could not change.

Company D was not the only unit with problems; there is merely more information in the extant archives about it. Company B, for example, also had a few difficulties; the company had sufficient forage and supplies but could not scout because the horses were down with "Epizootic in a very bad form. Three of best horses having died from its effects." Only one man had been sick, but the first sergeant was afraid there were signs of scurvy and asked if fresh fruit or something similar could be sent.[40] There is no reply to this letter, but if Jones could have found fresh fruit in December, Company B would have had fresh fruit.

The Frontier Battalion entered the New Year expecting another active Indian campaign, but the anticipated raids never developed and the troubles that had plagued Mason County did not recur. The year 1876 was to be one of the quietest periods in the Frontier Battalion's history.

In the opening months of 1876, Ranger companies in the battalion had been reduced to an average of twenty enlisted men and one officer, but there had been no corresponding reduction in responsibilities or territory. It was too small a force to patrol an area of thousands of square miles. With Major Jones' using Company A as his escort, there was yet another [Company C was still deactivated] unit unavailable for service on the frontier line. Despite these difficulties, the company commanders managed to keep at least one patrol on scout most of the time. Jones adopted a somewhat different plan during the year, calling in reinforcements from two companies to join his escort on extended scouts through terrain favored by Indian raiders.

Jones was fortunate to receive a slight increase in funds, enabling the force to add a few new men, and on March 1, 1876, commanders were told to recruit back up to three sergeants, three corporals and twenty-six privates, effective April 1.[41] The extra men allowed Jones to form stronger units for major scouts and still retain sufficient strength in the base camps. There were also some shifts in officer personnel; Sergeant C.H. Hamilton was promoted to second lieutenant and placed in command of Company B. Major Jones' old friend, Dr. Nicholson, came out of retirement and once again became the battalion surgeon.[42]

In late June 1876, Major Jones left on an extended scout to block raids from the west and out of Mexico by Apache and Kickapoo Indians. He reinforced Company A with nineteen Rangers from Company D commanded by Sergeant Reynolds and a detachment from Coldwell's Company F. To support this large force, he brought in three wagons and twenty mules. The combined party was large enough to fight any raiding band, and even strong enough to divide into smaller, combat-capable units.[43]

This large scouting party left from the camp of Company D and moved west and south to the Nueces, down that river, and turned west along the Lower Road leading to Fort Clark. Here Major Jones detached Ira Long and Company A, sending them along the road to old Fort Lancaster, established to guard one of the few fords on the Pecos near the Immigrant Crossing; Jones did not want to enable a war party to pass him to the north while he was scouting along the Rio Grande. He sent Long and the wagons along the easy road, instructing him to watch the ford and wait near Lancaster until the rest of the party joined him.

Crossing Devils River, Jones and the rest of the party marched southwest to Shafer Crossing and then scouted up the west bank of the Pecos. They spent ten days in extremely rough country and found several abandoned Indian camps but no fresh sign. They continued up the Pecos and probably used the crossing near abandoned Lancaster to rejoin Long and Company A. The entire force moved up Live Oak Creek to its head and out onto the level plains. Crossing the headwaters of the South Concho, they filled their water kegs and continued on for another ten miles before making a dry camp.

During their trek in late July, hot, dry, with all the usual water holes dried up, the Rangers hoarded both the water in their canteens and in the water kegs, and the animals began to suffer. The streams they crossed were dry, dusty beds or rapidly drying bogs. Buffalo carcasses revealed where the thirsty animals had been trapped in the mud trying to reach water.

The second dry day since leaving Fort Lancaster on the Pecos River, the Rangers were up and moving at four in the morning, taking advantage of the cooler air to reduce thirst and strain on the horses and mules. By luck they found fresh water the third day, killed a few buffalo for fresh meat, and camped for two days to rest the men and animals. The remainder of the trip was accomplished in easy stages across familiar country back to the camp of Company D from where the detachment from Company F returned to its base camp. The Rangers had covered about 560 miles during a month on the trail.

Once again a scout had returned without a fight, but the large party had left a broad track across Indian country to show there was no part of Texas safe for raiders. The Rangers had also explored new country and learned much about water holes, terrain features and travel routes. This new knowledge would help later Ranger scouts and be of value to people settling the country.

Lieutenant B.S. Foster and a party of eleven Rangers from Company E had the only real Indian fight of 1876 on July 11 when they crossed the Colorado River to follow a fresh Indian trail. About four in the morning after traveling thirty-five miles, they came upon an Indian camp and attacked the tepees without conducting a thorough reconnaissance. In the initial charge they wounded an Indian, drove the party from the tepees and captured a number of horses. By daylight both parties regrouped, and Foster saw he had charged a large number of tepees containing at least fifty warriors.

The Indians were able to retake most of their captured mounts because Foster's command, with tired horses, was too small both to guard the Indian horses and fight off the superior enemy force. He fell back, as did the Indians, but he had broken up a major base camp and captured a considerable amount of camp supplies, forcing the Indians to return to the reservation.[44]

Shortly after this skirmish, most of Company E joined Jones and his escort on another long scout, leaving July 26, 1876, and returning August 9.[45] They found a recently abandoned camp of seven tepees and, six miles away, another larger camp of twelve tepees, also hastily abandoned. Both camp areas were littered with discarded blankets, saddles and camp gear. The trail could not be followed because the prairie had been burned, possibly by Indians obliterating their tracks.[46]

In August, frequently a time for expanding or decreasing the battalion, Jones again warned his commanders of a change to take effect on September 1 at the start of the new fiscal year. Under the new allocation of funds, each company was cut to two sergeants, two corporals, and only sixteen privates. As he always did, Jones reminded his commanders that Rangers must be of good character, unmarried, sound, in good physical condition, without any indictments. He stressed the need for good horses, a condition that had recently been neglected to some degree.[47] Ira Long took advantage of the coming changes to resign.[48]

Company A was retained as escort company. In his correspondence, Jones listed the locations of the other companies as well as the location of the nearest telegraph office, a new type of entry which reveals the importance Jones placed on rapid communication between commands. He concluded with a caution for his commanders "to give particular attention to the maintenance of Law and Order and the arresting of criminals and fugitives from Justice, large lists of whom with orders for their arrest will be forwarded in a few days."[49] This is the first written indication of a shift in duties for the battalion; the Rangers would still scout for Indian raiders, but from now on their major emphasis was to be "criminals and fugitives." Coldwell and his Company F had already spent the earlier part of 1876 chasing horse thieves and murderers,[50] although in April and May they were again looking for Indians.

During the reorganization of the companies in September 1876 there were a number of enlisted personnel changes. When a number of vacancies opened in Company A, Company D Rangers N.O. Reynolds, Charles Nevill, Jack Martin, Bill Clements, Tom Gillespie and Jim Gillett all requested reassignment to the escort company because, as Gillett explained, of the opportunity to see new country all the time. They were no sooner in Company A than Jones marched south almost to San Antonio, then north again to settle into winter camp before bad weather struck.[51]

On the ride back north, some of the Rangers may have wondered why Major Jones pushed so hard in a forced march only to return to camp; many years later Gillett learned the major was eager to go on leave and visit Houston. The Masonic Order's Grande Lodge was having a convention to elect a new Grand Master of Texas and Jones was in line for the position.[52]

There were two other major changes in September, involving company commanders; both Neal Coldwell and Dan Roberts resigned. Why Coldwell resigned is unknown—probably because he was still a lieutenant—and Roberts merely mentions that he and his wife left and went to live in Houston.[53] With Coldwell gone Company F needed a commander, and Pat Dolan was promoted to lieutenant and given the company.

Coldwell's resignation did not last long. When the lieutenant commanding the escort company resigned because of ill health, Jones managed to obtain money to pay a captain and offered Company A to Coldwell at his old rank. He accepted and returned to duty. The same day, December 8, 1876, Doctor Nicholson again resigned.[54]

Winter set in, and the remainder of 1876 was uneventful.

Captain Lee H. McNelly, commander of the Special Company. A true legend in his own time, McNelly is ranked among the greatest of Ranger officers.

— 4 —

McNelly's Boys
1875-1876

During the spring of 1875 a command not part of the Frontier Battalion was active in South Texas. Neal Coldwell's company of the Frontier Battalion had been stationed for a time in the south, but the situation along the Rio Grande became so unsettled and troublesome that it was deemed necessary to send a special unit to the region. Taking advantage of the act allowing the governor to establish special companies, the Fifteenth Legislature authorized another company to combat crime in the Nueces Strip.[1] The Selection of Lee H. McNelly, who had commanded an earlier special company during the Sutton-Taylor feud, to lead the new Ranger unit was one of those fortunate times when the right man was chosen to meet the situation.

The early days of McNelly's new company are not well documented. News of the new Ranger unit evidently spread through the troubled Nueces Strip, the scene of almost continuous burnings, shootings and cattle thefts. On April 18, 1875, the sheriff of Nueces County, John McClure, telegraphed Adjutant General Steele asking when McNelly was coming. He informed Steele that five ranches had been burned by masked men in the past week.[2]

McNelly had already enlisted at least a cadre and had established a camp three miles outside Burton, on the road to Corpus Christi. George Durham, who became a member of the company, describes being in the post office in Burton, Washington County, in April 1875 when a "little runt of a fellow" came in to pick up mail from Austin. Durham, waiting to catch a glimpse of the celebrated Civil War partisan who had "led the Texas Scouts in Louisiana during the war," found it hard to believe this was the hero his father had said was such a great irregular-force commander.

Durham had initially wanted only to see McNelly because his father had served with him in Louisiana, but he decided he wanted to serve with him as well. He rode out to the camp, was inspected and signed up on, as he remembered, April 25, 1875. The new recruit from Georgia found that neither the men already in camp nor the captain were much for talking. The first sergeant was named John Armstrong; another, older man was Jim Boyd. One Ranger, who had signed up under the name Parrott, was a photographer and had some of his gear with him. No one made much fuss over young Durham.

By nightfall when McNelly told them to fall in and count off by eights, they had twenty-two men signed up. Each eighth man was appointed an acting corporal, and McNelly gave them instructions on bedding down and posting guards.[3] They were not yet in hostile territory, but the little captain was testing them, getting them accustomed to the dangers ahead.

The next day more men rode in, talked to the captain and were accepted or rejected. Sergeant Armstrong reported they had forty-one men when McNelly called them together and announced that L.B. Wright and J.B. Robinson were their lieutenants, John Armstrong the first sergeant, and R.P. Orrell and L.L. Wright the other sergeants. The company was to be ready to move in fifteen minutes—and it did.[4]

This company would have several official designations; it was usually listed on the monthly returns as the Washington County Volunteer Militia, but sometimes it was called Company A. To everyone they were Rangers and they considered themselves as such when McNelly had them fall in, sending Sergeant Orrell and two men out as advance guard as they began a march towards Corpus Christi and a place in Texas history.

When the Rangers reached Corpus Christi they found the little town, fearing an expected raid by bandits, almost deserted. Several outlaw gangs had crossed from Mexico into Texas, raiding deep into the interior and almost to Corpus. One of the biggest raids had been upon Nuecestown, where they had stolen eighteen new "Dick Heye" saddles which would become critical evidence within a few weeks. McNelly had the saddles described to his men and gave orders "to empty those saddles on sight. No palavering with the riders."

Sol Lichtenstein owned the largest general store in Corpus, and McNelly, without funds and needing supplies, weapons and ammunition, asked him for help. The Ranger explained all he could do was sign receipts which the state might not honor. The merchant shrugged and said he would rather trust the Rangers than have the outlaws steal his merchandise. He loaded the men with food, ammunition, and thirty-six new Sharps carbines. McNelly turned down the offer of Winchester, Henry and Spencer repeaters in favor of the big, single-shot buffalo guns, saying, "I don't want men who miss."[5]

Before he left town McNelly told Pat Whelan, leader of one of the vigilante posse groups, to disband his men and to give the same message to other gangs and so-called vigilantes, unless they had been officially deputized and were under the command of the sheriff. McNelly had seen how these groups operated in DeWitt County and knew they were little more than an excuse to justify killing enemies and to settle old grudges. One of the men in Corpus Christi openly boasted to the Rangers that they had killed eighteen men before the Rangers arrived.[6]

The adjutant general described conditions in the Nueces Strip.

> Soon after the raid of Mexicans in Nueces county, some raids occurred of a different character. Bands of Americans went to a place called La Para, where a store was burned and several persons killed. This was incited partially for revenge on the Mexicans, and partially to suppress the killing of cattle for their hides.
>
> There is considerable element in the country bordering on the Nueces and west, that think the killing of a Mexican no crime, and the effect has been to stop, to a considerable degree the trade between Laredo and Corpus Christi.

It was not a one-sided fight. Steele continued his summary of border conditions.

> The thieves and cut-throats, who have collected on the border, think the killing of a Texan some-

thing to be proud of, and they kill anyone, even their own nationality, should he happen to encounter them with stolen cattle, unless they have confidence in his discretion.

The adjutant general drew some broad conclusions about border conditions—the cattle thefts were being made with the full knowledge of Mexican authorities, and a number of merchants in Corpus Christi and other towns supported and profited from the raids, buying the stolen hides for resale. He concluded that the Americans near the Nueces who had banded together to fight the raiders had become as much of a threat as the Mexican bandits. As a result of atrocities on both sides, the country near the Rio Grande was becoming depopulated. Sadly, he felt the black soldiers offered little protection, but if the country could be defended and made peaceful, the country would be settled in short order.[7]

McNelly was probably not aware of all the problems within the Strip, but he did understand that the Rangers were facing a major fight. When they left Corpus, the Rangers took the old Taylor Road south and rode to the King Ranch where they were resupplied with good horses by Captain Richard King; like the merchant, King would rather give the horses to the Rangers than let the bandits take them. When they again started south, McNelly's Boys were on decent mounts and well armed. Most of them still had no more than the clothing on their backs, but it was now a force that could move with the outlaws.[8]

They had their first test soon after leaving the ranch. Now operating on a combat basis, the Ranger outriders saw men ahead and signaled the alarm. The company scattered to each side of the trail as two large, disorganized vigilante groups approached. Their spokesman announced "We're going to pitch in and help you, Captain." McNelly told them he didn't need help and gave the startled men ten minutes to surrender their weapons or he would open fire. The amazed men gathered to discuss the ultimatum, but when the ten minutes was up every Ranger pistol had been drawn. One of the vigilantes rode over and offered McNelly his pistol, but the Ranger told him to keep it, and to use it only to defend his home. Durham believed that moment was when some degree of law returned to the border country.

This was just a skirmish, an easy one at that. McNelly later told his men they were in a war. They must respect the law and private property and not enter a house unless invited or accept any gift from anyone, not even a "roasting ear or melon unless he tells you to." They must let people know the Rangers had come as friends to protect them. As for the others, the outlaws of either side, they were to be arrested and brought in. If an attempt was made to free a prisoner, the prisoner would be killed immediately. His calm, cold blooded recital of the rules of war according to McNelly frightened a few of the men, and five were discharged on the spot.[9]

A few days later, McNelly ran into Neal Coldwell and his company from the Frontier Battalion returning to their old station at Concepcion. Young Durham thought Coldwell was not too happy about being ordered out of the Strip, considering it a reflection on the work he had been doing. If so, Coldwell nevertheless cooperated fully with McNelly, giving him advice about the spy network the bandits operated along the Rio Grande. The Mexicans undoubtedly knew Coldwell's Rangers were leaving, but they probably had no idea another company was coming in to replace them. McNelly took his men into the bush, avoiding trails and inhabited places.

In the brush, the Rangers were joined by J.S. "Old" Rock, who had worked with McNelly when the Ranger had served on the Rio Grande with a congressional commission, and by a Mexican named Jesus Sandoval, both of whom knew every inch of the border region.

McNelly moved his company to an abandoned ranch near the present town of Edinburg, at that time a desolate place belonging to whomever had enough guns to hold it. There the dapper Ranger, carefully dressed in duck pants and brush jacket, with calf-skin leggins and a fine beaver hat, began planning his campaign. At five feet five inches, weighing about 125 pounds, he hardly fit the popular idea of a feared manhunter. None of his men sensed he was slowly dying from consumption; the low voice seemed to his men just part of his carefully controlled manner.[10]

McNelly knew intelligence was the key to fighting the raiders. The man they called Old Rock knew the border and managed to slip a spy into the headquarters of Juan Cortina, the chief contractor in Mexico for stolen beef. Besides being mayor of Matamoros, Cortina operated a thriving business based on stolen Texas cattle, selling most of his loot to Cuba. He had been in business for decades, resisting efforts of earlier Rangers, U.S. troops, and his own government to bring him to justice. In his operation he had a number of Americans working at various jobs; McNelly's spy, George Hall, fitted easily into this company and was able to write McNelly full details on how the thieves worked, providing complete information on strengths, dates and destinations of proposed raids.[11]

Thus armed with good intelligence, the Rangers caught up with one group of raiders, but unfortunately not until they had already crossed over to the Mexican side of the Rio Grande with an estimated three hundred head of cattle. It was a worried Lieutenant Robinson who reported this failure to his commander. Another Ranger patrol brought back an American prisoner riding one of the stolen Dick Heye saddles. The Rangers explained they had not killed him because he might have information on outlaw activities. McNelly agreed and turned the man over to Jesus Sandoval. In a few minutes "Casoose" Sandoval had the man dangling from a rope. At first he refused to talk, but a few jerks refreshed his memory and he admitted he knew about a raid in progress. The outlaws had gone into Texas and were circling to come back with the stolen herd between the Taylor Road and the Laguna Madre, well off the usual path for such raids. He thought they would be recrossing the river in eight or nine hours. The wilted prisoner was turned over to Sandoval while the Rangers readied themselves to ride; Durham said it "just about turned my stomach" when he heard what happened to the man.[12]

This "interrogation" probably occurred on June 5, the date McNelly said he first heard of the raiding party, but he did not explain *how* he learned of the outlaw crossing. In his report he never mentioned either his own spy, Hall, or the American prisoner, which lends some credence to Durham's account. He did state that a patrol led by Lieutenant Robinson captured one of the raiding party who talked freely and admitted to being part of the bandit rear guard. On June 11 the Rangers captured another man, part of the advance guard, who told the Rangers the rest of the gang were on the way south to the Rio Grande and planned to cross the next day.[13]

Although exact movements and events between June 5 and June 11 are not outlined in McNelly's report, the Rangers were obviously traveling towards the Laguna Madre. Durham suggests the company moved out after the American was "questioned," but it is also possible that a patrol sent out with Lieutenant Robinson captured another man, as suggested in McNelly's report. McNelly only reported that he stationed his men in a "motte," remaining there until about two in the morning until his scouts reported they had found the trail of the cattle four miles to the east. He ordered his men into the saddle, and they sighted the bandits and the stolen cattle about seven o'clock. [14]

A third account of the scout sheds light on some of the mystery about movements; William Callicott, another young Ranger with McNelly, also wrote his version of service in the company. On this occasion he stated the Rangers made several moves and caught a number of men, all questioned by Sandoval. The last prisoner was taken June 11, which agrees with McNelly's report. Callicott, like Durham, was quite frank about the fate of any prisoners. [15]

The Rangers found a clear trail out on the prairie; the raiders had several hundred cattle with them, flattening the grass and making tracking simple. When they came in sight of their quarry, the Rangers were several miles behind the thieves. At first the outlaws seemed confident they could hold off any pursuit, civilian or army, but as the Rangers continued to close the distance, the outlaws began to gather the herd more compactly and tried to increase their pace. They were not accustomed to a determined pursuit. McNelly carefully studied the enemy through a spyglass and had his men check equipment, then they started after them at a gallop. He was riding a splendid mount, the gift from Captain King, and easily outdistanced his men. Seeing they would be overtaken, the outlaws halted and waited for the Rangers.

Riding close, McNelly directed Lieutenant Robinson to continue with the direct approach through the shallow water they were entering, but not to start firing until they were on firm ground. He called to Sandoval and several of the nearest men to join him, then rode to the flank to cut off any attempt to reach the shelter of a motte of trees.

The main body of Rangers continued to move through

the shallow waters of the lagoon at a steady walk, as fast as
their horses could go. They never fired or called out, even
when bullets began splashing the water. This silent, calm
advance began to unnerve some of the waiting bandits, who
evidently expected to exchange a few shots across the water
and then ride away with the stolen cattle. Their shots were
not all wasted; a few Ranger horses were hit. Corporal W.L.
Rudd's horse went down, but he jumped clear, held his
Sharps above his head and continued to advance. The
bandits began to fall back from the edge of the water, look
for their horses and run.

They rallied, however, and a vicious fight spread across
the prairie in the high grass. McNelly reported:

> I have never seen men fight with such despera-
> tion. Many of them, after being shot from their
> horses and severely wounded three or four times,
> would rise on their elbows and fire at my men as
> they passed.

Durham lost his horse and was afoot in the muddy water
when a man suddenly rose from behind a bush in front of
him. First a fancy beaver hat appeared, then the rest of the
outlaw, turning to look for his horse. Durham had a clear
shot, and the bullet hit the man in the head; "Right there I
quit being a scared country boy. I was a man. A Ranger."
Firing was heavy all about him as the Rangers, some on foot,
began moving through the high grass and brush.

Separate fights broke out as the mounted Rangers began
chasing the outlaws who had reached their horses, but the
Ranger mounts were tired from the long scout and the rapid
chase at the beginning of the battle. The Rangers dismounted to be able to fire more accurately at the rustlers'
mounts, then finished off the riders on foot. None of the
bandits made any effort to surrender. The last man ran into
a dense clump of Spanish Dagger and McNelly, with only
one shell left in his revolver, started cautiously into the
thicket. The bandit, his pistol empty, drew a large knife and
waited, until the Ranger yelled duplicitously that his pistol
was empty and to bring more shells. The hidden man must
have understood English, for the ruse worked and he suddenly leaped up about eight feet from the Ranger and,
grinning, yelled "Me gotta you now, me gotta you." McNelly

sighted carefully and shot him in the mouth with his last shell.

Fighting also continued between the dismounted men of both sides. Lieutenant Wright, on foot, saw two rustlers run towards a horse, scramble on the animal and ride off. Wright had a clear shot and fired with his rifle. The rear man fell sideways, the other man continued riding for twenty paces or so before dropping to the ground; the heavy .50 caliber bullet, intended to stop buffalo, had easily penetrated both bodies.

The fight was almost over, but the last engagement did not have a happy ending. Spencer Adams and Berry Smith had come upon the last of the rustlers whom Smith, the youngest of the company, had hit with a pistol shot. Elated, Smith dismounted and followed the wounded man into the dense cover but was killed by a single shot at close range. Adams, more experienced but with a wounded horse, remained outside the thicket, making sure the man did not escape. He waited until other Rangers came up and, together, they surrounded the thicket. McNelly joined them and directed they fire at any movement. At length they went in and found a dead bandit.

The fight was over by early afternoon, and there was plenty of daylight left. Sandoval was directed to bring in the bandit bodies and hauled the corpses in by roping them and dragging them along the ground behind his horse. Callicott said they killed sixteen men that day, all of them Mexicans except for an American bandit identified as Jack Ellis. Two Mexican ranch hands joined Sandoval in bringing in the dead rustlers, and McNelly asked them to go back along the route of the fight and bring in any horses still alive, as well as saddles, blankets, weapons or other gear dropped during the running battle. The Rangers recovered Smith's body and started towards Brownsville, several of them riding captured horses.

During much of the chase a posse, led by Sheriff James Browne of Cameron County, based in Brownsville, was in sight, but McNelly reported their horses were too tired to take any role in the fighting. Members of the posse, all from the Brownsville area, identified the dead rustlers, also all from the Brownsville area and known by name and sight; several were leaders in the rustling operation.

McNelly had four Rangers escort the wagon bearing the

body of Ranger Smith; he and the remainder of the Rangers rode to the outskirts of Brownsville and established a camp. McNelly rode into town and registered at the Miller Hotel, taking two front rooms, and then sent a messenger to guide the company into town. He next sent for the brand inspector and the Brownsville marshal, telling them of the fight. The Ranger asked them to take wagons to the Palo Alto prairie and bring in the bodies, booty and cattle. He wanted them to return the stolen cattle to their owners if possible; if this could not be done, McNelly wanted the cattle and equipment sold.[16]

Marshal Joseph P. O'Schaughnessy, with two wagons and a detachment of troops from Fort Brown, could find only eight bodies. In his report he explained more had been killed but could not be found; it was supposed that relatives had gone out in the late afternoon and found the other corpses. While not stated, this would indicate that many people in Brownsville knew about the raid, knew who was in the party, and went looking for relatives when news of the fight reached town. John J. Smith, the Inspector of Cattle, swore that the cattle captured by the Rangers were turned over to him. He was able to identify ninety-seven head with Texas brands, out of 216 brought in. The Mounted Inspector of Customs, Herman S. Rock, was certain they were all stolen because he could identify many brands belonging to Texas ranchers as well as a number that had brands of Mexican ranches on the U.S. side of the Rio Grande. A number of the captured horses were traced to two ranches in Cameron County.[17]

When the outlaw bodies were brought in, McNelly had them stacked in the main plaza and placed armed guards over the pile, with orders to arrest anyone who tried to identify the dead. Next, he went to the fort and had the soldiers close the ferry to Matamoros for the night. That done, he returned to the hotel and went to sleep. Next morning the rest of the company, the camp guards and wagons and supplies, rode in and set up a new camp outside town. McNelly had the soldiers relieve his men of patrol duties inside the town, inspected the new camp, and rode to Fort Brown to use the military telegraph to report to Austin.[18]

What must be the telegram McNelly sent to the adjutant general is in the archives in Austin, but it was sent from Matamoros by way of Camargo on June 14, 1875.

Had a fight with raiders, killed twelve and captured two hundred and sixty five beeves. Wish you
were here.

> L.H. McNelly
> Capt comndg.[19]

The almost flippant "Wish you were here" was not in
character; McNelly was not a man for joking. What is
interesting is McNelly's mention of twelve killed.

The several accounts of this fight agree in large measure
except for the rustler casualties. Callicott said the spies
reported there were seventeen Mexicans and the American,
Jack Ellis, in the raiding party. He recalled all being brought
in except for one left for dead who had only been wounded
and had managed to crawl away. Durham thought the
marshal had said he picked up sixteen corpses, although
he reported finding only eight. McNelly's initial report, the
telegram on June 14, listed twelve killed, but when he made
his final report McNelly said he had counted twelve raiders
at the start of the fight and that, when he had twelve bodies,
he believed he had killed them all. He added that two
wounded rustlers had escaped and that one had died in
Mexico from his wounds. This supports Callicott's account
of at least one wounded man's escaping.

McNelly reported two prisoners by name, members of
the raiders whom he turned over to the sheriff, but no
account, including McNelly's, mentions any prisoners taken
during the chase and fight. Regardless of the exact number
of dead bodies and/or prisoners taken, it was the first time
in decades any serious blow had been struck at the Cortina
operation.

McNelly was fully prepared for any attempt at retali-
ation. Durham remembered that when McNelly returned
from sending the telegram, he held a roll call and told his
men not to go into town; he wanted to be ready for anything.
Durham wondered if piling the bodies had been an attempt
to goad the Mexicans into attacking.[20] The preparations for
a fight, however, possibly even crossing into Mexico, did not
sit well with a few of the men who had not been in the battle
on the prairie. One asked if the captain was going to cross
the river. McNelly did not answer; instead he asked a
question of his own, "You want your discharge?" When the

man whined that he wasn't going to cross the river to fight, he was discharged along with five others.[21]

Later that same morning, a messenger arrived from Fort Brown and saluted McNelly, telling him the Rangers were invited for breakfast. The hungry Rangers had a good meal in the army mess while their captain and Major Alexander made plans for Smith's funeral. They buried the boy-Ranger that afternoon with full military honors, the first time since the Mexican War a Ranger had been so honored. A light wagon carried the box, draped with an American flag. McNelly and his men led the procession, marching on foot followed by several squads of soldiers. They circled the town and marched to the post cemetery where the soldiers took over for the burial ceremonies. The same afternoon, McNelly allowed the sheriff to remove the bodies of the rustlers.[22]

Passion ran high in the town for days following the Ranger funeral. At least five of the slain outlaws had lived in Brownsville, and there were veiled threats in town and more open ones from across the Rio Grande. How much NcNelly knew about the identity of the slain raiders is unknown. Although they had been identified by the sheriff's posse, the Rangers had had no contact with the posse on the day of the fight, and the bodies still on the field had been brought in by Marshal O'Schaughnessy and piled in the main plaza. There is nothing to indicate whether or not the marshal told the Ranger captain the identity of the dead men.

Durham speculated that his captain may have believed, or hoped, that Cortina might be enticed into making a raid to recover the bodies, but it seems very unlikely that McNelly would have knowingly used citizens of Brownsville and the surrounding area as bait for Cortina. It seems even more unlikely that Cortina would have risked a major fight to recover the bodies of people living in Texas. Nothing in McNelly's record suggests he would have forced such an indignity on people living in Texas. He was satisfied he had caught men engaged in recent cattle thefts—nine of the Dick Heye saddles recently stolen in the raid on Nuecestown were recovered from men killed on the Palo Alto prairie. He knew he had killed raiders and bandits, and he probably thought they came from Mexico.

The company settled into a quiet routine. By now McNelly was ill, the first indication the Rangers had of his condition, and seldom left his rooms. A local banker, Charles Stillman, came to the aid of the Rangers, cashing their state script without discount and seeing that the sick Ranger obtained a better room at the Brown Hotel. Most people had a fear of any consumptive and hesitated to go near them. The medical staff at Fort Brown did everything possible to make McNelly comfortable, sending him goat milk each day. Few of his men ever saw him, as he limited his visitors to Lieutenant Robinson, Old Rock and Stillman.[23]

The Rangers had orders to leave their pistols in camp when they went into Brownsville but, considering the feelings in town, most of the men wisely refused to go under those conditions. The orders were changed to allow no more than three armed men in town at one time, and then only if they were accompanied by their corporal. They could not go into bars and were not to draw their weapons unless signaled by the corporal. The men were eager to get to town; they had a little spending money now and needed necessities. McNelly had given strict orders about not accepting any gifts.

The wisdom of restricting the men was shown a few days after the fight when Ranger Durham took some papers to Sheriff Browne, who wanted to know if the Ranger had a *List of Fugitives*, then he proceeded to tell the young Ranger that most of the names were out of date, many had become good citizens, some elected to public office. Durham said the captain was the one to answer that and took the list of the men the sheriff had buried and returned to camp. From his account, there is little doubt the local sheriff wanted the Rangers out of his county.[24]

Durham paints a gloomy picture of the months following the destruction of the rustler gang, with his captain's becoming sicker all the time. McNelly did report one scout in July, without any definitive result.[25] Another raid was broken up and the cattle turned loose on the Texas side of the river. The bandits, for all their brave talk, had no intention of being caught again. The captain still had his scouts and spies in place and was aware of any major movement. He reported in August that there were rumors of a raid upriver, but he was unable to find anything.[26]

The army medic at Fort Brown had sent for Mrs. McNelly and their son to come to camp without saying anything to McNelly. She provided good home cooking and was a comfort to him during this depressing time. There is a possibility McNelly deliberately spread word of his condition, hoping to lull the raiders into making a false move. Durham hints at this, describing a conversation with Lieutenant Robinson while the captain was supposedly deathly ill. Robinson said the Ranger was using the time to build a spy network. George Hall was still active in Cortina's headquarters, and McNelly received reports almost daily from his various agents.[27]

While largely inactive, the company's size increased considerably. Although nine men left in August, fifty-three men are reported for September and fifty in October. No scouts are reported on the monthly returns.[28] Durham mentions a number of scouts with McNelly, more than the reports or returns show, but they evidently came to nothing worth reporting. During this period—late summer—McNelly sent Ranger Parrott on what was to be a very lengthy secret mission into the Eagle Pass country. McNelly was obviously concerned about the outlaw King Fisher, who was building a reputation as cattle thief and local bandit chief in the Eagle Pass area. Parrott was a photographer in civilian life and still had his equipment, a perfect cover for a spy.

McNelly became so ill he had to turn over the company to Lieutenant Robinson and return to his home in Burton.[29] With the lieutenant in command, the Rangers sat about for days before Robinson started them patrolling again. In late October Sergeant Armstrong and a small group caught two suspicious riders out in the brush and asked them how many were in their party. One man said just the two of them but changed his story when Armstrong jabbed him in the stomach with his carbine, almost knocking him from his horse; he suddenly remembered there were really sixteen of them. Armstrong told him to go and bring in four of his friends. If they tried any tricks, he would kill the other man. The threat worked, and in short order all sixteen riders were taken prisoner. Durham recalled they seemed amused as though it was some game.

The Rangers found out how much of a game it was when they took the riders into town and tried to turn them over to the sheriff at Brownsville. The officer refused to accept the prisoners or sign a receipt; he informed the Rangers he didn't do law the way McNelly did. Where was the evidence? What were the charges? Besides, where was McNelly? He had heard the Ranger had run out and left his company. The disgruntled Armstrong tore up the list of names, told his men to return the weapons of the prisoners, and stormed out of the jail. As a parting shot, the sheriff told the Rangers not to get drunk in his town or he would arrest the lot of them.[30]

The Rangers did little after this fiasco. Durham said a few of the oldtimers and the sergeants kept the company together, but a lot of the men were thinking about going to work on the ranches until word should come down from Austin to disband the unit.

Instead, they received word of a different sort. An army messenger rode out in mid-November and gave Lieutenant Robinson a message received on the military telegraph. The officer read the paper, went outside, gave a wild yell, threw his hat up in the air and shot it twice as it descended.[31] The formerly sleepy camp was suddenly a scene of wild activity. Robinson had the bulk of the Rangers in the saddle in minutes, heading for Ringgold Barracks at Rio Grande City, the camp crew and guards to follow as soon as possible.

While he had been away from his company McNelly had not been inactive, even from his home in distant Burton. Under his wife's care he had regained strength; evidently he kept in touch with his spies all during this time and suggested as much in a letter to Adjutant General Steele. He had also been in communication with Commander Kells of the U.S. Navy, commander of the ironclad *Rio Bravo*. What scheme these two devised and how much official approval they thought they had for provoking an international incident will never be known.[32]

Nor is there anything in the records to explain definitively why McNelly had decided to travel to the Rio Grande at this time. Despite his spy network, he could not have known that army troops had chased, but failed to stop, a large cattle raid into Texas from Mexico. He had traveled with his wife at a leisurely pace in a wagon from Burton to Rio Grande City, where he learned there was a considerable army force on the river bank trying to decide what to do about the stolen cattle in Mexico. McNelly saw his opportunity, and he had used the army telegraph in Fort Ringgold to order his company to join him at Rio Grande City.

They did not keep him waiting long; Robinson had them on a forced march, covering the almost sixty miles in five hours. The Rangers traveled light, pockets and saddle bags stuffed with extra ammunition, everything else to follow with the company wagon. Durham recalled he had a hundred pistol cartridges with twenty rounds for his Sharps in his pockets. Callicott had forty rounds for each of his weapons.[33]

Although the Rangers made remarkable time, they arrived with worn-out horses. McNelly met them and told them to rest their mounts, to eat well and get what rest they could. The slight captain was dressed, as always, as though going on parade. His breeches were clean and pressed, his beard neatly trimmed. He even wore a small necktie. Durham thought he may have gained a little weight.[34]

It was November 18. Later in the day McNelly sent a telegram to Adjutant General Steele.

> A party of raiders have crossed two hundred and fifty cattle at Las Cuevas. They have been firing on Major Clendenin's men. He refuses to cross without further orders. I shall cross tonight if I can get any support.

Later that night he sent a second message.

> I commenced crossing at one o'clock tonight. Have thirty men. Will try and recover our cattle. The U.S. troops promise to cover my return. Lieutenant Robinson has just arrived making a march of fifty-five miles in five hours.

He signed the message "Capt. Rangers."[35] In such quiet and brief fashion McNelly announced he was going to invade Mexico. The Ranger had also told the senior U.S. Army officer on the site, Major D.R. Clendenin, what he planned. Clendenin said he would cover the crossing into Mexico and the return, but he refused to go with the Texans. There is no doubt McNelly believed he had a promise, implied or spoken, to come to his assistance if he became surrounded in Mexico. There is also some evidence that McNelly intended to draw the U.S. soldiers across the river into Mexico.[36]

When McNelly returned to his men, however, he told them they could not depend on the army for help. Both

Durham and Callicott remembered he told the Rangers it was a volunteer mission and asked if they were willing to cross. He was certain of his men; they would have followed him across more than a river.

McNelly managed to get five men and their horses across the river, but the opposite bank was so muddy and torn up from the cattle crossing that the horses bogged down. He changed his plan. Someone had noticed a small boat on the Mexican shore, and Matt Fleming swam across and brought it back. The Rangers went across in the boat, a few men at a time.[37]

It took time to ferry the men across to Mexico. McNelly had planned to attack the ranch at Las Cuevas at dawn; it was four in the morning before they were all assembled on the Mexican shore, supposedly about three miles from their objective. There were thirty Rangers for the fight ahead. The roll showed forty-nine, but the others were on special duty or still on the road escorting the wagon and supplies.[38] Twenty-nine men and McNelly.

There was a dense fog that morning, with visibility down to a few feet. Fortunately they had a cattle trail to follow through the high grass, trees and underbrush. Led by the five mounted men, the Rangers walked along as quietly as possible, with Sandoval's acting as point. The plan was simple: when they reached Las Cuevas the mounted Rangers would rush through the settlement, firing and yelling to draw attention to themselves. With this distraction as cover, the dismounted men would move through the place in skirmish order, killing all the men they found.

They came to a fence line, which agreed with the description of Las Cuevas although it was closer than they expected. Durham remembered that a shot was fired here, almost hitting Armstrong, but McNelly was also near and killed the sentry with a pistol shot. Able to see better in the thinning fog, the Rangers shot at every man they saw. A few men had been outside, cutting wood; there were some women cooking breakfast. Several men ran from the small houses into the brush. One woman, who never stopped patting her tortillas, informed the Rangers they had attacked Cachuttas, a line camp for the main ranch at Las Cuevas further on. Somehow Sandoval had become confused in the fog and veered too far to his right, missing the main trail to their objective.

McNelly talked to Sandoval for a time, not angrily, just planning his next move. Then, Durham recalled, he formed them again and they started toward the main ranch, almost running, aware that the element of surprise had been lost.

Sandoval halted them and pointed into a slight depression where the ranch occupied a large area. There were a number of houses, even a chapel, enclosed on two sides by a six-foot stockade. To the Rangers' surprise, there was no sign of undue alarm in the place although the men were saddling horses. A column of men rode out from the stockade, and after a time four of the men rode forward as scouts. The concealed Rangers waited for McNelly's signal. He let the scouts draw near and shot one, then a volley from his men dropped the other three. The Rangers scattered out and began deliberate fire on the column at rather long range but well within the capabilities of the Sharps. The heavy rounds blew the column apart, and the survivors fled back into the stockade.[39]

It was evident the men in the settlement had no clear idea what they were facing; it never occurred to them that dismounted men would dare come this far from the river, and they must have believed they had faced riders who had fired and then retreated. Apparently thinking to cut off any retreat, a number of the Mexicans mounted and began riding towards the river. The Rangers were hidden in the grass and bushes and again waited for McNelly; when he shot the first man, the Sharps began booming, dropping men and horses. Those Mexicans who still could fell back, and there was a lull during which Durham checked his ammunition. Beginning with twenty carbine rounds, he had only five or six left but didn't think he had wasted many.

The break in action ended when a large group of horsemen galloped in from the direction of Camargo. Leading the advance was a handsomely dressed man, his saddle and trappings silver-mounted. McNelly decided the leader was Juan Flores Salinas, *alcalde*, who took immediate charge of the disorganized rabble inside the ranch buildings; shortly he had at least a hundred men mounted and acting in a disciplined manner. They split into groups, fanning out to cut off the Rangers from the river.

Their actual numbers vary with each report, but Durham thought they mustered a hundred riders. McNelly said there were that many riders, with another 150-200 on foot.

McNelly yelled for each man to break and make his own way back to the Rio Grande while the five horsemen stayed back to cover their retreat. NcNelly said they had no real pursuit, but Durham thinks it was because the Mexicans had already tried three frontal attacks and still believed the Rangers were trying to lure them into another bloody ambush.

The Texans reached the river bank and dropped down into the shallow water near the shore. Fortunately this area was free of quicksand, with firm footing. The exact sequence of events following their return to the Rio Grande varies slightly, depending on sources, but all versions agree on major details. Probably thinking they could now catch the Rangers trying to cross the Rio Grande, a large party led by Juan Flores charged the bank, yelling and shooting, but was easily repulsed. Flores and many of his *bravos* were slain.

Durham stated the Rangers, having fired all their carbine rounds, could only fire their pistols, but they did good execution while McNelly stood on the bank giving directions and selecting targets. Major Clendenin had been joined by a Captain Randlett with a company of the 24th Infantry when the firing on the riverbank began. Randlett crossed the river with about forty soldiers and joined the fighting that led to the repulse of Flores' charge. A Sergeant Leahy had command of an emplaced Gatling gun and also opened fire, so the Rangers had considerable assistance during this skirmish on the river bank. Durham's account suggests the fire from the Gatling gun may have killed Flores and many of his men; Callicott does not mention the Gatling gun's being fired, although he did note that the weapon was there.

Callicott remembered the skirmish more as a charge by the Rangers, even to a counterattack by the Rangers on the retreating Mexicans. He said they rushed after the *bravos* all the way into the brush, where McNelly picked up a Smith & Wesson belonging to the dead Flores and ordered them back to the shelter of the high bank.

The soldiers definitely came to the aid of the Texans; Durham says they were glad to have them. The infantrymen had rifles which could engage the Mexicans at long range and keep them well back from the river. All army officers in the fight admitted they supported the Rangers, justifying their actions by explaining they believed the riders from Las Cuevas were invading the U.S. when shots fell on the Texas side.

With most of an infantry company on the Mexican side, McNelly tried to convince Randlett to join him in another attack on Las Cuevas! The officer refused to go further into Mexico, but he did offer to remain with the Rangers until his superior arrived. In his report of the engagements, Randlett wrote that the Mexicans came over with a flag of truce and offered to return the cattle the next day. They also promised to arrest the thieves and requested the American troops return to the Texas shore.[40] When Major Alexander reached the scene, he ordered Randlett and all troops to leave Mexico.

Durham has a different version than does Randlett of the events following the arrival of the soldiers; he does not mention either Randlett's meeting any Mexican emissary with a flag of truce or any negotiations involving Randlett, the emissary and McNelly. Durham picks up his story by recalling that McNelly had the Rangers get out of the water and dry their socks. While this was taking place, Major Alexander arrived and was rowed over to McNelly. Major Alexander was bringing a message from Colonel Potter in Fort Brown, the senior army officer on the lower Rio Grande, who had ordered his troops not to support the Rangers even if they were attacked. In a polite exchange, McNelly refused to leave, but he asked the soldiers for food because his men had not eaten since they started out the day before. Alexander said he had been ordered not to support the Rangers in a fight; he did not believe the order applied to food, and the officer arranged to provide the hungry Rangers with a meal. McNelly returned across the river with Alexander to look at some telegrams that had just arrived.

Across the river a small party rode out of the bush waving a white flag. Lieutenant Robinson, in command, sent a sergeant across the river to notify McNelly, then went out with a few men to meet the truce party.

Durham said he went with Robinson, Armstrong and Jim Boyd to see what the Mexicans wanted. The leader of the truce party was an American named Doc Headly, one of the outlaw leaders known to the Rangers from descriptions sent back by Hall from Cortina's headquarters. The man was also in the *List of Fugitives*. Headly, half drunk, held a letter drafted by the chief justice of Tamaulipas. He complained the Rangers had killed the beloved *alcalde* of Camargo and another eighty citizens. He told the Rangers he would only deal with their commander.

Boyd turned to Lieutenant Robinson and asked if he could have Headly's pistols and hand-tooled leather belt if he killed him; Armstrong immediately asked if a second shot would earn him Headly's saddle. The outlaw was drunk, but not so far gone as not to recognize danger. He quickly extended his rifle and the letter.

McNelly rejoined his Rangers about then and reread the letter from the chief justice, who promised to consider the complaints if the Rangers and the troops left Mexico, but the Ranger said he would negotiate only after the cattle were returned. Headly suggested they all declare a truce until the next day, Sunday, but McNelly again refused unless the cattle were returned. Headly said the cattle were penned in Camargo and could not be brought up immediately. Taking out his notebook, McNelly wrote out an order for the release of the cattle and had the outlaw sign it. In his report later, McNelly stated he promised to give them an hour's warning before he commenced active operations. About six in the afternoon the Rangers, once again alone on the river bank, could see a considerable gathering of Mexican forces back in the brush, out of range.

A small boat brought over plenty of food, the meal promised by Major Alexander, and McNelly informed his men they would spend the night in Mexico. Ranger Callicott described how his captain moved them to a better position and sent across the river for some shovels so they could dig in against the possibility for a last ditch defensive stand; Durham does not mention these endeavors.

By the dawn of November 20, McNelly was a famous man. He crossed back to the Texas side of the river and sent Adjutant General Steele a telegram, informing him he had crossed the Rio Grande, killing four men before reaching Las Cuevas and five afterwards. He reported his retreat to the river, the attack, and the aid of the U.S. troops. McNelly estimated there were now four hundred Mexican troops opposite his position, and in closing he asked the adjutant general what to do.[41] It seems out of character for McNelly to ask for advice, certainly this late in the game. He may have been hoping Steele would tell him to stay, or even to attack. Or he may have wanted Steele to order him out. There is no record of any answer from Steele.

Durham wrote that McNelly refused to return to the U.S.

side after Major Alexander brought him Colonel Potter's
message on November 19. This actually occurred on November 20, but regardless of the date, the answer was clear.
Durham quotes a message McNelly sent back to the senior
commander, telling him and the Secretary of War to go to
hell; if this message was actually sent it has not survived.
McNelly more probably expressed his sentiments verbally.

The State Department was now involved, as well as the
War Department. The U.S. Consul in Matamoros wired
Lucius Avery, the Commercial Agent in Camargo, arranging
for the surrender of the Rangers. Avery went at once from
Ringgold Barracks to the river bank and presented the
telegram to McNelly. The Ranger mentions Avery's visit in
his report, but he knew the border too well; once they
surrendered, the Rangers were dead men. McNelly said he
"couldn't see it."

There was one other interruption when a large party
came out under a flag of truce and began loading bodies in
several wagons. All of the official reports mention nine men
killed during the fighting. Durham says he learned later they
had slain twelve at the line camp. Casualties at Las Cuevas
are uncertain, but Headly mentioned eighty. It had been a
sobering experience for the rustlers, whatever the loss. To
cap the experience, late in the day McNelly informed the
Mexicans he was coming after them! If they wanted to escape
another fight, they could deliver cattle and thieves to Ranch
Davis. There was considerable talk among the men in the
brush, and the answer came back that the cattle and
rustlers would be sent to Rio Grande City the next day at
ten o'clock.

The weary Rangers recrossed the river in the same small
boat that had taken them over. They found Captain Randlett
had taken good care of their horses, and the tired men rode
to Rio Grande City opposite Camargo. The morning of
November 21 McNelly and some of his company returned to
the river bank. It was probably no great surprise to them
that the cattle were still across the river in pens, well
guarded. McNelly began trying to get them back. Using a
Mexican messenger, he politely asked Diego Garcia, the
senior official in Camargo, to return the cattle. Garcia sent
back an oral reply that he was busy and could not see the
Ranger until noon the next day, November 22, but later he
sent a written reply that he would send the cattle across

early the next day.

McNelly replied in writing, outlining the agreement with Headly on the river bank and reminding Garcia the cattle were due back in Texas by 10:00 a.m. *that* day, November 21. In a subtle but quite clear closure, he requested an early reply because the commander of the United States troops was awaiting Garcia's action. Garcia understood and shortly sent a second written message; he had discovered he did not have such pressing business after all and the cattle would be at McNelly's disposal on the banks of the river at three that afternoon.[42]

Garcia's failure to specify the *Texas* bank of the river must have been clear to the Ranger captain. He could see the cattle in a pole corral, guarded by a few men who obviously had no plans to move them. He had the company ride back to Rio Grande City not far from the river. It was a lazy Sunday morning, and he treated the Rangers to coffee and *pan dulces* in a little cafe. They sat about and talked to a few people and killed some time before McNelly took them back down to the river and the ferry crossing to Camargo.

He stepped on the ferry and smiled at the operator. Turning, he told Armstrong to "cut off" the first ten men from the head of the line and have the others stand back. Sergeant Armstrong counted off what later became known as the Death Squad because they never expected to return. Durham never forgot the names: Lieutenant Robinson, sergeants Hall and Armstrong, Corporal Rudd, and privates Pitts, Callicott, Maben, McGovern, Durham and Wofferd. They boarded the ferry as though they were going across into Mexico on a Sunday picnic.

McNelly jumped onto the Mexican bank, snubbed the ferry for the operator and dusted his hands. Five customs officers were waiting for them; the captain commanding the group was the man who had acted as a messenger earlier in the day, now dressed in uniform and armed. McNelly shook the man's hand and had McGovern tell the official it was now three o'clock and he had come to take delivery of the cattle. He asked the captain to have his men herd the cattle to the bank and cross them to the Texas side. Equally polite, the Mexican said he had forgotten it was Sunday and against their religion to work. McNelly drew his pistol and knocked the man down, kneeing him in the belly as he fell. The other Rangers had taken defensive positions on Robinson's signal; Bob Pitts shot one Mexican who managed to draw a pistol, and the others surrendered quickly. The Rangers disarmed them and herded them out of the way.

McNelly jerked the dazed customs man to his feet and had McGovern tell the others they were taking him back across the river. The groggy man must have understood English because he started shouting orders to his men, who began driving the cattle from the pens, down to the bank and into the water. As the animals swam the river to the Texas shore, they were herded together and driven away from the water to the waiting Rangers.

Callicott, one of the ten men who crossed with McNelly, also wrote about this incident, but his recollections vary considerably from Durham's. In his account, Callicott said the Rangers were facing twenty-five armed Mexicans, whose leader explained to McNelly the cattle could not be returned until they were inspected. McNelly instructed Tom Sullivan [see footnote #43] to tell the man they had been stolen without being inspected and could be returned the same way. When this did not lead to any movement of the cattle, McNelly had his men cover the Mexicans, and Sullivan told them they would all be killed if the cattle were not returned in five minutes. This was enough for the Mexicans to rush the cattle into the water. All crossed except for one tired animal that had to be roped and assisted. Callicott said McNelly gave the animal to the ferry operator as fare for the trip across and back.

Just how many cattle were returned is another disputed matter. Durham said they retrieved more than four hundred, which seems high. Major Alexander reported on November 29, 1875, that seventy-six head were brought back, obviously a low estimate.

Major Alexander's report is yet another version of the Las Cuevas crossing but contains few details and merely states that, after receiving Colonel Potter's message on November 20, he advised McNelly to return. The Ranger complied, then Alexander proceeded to Ringgold alone and reached the post, at 1:00 a.m. on November 21, where the cattle were returned. He suggested the return of the cattle showed the effect of the "demonstration," apparently referring to the Rangers' crossing of the river and the slaughter of the Mexicans.[43] The major and the other military officers involved distanced themselves from McNelly as much as

possible, probably sensing the furor that the crossing into
Mexico had provoked.

McNelly didn't mind, at least as far as anyone could tell;
he had brought back the stolen cattle, or at least some of
them. As far as possible the animals were identified by
brands and sent back to their owners, the only time this
ever happened. There were over thirty head belonging to
Captain King which McNelly sent back to his friend, escorted
by Corporal Rudd, Bob and Ed Pitts, Durham and Callicott.
Durham had hinted strongly to Armstrong about going on
the trip—he had fallen for one of the girls at the King
Ranch—but the big sergeant pretended not to understand
what the young Ranger was after. Finally Armstrong re-
lented and allowed Durham to go. They left the camp, which
was beginning to assume some degree of comfort since the
wagon and supplies and the remainder of the company had
finally caught up with them, and reached the ranch without
incident, much to the delight of the people at King Ranch.
There had been wild rumors all over the valley that McNelly
and his entire company had been wiped out at Las Cuevas,
and their demise had actually been reported over the army
telegraph by an excited young officer who had seen the first
charge of the Mexicans against the Rangers at the river.[44]

After telling King and his people the real story, the
Rangers were invited to eat. They had not bathed or shaved
in many days and, as Durham put it, "even with all the
clothes in the catalogue" they never could have "looked too
neat" except for Corporal Rudd, a careful dresser "who could
tidy up some, like Captain, and look like a human being."
Durham was still wearing the same threadbare clothes he
had worn when he came from Georgia a year earlier. The
Rangers were provided shaving materials, wash bowls and
clean blankets and had a chance to relax in a large room
over a warehouse. That evening a huge meal was brought
over for the hungry men. The two King daughters had made
two big poundcakes on which they had written:

Compliments of the two Miss Kings
to
THE MCNELLY RANGERS.

Callicott recalled that Durham ate so much he had a
nightmare and almost shot the others; understandably,

Durham overlooked this incident in his memoirs.

King had the returned cattle turned out to pasture, with one horn sawed off so they would never be sold. The Rangers returned to camp and a less elaborate lifestyle. Durham managed to obtain a glimpse of his lady love, though she never saw him, but the story has a happy ending; in later years they were married.

The rest of the year was quiet. For a time the Rangers were bothered by family or friends writing to claim the bodies of the Rangers supposedly slain at Las Cuevas, but soon the true story, although considerably enhanced, became known all over the country and made McNelly a folk hero everywhere except in Washington and Austin. To the people along the Rio Grande he became a favorite. The company established a camp at a place called Retama, and the families in the area sent them all the food they could eat. Durham said he got fat. When Mrs. McNelly mentioned her husband needed goat milk for this health, the neighbors "mighty near flooded the place with it." There is nothing in the records about the state of McNelly's health, but Durham said he was sick again and leaving the Rangers' activities to the other officers.

The area ranchers, encouraged by the result of the Ranger actions, began taking care of the few raids from across the Rio Grande. Durham rode on one patrol downriver to their old camp and ran across an elderly Mexican who told the Rangers a revolution under Porfirio Diaz was brewing in Mexico. The old man had good sources.[45] Toward the last of the year the Washington County Volunteer Militia mustered forty-five men for duty, with McNelly still commanding but with Lieutenant Robinson the only other officer.[46]

There is some confusion about McNelly's actions and location during early 1876; Robinson signed the monthly returns for January and February.[47] Durham said his captain went to Washington at his own expense to help two army men being tried for their role in helping the Rangers at Las Cuevas. He evidently cleared up the matter and the men were reinstated,[48] but his trip is not recorded in Ranger records.

McNelly, having come close to starting a war with Mexico, could not have been a very popular man in the nation's capital. Naval Commander Kells may have believed McNelly had authority for provoking an international incident; McNelly evidently thought so, but he was acting as a Ranger after stolen cattle, not trying to start a war.[49]

There was some activity during the two months McNelly was away from the company. In early January Robinson sent a scout for stolen cattle to a slaughterhouse where a rancher, caught in the act of butchering animals, tried to bribe his way free. When his offer was turned down, the man made a run for safety and was shot. A minor raid in Cameron County at the end of February succeeded in driving off a few cattle.[50]

In his first report of the year, possibly written at the King Ranch, McNelly told the adjutant general that he had traveled south through DeWitt County and found the old feud had broken out again. Probably wishing to make a name for himself, the sheriff of Henderson County had gathered a posse of so-called Sutton supporters and tried to serve a writ in Sinton for one of the Taylor faction. In the resulting fight, a deputy from DeWitt was killed, and the wanted man and one of his friends were wounded. A large party of Taylor partisans took their injured man to safety in Gonzales. When an equally large party of armed Sutton followers rode to Gonzales to capture him, they found a dying man. Because there seemed no point in fighting over a man who would be dead soon, both sides dispersed. For the time being, there was calm.

In the same letter McNelly told Steele he had received disturbing reports of events taking place in Nueces County where the sheriff was powerless to stop large-scale rustling. Stolen cattle were being sent up the trail to Kansas, and there was talk the Hardin gang was providing protection for the rustlers; apparently it was not widely known that Hardin had long since fled Texas. The Ranger was afraid the Devils River would become another DeWitt County.[51]

Before McNelly could make any plans, the Diaz Revolution began with the capture of Matamoros on April 2. As usual the Ranger had good information sources, and his spies kept him informed of plans and events. The revolt went fairly smoothly and most of the Federal troops joined Diaz, who began impressing the local *bravos* and formed an army for the march on Mexico City. Many of the Mexican cattlemen and workers had no interest in reforming Mexico, or furthering Diaz's personal ambitions. They swarmed into

Texas, bringing on an increase in stealing and minor crimes.[52] The biggest event for the Rangers in April, however, was Captain King's sending them thirty Winchester carbines and ammunition,[53] a welcome gift that also reveals the increasing trend in favor of repeaters.

His spies kept McNelly aware of planned raids, and he began making plans of his own to counter the next attack set for early May. Unfortunately his guides became confused in the darkness, and they reached the Rio Grande on the night of May 17 just after a stolen herd had been pushed across. A few cattle were still on the Texas side being hurried along after the others by four *bravos*, who opened fire on the Rangers. Two *bravos* were killed immediately and a third wounded; in the confusion the fourth escaped. The outlaws on the Mexican bank of the river opened fire as soon as the Rangers appeared, but the Rangers did not return their fire.

The Rangers gathered up a half dozen horses, with saddles, bridles and camp equipment the rustlers had not been able to transport across the river. McNelly wrote a note to the senior army officer in Edinburg requesting his help in recovering the stolen herd. The next morning, Captain H.J. Farnsworth arrived with a company of the 8th Cavalry but refused to cross the river. He did agree to aid them if they needed assistance in returning.

The Mexican guides with the Rangers believed the cattle were on a ranch just south of the river. Taking three men, McNelly crossed into Mexico and scouted the land near the ranch. They could find no cattle but discovered a clear trail leading towards Reynosa less than two miles away. There was little point in further pursuit because Reynosa had a large garrison; McNelly, never foolhardy, returned to Texas.

He was not through, however, just changing course. In Edinburg McNelly sent for the Reynosa *alcalde*, told him of the theft and demanded the return of the cattle and the rustlers. The Mexican official was very cooperative, promising to return the cattle, but the thieves would have to be sent over during the night because he was afraid to do this openly. McNelly also obtained a promise from the chief of the Rural Police that he would catch the guilty men.

The aspect that most galled the Texans about this raid was the clear indication the cattle had been taken to feed the troops of the senior Mexican commander, General Escobedo, who had been visiting Farnsworth in Edinburg.

While the cattle were being crossed into Mexico, his band's playing helped muffle sounds of the move just a short distance away. The cattle trail led directly to his headquarters in Reynosa, but McNelly couldn't do anything about it.[54]

It was the last time McNelly was to cross into Mexico, and his last affray with outlaws on the border.

It will be remembered that in late summer of 1875 McNelly had sent Ranger Parrott into the Nueces country to pose as a photographer, in one of the earliest undercover missions in the Ranger service. A professional photographer, Parrott lived with both rustlers and legitimate stockmen in the rough, largely unsettled country. When he rejoined the company in the spring of 1876, Parrott brought evidence of considerable cattle rustling and tales of several killings. The entire region was controlled by King Fisher.

John King Fisher is another notorious figure in Texas frontier history. Like Hardin, he began his career during Reconstruction by killing Republican police, and he is a subject of dispute among historians and family partisans; unlike Hardin he was a dandy, dressed carefully and wore two revolvers. Just how many people he killed, if any, is unknown. Within his territory in the Eagle Pass country he became a leader; no one operated or moved anything without his approval. He was wanted by the state of Texas, and several of his workers were wanted on warrants from other states. On the last day in May the company left Laredo and started for King Fisher country.[55]

At Pendencia, about ten miles from a small settlement, now Carrizo Springs, the Rangers quietly surrounded Fisher's ranch headquarters, rushed in from all sides and captured everyone without a shot's being fired. McNelly did not quite know what to do with his prisoners and finally sent the nine captives under guard to Eagle Pass, the nearest sheriff and jail.

There the Ranger had his first experience with a defense lawyer and began to understand why Fisher and his men had not put up a fight. Most of the prisoners were listed in the *List of Fugitives*, clearly identified, but the lawyer wanted to know if the courts had upheld the legality of the document. Could McNelly guarantee that the states with warrants for some of the men would actually show up to claim them? The questions, which went on and on, were a new experience for the Rangers. Young Durham became so angry he slapped the lawyer across the room and was run outside by McNelly, who finally ordered Lieutenant Wright to give their guns back to the prisoners.[56] At variance with the prompt release of the prisoners according to Durham, the official account states that the prisoners were held while McNelly went to obtain witnesses but were released by local authorities before McNelly returned. The official report better accounts for the two-day lapse between the Rangers' arrival in Eagle Pass and the release of the prisoners on June 6.[57] The Rangers never would be able to make a case in court against Fisher, although they tried several more times. The ease, however, with which the Rangers had ridden into Fisher's supposedly untouchable territory and arrested him and his men seriously tarnished his reputation.

To great extent this was the end of the McNelly saga. The gallant Ranger would still serve, but once again he was barely able to ride and was coughing up blood. His wife heard about a doctor in San Antonio who had a special medicine that thickened the blood and stopped the bleeding, and they decided to visit him.[58]

In July the Washington County Volunteer Militia was disbanded and a new command of Special Troops, Captain McNelly's Company of Texas State Troops, was sworn into service in San Antonio for a period of six months, unless sooner disbanded. McNelly was captain, but no lieutenants were listed. The same sergeants and corporals reenlisted for the new command, but there were a number of changes among the privates. Callicott left, but Durham stuck with his leader, as did Jesus Sandoval.[59]

Old Casoose had no place else to go. According to testimony he gave before a committee investigating the troubles along the lower Rio Grande, Sandoval had lived since 1846 on a ranch fifteen miles north of what became Brownsville. During the Mexican War he served in the U.S. Army Quartermaster and stayed on to live in what became Cameron County, becoming a citizen in 1853, voting and holding office. Mexicans on both sides of the river considered him a traitor, and his life became increasingly difficult. He spent most of his time hiding out in the brush, visiting his family when he could. His wife and child were threatened with death. He was well acquainted with cattle thieves and held them responsible for most of his troubles. Anything he could do to reduce this element—by whatever means—he considered justified. In the days of no rules for frontier warfare he was perfect for the job of scout and chief inquisitor, but those days were coming to an end.[60]

Another new man in the company, N.A. Jennings had actually enlisted earlier in May. According to Durham, he was signed on as a clerk.[61] Jennings would have some Ranger service, but the accounts in his memoirs are more fiction than fact.

McNelly was still in San Antonio, staying at the Menger Hotel with his wife. Robinson was still with the Rangers, in command of the main detachment of the company. McNelly had him send Corporal Rudd and privates Durham, Maben and Adams to San Antonio. When they arrived in the city, McNelly told them to spend a little of their accumulated pay on new clothes and to be seen about town, but not to get drunk or into any trouble. He wanted a favorable Ranger presence in San Antonio to combat the stories circulating about his men's being a bunch of killers. It was a heavenly assignment to young Durham and the others. He went out and bought the first new clothes of his life.[62]

The company gained a new officer in August 1876 when Governor Coke assigned outsider Lee Hall to the Rangers. Hall had been Sergeant-at-Arms of the Twentieth Legislature, and his assignment to the Rangers was possibly a political selection, but he also had considerable experience as a deputy sheriff and town marshal before taking the job at the legislature. His name was actually Leigh Hall, but he had so much trouble convincing people to spell his name correctly that he switched to Lee.[63] Hall was sent to the company as second in command. The bypassing of Robinson gave the Rangers an idea of what was in store for their commander, and McNelly recognized the handwriting on the wall.

The new lieutenant and eleven Rangers from San Antonio went to Goliad, on detached service from the company, where a bank had been robbed on August 24. The sheriff had given up on maintaining order and had left the county. When the Rangers reached town they found vigilante groups busily enforcing their own brand of law and order. Most of the groups were led by landowners who had hired gunmen to clear out drifters, squatters and anyone else who might possibly want to settle in their territory. Hall, no McNelly but copying his methods, faced these groups in Ranger style and was able to disband all the vigilantes. After a few days he sent four men back to the camp in Oakville, but he and the other Rangers remained and brought a degree of peace to the community. He later arrested one of the bank robbers and obtained the names of all who had taken part in the crime. It is significant that Hall's report was made directly to the adjutant general and not through McNelly, his nominal captain.[64]

When Hall made his report concerning his stay in Goliad, he could honestly say the county was once again in the hands of decent people and business was thriving. The new Ranger, possessing the ability to earn and keep the good will of influential ranchers and businessmen, had made a considerable impression on the citizens of Goliad. When the Rangers returned to camp, Hall had established a solid reputation where it counted—in Austin. The citizens of Goliad, fearing there would be a return to vigilante days, sent the governor a petition asking for the Rangers to remain in the town.[65] The men were needed elsewhere, but the petitions played a part in Hall's promotion the next year.

In the meantime Sergeant Armstrong had been busy. Still in San Antonio in the latter part of September, McNelly sent Durham and the other three back to the Oakville camp with instructions to sweep the King Fisher country again. As Durham recounts the story, Robinson ordered Armstrong to take twenty-five men and check on reports of stolen horses and cattle. The first sergeant gave the men ten minutes to get ready to ride, on what was to be a swift strike.

They rode all night, made a dry camp, remained until dark, then struck Carrizo at night. Armstrong had ordered them to arrest anyone they saw, and during the night they apprehended five men, mostly ranch hands who had been unfortunate enough to be out after dark. One of them, however, after the Rangers "heisted him a couple of feet off the ground," knew of an outlaw camp where stolen horses were being held for a drive up Devils River.[66]

Armstrong split his force and sent Corporal Williams and ten men to the Pendencia while he took the rest to Espinoza Lake. About midnight they approached the lake, where Armstrong again divided his men. Sergeant Wright and a few Rangers covered the lower end of the lake while

Armstrong, Durham, Devine, Evans, Boyd, Parrott and Jennings crept upon a group outlined against a campfire. The Rangers still had the prisoner who had told them about the outlaw camp, and Armstrong left him in the custody of Evans and Devine before heading with the remaining Rangers towards the glow of the fire.

Almost at the campfire, a sentry rose from the brush and shot at Armstrong, who was leading his men. He missed, but the sergeant did not and the fight was on. The five Rangers charged towards the fire, shooting as they ran. The seven men around the campfire held their ground and returned fire on the charging lawmen. Although outnumbered, the Rangers had the advantage of being in the dark, firing at men outlined against the flames, and the fight was quickly over. A survivor drew a large knife and rushed Boyd, the nearest Ranger. Boyd's Winchester jammed and he tossed the weapon aside and drew his own knife. He was a skilled knife fighter and finally killed his much larger opponent, although he himself was wounded.

The only other bandit still alive, a man they identified as Jim McAllister, lived about thirty minutes after the fight was over. Durham's claim that they recognized four of the seven bodies is puzzling because Armstrong, reporting directly to McNelly, said they slew four men. He told McNelly there were others, but they ran when they heard the Rangers were in the area.[67]

When the Rangers returned to their horses, they found the prisoner had tried to escape and been shot by Evans and Devine. Armstrong reported that the horses stampeded when the shooting started, the prisoner tried to use the stampede as cover for his escape, and the guards shot him when he refused to halt and return. Armstrong's report mentions another fight that night, a skirmish not described by Durham. The Ranger detail had heard about a "bad" Mexican at a ranch about eight miles away, and Armstrong sent three of his men to bring him in but he put up a fight and was killed. Armstrong sent word to the nearest judge, so that all the bodies in the encounters could be brought in, and started back.

Along the way they rounded up every man they met, trusting that honest riders would not be operating in King Fisher territory, and ended up with twenty-two prisoners lashed bareback to their horses. Armstrong took eight men

and escorted this column of embarrassed felons, or whatever they were, the thirty-five miles to Eagle Pass. Apparently none of the prisoners stayed long in jail, but the ride
did give them something to think about and further diminished the reputation of Fisher as absolute boss of the land.
Durham said that Jennings slipped away from the detail
and telegraphed a version of the scout to the San Antonio
Express. This story, Durham believed, probably figured in
the political decision to remove McNelly; there is little doubt
that the rest of the men in the company had little fondness
for the writer-Ranger.

The company record of scouts for September shows yet
another version of this engagement and states the Rangers
killed five men, wounded one, and captured fifty horses and
thirty-two head of cattle.[68] The various versions are not that
important; what was important was the skill and forceful-
ness of John Armstrong. He was on the way to becoming
one of the Ranger legends.

Captain McNelly's Company of Texas State Troops was
active the rest of the year. The November monthly return,
written in San Antonio, shows almost half the unit on
detached service. There were arrests made in Wilson,
Guadalupe, Blanco and Gillespie counties, plus a detachment sent to Caldwell County to investigate a reported store
robbery.[69] It was the beginning of the use of the Special
State Troops as troubleshooters to go anywhere in Texas,
leaving the Frontier Battalion free for Indian troubles and
the outlaws along the frontier counties.

In December 1876 Lee Hall was back in the news. The
old Sutton-Taylor troubles had broken out yet again in
September, although the players were mostly new. A prominent physician, Phillip Brazell, had been called to appear
before the grand jury in DeWitt County, the first time this
body had met in several years. Before he could testify, a
group of men visited his home near Clinton about dusk,
asked him to step outside, then took him to a nearby barn
and shot him to death. His twelve-year-old son followed his
father and was also murdered. Judge Clay Pleasants, the
presiding judge, called on the governor for help.

The Ranger company was so scattered on special assignments that it took some time to collect enough men to go to
Clinton, but by early December Hall had about twenty men
there. Conditions had reverted to the old anarchy of several

years earlier. Hall reported numerous murder cases on the court docket, but people were either afraid to testify or they were actually involved in the crimes. The Ranger did not expect an easy time in the county and asked for Winchesters and breech-loading shot guns to replace their old Sharps.[70]

The Rangers camped outside Cuero and began guarding Judge Pleasants. Their arrival changed how people began looking at the law. McNelly, the man who had performed legendary deeds along the Rio Grande, was sick; for all practical purposes he had been replaced by Hall, but no one knew this. Pleasants, with questionable legality, told Hall to round up the grand jurors and hold them in session no matter how afraid they might be. The jurymen regained their courage and indicted seven men for the murder of Doctor Brazell and his son. On December 20 Hall began planning the arrests of the seven.

Joe Sitterlee, one of the indicted men, was getting married; Hall believed most of the indicted men would be at the wedding and decided to capture them all at once. He and twelve men, all that could be spared from other duties, rode the several miles to the home of the bride's parents where the wedding was to take place, dismounted, secured their horses and circled the house.

A celebration was taking place inside, where Sitterlee had been married about an hour earlier. He and his bride were dancing to the music of a fiddle band when Hall walked into the big room and announced he was a Ranger and that Sitterlee was under arrest. Sitterlee told Hall both to go to hell and to come and get him if he had enough men. The Ranger replied calmly he had enough men and also had warrants for six more men. He read off the names; as hoped, they were all at the celebration. Hall told them to clear the women and children if they wanted to resist, and there was some discussion and argument. Only Sitterlee and Bill Meader, ostensibly lawmen, were armed; the others had surrendered their weapons when they entered the house. Whether drunk or sober, it was clear to all that Hall intended to take them dead or alive.[71]

One of the women defused the situation, probably saving many lives, when she asked why not let the party continue and the men surrender in the morning and make bail. Both sides agreed. Hall had one of the indicted men come with him as a hostage, but he allowed Sitterlee to stay. It was, after all, his wedding night. Never say the Rangers lacked compassion!

In a few minutes it was as though nothing had happened. The fiddlers again started playing, couples danced, and the whiskey flowed. The party continued all night. Hall took no chances on the honor system and had guards working in shifts around the house; Rangers not on watch were allowed to visit inside and enjoy the refreshments. At sunup Hall moved the seven indicted men outside. They offered to make bail, but Hall said only the judge could set bonds. Sitterlee protested loudly, but he and his friends were taken to the Ranger camp and placed under a heavy guard.

The prisoners were kept in custody at the camp for several days. Most were prominent figures in the community, with many friends and relatives, and the camp was visited daily by armed groups of men trying to overawe the Rangers. Judge Pleasants kept out of sight, guarded by Rangers, but he knew that he could not long delay a hearing on bail for the prisoners.

The judge sent for McNelly. Although ill, the captain rode down from San Antonio and took the prisoners under a heavy Ranger guard into the open court. The old magic was still there. Although captain in name only, McNelly informed the large crowd of armed men in the courtroom that anyone who tried to interfere with the proceedings would die. Judge Pleasants came in and the examining trial began.

The prisoners were represented by two able lawyers, but this time the Rangers were satisfied with the legal proceedings. One by one Pleasants read the indictments, and each time McNelly and his Rangers raised their pistols in warning. In about an hour the judge had refused bond and remanded all the prisoners to the custody of the Rangers. There was cursing and wild threats, but no man in the court or outside on the streets was bold enough to challenge the decision.

Judge Pleasants knew it was dangerous to keep the prisoners too long in the Ranger camp, and putting them in the county jail was foolish, so he ordered the Rangers to take them to Galveston where there was a secure jail away from their friends. When Hall wired the adjutant general from Flatonia that he and McNelly were on the way to Galveston with the prisoners, he was also reporting McNelly's last service as a Ranger; by early January 1877 his era was over.

It was also the real end of the feud in DeWitt, which had long since outgrown its Sutton-Taylor origins. The prisoners went through trial after retrial and appeal upon appeal, but none returned to reopen old wounds. The entire episode occupies only a few lines in the monthly return of the Special State Troops, reporting seven men arrested for murder in Clinton on December 22. Also listed were two men killed resisting arrest, one in Wilson and another in DeWitt County, both wanted for murder.[72]

Before he left for Galveston, McNelly spent a day resting at Judge Pleasant's house. Young Durham came around to tell him goodbye, but there wasn't much to say. McNelly invited the Ranger to visit his farm if he ever traveled up to Burton; he had hopes of starting up his farm again.[73] In January he was dropped from the rolls and his company was reorganized. A great deal of bitterness ensued, but Steele defended his action saying he had kept the best men in service and the state of Texas could not afford to pay McNelly's medical bills.[74]

With less than three years service, McNelly became a legend, a Ranger of myth and romantic fiction. He came to the border during a time of chaos and anarchy, charging through hell to restore some degree of order, destroying any gang, Mexican or American, that got in his way. In a harsh time and land, he was a harsh master. Some complained that he made small distinction between *defending* the law and *being* the law, but during a period when more legal methods were seldom effective, McNelly did whatever he thought necessary to preserve or restore peace. When he could have simply killed men, however, such as when he captured King Fisher and his men, he obeyed the letter of the law and was forced to endure the humiliation of seeing guilty men turned free by clever lawyers taking advantage of legal technicalities.

Even within a service where outstanding men were the rule, McNelly occupies a special place.

*Captain John Armstrong. Photo courtesy of the Texas Ranger
Hall of Fame and Museum, Waco, Texas.*

— 5 —

Changing Missions
1877

The major Ranger activity of 1877 would involve the Frontier Battalion, for which an organizational review is in order. The company muster rolls for January 1877 list the following units and commanders: Company A continued to be commanded by Captain Neal Coldwell; Company B's commander was Lieutenant G.W. Campbell; Company C, reorganized in October 1876, was commanded by Captain John C. Sparks; Company D's leader was Lieutenant F.M. Moore; Lieutenants B.S. Foster and Pat Dolan commanded Companies E and F respectively.

The Frontier Battalion was in winter quarters. It was too cold for much Indian activity, but the Rangers were nevertheless on the alert. There had been a few raids within Company A's territory during December, and Captain Coldwell believed the Indians might attempt more raids during the next "moon" despite the weather. He outlined his plans to Major Jones.[1]

Coldwell proposed sending Sergeant Reynolds and five men up the Sabinal, about thirty-five miles from the company's camp, to leave five days before the full moon. If Indians were to enter his area, Reynolds would first send a courier to warn the camp before following their trail. A separate patrol consisting of Corporal Woodward and four men would leave on January 24 for Woodward's Pasture on the Llano about eighteen miles southwest of the company's camp. Should a raiding party come near them, they would also warn the camp, then they were to join with settlers in the vicinity to trail the Indians. The rest of the company would remain in camp during the full moon but would make short scouts in the directions not covered by the two patrols.

If any of the scouts and patrols sighted hostiles, the bulk of the company would follow at once. If unable to catch the Indians before they crossed the Rio Grande, the company would gather and cross after them. He concluded his report by stating the health of men and animals was sound. He also inserted a mild protest against the transfer of T.M. Sparks to Company C. Jones' reaction to Coldwell's proposal is not recorded; after the commotion following McNelly's crossing the Rio Grande, it would seem Coldwell would have been less venturesome, but possibly he believed the Mexican authorities would be favorably inclined to an invasion of Mexico if it were a chase after Indian raiders.

Coldwell's report is devoted primarily to Indian activities. It also, however, began what was to be an ever-increasing mention of Sergeant N.O. Reynolds and Sergeant G.W. Arrington in letters and reports. Major Jones also had the opportunity to observe both these men, since they were part of his escort company, and soon marked both for future promotion. The two Rangers had little in common other than ability. Reynolds, tall, well-built and of a commanding presence, was another example of the Ranger of legend; Arrington, at five feet five inches and slight of build, was probably the only man in the battalion smaller than Major Jones.

Arrington's name was actually John C. Orrick, Jr., but he began using his mother's maiden name during his Civil War service, possibly while spying with Mosby. After the war he killed a man in Alabama and eventually came to Texas. For a time Jones refused to enlist him in the Rangers because of the old indictment, but finally under the name George Washington Arrington he was allowed to join Company E in 1875. He transferred to Company A when Coldwell assumed command in December 1876.[2] During January and February 1877, both Arrington and Reynolds led a number of patrols.[3]

The other companies in the battalion also kept active, as much as the cold weather allowed, although there were no major actions. Company B reported a somewhat rare arrest when a man named Ben Allen was brought in for rape, a crime that figured occasionally in arrest reports.[4] On the average the companies continued to muster twenty men in accordance with the September 1876 reduction and reorganization.[5]

Company B made news when two of the Rangers, carried away by festive spirit and spirits, joined in shooting-up part of Belknap. Major Jones was required to spend considerable time answering questions about who would pay for the bullet holes in various town properties. The company commander was on a scout, and the first Sergeant, George Kisinger explained to the major that the two Rangers had joined a large crowd of buffalo hunters and other citizens for some harmless fun in town, but the Rangers had been blamed for the whole show. The two men, however, knew they were in the wrong and had paid fines.[6] Two weeks later Lieutenant Campbell was still explaining the disciplinary problems in his company to Major Jones.[7]

During March Jones was in Austin. Among the mass of correspondence for this period is a letter from Coldwell asking for additional Winchesters for Company A. By this time a considerable number of Rangers had switched from Sharps to Winchesters; Coldwell stated there were thirteen of the new rifles or carbines in his company; the eight more he requested, if the men could obtain them at a special price, would have given every man in the unit a new weapon. He included news from the frontier; Pat Dolan's men in Company F had sighted Indians, but there was nothing in Company A's area.[8]

Although In Austin during most of the bad weather, Major Jones was not idle. In late March he instructed the battalion to concentrate on white outlaws, with special attention to cattle drives for which the Rangers were to check cattle brands. There would be no more routine scouts to look for Indian signs; only definite trails or information of a raiding party would be cause for a scout to the west.[9] There was certainly no intention on Jones' part to allow Indian raids along the frontier; actual Indian forays were few now, and it was the problem from outlaws of every degree that was increasing.

With the approach of spring Jones left Austin and joined Company A for a trip up the line. In early April he was in Frio City, still attending to public relations; on the way he had also stopped in San Antonio and talked with a number of prominent citizens. Major Jones was constantly being asked to station a Ranger company in a specific locality, usually near property of an influential person; he had received thirteen such requests in one month. He diplomati-

cally answered all of them, explaining his men had to go
where there was the greatest need rather than the most
political or financial influence. In turning down one such
petition and plea, he gave an indication of the next big
Ranger mission, "This company, Capt. Coldwells, goes at
once to Kimble County which is in worse condition than any
on the frontier at this time."[10]

Along the advancing frontier, the area of Kimble County,
organized as a separate county on January 3, 1876, seemed
most in danger. In Junction City, the second and permanent
county seat, the first business, a log store, had opened in
1873. By 1877 a general store was in business supporting
the hard-working, honest people who were settling the
county, along with a group of drifters, out-of-work cowhands and numerous others running from the law.[11]

In February 1877, a settler in Kimble had written Major
Jones describing conditions in his new home. Cattle, hogs
and horses were stolen every day; crime, from simple theft
to murder, was commonplace; any stranger was viewed with
suspicion and likely to be killed by outlaws as a possible
detective.[12] This claim was verified by Ranger H.B. Waddill
of Company C, who rode through the county and reported
to Major Jones that it was "a theaf's stronghold." The Ranger
was a keen observer, sending Jones the names of several
known outlaws as well as lists of honest men.[13]

On March 30 Judge W.A. Blackburn of the 17th Judicial
District informed Jones from Lampasas that he had not yet
held court in Kimble County because he had reports that
anywhere from forty to a hundred armed outlaws could be
raised on an hour's notice. Blackburn wrote again on April
2 telling the major he wanted to hold court in the county,
fearing if he did not the honest people would lose heart and
leave. Local peace officers were no help because the sheriff
and county judge were in league with the thieves and
murderers! On April 6 he wrote Major Jones yet again,
asking for Ranger assistance because he was afraid even to
travel in Kimble, much less try to hold open court.[14]

The conditions in Kimble were a direct challenge to the
power of the state. For the first time since the Rangers had
returned, there was a chance that an organized county
could actually be taken over by outlaws. The major answered the judge, saying he would move with three companies about April 15.[15] His decision was more than justified;

he soon learned the outlaws had bought all the ammunition available in Kimble and were trying to find more in adjacent areas.[16]

Jones was a careful planner, well aware of the necessity for good intelligence and secrecy. There had been no Ranger presence in Kimble County since Waddill had ridden through in February, and so far as any of the gangs knew they were safe and had matters under their control. From his temporary headquarters in Frio City (now Frio Town) on April 11, Jones began issuing instructions for the move on Kimble. He ordered Lieutenant Moore of Company D to send three men who knew "where every body lives on both Llanos and Johnsons Fork to meet me at Paint Rock on South Llano next Wednesday evening, the 18th inst." The men were to bring rations enough for two days after their arrival. Leaving only two or three men to guard Company D's camp, Moore was to take ten days' rations and march for Junction City, to arrive the evening of April 20 and remain until he heard from Jones. He cautioned Moore not to mention anything about the plan, except to the three men on the special scout who were to be warned not to talk. Jones continued, "I will bring Coldwells and Dolans Companies with me and will make a general 'round up' of Kimble county but want it kept secret until we are ready to make the break." Jones' message to Pat Dolan was brief, merely warning him that the major would reach his camp on April 16 and wanted Dolan to be in readiness to move with his men, less camp guards, the next day on a ten-day scout. Always with an eye to administration, Jones informed Dolan he was sending two recruits, Williams and Callahan, sworn in on the first of the month.[17]

The same day, Jones completed his plans by ordering supplies from a store in Kerrville. Not sure of what supplies might be available in Junction City, he included corn for the horses, soda, soap, candles, salt and pepper as well as the usual flour, bacon, beans, rice, "and 12 gals. Pickles." The supplies were to be delivered in Junction City on April 20 or 21, neither earlier nor later; the teamsters were not to know where they were going until they started from Kerrville. In case the entire order could not be shipped immediately, Jones wanted half of each item with the balance to follow in ten days.[18] Jones briefed the adjutant general the next day, telling him he had spies in the area and knew where most of the wanted men lived.[19]

Dolan brought his company up the Nueces Canyon, and Jones with Coldwell and Company A also swept up from the south. Both Ranger commands reached Junction on the evening of April 19. On the way they picked up every man they met, presuming guilt and not releasing them until properly identified and vouched for by a reliable citizen. The ones not so lucky were hauled into Junction and chained to trees.

The initial sweep into Kimble County was a complete surprise, and Jones was able to report two prisoners and no organized resistance by the time he reached Junction City.[20] On April 20 the Rangers moved north of town and began the tiring and potentially dangerous task of checking the numerous ravines and creek beds that cut into the hilly countryside. By this time an alarm had probably spread, but in his next report Jones told the adjutant general that he had twelve prisoners and his scouts were bringing in more. He asked for information on an individual who was possibly wanted.[21]

Some of the wanted men undoubtedly escaped as the operation continued, but Jones maintained three to five patrols out each day. By the end of the third day, the Rangers had captured twenty-nine fugitives.[22] It must have been a very-satisfied Major Jones who wrote Judge Blackburn that he would have plenty of work for his court in about a week.[23]

The Rangers picked up men wanted in several counties. Jones wrote the sheriff of Lavaca County he had arrested two men from his area and was sending them to jail in Austin where they would be held subject to the sheriff's order. He had also picked up another fugitive, but the man had made bond. Jones noted with some bitterness that the two men who signed the bond had no property and the paper was therefore worthless. He asked the sheriff to send an arrest warrant to Lieutenant Moore, care of Fort McKavett, so they could rearrest the man.[24]

The Rangers placed prisoners in whatever jails were available; eight men were jailed in Fredericksburg. The Kimble facility was full and men were still being chained to trees. By the time of Jones' final report on May 6, forty-one arrests had been made, thirty-seven in Kimble County. The law-abiding element of the region had cordially supported the Rangers, coming to their temporary camp and offering assistance in any way they were able.

Not every man arrested was on the fugitive list; some had been picked up on suspicion, and a few had probably drifted in recently to join one of the county's gangs. When court was held, twenty-five of the prisoners were indicted by a grand jury. They would have been tried immediately, but after the grand jury's jurors were excused there were not enough honest men remaining to serve on a regular jury. Even the sheriff and county judge had been indicted; both resigned. Jones released some of his force and moved to Fort McKavett, but Lieutenant Moore was kept in camp near Junction in the event there was any attempt to reestablish the gangs or any attempt by uncaptured fugitives to return to Kimble.[25]

Kimble County was a classic Jones operation. Not a man was wounded or killed in the sweep. The surprise was so complete, the Ranger force so large, that the outlaws were completely overpowered and unable to make any resistance. This duty was extremely tiring on both the Rangers and their mounts, but the results were worth their efforts. Many of the Rangers did not realize just how much they had accomplished; Gillett took part in the operation, but his memoirs contain only a few paragraphs recounting briefly how they split into groups and converged on Junction, picking up many wanted men. "We bagged several men wanted for murder and some horse and cattle thieves. Old Kimble County had never had such a clean-up of bandits in her history."[26] Jones had driven out a number of criminals, eliminated a crooked sheriff and judge, and returned a county to its honest citizens. Once again, Ranger enforcement made possible the operation of the law.

Kimble County never again posed a major threat to law and order, although a few individuals and families would be wanted in later years. Two families, the Dublins and the Potters, were not on any wanted list during the Ranger sweeps in April 1877 and escaped Ranger attention, but their turn would come later.

With the major sweep out of the way, Major Jones and his escort moved north to inspect the other companies and picked up several fugitives on the march. They stopped at Fort Griffin before starting the return to Austin, but in mid-June the Rangers halted at Lampasas, where Jones learned of trouble between the Horrell and Higgins factions.

He decided to stay and bring the trouble to an end.[27]

The Horrell brothers were no strangers to the law and to peace officers. As described in Chapter One, they had left Texas after shooting up a detachment of State Police, but they managed to get into trouble in New Mexico as well; one brother was killed, and the rest returned to their native state when the Democrats returned to power. They surrendered to peace officers and were tried and acquitted of the killings in Lampasas. The four remaining brothers settled down and went into the cattle business.

In early 1877 the Horrell brothers were gathering a herd and, as described by Gillett, may have picked up a few head belonging to Pink Higgins. At least Higgins believed they had, which was the same as stealing them. A rough man, Higgins reacted in frontier fashion; he walked through the rear door of a saloon where Merritt Horrell was taking his ease in a chair and shot him to death. When the news reached the other brothers, Mart and Tom Horrell hurried into town only to be ambushed by Higgins and some friends. Mart Horrell was wounded; his brother Tom had his horse killed but, afoot, rushed the hidden men, firing as he came. The bushwhackers fled. In short order the county was turned into a battlefield, and a gunfight in Lampasas resulted in the death of a man from each faction.[28]

In April Pink Higgins and Bob Mitchell, allies and companions on cattle drives up the line, came in and surrendered to Captain Sparks of Company C and made $10,000 bail. The local paper noted that no one had been killed in a week or more.[29] Although the fighting had stopped, at least for the moment, all the courthouse files and records of the troubles between the two groups vanished on June 11, with no clues as to which side was responsible. There seemed to be honest effort by both sides to avoid further trouble, but both gangs, apparently inadvertently, came into town on the same day, June 14. They attempted without success to keep away from one another in the small town, but shots were fired and a day-long skirmish ensued. Frank Mitchell of the Higgins' faction was killed and possibly one of the Horrell supporters. Captain Sparks finally was able to stop the shooting.[30]

Major Jones rode into Lampasas late in the afternoon of June 14 after the fighting was over. After talking to Sparks, he wrote the adjutant general that he would stay and try to put an end to the fighting, but there was a break of some weeks following these events. Major Jones was in and out of Lampasas, busy with matters such as guarding prisoners for which he had to split his escort company. Sergeant Reynolds had left the company on July 11, taking prisoners to Austin,[31] and did not return to Lampasas until later in the month. On July 16 Jones wrote Steele about the murder of a man named Graham in the far north of the county. Graham was thought to be a Higgins supporter, hence his murderers must be on the Horrell side.[32] Whether they were involved or not, this murder brought the Rangers again into Lampasas County after the Horrells.

On the evening of July 27 Sergeant Reynolds and a Ranger detachment captured most of the wanted men of the Horrell faction. Amazingly, no shots were fired and no men, Ranger or fugitive, killed or wounded. There is no official documentation of the particulars of the arrest, but the Ranger detachment did return with a number of prisoners to their camp, where they were closely guarded. Gillett said people came from miles away to see the famous Horrell brothers and the man who had taken them without a shot. Even Major Jones hurried out from Austin after the arrest,[33] and on July 28 he announced he had arrested the entire gang and was holding them prisoner, mentioning he had only ten Rangers but was satisfied he could protect the captives from either friends or a lynch mob.[34] In none of his dispatches does he mention Sergeant Reynolds.

There is little doubt Reynolds was the key player in the drama. Only a week later he even wrote his own version of the capture which was published in the *Lampasas Dispatch*.[35] Evidently writing to set the record straight, Reynolds gives considerably more detail than either Gillett or the sparse official reports.

As Reynolds remembered, Jones had received a tip that the Horrells were hiding on School Creek, ten miles from Lampasas. The major sent Reynolds and six Rangers with, unmentioned in other versions, two of the Mitchell brothers and William Wren as his guides. On the way they received fresh information about the fugitives and changed direction, going instead to Mart Horrell's place. It was raining when they arrived, a miserable night during which they waited for enough light to go inside. About five in the morning they moved in, leaving the guides outside because they were allied with the Higgins faction and Reynolds was afraid they might shoot the prisoners. Reynolds said the surprised men were confused and could not decide whether to surrender or fight. One man grabbed a Ranger rifle and a shot was fired, but the Horrells finally realized they were facing Rangers and would receive fair treatment.

During the return to camp, Reynolds played it safe and secured the three Horrell brothers but allowed some of the others taken in the house to ride beside his Rangers as guards to insure the prisoners were not harmed. A few of the men taken were not wanted and were released; the rest reached camp without trouble.

Just why Jones never mentioned Reynolds is unknown, he usually gave credit where credit was due, but Major Jones was soon to play a more personal and active role in ending the fighting between the two factions. In addition to the Horrells already in custody, the major picked up the prominent men in the Higgins faction, and he also called in Company C as a reinforcing precautionary measure.

The Rangers acted impartially. They had twelve prisoners secured in their camp—five on the Horrell side, three from Higgins', and four others for varying other offenses. Jones had reported that this was one of the most perplexing cases he had ever encountered; putting men under bond was not sufficient to prevent either side from fighting if they met. Jones wrote that, in the interests of peace and quiet, he was going to attempt something not necessarily in accordance with the strict letter of the law. He was familiar with both factions by now and hoped he could effect something in a few days. He was obviously referring to some kind of peace treaty.[36]

Jones most assuredly held hopes of settling the feud without more bloodshed, but he must have been pleasantly surprised when the Horrells made a written offer to hang up their guns, forget the past and make peace.[37] A few days later the Higgins faction wrote and accepted the truce.[38] Each document was witnessed and signed by Jones, who undoubtedly was the driving force behind the truce's being signed. On August 9 the *Lampasas Dispatch* announced the troubles were finally over and gave much of the credit to Major Jones.

The peace treaty ended the fighting in Lampasas, at least officially. The Horrells made bond and went their way, but six months later they were accused of murdering a store-keeper. There was no real proof they had anything to do with the crime, and two of the brothers voluntarily surrendered. They were placed in jail in Meridian in Bosque County, supposedly far enough distant to rule out mob violence. It was not distant enough; a mob stormed the jail and lynched them. Pink Higgins was tried for the killing of Merritt Horrell, the act that had begun all the violence, but he was acquitted, returned to ranching, and died of a heart attack on December 18, 1914.[39] Sam Horrell, the only survivor in his family, returned to peaceful work and was not further involved with the law.

Lampasas County did not automatically revert to a land of calm, but at least there were no more street battles. Almost a year later, Sergeant Collins and a Ranger detachment had to return to guard a court session, which they did by merely disarming most of the men in town, without resistance. It was a far cry from earlier times.[40]

The capture of the Horrells made Reynolds well known in Texas. The Rangers' activities in Kimble County and during the Horrell-Higgins feud attracted considerable attention and overshadowed the less glamorous work by other units and individual Rangers. This was true throughout their history; the necessary work such as scouting and protecting court sessions usually went unnoticed. The better-publicized Ranger activities, however, were not their only duties during the spring and summer of 1877.

With what he had of Company A, Coldwell worked through Kerr County in mid-June; by the time he reached Bandera they had captured several known criminals. When he returned to his base camp in Frio County he had even more. One of the prisoners was well-known, a man named Wolfe, a major catch which advertised that the Rangers would arrest anyone, regardless of position. Wolfe was placed in jail in Castroville.[41]

An action by Company D in mid-spring was also important, although not headline-quality, work. Apparently unable to write himself, Lieutenant Moore had the county clerk of Coleman telegraph Adjutant General Steele that he had captured William Taylor, wanted for the murder of a man on the steamboat *Indianola*.[42] In June Pat Dolan of Company F reported scouts' covering 1,100 miles and observing much activity by hide thieves and a few Indian trails.[43] In early

June Arrington and thirteen men were checking on suspicious characters in Eagle Pass, showing how extensive were the sweeps by Company A.[44]

Major Jones had a number of personnel changes to consider during this period, and the chronology of the battalion's history can be organized by such important shifts in officer assignments. Jones was concerned with Company D, which occupied a critical location on the frontier, in effect the anchor of the frontier line and, as such, requiring the best possible commander. Nothing in any of the correspondence, including Roberts' memoirs, suggests Jones was dissatisfied with Lieutenant Moore's performance as commander of Company D, but Jones was nevertheless required to find a new commander, possibly because of Moore's ill health. Moore's last day as an officer was August 31, 1877. For a time, Jones considered moving Neal Coldwell, the senior company commander, to Company D, then promoting Arrington and giving him Company A.

First, in a well-deserved move at the end of August, Jones recommended Reynolds' promotion and his assumption of command of Company E *vice* Lieutenant B.S. Foster.[45] At the same time, Company E was transferred from its old base in Coleman County to Lampasas and then to north of Austin. Jones' plans to move Coldwell and promote Arrington came to a halt when Arrington suddenly resigned. If Jones moved Coldwell to Company D, Company A would have neither officer nor sergeant, an impossible situation. Jones solved the problem by convincing Dan Roberts to return to Ranger service as a captain in his old company, and the November monthly return for Company D shows the familiar signature.

Another major change was brewing in Company C, whose muster rolls for September, October and November show Captain Sparks in command, but he evidently did not play a commanding role in the company's affairs. Sergeant Arrington's name reappears on Company C's roll for November, possibly as part and parcel of Jones' planning. All necessary and important with long-term impact on the Ranger service, these changes nevertheless attracted little attention; the newspaper headlines were about to focus upon a location hundreds of miles to the west.

Far West Texas, the country west of the Pecos River, was largely unknown in the 1870's. Geography and climate had limited travel and settlement to only a few areas. The Pecos, not a major stream, flowed through a rock canyon for much of its lower route, then joined the Rio Grande where that river was also constricted between high walls. The intersecting canyons blocked travel east and west and to some extent north and south in and out of Mexico. Persons traveling west from San Antonio had to detour far to the north to the first crossing where the Pecos could be forded without contending with impassable canyon walls. The U.S. Army blasted a steep wagon road into the Pecos Canyon just above the Rio Grande in 1875, but it was seldom used by civilians. Wagon trains, stagecoaches and other civilian travelers went by the roads surveyed in 1848.

The army had established a few military stations along the stage trails, largely to protect major springs and provide some protection against Indian raids. A few settlers and traders lived near the army posts, but there were no real towns west of Castroville not far from San Antonio. Indian country where the Comanches ruled east of the Pecos and the Mescalero Apaches to the west, it was nevertheless all Texas, at least on maps, divided into two huge counties. There were settlements of several hundred inhabitants at the extreme western tip of the state, across the Rio Grande from the Mexican town of El Paso del Norte, the only town of any size in the region. This U.S. settlement had a county government and contact with Austin through the army telegraph to San Antonio, but the mail stage took days; travel by horse or wagon to the area was a matter of weeks.

The only settlements were near El Paso. Ysleta, perhaps the oldest town in Texas, had been established by Spaniards driven out of New Mexico in 1680 during the Pueblo Revolt. In 1772 San Elizario was settled and in 1850 became the county seat of El Paso County.[46] Neither place saw many American settlers until after the Mexican War and the discovery of gold in California. In 1854 a small army garrison was established a few miles upriver, to protect the stage road to the Pacific, near another tiny settlement established about 1827, the ancestor of present-day El Paso; a number of people stopped here during the gold rush days and by 1852 the place was called Franklin. In the latter part of the Civil War, a column of California troops managed to travel that far east before disbanding in the semi-deserted town. A number of the Union soldiers remained in the area when the war was over and took over confiscated or abandoned property and buildings.

Although the population was largely of Mexican descent, the few Anglo residents held most political offices. Austin was a long distance away; Washington was little more than a concept. In 1870 the Davis administration had formed a Ranger unit in the area under Gregorio Garcia, and the Democrats had authorized Telesfero Montes to form a Ranger detachment in 1874, but these forces had probably been seen as little more than a barrier to Apache raids. People in the El Paso region, Mexican or American, depended on themselves. Their loyalties were to whomever was in power at the moment and, for the Catholics, to their local priests.

In the takeover by Republicans after the Civil War, El Paso County became, and remained, Republican. The Union soldiers who had remained were the first sizable influx of Americans and soon dominated the political process. The one exception was Charles E.H. Howard, a staunch Democrat, who made alliances with those in power and became a political force himself.[47]

In 1872, with Texas under Republican control, Howard formed a political alliance with Louis Cardis, the local political power. Nothing changed after the Democrats assumed control of the state in 1874; El Paso County, controlling the Hispanic vote, remained Republican. Howard and Cardis remained friends, although a rivalry was developing over who would run the county.

The alliance disintegrated over the question of who would control the salt deposits east and north of the settlements, used first by the Indians, then the Spanish, and now by local inhabitants. Howard, a businessman, began to develop the commercial possibilities of the valuable salt deposits, there for the taking. He wrote his father-in-law in Austin to send him land certificates so he could file claim on any land not already owned, then he forbade any more taking of salt except with payment. The people in the area, in both Texas and Mexico, had been driving wagons and mule trains to the salt flats for years and saw no reason to desist because some *gringo* had obtained some papers. The armed struggle known as the Salt War of San Elizario ensued.

Howard's actions caused a break with his friend Louis

Cardis. An Italian by birth, Cardis had arrived in the area in 1864, married a Mexican woman, was considered one of the locals, and prospered with his financial interest in the stage line and mail route through Fort Davis. Over the salt issue, however, he broke with Howard and told everyone they were not required to pay for the salt. Cardis was allied with the local priest, Padre Borajo, who controlled the local votes. When Padre Borajo discovered he was not to be a partner in Howard's enterprise, he turned his people against the entrepreneur.[48]

The open break between Cardis and Howard included Howard's physically assaulting Cardis on several occasions. There were continued efforts by local residents to gather salt; when Howard had two men arrested in early October, an armed group of Mexican and Mexican-Americans rioted and held Howard at San Elizario for several days. Howard was placed under a heavy bond on condition he leave El Paso County; Howard accepted the terms, several of his friends signed the bond, and he left for Mesilla, New Mexico.

His departure made little difference because the underlying problem of who owned the salt remained unanswered. A detachment of U.S. troops was stationed in the town for a time but took no part in maintaining the peace. The district judge wired Governor Richard B. Hubbard there was no civil law and that the mob was well organized and firm in their demands.[49] The county sheriff also informed Austin he was powerless to act because there were only fifteen Americans willing to serve on a posse.[50] Cardis, a state legislator, told the governor matters had quieted down and modestly took credit for bringing about peace.[51]

Governor Hubbard had decided to send help, but he was not sure about how to do so since it would take a Ranger company almost a month to reach the area, and none could be spared from their assigned locations. He decided to send Major Jones to observe conditions and make a recommendation for a solution. Jones traveled by train from Austin to Topeka, Kansas, and from there he took another train west as far as it ran into New Mexico. Then he rode by stage down to Franklin, Texas, arriving days ahead of the usual mail stage across West Texas. Unannounced, he obtained a good idea of local conditions and, on November 7, wired a none-too-reassuring report to Austin: the mob in San Elizario had not disbanded and had surrounded Howard's bondsmen;

no help could be counted upon from the army garrison, nor were there enough dependable civilians to form a posse; he was going down to San Elizario for a close look at conditions.[52]

It was typical of Jones that he continued to carry out his administrative duties as battalion commander even though he was five-hundred miles away in the middle of potential danger in El Paso County. He prepared and dispatched a message to B, C and E companies, instructing them to discharge four men effective November 30, 1877.[53] He was never very far from the realities of matching men and money.

Jones, convinced there was a need for more police protection than the sheriff *could* provide or than the army *would* provide, began forming a Ranger detachment in San Elizario. On November 10 he enlisted John B. Tays as commander of the new unit with the rank of second lieutenant, and during the next two days he found enough men to form the detachment. Recruiting continued during the month; the November muster roll reports twenty-three men for duty. Jones evidently wanted to retain command of the men and formed then as a detachment of Company C of the Frontier Battalion rather than as a special detachment of the county. They drew the same pay as other Rangers and furnished their horses, equipment, etc.

This unit is one of the most controversial in Ranger history. It is a wonder Jones was able to find enough men to volunteer; the pool of possible recruits was very small and not up to the standards of the force. Gregorio Garcia, who had commanded a Ranger company in 1870-1871, enlisted on November 19 as a private, but no other frontier-fighting experience is revealed by the records, including Tays'. The men who would serve in the detachment ranged in age from eighteen to sixty-one. The shortest was five feet; the tallest six feet and two inches. Most had been farmers or miners, with a stray saddler, a doctor, a cook and a pair of cowboys for good measure. They came from various states and several foreign countries; Tays was a Canadian, two or three were native Texans, one was from Mexico. This varied and inexperienced, often transient, population would also hamper Ranger recruitment in the years ahead in El Paso County.

It was the best Jones could do. He furnished Tays specific written instructions on operations and the neces-

sary reports and administrative details incidental to commanding a Ranger unit,[54] then he spent a few busy weeks
meeting with everyone he could find who might have any
influence on settling the problems in the county. Evidently
he kept the telegraph busy, because the adjutant general
finally replied, saying he had not answered all the messages
because he had no reason to give instructions by either wire
or by slower mail. He had been trying to send additional
arms to Jones, but was having trouble finding the state
agent. He suggested Jones might be able to locate some
weapons belonging to the state that had been sent to Cardis
to protect his stage stations. The blankets Jones had wanted
had been sent several days hence. Steele wanted to retain
the Ranger detachment in Austin because unknown parties
had tried to break into the office of the attorney general,
probably to steal evidence in a land-fraud case. Steele told
Jones the governor wanted a full report as soon as possible,
especially with whatever evidence he might have of parties'
outside the U.S. being part of the mob. As a final word, Steele
said the major had a lot of mail but he was doubtful about
forwarding it.[55]

None of this was of much moment to Jones, who was
winding down his task. On November 18 he brought Howard
down from Mesilla and he was placed under a new bond.
There was considerable excitement over Howard's return,
with many threats, but Jones said he had twenty good men,
obviously referring to Tays and the new Ranger detachment.[56] In a final report from the county, Jones told Steele
the mob had disbanded and its members had promised to
submit to the law. Howard was back in Mesilla, and Tays
was in San Elizario. His job done, Jones said he was leaving
the same day, returning to Austin via Coleman and Kimble.[57] His report was overly optimistic.

Howard wrote Major Jones a letter a few days later. Just
when Jones was able to read it is not known, but it made
no difference. Howard told the major that Tays was a good
man, but slow, and warned Jones not to trust the Mexicans.
As for his part, Howard was as adamant as ever about
making people pay for salt.[58]

Tays had his detachment organized and made his first
report at the end of November. He noted the Rangers were
stationed in San Elizario, but he had ridden to Franklin on
November 28. There had been some trouble at first when

Howard had returned from Mesilla, but things were quiet.[59]

The first indication of the renewal of fighting was a telegram on December 15, 1877.

FIGHTING IN SAN ELIZARIO.
RELIABLE REPORTS ELLIS AND SIX RANGERS KILLED.
MARTIN LOHMAN[60]

As with many initial reports, this one was exaggerated, although two men *had* already been killed. Early in December a Mexican wagon train had traveled to the lakes to obtain salt. Hearing of this, Howard accompanied a small party of Rangers down to San Elizario, where they met a growing mob. Tays hurried out with more men and escorted Howard into their quarters in some store buildings. The Rangers, heavily outnumbered and with even more men's riding into town to oppose them, requested aid from the army. A small army detachment came down from the post near Franklin, and Captain Thomas Blair talked with the mob leaders and assured them he had no intention of interfering in a civil matter. He then returned to Franklin. His lack of decisive action guaranteed trouble; the mob was now convinced they had nothing to fear from U.S. Army troops and began concentrating men for an attack on the buildings occupied by the Rangers, Howard, and Howard's bondsmen.

One of the Americans, Charles Ellis, who owned a store in San Elizario and acted as commissary agent for the Ranger detachment, stuck a pistol in his boot and went outside to talk to the mob surrounding his store. As he was speaking to one of the men, another rode up and threw a rope about his neck and galloped off, dragging Ellis along the ground. After a time the rider stopped, dismounted, and cut the unconscious Ellis' throat.

Gregorio Garcia and several other Mexican Americans garrisoned Ellis' store. After Ellis' murder Garcia asked for reinforcements, but Tays had no men to spare. The small Ranger detachment and Howard's bondsmen were heavily outnumbered by the mob, which was growing every hour. John Atkinson, one of the bondsmen, brought in $11,000 and tried to strike some sort of deal with the mob leaders but was told nothing except the surrender of Howard would be acceptable. Both sides prepared for battle. The Rangers cut firing holes in the adobe walls of the buildings they occupied, while the mob scattered throughout the small village and maintained random firing. Going from one building to another, Sergeant C.E. Mortimer was hit and mortally wounded by a sniper; Lieutenant Tays ran out and brought the dying man into one of the houses despite fire from the mob. Firing stopped for a time on December 13 after a white flag brought on an informal truce for the night.

The truce did not hold, and firing resumed throughout December 15 and 16. Garcia and his men were forced out of the store and joined the Rangers in other buildings. Another parley and truce was used as a cover by the mob to place gunpowder under the Ranger quarters.[61]

Accounts of the next few hours vary, depending on the man reporting. Tays said he went out the next morning to resume peace talks but was told the Ranger buildings would be blown up if Howard was not surrendered. Howard realized the game was ended and volunteered to surrender to the mob to save the others. There could have been some dissension among the Rangers over dying for something less than a noble cause; the fee for salt did not seem too important to some of them. Because neither Howard nor Tays could speak Spanish, they asked for Atkinson to serve as interpreter, but when Atkinson arrived he was not allowed to see Tays, who later claimed Atkinson betrayed them and made a deal with the mob. Atkinson supposedly returned to the Ranger quarters and told the men that everything was arranged, to come outside with their weapons because the matter had been settled peacefully. The Rangers complied and were disarmed and taken prisoner.

Another version has Tays' going outside to talk to the leaders of the mob. As they were talking more Mexicans began to approach and listen; before Tays realized what was happening, forty or fifty armed men had his peace party surrounded and helpless. Tays then went back inside and told his men to give up. There was considerable bitterness over this; one young Ranger called his lieutenant a skunk![62]

There is no dispute over what happened following the surrender. Atkinson, whatever role he may have played before, gave the leaders of the mob his $11,000, but it made no difference. He and Howard and Sergeant McBride were dragged outside for execution. Chico Barela, the pre-eminent leader of the mob, had promised the Americans would not be harmed, but he was overruled by Padre Borajo, who was directing matters from Mexico. The priest sent word to kill all the *gringos*, and he would absolve them.[63]

Howard was led out first and shot, but he did not die from the firing squad's volley. One of the mob ran up and tried to kill him with a wild machete slash, but instead cut off two of his own toes. Others came over and finished the job, tossing the mutilated body into an abandoned well. McBride died instantly in a single volley of shots. Atkinson faced the firing squad and himself gave the command to fire in Spanish. The hail of bullets staggered him, whereupon two more rounds were fired. Still alive, he managed to motion towards his head, and the commander of the firing squad finally killed him with a shot to the brain.

The mob was looting Atkinson's store and house even before the bodies had been dragged away. They took everything, clothing, jewelry, furniture, bedding. Garcia and the other Hispanics who had stood with the Rangers managed to slip away, most hiding in Mexico where they were saved from the wrath of Borajo by friends.[64]

Meantime, the captured Rangers were in a precarious position. There were insistent demands from across the Rio Grande that all the Americans must be killed, but Chico Barela would not allow this to happen and there is no doubt the man who led the mob was responsible for saving the lives of the remaining Rangers. He allowed them to take their horses, but not their weapons, and ride to Franklin. Even Tays credits Barela with saving their lives, including this fact in the report he wrote December 20, two days after they arrived safely in Franklin.

There was considerable activity in Franklin. Sheriff Kerber gathered a posse and saw to the rearming of the Rangers, and a group of Americans arrived from Silver City. The revenging expedition was not a glorious one; the combined Ranger/posse/Silver City contingent first moved on Ysleta, taking a wagon with coffins for the murdered Americans. They captured two men in Ysleta who were shot the next day, possibly murdered but possibly killed while "trying to escape." In Socorro they first killed a man and wounded a woman, then killed the man who had tried to kill Howard with a machete. They then killed another Mexican. Hearing the road to San Elizario was lined by armed men, the posse and the Rangers went no further, and it was not until December 28 that the bodies of the murdered men were brought from San Elizario to Franklin for burial.

In a final report to Major Jones written December 30, Tays said San Elizario was deserted except for a few people; the Mexican population had fled to Mexico. Despite his situation, Tays completed and forwarded a monthly return for December 1877. It did not contain any details of the fight and merely listed Sergeant Mortimer killed on December 13 and McBride murdered on December 18. It showed seven men discharged during the month.[65]

The furor over the killing of the Americans and what was thought to be an invasion of the United States by armed forces from Mexico reached all the way to Washington, and President Rutherford B. Hayes appointed an investigative board which included Major Jones as one of the three members. The meetings of this board and the findings, including Jones' minority report on some of the opinions, are not part of this narrative. However, even the countless documents reveal that all of the facts are still not known.

Part of the inquiry dealt with whether there was an actual invasion, of sorts, from Mexico. On December 20, Jones' reply to an inquiry by the Secretary of the Texas Congressional Delegation had stated "that of a hundred and fifty of the mob which fought him (Tays) at San Elizario and killed three of his men and three citizens and to which he was forced to surrender were Mexican citizens...." In addition to the unresolved speculation as to nationalities, the question of why all three of the Rangers which Jones reported as killed were not listed on Tays' December monthly return is also unanswered; the third man was probably Atkinson. Even though his name does not appear on muster rolls, it does appear on a worksheet, in the Ranger Papers in Austin, which was used to prepare the 1877-1878 Report of the Adjutant General. When the report was published, however, all the names were omitted and only numbers used to show the losses.

Tays' role in the surrender is debated to this day. In the long history of the Rangers, this is the only unit which ever surrendered; some brand the lieutenant a coward, as did some of his own men. Others of the detachment merely believed he made an error in judgment.[66] If Tays' account is reliable, he showed considerable courage in bringing in his wounded sergeant. His fault was in his lack of experience and judgment; he should never have agreed to meet the

Mexicans out in the open where he could be cut off and surrounded. An experienced leader would have held the talk nearer his own men where the Mexicans, rather than the Americans, could have been taken hostage if necessary. Jones, however, had been required to enlist the men he was able to find in the county, and his choices had been limited. Had the Rangers been able to hold out for a few more days, help would have arrived from Franklin where the sheriff and the Silver City vigilantes were forming. It is easy, however, to identify a more perfect solution a century and more after the incident.

Contemporary discussion may be of academic interest. So far as we know, Major Jones did not relieve Tays or censure him in any way. Tays did resign in March of the following year, but he was reenlisted and continued to command the detachment. There were numerous personnel changes in the unit; Private S. Frazier "died" January 31, 1878, in "a personal difficulty" which was probably a suicide. There must have been some patrolling by the unit during the following year because Private A.A. Ruzin was killed by Indians on August 10, 1878. The unit was down to fifteen men on August 31, 1878, when the men were all discharged, but conditions remained chaotic in El Paso County, with a need for a Ranger presence to assist the civil authorities. According to the detachment muster roll for May 31, 1879 - September 5, 1879, a new unit was mustered into service on December 1, 1878. M.H. Ludwick, who had been a member of Tays' command, was promoted to sergeant and placed in command. The further actions of this unit will be described in Chapter Seven.

In describing Ranger actions during a given year, it is seldom possible to use a strictly chronological organization. Major actions usually take center stage, and less-important events at different locations appear only after the major actions have been described, and as space permits. The reader will remember that McNelly's company was disbanded at the end of 1876 and a new unit, the Special State Troops organized. The new unit was obviously organized under the authority of the legislation authorizing county units, but this new command had no county origin nor was it formed from personnel of one county. The first muster roll of the Special State Troops, dated January 25, 1877, listed Second

Lieutenant Lee Hall as company commander, and Armstrong as sergeant.

It was a drastically different unit, with many of the earlier Rangers no longer in service, but the company continued to do good work. Hall made a sweep of the Eagle Pass region in February, following earlier patrols to the southwest, and Armstrong scouted along the Rio Grande, moving in on Eagle Pass.[67] The Special Rangers made additional and sudden sweeps through this area in the spring, and they cooperated with the Frontier Battalion Rangers from Company A on several occasions.

Hall and Armstrong again hit Eagle Pass in May, and their unexpected assault caused the outlaw population to flee in panic across the river. Hall, Armstrong and Sergeant Parrot crossed to Piedras Negras in search of a fugitive, hoping the Mexican authorities would help in his extradition, but spotted the wanted man and arrested him before they could talk to the Mexican police. The report says they extradited him "according to law."[68]

Once more the Rangers arrested King Fisher and brought him to jail only to see him go free again. They guarded jails and provided protection for courts and witnesses. Armstrong, active in all of these activities, also led independent scouts during April and May. The Rio Grande trouble spot continued to be patrolled by Company A of the Frontier Battalion as well. On April 5, prior to his resignation in the autumn, Arrington and eleven Company A Rangers arrested a fugitive named Sam Williams in the area.[69]

Hall's men were so critical to maintaining some degree of law and order within the area that there was a public outcry when it was believed the company would be disbanded by yet another economy move. Governor Hubbard had the authority to form a company by using his discretionary powers, but it was up to the legislature to provide the funds for salaries and other expenses. When it seemed that some of the legislators from eastern areas of Texas would block funds for the Special State Troops, a number of cattlemen met in Goliad and quickly agreed to raise the money themselves! Representatives from twenty-four counties, members of the West Texas Stock Association, raised enough money to keep the company active until a regular appropriation could be passed. The funds were deposited in a Cuero bank and could only be disbursed by the adjutant general,[70] eliminating any appearance that the stockmen were in control rather than the state.

In early August while Porfirio Diaz was slowly overcoming all opposition to his revolution in Mexico and a lot of out-of-work *bravos* were crossing into Texas, Hall and his Special Troops again joined forces with Company A to investigate rumors of a large camp of Mexican fighting men east of Eagle Pass. Working with Arrington, Hall dashed through Eagle Pass and overran the camp, but somewhat belatedly because a hundred men managed to escape across the river. Nevertheless, the Rangers captured fifty men and identified several of them as being wanted on the fugitive list. Later they picked up more suspicious characters and delivered sixteen known criminals to the jail in Castroville, seven of them wanted for murder.[71]

Hall maintained pressure on the outlaws, but the work was routine and made no newspaper headlines. John Armstrong, now a lieutenant, was the Ranger who next attracted statewide attention by capturing the most wanted gunman in the country.

John Wesley Hardin had followed his usual pattern of escapades and killings in Louisiana and Alabama after he left Texas. By August 1877 he had settled in Polland, Alabama, where he went into the logging business.[72] Lieutenant Armstrong became interested in the search for Hardin after capturing a braggart claiming *he* was the noted desperado; there was also a $4,000 reward for the taking of Hardin. While recovering from an accidentally inflicted wound, Armstrong asked for permission to work on the Hardin case; the adjutant general agreed and assigned John Duncan, variously described as a Special Ranger and a detective, to assist the Ranger.[73]

Duncan played a key role in the eventual capture of Hardin. Unrecognized as a lawman, he was able to rent a farm near Hardin's father-in-law and made friends with several friends and relatives of the fugitive. Hardin stated that his brother-in-law Brown Bowen visited Hardin and his wife in Alabama and wrote home to his father; subsequent letters back and forth, observed by Duncan, were the clues that eventually let to Hardin's arrest by giving the address and aliases, Swain and Adams, which Hardin was using in Alabama.

Armstrong and Duncan both traveled to Austin for a talk

with Governor Hubbard and to make arrangements to have warrants sent to them by mail. Expecting the proper papers to be awaiting them, the two Texans started for Alabama. When they reached Polland, they took the local sheriff into their confidence, but Hardin was visiting in Pensacola, Florida. The railway people promised to aid the Texas lawmen.

Armstrong, Duncan, the sheriff and several deputies rode the train to a station outside Pensacola, where Hardin would have to stop on his way back to Alabama. When the train arrived, they could see Hardin sitting forward next to a window. They decided Armstrong would enter one end of the coach, facing Hardin, and the peace officers the other end behind Hardin; Duncan would grab Hardin's arm through the open window. No one, however, was in position when Armstrong entered the coach. Handicapped by his wound and carrying a cane, he moved slowly; Hardin evidently paid him no attention until he saw the revolver Armstrong had just drawn. He cried out, "Texas, by God!" and tried to draw his own weapon, but the hammer caught in his clothing. One of the four men with Hardin fired at Armstrong, whose return shot struck him in the chest. The mortally wounded man managed to jump through a window and stagger a few steps before he died. Hobbling as fast as he could, Armstrong approached Hardin but was kicked back into an empty seat. Jumping up, he slugged Hardin across the head with his gun barrel and knocked him unconscious. The other men with Hardin surrendered.

In his memoirs Hardin tells a somewhat different story. He describes at length how he wrestled with a number of deputies and was constantly struck by gun barrels before he was finally tied up. He barely mentions Armstrong but does say the Ranger told the deputies not to harm him and that he would kill any man who shot Hardin. Understandably, Hardin was reluctant to admit he had been taken by only one man.

The train conductor was informed of the situation and agreed to follow Armstrong's orders. He started the train towards Alabama; along the way Hardin's friends were dropped off, with their guns but without ammunition. From Whitney, Alabama, Armstrong sent a telegram to the adjutant general, telling him he had Hardin and describing the fight and the killing of one man.[74] Armstrong was in a tight spot; Hardin had many friends who threatened to rescue him. Armstrong's answer to the threats was the standard Ranger tactic: he would kill the prisoner first, then fight as long as ammunition and life allowed.

The prisoner was lodged in the Montgomery, Alabama, jail, and everyone managed to get some sleep. Hardin contacted an attorney, who agreed to obtain his release for $500. It took considerable talking for the Ranger to convince the judge that Hardin was a dangerous man, wanted in Texas. He showed his Ranger credentials and explained a warrant was being wired to him. Fortunately, he had a telegram stating Governor Hubbard was wiring the warrants, and he finally managed to convince the judge to hold Hardin until Wednesday. He at once wired Steele about the necessity of sending papers by messenger or express because the warrants had evidently been lost in the mail. There must have been other talks with Alabama officials, because the Ranger sent another message stating the governor of Alabama would issue a warrant after all, on the strength of Hubbard's telegram, and they would leave early the next morning. There was a final telegram:

IT IS ALL DAY NOW. ON OUR WAY. PAPERS O.K.[75]

There were no more interruptions or trouble on the rest of the trip to Texas, although Hardin says he almost escaped once. At every stop, huge crowds gathered to see the famous gunfighter. When they detrained in Austin, they had difficulty getting to the jail because of the crowd of curious onlookers.

This was the last major event in Armstrong's Ranger career, but it made him famous; forever after he was the man who captured John Wesley Hardin. He received the $4,000 reward and continued in service for a time, but his improved financial situation enabled him to marry into a pioneer Texas family in 1878.[76] A legend at age twenty-eight, he retired from the Rangers and went into real estate. Later he joined with his mother-in-law in a major ranching enterprise, in South Texas, which is still owned by the Armstrong family.

Lieutenant Reynolds and Company E were given the task of guarding Hardin. Composed of men from the earlier Company E, augmented by transfers from Company A and by new recruits, the company was considered one of the premier units. Gillett felt honored to be allowed to transfer into E, "the most formidable body of men I had ever seen." Gillett, at five feet nine inches was the smallest man in the command. Most of the others, including Reynolds and all the non-commissioned officers, were six feet or taller.[77]

Reynolds was one of the great Rangers of his time. He had already had a distinguished career as a sergeant; now he was to show what he could do as a company commander. He was a handsome man, well-built, blond and blue-eyed but also something of a mystery. His nickname was "Maje," short for major, supposedly because he had captured a Union major during the Civil War and appropriated his uniform. He answered to the name but never explained its derivation. He said he was from Missouri, but his family name does not appear on any census records from the county he claimed. There is a family listed on Pennsylvania records with the right name and a child about his age.[78] Gillett, who idolized Reynolds, once tried to discuss his past and the origin of the nickname, but Reynolds informed him that his early life was of no interest to anyone.[79] At the time he became commander of Company E, Reynolds was probably about thirty.

His first major assignment as an officer was to guard Hardin in Austin until he could be tried. Hardin was still under indictment for the killing of Charles Webb in Comanche County, and the prisoner was taken there for his trial. The entire company escorted Hardin, who rode in a buggy with the sheriff and who was so heavily shackled that he could not walk and had to be carried into the jail.

Hardin's return to Comanche City attracted the same attention as elsewhere. There was considerable sentiment for forming a lynch mob and saving the state the expense of a trial, but Hardin admitted that he had misjudged the Rangers, especially Reynolds, when he believed they would not protect him. Reynolds guarded the jail on all sides and positioned men inside with Hardin to avoid mob action. He also let it be known that if there *was* any mob action, he would arm Hardin and the other prisoners.[80]

Hardin's trial was short. He complained bitterly that he had not obtained justice—his shooting of Webb had been in self defense. He was sentenced to twenty-five years in prison, and Company E and Reynolds returned him to the jail in Austin to await the outcome of an appeal. Almost a year later, in September 1878, his appeal was denied and the Rangers escorted him first to Comanche for resentencing and then to the penitentiary at Huntsville. Hardin, possibly the premier gunfighter of the Old West, remained in prison until pardoned in 1894. He was murdered in El Paso in 1895.[81]

After placing Hardin in the Austin jail in October 1877, Reynolds and Company E went back to Kimble County and the routine of Ranger life. As the year ended, Major Jones settled his companies into winter quarters. Despite the new emphasis on white criminals, he did not overlook the possibility of Indian raids and ordered Coldwell to take Company A and select a location for winter camp in Frio County. With Dolan at Camp Wood, Roberts on the Sabinal, and Coldwell in Frio, Jones believed he would be able to spot or block any raids during the winter. He instructed Coldwell to report his exact location to the other two company commanders because he wanted them to work as a team rather than as separate commands. He expressed his usual concern for forage and supplies and brought Coldwell up-to-date on the new men being sent to Company A. He also sent along the battalion news, informing Coldwell that Captain Sparks had resigned from Company C and that Arrington was to be promoted and given the company. As a reminder, he mentioned there was a $500 reward for Richard Dublin and John Beard, and a $300 reward for Thomas M. Childers.[82]

Coldwell soon reported that he had selected a good campsite and was sending the location to Roberts and Dolan. He stated the people in the county were very gratified at having the Rangers back in their area.[83]

All in all, 1877 had been a good year for the Rangers, despite the Salt War. A newspaper editor summed up the year.

> If there is any one thing more than another the People of Western Texas have to congratulate themselves upon in connection with the progress of the year 1877, it is the breaking up and almost entire eradication of the cutthroat desperadoes that infested our section a year ago....the Rangers entered in among them and their presence gave encouragement to the officers of the law....[84]

— 6 —

Sam Bass and Other Bad Men
1878

Early in the new year, Major Jones began supervising the reorganization of Company C. G.W. Arrington, newly commissioned, took command of the company, a move that would transform a fine sergeant into one of the famous Ranger captains. Jones had Arrington report to Austin, where most of C and E companies were camping. From Austin, Company C would relocate to Coleman County.

In his letter of instructions, Jones outlined where Arrington would find supplies, who would supply corn for the horses, and how to obtain funds for incidental expenses. The major overlooked nothing. There was the matter of a cow, killed by the Rangers two years previously, that had to be settled. Jones had supposed the previous commander had settled the debt, but evidently he had forgotten and Jones, wanting the debt paid at full value but no more, instructed Arrington to "Pay him the customary price."

Company C had not been strongly officered for some time, and Jones did not want Arrington to jump in too hard at first.

> In assuming command of the company it will probably be better not to be too rigid in the enforcement of discipline at first, as you are not acquainted with the men & they have been under pretty slack rule for some two years. As you become better acquainted with them you can draw the reins tighter & gradually bring them to proper discipline & duty.

He continued his letter with the news that he had

discharged Sergeant Sparks and Private Taylor but had
returned them to duty on January 3, as they had promised
to repent and perform in the future. All the members of C
and E companies had asked him to give the two men another
chance, but the time lost would be deducted from their pay.
Jones was a strict disciplinarian, but a fair commander.
What brought about the discharges was not stated. Sparks
figures favorably in the monthly returns of Company C prior
to this incident and seemed a good leader. Easy living in
Austin may have been too much for him.[1]

In February, the first month for which Arrington signed
a monthly return, Company C was camped at Pecan Springs
in Coleman County with only one officer and nineteen
enlisted Rangers.[2] In March, Arrington had five men on duty
in Lampasas, one with Major Jones, and it was not until
May that the company again assembled in Coleman. They
had a large territory to cover and scouted 1,566 miles that
month.[3] Their tasks were sometimes exciting, often boring;
Arrington, his great days still ahead, was shaping and
training his company.

While not under Arrington's control, the detachment of
Company C under Lieutenant John B. Tays in El Paso
County was still operating and was still as large as most of
the companies. Gillett's statements that Tays resigned
shortly after the events of the Salt War and that a few
Rangers hung around Franklin until a regular unit arrived[4]
are compressing events and unfair to the men in the detachment.

There are monthly returns for the detachment for most
of 1878. Tays remained in command until his resignation
on March 30, 1878. Evidently Jones was satisfied with his
performance, because he had made no effort to relieve him.
By March the detachment was down to sixteen men, still
almost as large as the regular companies. For several of the
months there are no entries on the returns other than the
strength figures; other returns list scouting, cooperation
with the sheriff in arresting felons, and patrols after stolen
cattle and property. There is a puzzling item on the July
return, which is signed J.A. Tays rather than J.B. Tays.

In July the detachment was in Ysleta, still with sixteen
men. The following month the detachment had its biggest
action since the Salt War during a patrol's return to camp
after escorting stock to the Guadalupe Mountains. The

Typical General Order of the late '70s. This GO designates newly promoted 2nd Lieutenant N.O. Reynolds as commander of Company E, Frontier Battalion. Courtesy of the Texas State Library.

patrol was ambushed by Apaches on August 10. Ranger H.H. Ruzin was killed and two horses shot, and there were no known Indian losses.[5] If the detachment did not accomplish great deeds, it at least maintained a Ranger presence in the region. There was certainly a need. The local sheriffs in El Paso and Presidio counties did what they could, but they never had enough dependable men to form a posse. Many of the men who were available were men the posse should have been chasing.

Jones somehow managed to keep the frontier line and the Trans Pecos under observation. In February he wrote Lieutenant Campbell, commanding Company B, enclosing Special Order No.20 and a letter from Private H.D. Lynch who was requesting a discharge. Jones wanted the problem of Ranger Lynch settled and sent Campbell a discharge for the man, "not because he applies for it, but because he has always been troublesome, and has not made a good ranger." Jones stated his policy of not discharging men, before their time was up, merely because they wanted out. Rangers would be discharged only for cause. While this was official policy, it was generally agreed that a Ranger who had served time honorably and wanted a discharge should be released; the officers wanted men with good morale, and an unhappy Ranger was not likely to be very dependable.

Jones also told the lieutenant he had made arrangements for company supplies, for the next quarter, which would be hauled to the company's camp. Campbell was to take ten men and supplies for twenty days to Clay County to help the sheriff there track down fugitives. In closing, Jones mentioned he would be in El Paso for four to six weeks on the Congressional Committee investigating the Salt War and would tour the frontier when he returned.[6]

There was a good deal of correspondence back and forth between Jones and Campbell in the following months. The lieutenant sent the major a letter on April 3 outlining conditions in his area. Campbell said two men had just arrived at his camp with a prisoner, picked up at Castroville upon the order of Lee Hall. The prisoner, William A. Martin, was better known as "Hurricane Bill" and was wanted for murder.

Hurricane Bill Martin had experienced a change of heart, but he did not want to turn state's evidence. He did, however, want to stop the murderous "Tell Not Committee" and would give the names of citizens who had seen murders in the past several years. The witnesses needed protection from the Vigilance Committee. Campbell did not give details on either of these "committees," but it is evident they were a major power in the area. Martin also offered to show the skeletons of seven victims of mob brutality. Campbell told Jones he was sure there were people who would give testimony if they could be assured of protection.

He asked Jones' advice on proceeding and thought it would be a good idea if the major could attend court. Campbell had thirteen prisoners under guard at Albany and felt confident he could hold them, even though there was no jail. He proposed to arrest other suspected men when they showed up for court, either out of curiosity or to intimidate judge and jury. Martin could then testify against them.[7]

Not much resulted from Campbell's proposals. The situation in Albany was one of several in which outlaw groups took over an entire area, with the elected officials either powerless to stop them or themselves actively supporting the vigilantes. Coming from outside the area, with no local loyalties, the Rangers could stand up to the outlaws without fear of family reprisals. They also had sufficient numbers to wage war, and the vigilantes seldom had the nerve for an open fight. The restoration of local law was the most significant contribution the Rangers made in the years following Reconstruction, far outweighing the spectacular battles along the Rio Grande or Indian chases.

Even though Campbell was very active, Jones evidently had some doubts about him and queried local citizens about the officer after Judge J.R. Fleming wrote to Governor Hubbard and initiated an investigation of the Ranger. Later, in a letter that has survived, Fleming wrote Major Jones that he hoped he had not given a wrong impression of Campbell, who had done a good job as far as he knew. He added, however, that there had been a few complaints, and it might be a good idea to send the unit to another place.[8] It is possible Campbell was doing his job too well.

Nineteenth-century Ranger duty was much like today's police work with its often-boring routine and dead ends, and an occasional front-page case. The most newsworthy Ranger action of 1878 was the hunt for the young outlaw Sam Bass.[9]

The Rangers became involved in the spring of 1878, but Bass' infamy began in 1870 not long after his arrival in Texas from his home in Indiana. Young Bass had learned to play cards on the way to his new location in Denton. For several years he was a law-abiding citizen, working on a farm for the county sheriff, W.F. Eagan. Bass worked hard, saved his money, and bought a fine little mare in 1874. He won a number of races and made some money betting at the track. With a flair for cards, and winning at the track, Bass realized there were easier ways of making money than sweating as a teamster for his boss.

Bass went north to Fort Sill and began racing against Indians on the reservation, taking Indian horses as his winnings. He gathered up a herd of these horses, some of which were actually his, and headed south, under cover of night, to San Antonio. Bass was in his element in the bustling town, the largest he had been in, with its gambling halls and saloons. He made friends with Joel Collins, a kindred spirit, and they embarked on a business venture.

In August 1875 Collins and Bass started north to Kansas with a herd of cattle. From Kansas they shipped the animals to Sidney, Nebraska, to avoid a close examination of the title to the cattle, then drove the herd to the Black Hills and sold it. They invested their cattle profits in wagons and mules and went into the shipping business in Deadwood. Bad weather soon closed the roads, and the two businessmen went back to playing cards but lost everything they had. Collins also owed money he had borrowed, to pay some of the cost of the herd, and faced a big debt if he ever returned to San Antonio.

There was a simple way out of both their long term debt and their temporary poverty; they gathered a few new friends and began robbing stage coaches. Within a short time they had stopped seven stages and gained considerable notoriety but not much money. Their small gang, with the older Collins as leader, included Tom Nixon, Jack Davis and John Underwood, and was later joined by Bill Heffridge and James Berry.

There seemed to be little future in stopping stage coaches so the gang decided to switch to train robbery. They selected a water station at Big Spring, Nebraska, as the site of their first job, the robbery of a gold shipment aboard the Union Pacific. On September 19, 1877, they pulled off the robbery that made them the most wanted men in America, escaping with three thousand, brand new, $20 gold pieces and several thousand dollars from the train passengers. Peace officers in several states were alerted.

Bass and Davis were traced to Fort Worth, where their trail simply vanished. Joel Collins and Bill Heffridge were the first to be caught, at Buffalo Station of the Kansas Pacific Railroad by the local sheriff and some soldiers. When Collins and Heffridge drew hidden pistols and tried to escape, both were killed. The soldiers recovered $25,000 in 1877 gold coins.

Jim Berry deposited his gold coins in a bank in Mexico, Missouri, where the sheriff was not of a trusting nature; the newly minted $20 gold coins drew his suspicion. Berry, hiding out at his father's farm, was shot and captured. Although only wounded in the leg, the injury turned gangrenous and Berry died a few days later.

John Underwood was never found; Tom Nixon, believed to be Canadian, also vanished. The hunt turned to Bass and Davis in Texas, where by now the Rangers had their descriptions. As Gillett remembered, Bass was "Twenty-five to twenty-six years old, 5 feet 7 inches high, black hair, dark brown eyes, brown mustache, large white teeth, shows them when talking; has very little to say." Bass was eventually sighted in Fort Worth, then in Denton,[10] but Davis evidently left the country and was supposed to have gone to South America.

The last few months of 1877 after the Big Spring train robbery were busy times for Texas peace officers, as well as for the horde of outside lawmen who had come to the state looking for Bass. Special Company Commander Lee Hall had known Bass at least by sight. Hall happened to be in Dallas during late 1877, became interested in the chase, and made some effort to track down the robber.[11] Hall observed with some humor that the better hotels in Dallas were filled with clean-shaven northern detectives, Pinkerton men and newspapermen. Because they were easily recognizable among the bearded Texans, they attempted fanciful disguises, complete with slipping false beards and misplaced mustaches.[12]

None of the hunts came close to finding Bass. Even veteran Sheriff Eagan, now chasing his former employee, could not find Sam in the countryside near Denton, covered with dense thickets and cut by creeks and river bottoms. Sam Bass had plenty of money, spent it easily and freely, and was on his way to becoming a popular hero.

In early 1878, Bass became undisputed leader of a new gang which included, at various times, Henry Underwood, the brother of former gang member John Underwood, Ar-

kansas Johnson, Jim Murphy, Frank Jackson, Bill Collins,
Seaborn Barnes, Thomas Spotswood, Sam Pipes and Albert
Herndon. It is no surprise that Bass returned to the occupation which had provided his greatest financial success—
robbing a train. Dallas, not far from his hideout in the creek
bottoms of Denton County, was a rail hub with trains
running in all directions.

Trains were stopped and robbed on February 22, March
18, April 4 and April 10 at small stations within the same
general area about twenty miles from Dallas. There was
resistance at the Mesquite station and several of the bandits
were wounded slightly but they escaped with about $3,000.
Other than their success at Mesquite, the robbers obtained
little money but plenty of notoriety. Now generally believed
to be the Bass Gang, they became folk heroes to many. The
powerful railroads were not popular with the general public,
but they exercised considerable political influence. Governor Hubbard, probably under pressure and not caring for
the unflattering publicity his state was receiving, decided
something had to be done about Sam Bass & Company.

Two days after the robbery in Mesquite, Adjutant General Steele wrote Major Jones, then in Dallas, informing him
the governor had decided to raise a special force of thirty
men as a detachment of Company B of the Frontier Battalion
and directed Colonel E.G. Bower, a militia commander, to
muster them into service and see that they were supplied.
They would be in service for a month, or less, and work with
the U.S. marshal already in Dallas. The adjutant general
told Jones he would rather have sent experienced Rangers,
but the force was too extended.[13] The importance placed on
capturing or killing Bass is evidenced by the number of new
Rangers authorized; thirty men was a full company at a time
when the state was having the usual financial trouble
keeping the Frontier Battalion on duty.

In fairly short order the thirty new Rangers were selected; the position of the lieutenant in command went to
Junius Peak, who proved a wise choice. One can only
wonder if Jones experienced any qualms while selecting
another Ranger commander after his experience with Tays
in El Paso County, but if he had doubts, they do not show
in any of the correspondence.

The new detachment was in action immediately. Gillett
noted the new Rangers were inexperienced and did not

accomplish much at first; Bass and his gang knew the country and seemed to be having a good time eluding both the Rangers and the scores of private citizens and detectives after the reward.[14] Peak, however, even with his green men, was himself experienced and, once on the trail, never slowed. On April 22 he captured Sam Pipes and Albert Herndon near Denton.

Seemingly everyone in Texas was in on the chase, and no lead was overlooked even though some were pretty vague. On April 22 Steele wrote Jones that a man living south of Austin had received a letter from his brother-in-law in Chattanooga about overhearing some men discussing money that had supposedly been taken from the station agent at Eagle Ford, site of one of the Bass train robberies. Steele wanted to let Jones know about it. Even with the major absent on the Bass chase, the business of running the battalion had to go on, and Steele informed Jones that Corporal Wilson had come in the day before on business for Company A.[15]

At least one aspiring detective wrote directly to Governor Hubbard offering his services, stating he knew Sam Bass, Jack Davis and Henry Underwood and could find them through their kinfolks. Unfortunately he did not have the means to defray his expenses, but if the governor could take care of this detail, he could go to work right away and "please answer immediately." He was thoughtful enough to give references.[16] There is no indication he was placed on the state's payroll.

During this time Lieutenant Peak was working with Sheriff Eagan, Bass' former boss, who was chasing his ex-farmhand with grim determination. In Decatur, Peak and Eagan learned that Bass and his men had gone to Jack County, somewhat out of their territory. Peak asked the major for instructions and evidently received clearance to keep after the robbers.[17] Peak and Eagan and some civilians took up the hunt again and ran the fugitives down along Salt Creek in Wise County. In a brisk fight, Arkansas Johnson was slain and the outlaws' horses killed or captured.[18] The luck of the young outlaw still held; although on foot, Bass and the rest of his gang hid in the brush, managed to steal horses, and rode back to safer hideouts in Denton County.

Engrossed as he was in the Bass chase, Major Jones still

was never able to escape money shortages. In early May he
had to write Lieutenant Campbell that it would be necessary
to disband most of Company B, and told him how to manage
the transaction.[19] Later in the month, when details were
firm, he sent the lieutenant final instructions and the
Special Order making the action official. Sergeant Van Riper,
one corporal and six privates would remain to keep Company B active. Jones mentioned by name two privates who
could stay if they wished, but he could not be there to
oversee the reduction because he was a witness in Tyler on
the train robbery cases.[20]

Sergeant Riper remained in service as commander of the
reduced Company B and filed the next fifteen-day report as
required by battalion regulations. He reported that five of
the six men retained in Company B, and fourteen recently
discharged men, started out on a scout after Bass on May
31 and learned that he had either been able to recapture or
had stolen horses. Riper also reported that another six
ex-Rangers had been working with the Wise County sheriff
and were with him in another skirmish with the Bass gang
in that county. Of interest, Riper noted both that there were
Indians in the area and that there was the possibility of
another feud between the cattlemen and the farmers who
had been killing stock.[21]

Peak and his detachment continued to scout throughout
the area. On May 11 he wired Colonel Bower from Decatur,
asking the location of Major Jones because he had learned
Underwood had been in Stephens County the preceding
Thursday. Peak said he would await further orders in
Decatur.[22] The time of service for the detachment was
running out, facing Jones with another difficult decision,
and on May 17 he informed the adjutant general he had
discharged sixteen of Peak's men and would retain the
remainder on duty a few more weeks in Dallas and the
adjoining counties.[23]

Jones had every reason to be pleased with Lieutenant
Peak's conduct as a Ranger officer. Partially as a reward, but
more for the future, he wrote Steele and recommended the
promotion of Peak to captain, to become effective June 1,
1878. He praised the man as an efficient and energetic
officer whose "services I can use to better advantage in my
command with the rank of Captain than Lieutenant.[24] As
always the little major was thinking ahead, to the day when

Company B could be expanded again. For the time being, and in some manner, Jones managed to retain Peak and his remaining Rangers in service in Dallas County.

While these more dramatic events were taking place, Jones had been engaged in low-key, behind-the-scenes actions which would result in breaking the case. The plan was to arrest anyone even remotely connected to Bass on federal charges and jail them far from Denton County. The anonymous citizen of Denton County listed the numerous individuals jailed by federal marshals and sheriffs, and he clearly believed the law may have been stretched in the process; at times it seemed merely knowing Bass was grounds for arrest, and suspicion of sheltering him or gang members more than enough to be hauled to a distant jail. Whatever the legal niceties, people became afraid to have anything to do with the outlaw.

On or about May 1, Sheriff Everhart of Grayson County arrested and jailed Jim Murphy and his father for harboring Sam Bass. Because Jim Murphy was at least an associate of the gang, Deputy U.S. Marshal Walter Johnson took him from Sherman to the more secure jail in Tyler, where Murphy broached a plan to capture Bass. Johnson, impressed, promised to see what he could do. He brought Peak to talk with Murphy, and the Ranger soon asked Major Jones to come to Tyler.

The major was willing to do anything to capture the outlaw, and Murphy offered a chance to obtain advance information on the movements of the gang. They drew up a contract of sorts; Murphy said Jones promised him a share of the reward, to include Jones' share because the major wanted none of the money. In return for helping capture Bass, all charges against Murphy and his father would be dropped. The plan worked out very well. Murphy was in Tyler on bond awaiting a court hearing, and it was announced that he had fled, forfeiting his bond.[25]

Once free, Murphy began to carry out his part of the bargain. He rode back to Denton, hiding out until Bass and his gang returned from the disastrous fight on Salt Creek. Murphy finally managed to contact his old companions, but he was under considerable suspicion and several of the outlaws wanted to kill him. Frank Jackson finally convinced Bass to let Murphy stay, possibly because Jackson and Murphy were cousins.

In early June, Bass decided to leave Texas, working south and robbing a bank or two along the way to finance a trip to Mexico or South America. According to Murphy, he tried to warn officials about Bass' plans and on July 13 managed to mail a letter addressed to Sheriff Everhart and/or Marshal Johnson, alerting them to the possibility of a bank robbery in Round Rock, a settlement north of Austin. The letter, if actually mailed, was lost. Jones assumed Murphy had pulled a double betrayal or was dead, but at considerable risk Murphy managed to mail a second letter as the gang rode through Georgetown on July 17.

This letter reached Major Jones in Austin and caused an upheaval in the capital. The State Convention was taking place, and every politician and aspiring politician in Texas was in attendance. At stake was the gubernatorial nomination, and Hubbard and the adjutant general wanted the scalp of Bass for good political reasons.

It seemed like every fight with a lone rustler or a band of thieves during this period was reported as an encounter with the Bass gang. Sergeant T.A. Floyd of Company B reported to Peak that he had started after Sam Bass and party because the sheriff had come into town and reported Bass east of Denton. The sheriff and a Mr. Carter had been out the night before, looking for rustlers, were fired on and Carter badly wounded and the sheriff's horse killed. Next day Floyd wrote again, saying he and a posse had traveled to the scene of the fight but could not determine what happened. They assumed it was Bass, because Bass' crony Underwood was supposed to be in the country. Floyd closed by asking what he should do about corn for his detachment.[26]

These scattered scouting detachments and the numerous other searches for him were major reasons for Bass to decide to leave the area. He seemed to vanish. Captain Peak continued to drop in on all the old hideouts during July but found no sign of any of the gang. On July 15 he visited a small Ranger camp he had established near Denton with Sergeant Floyd and a Ranger detachment; three of the Rangers were sick, the other three were out making an arrest. In his report Peak mentioned there had been no definite sighting of Bass in two or three weeks, and he believed the robber had left that part of the state. He could only conclude that Murphy must still be with Bass.[27]

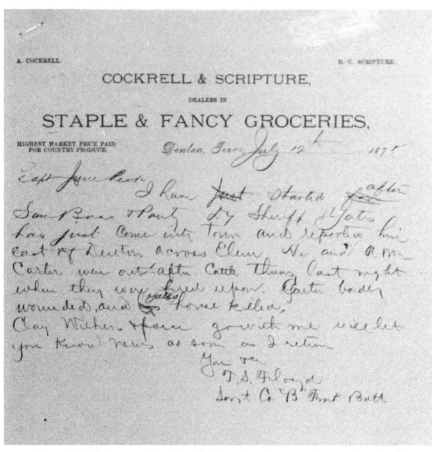

Report of Sergeant T.A. Floyd, Company B, giving some details of
a scout after Sam Bass. Like numerous reports and memos,
hastily written in the field, this is scrawled on the letterhead of a
Denton grocery store. When the Rangers made an infrequent trip
into town, they often borrowed paper to file reports, make out
requisitions and write letters. Courtesy of the Texas State Library.

Jones finally received Murphy's letter saying the gang
was on the way to Round Rock, just a few miles north of
Austin. Without being recognized, Bass and his shrunken
gang of three men had ridden down the stage road from Fort
Worth and Dallas into Waco, spending the last of the 1877
gold pieces. They had taken their time, talking freely, and
continued unrecognized through Belton and Georgetown.
With Murphy's letter, Jones now had a good indication that

his prey intended to rob a bank no more than twenty miles
away.

His elation at finally knowing the location of Bass was
tempered by not knowing how many men were with Bass,
nor an exact time of arrival, nor if Murphy might be playing
him false to mask some other move by the gang. Jones
nevertheless went into action.

The nearest Ranger unit was Company E commanded
by Reynolds, camped at San Saba a considerable distance
away but the best he could do. A few Rangers were in Austin
guarding the Land Office and the State Treasury, and Jones
sent Corporal Vernon Wilson to bring Reynolds and as many
Rangers as he could rapidly muster to Round Rock as
quickly as possible. The corporal was a nephew of former
Governor Coke and functioned as Jones' clerk helping with
battalion administration, but he held his job through merit
and not through family influence. There were no noncombat
positions in the Frontier Battalion.

Wilson rode all night, reaching Lampasas sixty-five
miles away at dawn in time to catch the stage to San Saba,
although the trip killed his horse. The fifty miles to San Saba
took most of the day. He hired a horse in the town and
galloped the three miles to Reynolds' camp, reaching it at
sundown July 18.

Reynolds had been sick and was unable to ride a horse,
but he had a small wagon hitched to the best mules in camp
and rode in it to Round Rock accompanied by eight men
with the best horses. Wilson, who had not slept in thirty-six
hours, tumbled atop some blankets in the wagon bed and
went to sleep.

Jones, in Austin, was caught in a guessing game. He
had no way of knowing when either Reynolds or Bass would
reach Round Rock, so he played the cards he had and sent
out the last of his Austin-based Rangers. Dick Ware, Chris
Connor and George Harrell left on horseback, with orders
to stable their horses in Round Rock and keep out of sight.
The same afternoon Jones left for Round Rock on a special
train, accompanied by Morris Moore, a deputy sheriff of
Travis County. Jones was understandably eager to acquire
all the help he could, but his choice of Moore would prove
to be a mistake.

In Austin on July 19, Steele quietly contacted Lee Hall,
who was in town acting as sergeant-at-arms for the State

Convention. Hall left immediately for Round Rock, in company with Armstrong and several of his men. They camped about three miles outside of the town, Hall rode in, and he and Jones decided Hall should stay under cover since Bass could possibly recognize him. In the meantime, Jones had also enlisted the aid of Deputy Sheriff Grimes of Williamson County.

Bass and his men had already reached Round Rock and camped outside town. They had decided to rob the bank on Saturday, July 20; on Friday afternoon they all rode into town to buy supplies and make one final survey. On the pretext of buying corn for the horses, Jim Murphy stopped at the edge of the little settlement while the others, Sam Bass, Seaborn Barnes and Frank Jackson, rode ahead.

About the same time, Reynolds and the Company E Rangers were approaching Round Rock after having ridden all night, stopping only for a thirty-minute breakfast. Gillett, a member of the detachment, recalled they made camp along a creek outside town about one in the afternoon. Reynolds did not want to give away their arrival, not knowing what might be happening in town, and went into town alone.

It was a hot Texas summer afternoon, between one and two p.m.; sensible people were taking it easy under shade. Ranger Dick Ware was waiting for a shave, the other two Rangers from the capital guard were half asleep, waiting for Ware, and Major Jones was in the telegraph office when Bass and his two companions walked into the town store. Among the few people on the street were the two peace officers, Moore and Grimes; Major Jones had suggested they check the streets for anyone they didn't recognize. Seeing three strangers, who almost had to be Bass and his men, the two lawmen entered the store. Grimes walked over to Bass, asked if Bass had a gun, and was shot and killed. Moore managed to get off one round but was shot in the chest and stumbled outside.

Dick Ware, the first Ranger on the scene, found the outlaws' trying to unhitch their horses and opened fire, but the three desperados turned and showered him with splinters from a shot-up hitching post. The other two Rangers ran up and also began firing; Major Jones heard the shooting and ran outside, drawing a small, double-action revolver.

A number of the town citizens began firing, inflicting no injuries but adding to the gunsmoke and confusion. As the anonymous citizen of Denton County tells the story, the outlaws entered a small alley in an attempt to get to their horses. Bass was hit in the hand here and rendered unable to fire his weapon. Ware shot Seaborn Barnes in the head, killing him instantly. Harrell shot Bass in the back, but the wounded man was able to continue hobbling towards his horse and Jackson, now mounted. Bass was unable to climb into the saddle, so Jackson rode over and tugged him up. Holding Bass, Jackson and Bass galloped out of town, side by side. Outlaw or not, Jackson was a man of rare courage.

About this time Reynolds rode into town, finding a confused scene. Still ill, he was in no condition for a chase, even if his horse had been fresh, but Major Jones, Hall and three of the Rangers had obtained horses and started out after the outlaws. The chase did not last long; for whatever reason, possibly losing the trail, the pursuers returned within a short time even though it must have been clear Bass was seriously wounded and needed Jackson's help to stay in the saddle.

Early the next morning, Saturday, their horses rested, Reynolds sent out a patrol commanded by Sergeant Nevill. Now a second corporal, Gillett was a member of this patrol. They did not have to ride far and soon found a man, lying under a large oak tree, who called out he was Bass and not to shoot. Bass was dying but talked freely with the Rangers, explaining he had made Jackson leave although his friend had been unwilling at first. The mortally wounded outlaw had been outside all night, tearing up his shirt trying to wipe the blood from his body. At daybreak he managed to walk to a house and ask for water, but the people who saw him covered with blood became frightened and ran away. Nevill and the Ranger patrol found him shortly thereafter.

Somehow Bass lived until late Sunday afternoon. Jones saw to it that the outlaw had the best medical care possible, but his death was merely a matter of time. In great pain, Bass was unwilling to talk about his friends and gang members. There was a final moment with the oft-quoted, "The world is bobbing around...." He was buried in the cemetery at Old Round Rock, where the gang had camped while scouting the bank; Barnes was buried beside him.[28]

The day Bass died, Major Jones wired Captain Peak to

be on watch for Jackson, believing he might return to his old haunts and his brother in Denton County,[29] but the Rangers never did find him. There was talk he did hide out for a time, hoping Murphy would show up. Captain Peak continued to scout for both Jackson and Underwood for some time after a reported sighting of Jackson eight miles from Denton, but by early August Peak had decided the two men had left the country and wanted to know if Major Jones had any orders regarding James Murphy.[30]

The death of Bass and the breakup of his gang was a major news story in Texas. The first account came to the governor by messenger, but when he made the announcement on the Convention floor there was a howl of derision; Hubbard had actively supported the Rangers, and his political foes saw this as a ploy to get him renominated. Not until the fight and capture of Bass was confirmed by the telegraph operator in Round Rock did many delegates become convinced the story was true. By then all the papers were headlining the story, giving the Rangers full credit. Even Hall received some credit for assisting, although his role was very minor.[31]

About a month after the fight, Murphy wrote Major Jones that he had heard from Jackson, who wanted to know if there was any way he could receive a reprieve. According to Murphy, the fugitive offered to help catch Underwood and others in exchange for his freedom. Murphy said he was willing to help Jackson because the man had saved his life when he was in danger from the other gang members.[32] Even if Murphy was telling the truth, nothing came of his proposal and the wanted man vanished.

The state of Texas paid a bill for $5.20 to cover the cost of a cot and bedding for Sam Bass as he lay dying in Round Rock. There was considerable correspondence about other claims and reward monies involved in the capture of Bass. Jones wrote Captain Peak about reward money offered by the state for the capture of Pipes and Herndon; there was no money to pay claims for the reward, at least until the next legislature met. Jones suggested the claims of Company B's Rangers might be sold for seventy-one cents on the dollar, which he thought fair. He outlined his system for paying reward money: each officer, noncommissioned officer and private was to share according to the "percentage of his pay."[33]

Late in August Jones wrote to the Texas Express Company, thanking the firm for a "donation" of $1,000. He informed the company the money would be distributed among the men entitled to it.[34] There is nothing to indicate either that Jones received any of this reward money or how it was distributed.

All the members of the Bass gang had been killed, imprisoned, or had disappeared except for Jim Murphy, a marginal member at best. He must have had a miserable life in the months following Round Rock; Bass still had many friends and admirers around Denton, where Murphy returned to live. Some of the correspondence between Murphy and Jones, probably over reward money and the selling of Murphy's horse, has not survived, but the ex-outlaw must have accused Jones of not playing fair and apparently received a scathing reply because, in a rambling, four-page letter, Murphy apologized again and again to the major, saying he had been mistaken about a $7,000 reward and asking Jones to forgive him.[35] Alone, afraid, distrusted, always thinking Jackson or Underwood might somehow return and kill him, Murphy committed suicide by drinking poison.

To this day there is dispute over which Ranger fired the shot which killed Bass. A coroner's jury decided George Harrell fired the shot, but Major Jones and others on the scene believed Dick Ware should have the credit. Even today it would be impossible to say; the fatal bullet that hit the young outlaw was so mangled not even modern ballistic tests would be able to match it to a specific revolver. The cemetery at Old Round Rock became a mecca for the curious, and several grave markers have had to be erected over the years as souvenir hunters chipped away each in turn. Sam Bass continued to be a folk hero, the first Northerner to become popular in Texas after the Civil War.

As fall began cooling Texas, Ranger business continued as usual; there remained plenty of other outlaws, maybe not as colorful as Bass but just as bad. There were also a few who had already crossed swords with the Rangers and lost; in early September, Jones instructed Reynolds to take half his company and report to Austin in time to have Hardin back in court in Comanche for resentencing by September 23. He wanted no trouble and offered Reynolds some of the Rangers on duty in Austin, if needed. He cautioned the

Ranger about preserving strict neutrality in all court appearances.[36]

Reynolds evidently did not ask for help; the region was quiet. He did mention to Jones that they had received some much-needed rain and added, for what it was worth, that Sergeant McGee had heard a mob was determined to kill Hardin this time.[37] It was an idle threat, and Hardin was sentenced and then escorted to the penitentiary.

Reynolds had his company reassembled in camp at San Saba and again at work by early October. On October 14 he wrote to Major Jones that Sergeant Nevill had started to "round up" a house containing fugitives, but had been ordered off by the local sheriff, a "sweet scented young man." Reynolds was of the opinion that nothing much would change in the area until they replaced the sheriff with a man who would impartially discharge his duties.[38]

The Rangers were required to work with elected officials, but they often felt it necessary to act unilaterally. When nothing was done about a murder in the county, Sergeant Nevill arrested the man everyone knew was guilty. None of the civil authorities had held any kind of investigation of the murder and the corpse had been buried without an inquest. The body was disinterred, but it was difficult to find a jury. Finally, "one of the Thorntons" was charged with the murder.

Up at Fort Griffin, Lieutenant Arrington was settling in as commander of Company C. On October 7 Major Jones ordered him to take fifteen men and attend court in Albany. He was also to assume command of a detachment from Company B that was guarding Judge Fleming while he made the rounds of his circuit. Jones did not give specific orders and merely told Arrington to protect property and the lives of civilians in the area. He was to serve such papers as might be given him by authorized officials.[39]

Arrington completed this assignment and was back in camp and out scouting again the following month. Also in November he worked again with the now-famous John Armstrong assisting the Ranger from Special Troops to arrest a man wanted in DeWitt County.[40]

The chase after Sam Bass and the retrial of John Wesley Hardin made up the major headlines of 1878, but the Rangers had accomplished much in addition to these media

I will give you all the true statement of the plan that was laid to catch Sam Bass. I J. H. Murphy was arrested Aug 1st 78 By Sheriff Everhart of Grayson county for harboring Sam Bass I was innocent of the charge I told Everhart so, I asked him why he did not tell me long ago that he wanted Sam Bass He gave me no answer of any satisfaction, But pushed me off from my Family & put me in Jail at Sherman He took my horse from me & gave me his word of honor that he would send the horse back to my Family, but I have never seen the horse since the proper Authority tells me that He had no right to take him whatever, Sheriff Johnson took me from the Sherman Jail to put me in Jail at Tyler; on the way to the Jail I hinted the plan for capturing Sam Bass to Taylor & He said that he would send Johnson to see me soon so Johnson came to see me after I had gave bond, I told that I could plan a job to capture Sam Bass if I was foot loose Johnson told me that he would see me again so He went off I came back with June Peak;

events. The Report of the Adjutant General for 1878 does not contain a great deal of detail, but it does have an interesting statistical summary. During the fiscal year ending August 31, 1878, the Rangers arrested 207 men accused of murder; ninety-three of these were charged with assault to kill. Animal theft of all kinds accounted for 395 arrests. Another 234 people were brought in for minor or unstated crimes. While they spent most of their time on major crime, the Rangers also brought in persons suspected of non-violent acts such as arson, forgery, perjury, swindling and embezzling. In all, they made 1,122 arrests during the fiscal year. They had followed twenty-eight Indian trails, made 916 scouts, and provided assistance to civil authorities on 217 occasions. Rangers returned 2,828 stolen animals and 1,686 stolen hides. They had killed or wounded twenty-eight criminals with a loss of five Rangers killed and two wounded.

In terms the legislators understood—money—the adjutant general made an eloquent case for the continued operation of the Rangers. In the frontier counties, property values had more than doubled since 1874. Several new frontier counties had been organized in 1875, largely due to Ranger protection against Indian raids, with an initial property assessment of $220,194; as a result of increased protection and continued settlement, these counties now had properties on the rolls valued at $1,445,157. Steele believed that at this rate of growth there would be no more frontier within a few years.[41]

Steele nevertheless cautioned there was much work still ahead. What had been accomplished could easily be lost if the Ranger force was dropped or drastically cut back in size. Letters from all parts of the frontier show that private citizens and elected officials shared the adjutant general's views. From J.H. Comstock, Sheriff of Menard County:

> Our county is at present enjoying comparative peace and quiet, but our citizens attribute it to the assistance rendered to civil authorities by the rangers. This necessity for protection will continue....Roving bands of Indians and Mexicans have also frequently raided through this section during the past twelve months, stealing and driving away horses and at times committing murder.

Ranger camp life in 1878. This photograph shows Captain Dan Roberts' Company D at mealtime. The scene is in their camp near Fort McKavett. Now part of the Rose Collection, this was shot by M.C. Ragsdale as part of a series he made on a visit to the camp.

In every case they have been speedily followed and driven out by the state troops, frequently having to leave behind their stolen property. Experience has shown that we have little to expect from the United States troops, as their movements are too slow and cumbersome.

And from William Wahrmund, County Judge, Gillespie County:

From my own experience I know that to the rangers the people of the frontier are most indebted for the security we enjoy now in our property and life, so much endangered by Indians, outlaws and desperadoes. But should this force now be withdrawn, I have no doubt the same state of affairs, of crime, riots, mob law and destruction of life and property would take place.

Steele printed fourteen such letters as samples in his report for 1878, one from Judge A. Blacker, of the Twentieth District, who wrote in September about "the absolute necessity of state troops to maintain law and order...."[42]

Judge Blacker wrote Steele again on December 4, 1878, outlining his views on the Rangers and the work they had done, praising the past conduct of the Rangers and pleading for their continued presence. He discussed conditions in far West Texas, the big counties that made up his district, and pointed out that men who had formerly been engaged in the troubles in Lincoln County, New Mexico, were now gathered in Pecos, Presidio and El Paso counties. Blacker quoted from a letter from Fort Davis in Presidio County, describing the lawless element that had settled below the small town near the army post; the primary interest of this element seemed to be the movements of the army's paymaster. The judge said men were running roughshod through the army posts at Fort Stockton and Fort Davis, as well as through any town they chose. He expressed his belief that if state troops were not provided there would be no courts held in the far western counties.[43]

It is very likely that Blacker's long and impassioned letter influenced the decision to reinforce the detachment in El Paso County and provide the unit with a qualified officer.

Unfortunately, this action had to be postponed for many months because of the chronic shortage of money and men.

— 7 —

The Changing Frontier
1879-1880

Adjutant General Steele resigned in January 1879,[1] and it was probably no great surprise to Texans when Major John B. Jones was named his successor. The promotion was well deserved; no man in Texas had a better understanding of the problems still ahead in attempting to bring law and order to the state. On February 8, 1879, Jones issued General Order No.1, instructing the Frontier Battalion's company commanders to send their reports, previously submitted to the battalion commander, direct to the adjutant general. There was no longer a Frontier Battalion commander— Jones carried the job with him, in fact if not in title, when he became the adjutant general.

Even though Texas still possessed a frontier, the frontier line was much less distinct than it had been five years earlier when the frontier could clearly be delineated with a broad line across Texas. In 1879 the demarcation was not so precise, and there were troubled areas even well back in the settlements. Civilization had spread into prairie and hills, and there were ranchers and farmers a hundred miles west of the 1874 frontier. Venturesome ranchers had staked claims on land that had been unexplored ten years earlier. Little towns were prospering in areas that had recently been buffalo range and Indian hunting grounds. Civilization was edging even into the last wild outposts in the Panhandle and the Trans Pecos. Railway surveys had been completed, and construction of southern routes to parallel the Union Pacific further north was about to begin.

Ranger operations had to adapt to the changing frontier. In 1874, six companies had patrolled their assigned sections of the frontier, while only one separate company worked in the interior or along the Rio Grande. Now companies could be and were ordered to any troubled location.

Jones had to preside over the changing mission of the Rangers as well as assume responsibility for all militia units in the state. The increase in his duties is revealed by the Reports of the Adjutant General. Steele's 1874 report had been dominated by Ranger activities, but in 1879, when the militia units were being organized into the regiments and brigades which were the forerunners of the present Texas National Guard, matters pertaining to the militia units take up almost the entire publication. Jones managed his new duties with his customary devotion and dedication, although there can be little doubt his beloved Rangers retained their special place in his concerns.

As adjutant general, Jones still had to face an old problem—money. The governor, Oran Milo Roberts, one of the giants in Texas history, had been a Confederate colonel and chief justice of the Texas Supreme Court until removed by Reconstruction authorities. He became chief justice again in 1874. Elected governor in 1878, Roberts was determined to reduce the state debt by following a pay-as-you-go program. He reduced pensions for Texas Revolution veterans, cut back on school funding, and abolished rewards for fugitives. To reduce the strain on crowded prisons, he instituted a liberal furlough and pardon system which reduced prison crowding but which also released a flood of criminals back into society.[2] Roberts held strict views on how peace officers should operate, and he kept a wary eye on the Rangers.

Always concerned about the next appropriation, Jones took advantage of any support he could muster with the legislature. He even wrote Captain June Peak to talk to some of his friends in the government.[3] He received help on administrative matters when Neal Coldwell was appointed quartermaster of the Frontier Battalion with the rank of captain[4] and charged with responsibility for the multitude of details concerning pay, supplies, forage and personnel of the battalion. It also gave Jones a trained Ranger captain to act as troubleshooter and inspector, a role which Coldwell filled for many years. Coldwell's appointment also set a precedent for filling the quartermaster post with a former Ranger officer, someone who could actually run the battalion, if necessary, or travel to the scene of trouble and act as coordinator or supervisor. The transfer of Coldwell removed the last of the original company commanders of the Frontier Battalion; and Dan Roberts, now commanding Company D, was the only remaining officer who had served in 1874.

Among the new officers in 1879, Lieutenant N.O. Reynolds now commanding Company E had made a name for himself even as an enlisted man. George W. Arrington had also served with distinction as an enlisted man, but he had not attracted popular attention until he became an officer and was given Company C. When it became necessary to move the company from the Coleman area, Jones received several compliments on the work done by the Rangers and requests to leave them in place. As he had on numerous occasions, Jones explained to the writers why the Rangers had to be moved but thanked them for their favorable comments.[5]

A full account of the Arrington scouts prior to the company's move to Fort Griffin would be repetitious, but he followed the Ranger practice of not taking sides in any dispute, served the warrants given him by proper authority, protected the courts, and refused the "help" of outside parties. On one occasion when he had a small Ranger detachment guarding fifteen prisoners, assisted by a few deputies and the local sheriff, fifty armed men rode to his camp and told him they had come to make sure the prisoners did not escape. The Ranger spread out his men and instructed them to shoot the first man who advanced. The vigilante band took the hint and rode away; the next day a smaller group rode up on the same mission, only to beat a similar hasty retreat before the Ranger rifles.[6]

At Fort Griffin, Arrington was operating just to the south of the Panhandle, a vast rectangle of largely unknown country although a few trails had been opened between Santa Fe and San Antonio during Spanish colonial days. In 1841 the Santa Fe Expedition had straggled across the lower part of the area, and the U.S. Army campaign of 1874 had uncovered the Palo Duro and Tule canyons and continued on into New Mexico. None of these crossings, however, had led to road building or settlement; even the buffalo hunters of the 1870s had only limited knowledge of the region.[7]

Now, confined to reservations, the Indians still roamed the area when allowed to go on supervised hunting expeditions. The policy that permitted small groups of Indians to leave the reservation and hunt seemed to be a fine idea, allowing them to retain their old skills, even if only for a time, leave the confinement of the reservation, and roam as they did in their days of glory. In actuality, the hunting trips often became depredating raids.

At the end of 1878, Arrington had reports of Indian raids and obtained permission from the adjutant general for a scout. There were several army posts below the Panhandle, but only Fort Elliott was actually in the eastern Texas Panhandle region, established to keep Indians in check and out of the area. Arrington took seventeen of his Rangers and started out on January 1, 1879, to scout for hostiles, or Indians on a hunt.

It was a typical Panhandle winter. The Rangers were soon caught in a snowstorm but were fortunate to be able to settle in at one of the scattered ranches, where they learned ten Indians had been sighted between the Brazos and Wichita rivers. When they could travel again, the Rangers managed to reach the divide between the Pease and the Wichita, but another severe storm forced them back to the shelter of the ranch.

On January 15 the Rangers were able to start again and found a trail made by about twenty Indians. Following the trail and seeing Indians ahead, they started in pursuit when the Indians began running. One Indian was killed before the Rangers came upon a camp with fourteen lodges and a large horse herd. Without waiting to ascertain the number of Indians, the Rangers spread out and rushed through the camp only to discover a number of soldiers with the Indians; a sergeant and a detachment of troops from the 10th Cavalry at Fort Sill were escorting the Indians on a hunting trip. It was later learned that the soldiers maintained little control over the Indians, who often were permitted to ride as much as thirty miles away from their escort and any supervision. The disgusted Rangers returned to their camp.[8]

Considerable friction developed over the incident. Wheeler County had just been organized, despite opposition from the post sutler at Fort Elliott who, with others, wished to keep settlers out of the area and retain control of the trade in the region.[9]

This animosity against outsiders would lead to trouble with the Rangers. After learning of Indians again in the Panhandle, Arrington had left his camp near Fort Griffin and ridden north with twenty men and rations for forty days. They camped on Sweetwater Creek near Fort Elliott on June 12, 1879. Arrington rode to the fort and was accosted by John Donnelly, an employee of the post sutler. Possibly mistaking Arrington's diminutive size for weakness, Donnelly demanded to know if Arrington was in charge of the Rangers and stated that "Gen. Davidson wants to see you immediately." The Ranger replied he might call the next day, if he had time. Shortly thereafter John W. Davidson rode up, and he and Arrington must have held a spirited conversation; the soldier wanted to know if the Rangers would fire on Indians, and the Ranger replied he would if they were armed.

On the morning of June 18 Arrington wrote the adjutant general a report of his move to Fort Elliott and events to that date.[10] Later in the morning, Arrington heard that Donnelly had stated that General Davidson had said he would order his men to fire on the Rangers if they killed or molested Indians in the Panhandle. This must have infuriated Arrington, but he wanted to be certain and wrote Davidson asking if Donnelly had correctly expressed the officer's policy, "not that I have any fears of you in the execution of the enterprise, but for the purpose of laying the matter before the Governor and the Legislature of Texas which is now in session." If Davidson replied his answer has been lost, but he did have Donnelly write a statement clearing the officer. To be safe, Davidson sent Governor Roberts copies of Arrington's letter and the statement by Donnelly.[11] There were no further exchanges, verbal or written. Arrington never seemed quite so short in stature after this; a man willing to stand up to bad whites, Indians, and the U.S. Army could not be measured in inches.

Arrington's brush with reservation Indians was not an isolated affair. Further south, Captain June Peak and Company B were having trouble with "hunting parties." On July 1 Peak sent Jones a preliminary report on a scout and fight by Corporal Douglas. Later Peak filed a full report.[12] He had sent Corporal Douglas and six men to the head of the North Concho to set up camp and watch for Indians. About twenty-five miles northwest of Fort Concho, the Rangers met a rancher who told them there were Indians in the area. The rancher joined the Rangers, and they soon cut a trail going east. On June 28 they came on the Indian horses, staked out near their camp.

Douglas charged the horses, cutting them loose, and came under heavy fire from the Indian camp. The initial volley killed two Ranger mounts and wounded the rancher's horse. The Rangers circled and tried to get behind the camp, but the Indians had slipped away to a rocky bluff close by. It was almost dark and Douglas fell back, taking eight Indian horses. As usual, the pack mules had been cut free when the fight began; they wandered into the Indian camp and vanished.

The Indians attacked Douglas during the night, but the Rangers beat them off and the Indians slipped away in the darkness. Next morning the Rangers found the raiding party had gone due west, evidently abandoning their raiding mission, and the Rangers followed them for a hundred miles, finally spotting the two pack mules atop a slight rise.

There was no sign of Indians but Douglas was cautious, directing some of his men to circle the little slope while the others moved in from the front. Ranger W.B. Angling rode in too close, before the others were ready, and was hit by a volley from the concealed Indians. Although wounded, he managed to free himself from his dead horse but was killed by a second volley. Two more Ranger horses were killed and Douglas pulled back. The Indians, able to fire with only their heads momentarily exposed, had located a perfect ambush site and had rifles and plenty of ammunition, firing "promously," as Peak reported. Corporal Douglas now had several men without horses and was without supplies. A long way from help, he pulled his men back towards their camp.

On the return trip they met a patrol from the 10th Cavalry, and Douglas left two mounted Rangers with them to act as guides so they could retrieve the dead Ranger. In his report, Captain Peak complained that the Indians had come down from Fort Sill, escorted by a Captain Nolan who had issued them rifles and ammunition. Instead of hunting, they had left Nolan and cut east of the Staked Plains, then east again towards the settlements. On the trip back to his camp, Corporal Douglas had crossed other trails but could do nothing with no supplies and dismounted men. Peak noted he was sending Sergeant Floyd to follow these trails and continued with the opinion that Captain Nolan might complain about the Indians' being attacked unnecessarily, but the ranchers demanded protection, "There is strong feeling expressed upon this subject here, by leading citizens."

Company B continued to have Indian troubles. In August, Captain Peak reported Indians' stealing horses and his departure after them the next morning. Corporal Taylor was on a scout towards Devils River after more Indians; another patrol under Sergeant Floyd was with some troopers of the 10th Cavalry.[13] On August 27 Peak wired Jones he had captured fourteen horses from the Indians. Taylor had followed his trail to the Rio Grande, where the Indians crossed into Mexico.

Action continued into September when Corporal Taylor again chased Indians as part of a larger army detachment. In disgust he explained to his captain why they had not caught any raiders; the army lieutenant in command, believing he had seen some Indians way off the trail, had suddenly sounded the charge and had run their horses into the dirt. Taylor said the inexperienced officer later ordered a second charge with the same result. With night at hand and their horses exhausted, the combined patrol lost the trail.[14]

By the summer of 1879 the location of Company C near Fort Griffin was no longer a satisfactory camp. It was too far east to block Indian raids and did not provide protection to settlers out on the plains. Ranger patrols found the Panhandle was being settled, no towns yet but with ranches on all the major streams. Settlers edging into the region were running into bad whites and occasional Indian raiders. Shackelford, a frontier county only five years earlier, was far to the east of what was considered the frontier in 1879. In September, Arrington moved his camp a hundred miles northwest, into Crosby County, and established Camp Roberts at the mouth of Blanco Canyon.[15]

It was an ideal site. The canyon had served as an east-west route for anyone's going up or coming down from the Staked Plains. Shortly before the Rangers arrived a party of horse thieves had crossed into New Mexico, but this type of traffic and easy passage was stopped. Arrington was monarch of several thousand square miles of unknown and unsettled territory. In 1877 Captain Nolan of the 10th Cavalry had tried to follow a war party out onto the Plains

Company C , Frontier Battalion, late 1870s.
Captain John Arrington is front and center. This photograph
shows the typical Ranger working dress of the day.

and had been lost for days. With no familiar landmarks nor known watering holes, it was more by chance than skill that Nolan found his way to Fort Concho. Two men had died and two others had been lost out on the sands, and the incident became a well-publicized horror story that hindered further exploration. [16]

Despite Nolan's near disaster, Arrington was curious about the lower part of the Staked Plains. Indians managed to come from the west on raids then flee back west into the desert, and it seemed logical to the Rangers that there was water somewhere in the wasteland.

An excuse to explore the region came on December 28 when two cowboys reported to Arrington that Indians had stolen some horses from the Slaughter Ranch the night before. The Rangers were alerted to the raid about noon; within two hours Arrington with twelve men and two mules loaded with rations for ten days were on the trail to the ranch. [17]

It took them three hours to ride to the ranch and pick

up the Indian trail, following it past Yellow House Canyon and up on top of the rimrock and out onto the Plains. Night came early in the winter, and the Rangers soon had to make camp. The winter mist that covered everything soon turned to ice.

Next morning Arrington followed the trail west, to some lakes they knew by name, then another thirty miles when dark again halted them. Not about to make the same mistake as Captain Nolan, Arrington sent Ranger John D. Birdwell back to camp for a wagon, water casks and additional supplies to meet them at Double Lakes. The Rangers then started northwest, marching for two days to a landmark known as the Yellow Houses on a marked trail running from the headwaters of the Brazos across the Plains to Fort Sumner in New Mexico.

Two brothers, George and John Causey, had a camp about three miles north of the high bluffs that gave the spot its name. Several caves, some large, cut back into the bluffs. The Rangers bought some buffalo hides from the brothers and used them to make slings to hold the water casks. When Birdwell arrived with the wagon and extra supplies, Arrington had the water casks slung on the mules and divided the extra rations among the men. They had four, ten-gallon barrels plus their canteens. He could expect to find fresh water at Silver Lake, but after that water sources were unknown. Arrington planned to move southwest from Silver Lake for two days and intersect the Indian trail. He thought they could continue two more days, then fill their canteens, give the rest of the water to the animals, and return without too much trouble. It would be hard, but should not be dangerous.

Despite all the traveling they had done, they were only about fifty miles west of their main camp when they left the shelter of Yellow Houses on January 12, 1880, and marched to Silver Lake. It was bitter cold, the lake frozen, and the Rangers had to break through the ice so their horses could drink. The next morning they started out to the southwest using a pocket compass as a guide. The land was flat, the dark sand covered by a heavy grass turf. After thirty miles they entered sand desert, deep, blowing in the wind, almost white in color; Arrington later said it was the most desolate region he had ever seen. There were no landmarks of any kind. Only their trust in the compass kept them moving to the southwest.

Movement was slow because the horses sank into the sand at each step. They camped that night in another desolate spot, then were up and on the way as soon as they had light enough to check the compass. That afternoon they crossed an old trail, probably Nolan's, but it did not go in their direction and Arrington had no wish to follow the meanderings of the unlucky soldiers. At the end of the day, January 15, they rode out of the sand hills and desert and onto firm earth.

At sunset the leading Rangers spotted a low hill, the first elevation in the landscape. The sun was almost down when they reached the hill, but there was enough light to see a dry lake bed, on the west of the slope, about a quarter of a mile wide and a mile long. The happy Rangers found several springs on the west side where a large group of animals had watered recently; there were horse tracks all along the lake shore.

Near the water they found a huge buffalo shoulder blade, the largest any of the Rangers had ever seen, which the Indians used to leave messages for others passing that way. The "bulletin board" had a notice of Indians' traveling, followed by a double set of shod tracks indicating the Indians knew they were being trailed. The Rangers camped near the water for two nights, resting their tired animals.

On January 17 Arrington started south, following a large trail. The Rangers tracked the Indians for twenty miles and discovered the first of four lake beds running generally north and south. Again they found a number of springs, with fresh water but somewhat brackish. Here again were numerous Indian and horse tracks; ashes in the fire stones were still warm. The mystery of the Indians' ability to appear from and vanish into the west was solved; the legends about lakes and water in the desert were fact not fable.

A large trail led southwest, and Arrington's inclination was to follow and punish the raiders. Common sense dictated another course. Arrington was not sure where he was; he was possibly in New Mexico where the Rangers had no jurisdiction. There were Indians in large numbers in the vicinity; his horses were in poor shape and his supplies were low. Arrington discussed the situation with his men and they camped in a sheltered location near another lake where they hid their horses in a large draw where they could graze.

Arrington and the rest of the party could see and intercept any Indians heading east; sentries were posted to watch for Indians approaching from the east. Evidently feeling at home, the Rangers named their lake Ranger Lake.

They had been out twenty days, and Arrington knew his superiors would be concerned about their absence. Taking several pages from his small note book, he wrote a brief but complete account of the scout. Short as it was, the field report showed distances, directions, gave all essential details and included a sketch map of the newly discovered lakes. This message was sent by courier to the camp of the Causey brothers and eventually reached Austin. Another messenger was sent to Camp Roberts, their main base, to bring the rest of the company and additional supplies.

Arrington planned to wait out the full moon, often a time for raids. There was little to do other than sit about, but scouts were sent out all the time. Water was no problem, but the supplies seemed to shrink at a rapid rate even after the rations were cut in half. The bacon gave out, leaving only coffee and flour, but even worse was the lack of forage for the animals. The weather was favorable, considering the time of year, the nights bitter cold but the days clear and comparatively warm. Although there was plenty of game, especially antelope, Arrington was afraid to waste ammunition that might be needed in a fight, and in the high, clear air a shot could be heard for many miles, possibly warning an approaching band of Indians.

Finally, needing food, Arrington sent three Rangers back to the four lakes to kill antelope, far enough away not to alarm any raiders riding near their encampment on Ranger Lake. They returned the following day with news there were about twenty Indians around the lakes who had tried to steal the Ranger horses. The Rangers managed to elude them, but from the signs the Texans were certain other parties were near.

Arrington decided it was time to return; their horses were in no condition for a chase or a fight. If all or even part of the Indians joined forces he would be heavily outnumbered, so on January 31 the Rangers started back. The first day the weather held clear. They shot an antelope and ate every morsel. It was their last good moment. The trip out had been difficult; the return was agony.

After arising the next morning, the Rangers were soon

Initial page of Arrington's report on his scout across the Panhandle. As was often the case, Rangers used whatever paper available for necessary correspondence. This is written on a small notebook Arrington carried. Approximately full size. Courtesy of the Texas State Library.

covered with snow. Pointing northeast, directly into the blizzard, Arrington took a compass reading and led the way, his men hunched over against the wind and driving snow. He estimated they were fifty to sixty miles from the Yellow Houses and shelter, and even with the compass he could easily miss the bluffs in the whiteness of the storm. The snow, a foot deep by nightfall, and the drifts tired the already weakened horses.

When John Birdwell's horse collapsed, he told his companions he could not go on. They tied him to an Indian pony they had found abandoned at Ranger Lake and started again. After eighteen hours the horses were almost spent, the men bent over in the saddle, wrapped in blankets trying to protect themselves from the wind and blowing snow. Every man was covered with ice, cracking as they shifted position.

To halt was certain death, and they continued on after dark. Suddenly the snow stopped and the heavy clouds broke. Arrington had done a marvelous job of guiding them with his small compass; they were almost at the bluffs. Another thirty minutes and they found where they had left the wagon. Not far away was a huge cave with room for men and horses. A search located the cache of mesquite roots they had collected earlier, and before long there was a fire going.

Ranger Birdwell was delirious and in great pain from frostbite. When they cut off his frozen gloves, he rolled over into the fire trying to warm his hands, but others carried him outside and rubbed snow on his face, hands and feet. Back inside the cave, he again tried to crawl into the fire. When they finally thawed him out, the Rangers took turns guarding him so that he did not crawl back into the flames.

The Rangers used the fire Indian-fashion, taking turns sitting close to the small blaze and rationing the precious roots. In the morning, Arrington sent two of the stronger Rangers and the pack mules to the Causey brothers; on February 3 they brought back buffalo meat, flour, sugar and everything else they had been able to find. Arrington said later, "The men were so weak from hunger and exposure to cold that they could scarcely stand up, and some of them, when attempting to walk, would turn blind." It was necessary for the stronger men to help their comrades, keeping them from eating too much at first.

With plenty of food and a little warmth, the hardy Rangers recovered quickly. They spent February 4 resting and eating and started back to camp late in the day. On February 6 they arrived back at Camp Roberts in time to forestall any reinforcements of men or supplies. In all likelihood they had been given up for lost. The next day Arrington wrote a fuller report than the brief account on the pages from his notebook, and the Ranger scout became a big newspaper story. The post commander at Fort Sill wrote and asked for a copy of the report, or a description of the route they had taken, because there had been rumors of "lost" lakes in New Mexico. The Rangers sent him full details of the scout.

Arrington had thought they might have been in Gaines County, but the Rangers had actually traveled well into New Mexico. His discovery of the springs broke up further raids across the Panhandle and opened another section of Texas to settlement, of far greater significance than many noted battles. Arrington summed up their accomplishments many years later.

> In my opinion, few men have suffered more and lived than did this little squad of Rangers....they penetrated a region of country that at the time was absolutely unknown to white men and discovered lakes of water in the heart of the Great Desert. They also discovered the hiding place of this band of hostile Indians which had been raiding the frontier of Texas....They were never known to make a raid on that part of the Frontier of Texas again.[18]

For a time, the only law in or near the Panhandle was the Ranger company at Camp Roberts. Arrington and his men would be active in the early months of 1880, but they were no longer operating in largely unknown territory. There was no immediate surge of settlement, but people did begin to move west and north into the area. Some of the buffalo hunters remained, and cattle ranchers arrived in some numbers. Mobeetie would form a base for the organization of Wheeler County in 1879, the first county in the Panhandle. Clarendon, in what would be Donley County, was another early settlement. Hispanic sheep herders along the western border with New Mexico created enough market for the town of Tascosa to develop, and on January 12, 1881, newly elected officers took the oath of office in Oldham County, the second county in the Panhandle. Another part of the frontier was vanishing.[19]

The activities of Company C have been followed in some detail because of the spectacular discovery of the Lost Lakes, but the other Ranger units were also active in this period. Their accomplishments in 1879-1880 depended on who was breaking the law and in what location. If some companies achieved more, it was not necessarily due to superior officers or better Rangers; location played the key role in determining which companies managed to make the records. Company D always managed somehow to be in on action, and this unit furnished more company commanders from among its ranks than any other Ranger command.

There were no major operations during 1879, largely a period for belt tightening. The Rangers existed on funds allocated by the previous legislature, and no one knew what the next body would do. Jones fell back on his system of cutting manpower to save funds, and the companies were reduced by four or five men a month for several months into the year. Company A, a typical example, had twenty-one men on the roll in March, sixteen in April, and only ten by the end of May.[20]

The Rangers made do. In early March Pat Dolan, commanding Company F, asked Reynolds' help for a big scout to the head of Devils River because of information that a large band of cattle thieves was operating there. Reynolds sent Gillett, now a second sergeant, and five men from Company E to beef up the scout, but the Rangers were gone most of the month, covering extremely wild country, without finding any outlaws. By the time Gillett returned to Company E, he had covered over five hundred miles.[21]

Gillett returned to his company to find his commander, the gallant Reynolds, had resigned. Ill health was probably the cause. Reynolds had always claimed to be a bootmaker by trade, and for a time he practiced this work, living at various places away from the frontier. The lure of action was too strong, however, and he eventually returned to Lampasas, where he had earned his reputation, and served as county sheriff for two terms.[22]

When Reynolds resigned, Sergeant Charles L. Nevill was promoted to lieutenant and placed in command of Company E. The unit was moved to Austin for reorganization; several of the Rangers retired, some transferred to other companies, one became an Austin policeman. Despite the reduction of spaces, Jones was unable to keep within the shrinking financial allocation for the Frontier Battalion and had to disband Company F. Pat Dolan left the service, the only company commander known at the time who had served in the Union army.[23]

Despite intensive efforts by the Rangers to run them down, there were several individuals and groups that seemed to bear charmed lives. The Dublins were one such family. The father, Jim "Jimmie" Dublin, had a farm on the South Llano, but neither he nor his sons had been listed on any of the fugitive lists in 1877 when the Rangers had swept through Kimble County. Shortly thereafter, however, the

oldest son Dick and his friend Ace Lankford, both known to
Gillett from earlier years, killed two men in Coryell County.
The county offered a $200 reward for Dick Dublin, and the
state added another $500. The Dublins moved to the pro-
tection of the brushy, broken country in Kimble, soon joined
by another son, Dell, who had killed a man named Jim
Williams. In late 1877 Reynolds made another sweep
through Kimble and, in a raid on a ranch hideout, captured
Dell and almost caught Dick, who escaped under heavy
gunfire. For some time the man seemed to live under a lucky
star.[24]

In early 1878, the sheriff of Tom Green County had
ridden into the Company E camp on the trail of cattle stolen
from the San Angelo area. Reynolds had sent Nevill and
some Rangers with the sheriff, and they found the stolen
cattle near the South Llano. Once again they had almost
captured Dick Dublin when he rode near some hidden
Rangers, but once again he had been able to flee through a
volley of shots. Nevill returned to camp with fifty stolen cattle
and the embarrassing admission that Dublin had escaped
again. Reynolds, disgusted, told him their Negro cook could
have killed the man; he could not understand how four of
his best men could miss an outlaw who had ridden almost
on top of them.

Reynolds next sent Gillett, with five Rangers, to scout
for Dick Dublin who, Reynolds explained, "seems to be a
regular Jonah to this company."[25] Gillett, with supplies for
five days, rode fifty miles to the headwaters of the South
Llano where some stockmen had built a pen to hold wild
cattle. The Ranger corporal believed the locale would be a
good place for Dublin to hide, but when they reached the
pen the stockmen had moved. The Rangers started back and
traveled about twenty-five miles the third day, timing their
ride to reach the Potter ranch at about nightfall of their
fourth day on the trail.

Mack Potter and his two sons were friends of the Dublins, living not too far from Jim Dublin's farm, and Gillett
knew that Dick Dublin often visited the Potter ranch. Arriving after sundown, Gillett left the horses with two guards
while he and the other three Rangers approached on foot.
They saw a rider enter the ranch yard surrounding the
one-room cabin with a wagon in front. Crossing the open
ground, even in the dark, the Rangers were soon spotted.

Mack Potter yelled for Dublin to run, but this time his luck was out. He reached the brush and almost outran Gillett, but the Ranger's second shot instantly killed Dublin. They never did receive any of the reward money, which had been offered for "arrest and conviction" rather than for "dead or alive." The other Dublin brothers, particularly Dell who was somehow again on the loose after his arrest in late 1877, swore to avenge Dick, but Gillett did not lose any sleep over the threat. Later, back in camp, he sent a letter to Ranger Ben F. Carter who was evidently on leave.

Camp Steele, Kimble Co. Texas, Ap 8th 1879
Mr. B.F. Carter

Dear Friend I received your letter last night and as I am to lesure to day I will write you an answer. Things go prity much as usual—the Dublins have maid some prity big threats. We arrested Mack Potter and I carried him to Menardville jail. I pumped all out of him I could. . . .[26]

During this period the Rangers also had trouble trying to stop robberies at an isolated stage station called Peg Leg, located at a road crossing on the San Saba River far from any settlement in extremely rugged country. About all the lawmen had to work with were victim accounts of several bandits, one possibly being a woman because they found small footprints after some of the holdups.

The general area around Peg Leg station, midway between Fort McKavett and Fort Mason, was Company D territory. Dan Roberts had tried to catch the robbers by putting a Ranger with a shotgun on each coach, but the scheme did not work and, needing his men for other assignments, Roberts pulled the guards; the coach was stopped on its next run. An army lieutenant among the passengers tried to use a small revolver to protect himself, but the other passengers prevented him from resisting, probably preferring robbery to death.

The officer refused to let the matter die; when the stage passed the Ranger camp, he gave Roberts a list of items stolen. The Ranger captain had a patrol on the trail within a short time which soon ran across a group of riders with rifles across their saddles, not normally the way innocent men rode. The Rangers, who looked like ordinary cowhands, rode up casually and waved, then covered the startled riders. Roberts noticed they had new clothing, so he had the riders strip to their stockings while the Rangers searched their saddle bags and rolls. They found nothing matching the articles stolen from the stage, putting Roberts in a quandary because he had arrested the riders without warrants or any reference to the fugitive list. He was positive they had done something but did not know what or where, and he came up with a novel way out of his predicament. If the men promised to leave the country and not return, Roberts promised not to hold them further. The worried men agreed and dressed as quickly as possible. After emptying their weapons, the Rangers gave them their arms and watched them gallop off. Later Roberts learned they had robbed a store, which accounted for the new clothing.[27]

Although Nevill had missed out on the initial capture of Dell and the death of Dick Dublin, he was able to round up Bill Allison, a son-in-law of old Jimmie Dublin. Wanted for cattle theft and unable to make bail, Allison remained in jail almost a year without a word from family or friends. He thought he had been forgotten and abandoned, so when Dick Ware and Gillett brought some prisoners to the jail in Austin in the spring of 1879, Allison was ready to talk.

The prisoner had known Gillett when they worked cattle years earlier. When he saw the Ranger, he called out through the bars and told Gillett he was tired of staying in jail while others were free; he wanted to talk and he knew how to break up the Peg Leg gang. Ware realized the importance of the information and told Allison he would inform Adjutant General Jones, and in short order Jones obtained the permission of the Travis County sheriff to interview Allison. Gillett and Ware escorted the prisoner to Jones' office, where the men talked privately for an hour before the Rangers returned Allison to his jail cell.

Jones had warrants issued for the remaining Dublins, Mack Potter and Rube Boyce, then turned the case over to Roberts and Company D in Menard County because they were closer to the wanted men in Kimble County than was Company E.[28]

Roberts' men were finally able to conclude the case of the Peg Leg robberies. A Company D scout under Corporal Ashburn, headed towards the Dublin home from Roberts' camp in Menard County, intercepted Mack Potter, Rube Boyce, and Dell and Role Dublin. In the running gunfight that followed, the Rangers shot Role Dublin in the hip and captured him. Dell escaped but the Rangers captured his horse and found blood on the saddle. Roberts later found a doctor in Junction who had treated Dublin, who had explained his severe wound by saying he had shot himself. The bullet had struck a knife in his pocket and broken into several pieces; the doctor cut out the fragments, but Dublin had escaped on a stolen horse before being properly treated.

The fight had taken place near the Dublin home, where the women gave the Rangers a terrible cursing, accusing them of murdering their men and hiding the bodies. Roberts was now confident he could run down the injured Dublin, as well as the other two wanted men.[29]

His confidence was justified. The later capture of the wounded Dublin as well as Potter and Boyce was the end of the Peg Leg robberies and mystery. The small footprints which had led officers to think a woman was in the gang belonged to the very small feet of Mack Potter. Boyce was not a member of the gang, but he had committed enough other crimes to earn him a prison sentence although he never served much time; his wife smuggled a pistol into the jail and he escaped to New Mexico. The other gang members talked freely about the robberies, from which they had been able to escape with ease because they had attacked the stages late in the day so they could ride away from the robberies in the dark, finding shelter at the Dublin home.

There was no adjutant general's report for 1879, but Jones published a report in 1880 covering some of the activities for the previous year. He devoted an entire section to the Peg Leg gang; during the two-year chase, the Rangers had killed three of the gang and sent nine others to the penitentiary. Jones gave companies D and E credit for the operation.[30] During 1879 the average strength of the Frontier Battalion was only 107 officers and men.[31]

Some mention must be made of the Special Troops because the company was active during this period. The legislature authorized its continued operation in August 1879 with Lee Hall as captain and T.L. Oglesby as lieutenant. With an average of twenty-seven men and based at San Diego in Duval County, Hall's Rangers operated all over South Texas. When army troops were temporarily withdrawn from Brownsville, the Rangers were sent to the city, whose local citizens welcomed the protection. Even General Edward O.C. Ord, the Department Commander and the senior U.S. Army officer in Texas, praised the men and asked they be retained on station.[32]

There was a recurrence of Indian trouble during the year, some of which has been discussed earlier. The seven actual fights during 1879 were about the last of the Indian skirmishes within Central and North Texas. By summer, Jones decided to bolster his forces in the Trans Pecos, where there were both Apaches and growing numbers of white outlaws. Neither had conditions in El Paso County improved much since the Salt War, and Governor Roberts and Jones decided something should be done to bolster the elected officials in the far West. It was impossible to move one of the Ranger companies, so they fell back on using the Detachment of Company C still in the area, plus reinforcements and an officer.

Jones and Governor Roberts decided to offer the detachment commander position to George W. Baylor, who had shown a previous interest in Ranger service during a period when there were no officer vacancies. A former Confederate colonel with experience fighting Comanches in central Texas as well as service in West Texas, he was a likely choice. Invited to Austin for an interview, he was accompanied by Jones when he went to see the governor. Roberts gave Baylor instruction on conducting himself and at the conclusion of the interview said, "Lieutenant Baylor, I want you to remember out in that far, wild country that you represent the honor and dignity of the great state of Texas." To which Baylor replied, "Governor, as far as an army of ten men can do it, you may rest assured I will."[33]

Jones could not spare many men because the Frontier Battalion was at a very low strength. From Austin he sent Sergeant Gillett and Private Henry Maltimore, all he could spare. The two Rangers joined Baylor at a little camp south of San Antonio on July 28, 1879. Baylor had Gillett as his second in command and five privates when they headed west on August 2, using the stage road to Franklin some six hundred miles away.

It was one of the more memorable marches in Ranger history, not just for distance but for the composition of the party. Baylor brought along his family—wife, two daughters and his sister-in-law. The women rode in a large hack pulled by a pair of mules. Another wagon carried the family supplies while the third wagon hauled the family possessions, including a piano and a coop of game chickens. Two travelers, bound for New Mexico and afraid they would not make it safely alone, took advantage of the Ranger rifles and rode along in a two-wheeled cart.

With the collection of cart and wagons' moving at the pace of the slowest pair of mules, progress was slow even on the well-traveled stage road. They journeyed west to Fort Clark, where the road turned northwest to cross the Devils River into frontier country in which the Rangers stayed alert for Indian sign. They moved very cautiously after passing, on a tributary of the Pecos, a burned-out wagon train ambushed a few months earlier.

They kept on the road, moving to the east of the Pecos and up to old Fort Lancaster. They did not use the Emigrant Crossing, probably because the slopes were too steep for the wagons, and instead traveled to the Pontoon Crossing further north. At this point they joined the Overland Mail Road. They had not seen a ranch or farm since leaving Devils River, nor would they see civilization, other than the stage stations at regular intervals, until they reached Fort Stockton many days ahead.

Fort Stockton seemed like a big city after the wilderness. They were able to buy supplies and obtain decent food for themselves and the animals and talk to people. The little town was bustling at night with off-duty soldiers, civilian contractors and visiting cowhands. It was the first Ranger association with a locale that would provide plenty of business for them in the years ahead.

After Fort Stockton they were delayed in camp for some time because Mrs. Baylor became ill. When she recovered, they resumed the march southwest to Fort Davis where the altitude, over five-thousand feet, brought sudden drops in nighttime temperatures even in August. The caravan kept on along the road, going through Quitman Canyon, past Fort Quitman, and northward near the Rio Grande until they reached Ysleta on September 12, 1879, forty-two days after leaving San Antonio.

Their arrival must have been a welcome sight for Sergeant Ludwick's detachment. By any standard, he had done a fine job. During March and August of the year he had led

scouts against Apache raiders important enough to be
mentioned by the adjutant general.[34] During August he had
fifteen men in the detachment, with ten on scout most of
the time, and had worked with the county sheriff to bring
in a number of prisoners.[35] But for whatever reasons,
Ludwick chose not to continue in the Ranger service; Gillett
mentions Ludwick asked to be relieved and resigned. According to Ludwick's last muster roll for the period May
31-September 5, he had nine men and himself on duty, but
they were all discharged on September 5.

Baylor's muster roll for September 1-December 1, 1879,
his first in his new station at Ysleta, shows the changes in
the new detachment of Company C. Gillett became first
sergeant, dating from September 12, and by September 15
Baylor had twelve enlisted men, four of whom had reenlisted
from Ludwick's previous unit. Before the reporting period
ended on December 1, several of Baylor's men would be
discharged for various reasons, the beginning of a series of
enlistments and discharges that would plague him during
his service in the region.

Baylor began settling his new command in quarters
before really cold weather set in. He purchased a home and
some acreage in Ysleta and quartered the Rangers in several
adobe buildings not too far away.

After becoming first sergeant, Gillett checked through
the papers Ludwick had left for him and found warrants for
a number of the mob members who had killed Howard and
the others during the Salt War. He brought the papers to
Baylor and suggested they could round up the men in one
sweep; the lieutenant told him Governor Roberts had sent
him to keep the peace, not start another fight.[36]

Baylor, an able diplomat, and his wife, a well-educated
and cultured lady who played the piano with great skill, were
a most welcome addition to the small town. The revitalized
Ranger detachment provided protection and stability to the
community, and Ysleta looked forward to a happier time.[37]

The Rangers had a little less than a month to settle in.
At midnight on October 5 a message arrived from Gregorio
Garcia in San Elizario, telling Baylor a band of Apaches had
attacked and killed a party of hay cutters near a stage
station. The lieutenant ordered Gillett to prepare ten men
for a scout. It took Gillett only an hour to wake the men,
collect supplies, load the mules, saddle up and leave about

one in the morning with Sergeant Tom Swilling, Juan Garcia and seven others.

Lieutenant Baylor led the patrol, reaching the stage station at daylight where it took repeated calls and much beating on the door to persuade anyone to open the door. Finally a man peeked through a crack in the door and admitted he was one of the hay cutters, the only one to escape alive. When he started to describe how his father had been killed, he broke into tears. The poor fellow was too distraught to accompany them to the site but gave them directions to a ranch where some of the slain men had relatives.[38]

They had ridden forty miles in the dark, and when they arrived at the ranch the Rangers broke for a quick breakfast. Their arrival had panicked the people at the ranch, but when they found the armed riders were Rangers they could not do enough for them. Discussion revealed that none of the hay cutters had been killed; when the Apaches had rushed their camp, the men had scattered into the dense brush and all had escaped while the Indians were looting the camp.

The Rangers picked up the trail and followed the Indians to the Rio Grande, where tracks indicated fifteen to twenty Apache raiders had crossed into Mexico. The Rangers entered Mexico about a mile from the little town of Guadalupe, and Baylor sent a Mexican guide to ask the town leader for permission to chase the Indians; the Mexicans welcomed them and offered to join the hunt with all the men they could raise.

The trail led south, following the stage road to Chihuahua. The combined party soon met a rider from a large ranch about twenty miles distant who told them the Apaches had killed a man on the ranch and stolen some animals, so the trackers rode on and reached the ranch at sundown. The Rangers had traveled almost eighty miles since departing their camp at one o'clock that morning, and men and horses were tired. They rested and ate a little, watching the silent women near the shrouded body of the slain herder. A few more men rode in to join the search, bringing Baylor's posse to twenty-five armed men.

They left the ranch at first light, picking up the trail along the base of some mountains. Baylor let some of the Mexicans take the lead because they knew the country. Near eleven in the morning, they came to a canyon in which the Mexicans believed the Apaches were hiding. Baylor had Gillett station two men to guard their horses while the rest climbed the mountainside on foot.

Dismounting did not make any sense to Gillett, who was accustomed to fighting Comanches, but Baylor told him the Apaches delighted in using rocky sides of canyons to ambush their pursuers. The Mexicans suggested they go into the canyon but Baylor refused; the Indians wanted just such a move. Instead, he said, they should climb up the side of the mountain and come down on the canyon from above. His plan was adopted.

Gillett and the other Rangers were impressed by Baylor's knowledge of Apache tactics, although it was actually second-hand information. Although an experienced officer, Baylor had never before fought Apaches. His older brother John, however, was an old hand; during the war, John Baylor had commanded the 2nd Regiment of the Texas Mounted Rifles and been stationed for a time at Fort Davis where he and his troops had gained considerable experience fighting Mescaleros in the Big Bend. They had learned about Apache canyon ambuscades the hard way when one of his detachments was wiped out in the Santiago Mountains.[39] The experiences of his brother would serve George Baylor well during his Ranger service.

Following Baylor's plan, the Mexicans started up the mountain on the left of the canyon while the Rangers took the right. As they walked along, Baylor pulled tufts of grass to stick in his hat band and suggested the others do the same to break the outline of their big hats. Gillett, eating some cheese while walking along, was certain there were no Indians within a hundred miles until a burst of firing on their left changed his mind.

The Mexicans took shelter under a ledge, trying to locate the Indians now firing from the sides of the mountain above. Baylor yelled for a charge, and the Rangers scrambled up the steep slope to scale one of the ledges that broke the sides of the mountain. Gillett found himself twenty yards away from a big Apache whose shot threw dirt and leaves in the Ranger's face. He yelled for the others to take cover, but they had already taken shelter under a ledge. A second shot tore away part of Gillett's hat brim. As the Apache worked another shell into his rifle, Gillett raised his rifle and both men fired together; the Apache was killed. The warrior had an old shirt sleeve, tied at one end, filled with over two-hundred cartridges, and it soon became apparent the other Apaches were also well supplied with ammunition.

From their positions high up the mountainside, the Indians maintained a steady fire, keeping the Rangers and their Mexican allies pinned below the ledges. Had they ridden into the canyon, all would have been slain, but as it was neither side could do much damage. When the Apaches climbed even higher, a careless Indian lagged behind and was shot by an alert Mexican, but the Indians controlled the mountain during the rest of the day and even killed one of the Ranger horses.

Under cover of night, the Rangers and the Mexicans withdrew from the mountain, leaving the Apaches blazing away in the dark. The posse had been without water all day and nothing more could be accomplished. The Rangers returned to Guadalupe, then on to Ysleta. They had been gone five days and had covered 226 miles.[40]

This introduction to Apache warfare began Baylor's service along the Rio Grande. A diplomat as well as a fighter, Baylor made a "treaty" with the *alcalde* of Guadalupe, allowing the Rangers to cross into Mexico after Indians. Baylor, in exchange, gave the Mexicans permission to cross after Indians and to kill any they found.[41] The detachment had a relatively quiet time during the rest of the month. A few more men resigned and new men enlisted, but the strength dropped to ten by the end of October.[42]

In November, Victorio left the Mescalero Reservation with over one-hundred warriors, and about the same number of women and children, and headed into Mexico. Geronimo has always been the more famous Apache of the period, but Victorio was one of the most skilled commanders any tribe produced. With him on the exodus was Nana, an elderly fighter and a master guerrilla commander. The band of Indians went into the Candeleria Mountains, territory they had traveled for generations. As always, they had no understanding of national boundaries or maps; they went where the hunting was good.

The wily leader sent a small raiding party after horses, which they found at the small village of San Jose. A confident band of pursuers followed the trail of the small number of Indians into a classic canyon ambush. The Apaches hid up on the sides of the canyon and killed all fifteen Mexicans who galloped into the trap, as well as their horses. When the men failed to return, a second band of fourteen men followed the same tracks, rode into the same ambush, and were slaughtered to a man.[43]

All of these men had ridden out after a few Apaches and simply vanished. The Mexicans gathered all the men they could from the small settlements along the river and sent word for the Rangers to join them. They mustered a hundred rifles, and on November 17 Baylor crossed the Rio Grande to join them with nine Rangers.[44] The Mexicans offered Baylor the command because they considered him the most experienced leader, but since the chase was on Mexican soil Baylor wisely declined and offered to serve under any man they selected. The Mexicans decided on Francisco Escajeda with Baylor as second in command. Several of the Mexicans in the party had been at Ysleta when Howard was killed, and Gillett had warrants for many of them, including Chico Barela, but the Rangers managed to let the men know this was in the past. All they wanted now was to stop Victorio.

The Rangers paired off with the Mexicans and rode cautiously along the trail, but Victorio had long since departed from the region. The bodies of the slain Mexicans were found and buried on November 20, and the Rangers were back in Ysleta on November 22.[45] The long scout accomplished nothing other than to give the slain men a decent burial. Detachment C finished the year without major incident.

The Rangers had no way to know that 1880 would bring marked changes, but they did know it was a hard winter, cold, very cold. Although not conducive to Indian raids, Company B was out in the field for twenty-eight days in January despite the extremely low temperatures. With better conditions in April, the company was again out looking for Indians but found no hostiles; the days of raids were over in their part of Texas. The Rangers did, however, discover two new springs, far more important than any fight with Indians.[46]

Baylor's move to El Paso County did not automatically stop the lawlessness that ruled much of the Trans Pecos region. Despite the garrison at Fort Davis, the settlement near the post was at the mercy of any lawless band that rode by. There was little civil law, and a band of outlaws rode up to one of the stores, robbed everyone in sight and rode off. The county attorney wrote the governor in May, requesting help because the town was defenseless.[47] The bandits were thought to be remnants of the Billy the Kid bunch from Lincoln County, New Mexico, who also operated in the vicinity of Fort Stockton from where Judge G.M. Frazer wired Jones he believed the outlaws were gathering on the Pecos; he even thought they had captured one of the Peg Leg robbers. The citizens wanted Rangers.[48] Frazer also wired Dan Roberts, saying five bandits had "sacked" Fort Stockton and ridden north towards Fort Davis, where they repeated the performance.[49]

For some reason Jones did not call on Baylor and instead gave the assignment to Company D. Roberts sent the ever-reliable Sergeant Ed Sieker, but he could only spare seven men to go with him.[50] Jones sent one more man, Sergeant L.B. Caruthers of Company E, who traveled from Austin by mail hack but missed connections in Fredericksburg and Concho and lost a day in each stop. When he arrived, Caruthers checked out the situation and wrote Lieutenant Nevill on June 8 that the people were on the lookout for outlaws but all was quiet in Fort Davis at the time. He gave details about some of the wanted and suspected men and explained that forts Davis and Stockton were layover and supply points for the gentry who preyed on the countryside. An Apache party had raided recently, killing a woman and wounding her husband, but the soldiers had not begun to follow the trail until five days after the attack, "How is that for an Indian pursuit? Of course they did nothing."[51]

Sieker and his men reached Fort Davis on June 6, 1880, and were busy the rest of the month trying to restore order around the area.[52] A number of known outlaws were "working" the area, many having fought in the disputes in New Mexico. Dan Roberts listed them as the three Davis brothers, Jesse Evans and John Gunter,[53] but these were aliases; their real names were unknown.

Caruthers cooperated with Sieker, but he evidently also worked on his own part of the time because he continued to report to his own company commander and to Jones in Austin. When some citizens in Fort Stockton captured a criminal named Ace Carr, the Rangers were given the task of guarding him, and it tied-up manpower.[54] About the same time, Caruthers also wrote the adjutant general that a man called Captain Tyson was actually John Selman, wanted in Shackelford County, but he had no papers for him. There was no help to be had from the local sheriff because outlaws had threatened his life, and it was impossible to find support among the local citizens.[55]

Caruthers devised a novel plan to eliminate both the outlaws and the need for Ranger guards at the Stockton jail. The Rangers brought prisoner Ace Carr to the Fort Davis jail and appointed John Selman the jailer and deputy, under Ranger supervision. Caruthers believed the outlaws would attempt to rescue their friend, and the Rangers could ambush them. It was a fine plan, but unfortunately the sheriff became drunk and boasted about the trick they were going to play on the bad men.[56] The outlaws gave Fort Davis a wide berth, but Selman continued as jailer for the time being.

Outlaw Jesse Evans, worried about the constant Ranger scouting and the close watch on the Fort Davis jail, made a plan of his own. The gang rode south to Presidio on the Rio Grande, where they bought some boots and talked about going into Mexico, but after leaving the town they doubled back and hid in the Chinati Mountains. The Rangers received a tip about the move; on July 1, Sergeant Sieker with a Mexican guide and five Rangers started for Presidio.[57]

The country in the Big Bend, a vast, harsh, unsettled part of the Chihuahua Desert, was largely unknown to the Rangers. They left Fort Davis about nine in the morning and traveled around the southern edge of the Davis Mountains and out onto the open land sloping towards the distant river. After camping for the night, they started again on July 3, reaching the mountains north of Presidio about one in the afternoon. The Rangers saw four men and some pack mules heading into the mountains from the open plain. When the men spotted the Rangers, they started firing and made a run for a draw cutting into the hills, and the Rangers pursued.

Sergeant Sieker, R.R. Russell, D.T. Carson and George Bingham were riding grain-fed "Ranger" horses that could keep a fast pace, but the other Rangers fell behind. When the four leading Rangers reached the base of the mountains and the draw, the outlaws again opened fire. Carson's horse was killed before he could dismount; another bullet ripped his hat. The other Rangers hurriedly dismounted and tried to locate the hidden snipers. A man later identified as George Davis stood up from behind a boulder and started to shoot at the Rangers but was shot by both Sieker and Carson. The other three outlaws tried to hide among the rocks.

The Rangers charged up the slope, searching among the rocks for the hidden men. One outlaw yelled they would surrender if they would not be killed, and Sieker called for them to come out, promising they would be safe. The three men tossed their rifles into the open and surrendered just as the Mexican guide and the other Rangers rode up to tell Sieker they had found a dead Ranger. In the rush up the hill and the search among the rocks, none of the men had noticed Bingham was not with them; he was lying about seventy-five yards out in the open, killed by the outlaws' first series of shots.

Russell worked a shell into the chamber of his Winchester, and the other Rangers swung their rifles toward the frightened prisoners, now begging for their lives. Finally Russell said, "Don't kill them." Sieker admitted in his report that "Had I known Bingham was killed at the time I should have killed them all."[58]

It was too late in the day to travel, and the Rangers and their tied-up captives spent the night in the mountains. Bingham was buried beside the road leading to Presidio. The Rangers lined up and fired three volleys over his grave and headed north to Fort Davis where the relieved citizens made up a purse of five hundred dollars. Fort Stockton contributed six hundred dollars. The Rangers had broken up at least one of the gangs that had been terrorizing the area.

Judge Frazer refused to allow bail, holding the prisoners for district court. Two of the prisoners, Jesse Evans and John Gunter, were convicted and sent to the pen. The surviving Davis brothers, whose true names came out during their trial and who were members of a well-known Texas family, eventually made bond, which they forfeited, but that was the end of their criminal activities. Dan Roberts, who knew their real identity, did not reveal their names even after forty years had passed.[59]

Despite Sieker and the other Rangers' good performance, Jones realized there had to be another Ranger unit in the Trans Pecos, a unit between Baylor in Ysleta and Dan Roberts far to the east in Menard County. Nevill's Company

E was not covering any part of what was left of the old frontier, and Jones sent him to a new station at Fort Davis. The company reached its new location on August 5, 1880, relieving Sieker and the detachment from Company D which returned to its regular camp on August 25, having been gone a little less than three months.[60] For the time being, trouble with white outlaws took a secondary role when a major Indian raid moved to center stage.

Victorio broke out of the reservation again in midsummer, slipping into Mexico then heading north into Texas. When he started north, Mexican authorities warned Colonel Benjamin H. Grierson at Fort Davis. The army alerted Baylor, who left Ysleta on August 2 with thirteen other Rangers to join in the hunt.[61] The Apaches and the soldiers played cat and mouse over a wide section of the Big Bend as the Indians tried to reach critical water holes before the soldiers could catch them. It was a military campaign, something the army did well, as opposed to smaller Ranger scouts after small raiding bands. Grierson, with most of his 10th Cavalry, a troop of the 8th and several infantry companies, outfoxed Victorio, beating him to the critical water points and turning him back in a number of skirmishes. The Apaches finally gave up and rode back into Mexico.[62]

Along the way, however, the Apaches ambushed the stage in Quitman Canyon and killed a Mexican sheep herder before escaping into Mexico. The Rangers with Baylor were following Grierson on his rapid moves, hoping to be in on a fight, but arrived after each of Grierson's engagements. With Victorio definitely in Mexico, the ranches and settlements along the Rio Grande decided on another joint venture and asked Baylor to join them. Baylor and his Rangers crossed into Mexico on September 17 and helped the Mexicans chase Victorio until October 3 when a considerable force of Mexican regulars and Indian infantry under General Joaquin Terrasas joined the Rangers and civilians. A senior general, Terrasas assumed command. The arrangement worked for a brief time, until a U.S. Army contingent with friendly Apache scouts joined the column. Distrustful of the Apache scouts, Terrasas ordered all the Americans out of Mexico; they had no choice but to obey his orders. Baylor and Gillett and the twelve other Rangers had been on scout twenty-eight days covering 525 miles, all for nothing.[63]

Terrasas kept after Victorio and finally cornered him in

the mountains at Tres Castillos. In a day-long battle, the Mexicans killed Victorio and most of his warriors. The remainder and all the women and children were captured. Unfortunately for the future, there had been considerable bickering among the Apaches before the fight; Nana and one band broke away, joined Geronimo and the Chiricahua in the Sierra Madre, and would later terrorize Arizona. Another, smaller band slipped away and headed for Texas where, in the months ahead, they would achieve fame of a sort.

Back in Ysleta, Baylor filed a report on the long and fruitless scout.[64] There had been a few changes in the battalion. Neal Coldwell had been shifted to quartermaster, as described earlier; his old Company A designation was given to Baylor's detachment.[65]

Nevill and part of Company E had played a lesser role in the chase after Victorio, returning to Fort Davis late in August. The chase by then was well away from their area, but they found the white outlaws were still active. He reported the prisoners were still trying to dig out of jail and still trying to get Billy the Kid to come break them loose.[66] The imprisoned men made a final effort to free themselves, digging with a spoon, but the Rangers caught them again.[67]

In the middle of September, Nevill left five men at Fort Davis to protect the jail and moved the rest of his company down to Musquez Canyon where the Rangers could watch movement through the natural corridors leading up into the Davis Mountains. At the new camp site, an abandoned ranch and one of the earliest settlements in the region, the Rangers could live in comparative security. Adobe walls six to seven feet high made an ideal horse corral. On September 17 Nevill informed Coldwell he had made arrangements for hay and had settled into three small rooms and the corral. It was a decent camp, but he needed some tents because his old ones leaked; they had tried to borrow from the army without success. Nevill also had given vouchers for some forage Ed Sieker had used and forgotten to pay for when the Company D Rangers had been in the area.[68]

When Nevill forwarded his September monthly return, he included a letter to Coldwell which brought the quartermaster up to date on local conditions. Company E had eleven prisoners in the Davis jail, including a few captured by Sieker. His Rangers were building a cover for the corrals to shelter the horses, but he was concerned about leaving his hay unguarded at the new camp because it was stored near a road and could be stolen if he had to send out all his men on a scout. He concluded by telling Coldwell that matters were generally quiet.

Matters remained generally quiet until December when the Rangers helped J.B. Tays, now a customs collector, capture smugglers with two thousand cigars and a number of horses and mules. Nevill had the usual multiple calls for help and pulled all his guards from the Davis jail for a short time, long enough for the prisoners to kick through the floor and drop to the lower story and escape into the mountains. The loss was not much because all the really bad prisoners had been sentenced and sent to the pen.[69]

Further west, the detachment newly renamed Company A was busy. Late in October, Gillett went into Franklin and arrested Frank and James Manning, wanted for assault to kill. On October 27, he picked up Diego Garcia and three companions for assaulting Antonio Apacaca. During November and December, Gillett's name appears frequently on arrest records for Company A.[70]

While the Rangers of companies A and E were settling back into their camps after the Victorio chase, Captain Roberts had his Company D in camp below Fort McKavett enjoying good grass and decent weather. He had worked out a plan for ranchers and settlers to warn him if there was anything suspicious within their area, and one of these, Sam Mark, rode forty miles through a heavy rain to report the theft of a number of horses near his place. The Ranger immediately had a scout out to find the animals and whomever was responsible for their loss.

Commanding the scout was Sergeant Rush Kimbell, a Ranger with an interesting story.[71] In 1878 he had fallen in love with a young lady who agreed to marry him after he had served three years in the Rangers. Men have done stranger things for less reason, and Kimbell went to Austin and enlisted as a Ranger on September 10, 1878. His initial assignment was with Lieutenant G.B. Broadwater in Company A, then in La Salle County. He transferred to Company D and saw hard service during 1879 and was promoted to sergeant.

Captain Roberts considered the pursuit important and gave Kimbell six men—R.C. Roberts, Ed Dozier, Mc Smith,

James Latham, Bill Dunham and J.J. Brown—with ten days of rations. His orders to Kimbell were to follow the trail "and if they stayed on top of the ground to get them." The orders did not seem unusual at the time; they would go over to the headwaters of the Llano River, pick up the trail, and catch the thieves.

The Rangers crossed over the divide to Beaver Lake on the headwaters of the Devils River and crossed the stage road between San Antonio and Franklin, the first sign of civilization they had seen. Here they found fresh tracks, too many for normal travel, and decided they were on the trail of the horse thieves. Up the road, they came to a water hole and found army soldiers on patrol who told the Rangers they had sighted riders several miles to the west, possibly Indians.

Encouraged that they were following the right trail, the Rangers went by old Fort Lancaster, where Kimbell sent a brief report to Captain Roberts, his first report in four or five days.[72] It was clear from the multiple tracks the thieves had continued north rather than following the road across the steep Emigrant Crossing. The Rangers kept on, moving along the east bank of the Pecos and following the trail until close to Horsehead Crossing.

Kimbell had been pushing men and animals hard, keeping close, covering fifty miles a day for many days. He had previously been able to exchange horses, but now ranches at which to do so were few and far between. His horses were about done, and near the Crossing he had to make a decision because most of the horses had become sick from drinking bad water at an earlier stop. Kimbell left all of his men except Bill Dunham, who had the only other horse able to move, and continued on.

By now, from observing the pattern of movement and probably from talking to men they passed, the Rangers knew they were not chasing Indians and suspected they were following some of the Potters. Kimbell lost the trail for a time and located it again, but his horse finally gave out, fortunately near the only ranch in the region.

The Hashknife Ranch was the only settlement for countless miles in any direction. Billy Smith, a young man at the ranch, gave them fresh mounts and offered to ride with them. It was almost dark, but Kimbell knew he was close and was afraid the outlaws would be able to cross the New

Mexico line and escape. Starting out at night, they rode steadily and, unknowingly, passed by their sleeping quarry.

With daylight Kimbell began to suspect what had happened. They should have long since come up to the outlaws so, turning back, he rode cautiously and often stopped to use his field glasses. In the early light, the Ranger spotted two men a few miles away, across the flat country. Kimbell estimated the distance between the two riders and spaced Dunham the same distance behind himself. He instructed Smith to get to one side "and just play where he saw he was most needed."

Kimbell, afraid the Potters might remember him from Kimble County ranching days, rode hunched over, his hat down over his face, and passed well to one side of the approaching riders. The Potters, worried about pursuit from behind, did not expect trouble from ahead and rode by the Rangers without comment until Kimbell yelled they were Rangers and to give up, whereupon

> everyone pulled rifles and the battle was open!
> After about eight or ten shots in which both of
> them and two horses, one of theirs and one of
> mine, were shot, I ordered, 'Shoot no more!'

There was no more danger of the outlaws' shooting any more; both the fugitives were on the ground, wounded. Kimbell identified the man with a thigh wound as Jim Potter and the other with a chest wound as the son, John Potter. Kimbell was beginning to think it was over until Dunham, watching a dust cloud on the back trail, shouted, "Sergeant, hell, this thing is just begun. Look yonder!" The three men saw a half-dozen riders approaching quickly. Kimbell and the others reloaded as fast as they could, and the sergeant spread them out, "so as not to let them thread more than one of us with one bullet." When the riders came close, Kimbell waved his hat in his left hand while keeping his Winchester ready in his right. To his relief the men were cowboys who had heard firing and thought it was a fight with Apaches. Kimbell even knew one of the men from his own cowboy days.

He asked them to stay with Dunham and the wounded prisoners while he rode to Fort Stockton, the nearest army post, between 120 and 140 miles away. He reached the fort without incident and wired Captain Roberts, over the army telegraph to Fort McKavett then by courier to the Ranger camp. The foresight of Jones in placing Ranger camps near army posts again paid dividends.

Separated by almost two hundred miles requiring days to send letters back and forth, Roberts used the telegraph to send instructions to Kimbell in short order. He told the sergeant to return to his men and stay at Popes Well on the Pecos until Lieutenant Nevill could come out from Fort Davis with a wagon for the wounded prisoners and supplies for the trip home. He then wired Nevill through the Fort Davis telegraph office. For the first time in many a long night, Sergeant Kimbell slept inside, resting comfortably atop some blankets on the pool table in the officers' quarters at Fort Stockton. Before he left, the post surgeon told him the man shot through the lungs would likely live, but the man with the thigh wound would die.

When Kimbell returned he found Jim Potter *had* died of his thigh injury. Dunham had buried him as best he could using an old hoe and a large knife to dig a shallow grave. They piled rocks atop the spot, but the coyotes kept digging up the corpse. Finally the wagon and detachment from Company E reached them, and they took the wounded prisoner to the Fort Davis jail.

Kimbell and Dunham stayed at Fort Davis until after the October election, waiting for John Potter to recover enough to travel. The sergeant took advantage of free time and the regular stage run from Davis to San Antonio and Austin to write his sweetheart. With Potter able to ride, he started back, picking up his men on the way. He had logged 1,118 miles on his excursion.

They turned John Potter over to the sheriff in Kimble County. Potter was taken to San Antonio to avoid any mob action, a wise precaution; when he was being returned for trial, security was relaxed and a mob ambushed the party and shot Potter to death.

With all the hardship and riding and shooting, it is nice to know there was a happy ending to the story. Ranger Kimbell served his three years and applied for a discharge, which was granted. His sweetheart was true to her word; they were married in October 1881 and, according to his memoirs, lived happily ever after.[73]

During the period covered by this chapter, there were several major personnel changes that have not yet been mentioned. The Special Troops underwent several officer changes: Lee Hall resigned in May 1880 and was replaced by Lieutenant T.L. Oglesby, who was promoted to captain; Sergeant S.A. McMurray was promoted to lieutenant.[74] Both men would continue to have outstanding Ranger careers.

Also in May, June Peak resigned as commander of Company B.[75] Peak had become well known for his part in the chase after Sam Bass, but he had served equally well on many a less-publicized scout and had earned the respect of his men. From Hackberry Springs in Mitchell County, First Sergeant Ed Hageman wrote somewhat more than just a monthly return for his captain to sign.

> That in parting with Captain June Peak, we desire to say, that during the two years, that he has been the Commander of our company, he has performed every duty to the State with promptness and fidelity; That he has shared with us every hardship and danger, fearlessly and unhesitatingly; in the camp and on the field, he has always been prompted by a stern sense of duty, ever ready, ever willing; That he was ever courteous, polite and gentlemanly; Ever eager and bold, keen and quiet, urgent and energetic; Never daunted, never uncertain, fearless in all things. . . .[76]

A copy was given to June Peak, one was sent to the *Galveston News*, a third copy went to the adjutant general where today it is part of the Ranger Papers. Junius Peak was a fortunate man; not every commander, Ranger or soldier, gains such respect from his men.

Ira Long, who had commanded Company A for a year until his resignation in September 1876 and who has figured previously within these pages, was given command of Company B. He was an interesting character, big, strong, bold, fearless and a superior scout leader. Shortly after his assumption of command, he received a new recruit, Jeff Milton, who was sworn into Ranger service at Swenson's Pasture outside Austin on July 27, 1880. Milton would have a fine career as a Ranger, but for the moment he was probably more interested in the latest exploits of the legendary Sergeant Dick Ware, also of Company B but now in charge of the Rangers' capital detachment at Austin, who was possibly the man who had killed Sam Bass.[77]

Assignment to the capital detachment was no excuse from field duty. Ware and Sergeant Ed Hageman had been on an extended trip and were in Fort Concho late in the afternoon of July 5 when they learned that the last of the Horrells and several companions had passed through the post early in the day. Evidently the wanted men had indicated they were going to a Camp Charlotte at the head of Main Concho, and Ware sent the word to Captain Long. Leaving camp the afternoon of July 7, Long and seven men traveled 115 miles and captured Horrell and two other wanted men without any trouble the next day.[78] Long took the prisoners to Fort Concho, from where he wired Austin for instructions on July 10.[79] Fearful of mob action at county jails, the prisoners begged to be taken to Austin and were escorted there by sergeants Ware and Hageman. Ware then took a prisoner identified as Snow to the pen at Huntsville before returning to his duty station at Swenson's Pasture.[80]

The exploits of Captain Long and Sergeant Ware in the capture of Horrell must have impressed young Ranger Jeff Milton, who was assigned to Company B at Hackberry Springs. Early in his service he discovered his company commander could not read, a secret he kept to himself. The big captain, however, had a remarkable memory; he was unlettered, not stupid. He knew arithmetic and could figure sums in his head faster than most people could do them with pencil and paper. He subscribed to the *Galveston News* and had it read to him by Dick Ware or by his brother-in-law, who was the first sergeant. The first sergeant usually made out company papers for the commander's signature, and the difference between the scripts was never noted. Illiteracy was not unusual in those days; Milton recalled obtaining a Blue Back Speller and teaching one of his Ranger companions how to write.[81]

Towards the end of 1880, Long was fretting about not being busy. Indian raids had stopped, and even the bad whites had moved along. Boredom probably brought about Long's resignation, although Jones listed it as a need to attend to business affairs.[82]

Long was followed by an outsider, Bryan Marsh,[83] who became another of the Ranger legends. Like most of the other commanders, Marsh had been an officer in the Confederate army, but he had lost an arm in battle, was below-average height, and had a truculent nature sometimes associated with short men. He had the heart of a giant and would face anything. Unlike most Ranger officers, he saw absolutely no virtue in sobriety and drank considerably whenever opportunity beckoned.[84] Marsh and Company B joined up in time to face a new year in Texas.

The year 1880 had been a landmark one for the Rangers; a considerable portion of the force had been shifted to West Texas, far beyond what was considered the frontier line. During October and November of 1880, Jones toured an area that had been considered frontier country during his last visit.

> I found the country wonderfully developed and improved since my last trip to the frontier, two years ago. The outside settlements are now from fifty to one hundred miles further west than they were then. The tier of counties which contained the border settlements three years ago, their only population at that time being stockmen, who lived in picket houses and dug-outs, are now settled and rapidly filling up by an industrious class of farmers, who are building handsome frame and stone dwelling-houses, store-houses, court-houses and jails. The stockmen have given up these counties to the farmer, and moved from fifty to one hundred and fifty miles further west and northwest. Many of the large stockraisers have established ranches at the foot of the plains and there is now almost a continuous line of large ranches from Devil's River on the Rio Grande, via the headwaters of the Concho, Colorado, Brazos and Red rivers to the Canadian, in the extreme northern part of the Panhandle. Three years ago there was not a single inhabitant on this whole line.[85]

With all the settlement and advancing civilization, Jones

could also foresee some problems. The railroad system designed to parallel the Union Pacific and tie the Atlantic and Pacific together on a southern route had already been constructed almost to Franklin, Texas, now El Paso, and would provide quick transportation across the vast arid lands between El Paso and San Antonio. It would also mean work for the Rangers. Jones was prophetic in another part of his 1880 report.

> Recently complaint has been made by the mayor and board of alderman of the town of El Paso, that their community is over-run and over-awed by gamblers, rowdies, thieves and murderers, who are congregating at that place in anticipation of a rich field for their operations as soon as the Texas pacific and Southern Pacific railroads reach there; and they ask that troops be sent there to protect them against these lawless characters. I have ordered Captain Baylor to move his company to that place, it having heretofore been stationed in Ysleta, and assist the civil authorities in maintaining law and order. Have also authorized him to increase his force to twenty men. [86]

The by-products of civilization would keep the Rangers busy for the years ahead.

Texas Ranger Ed Sieker, brother of Captain Lamb Sieker.

— 8 —

The Vanishing Frontier
1881-1882

Texas seemed poised for a leap into the future, but the initial Ranger activity of 1881 followed an old-fashioned Indian raid, one of historic significance. In early January, one of the bands that had left Victorio before his last battle, usually considered to be the band that had not departed with Nana, started raiding in Texas. Whoever they were, they displayed all the skill and cunning of the best Apache warriors as they roamed through their old grounds in Texas and Mexico, leaving a bloody trail.

On one occasion, some of Grierson's U.S. soldiers did not take the advice of their Pueblo Indian scouts, and a new lieutenant, not long out of West Point, lost a half-dozen soldiers in an ambush. The other soldiers fled, but the four remaining Indian scouts took shelter behind some boulders and repulsed the Apaches, saving the dead men from mutilation.

Turned back, the Apaches rode up to the Overland Stage Road, attacked an emigrant train on the way to New Mexico, and killed a man and a woman then vanished into Mexico. Soon they were back in Texas. An eight-man cavalry patrol was caught eating breakfast and seven of them were killed almost before they knew they were in danger; one soldier managed to escape on foot and reach safety. The Apaches used the long horse-staking pins carried by each cavalryman to pin the bodies to the ground. This gruesome bit of work completed, they vanished again for several months then reappeared to ambush the stage in Quitman Canyon, that deadliest of corridors. The driver and a passenger were apparently slain, but it was not immediately clear if the Apaches or white outlaws were responsible. No bodies were found, and there was a possibility that the driver and the passenger, a gambler named Crenshaw, had robbed the stage and made it look like the work of raiding Apaches.[1]

The Rangers were sent to determine if white men had committed a civil crime, or whether it was an Indian raid for which the army would be responsible. On the morning of January 16, 1881, Captain Baylor of Company A wrote Adjutant General Jones acknowledging receipt of a telegram of the same date and a letter written January 6.[2] Jones had ordered him to investigate the attack on the stage in Quitman Canyon and authorized the Ranger to recruit four more men and employ some of the Pueblo Indian scouts used by the army. At the time, Baylor had doubts about the stage's having been attacked by Indians and told the adjutant general he was hesitant about expending state funds until he was more positive. If he found evidence of an Indian attack, he would send for the Indian scouts and have Lieutenant Nevill of Company E join him at Quitman Canyon.

That same morning Baylor selected fifteen enlisted men including Corporal A. Harrison. Because of possible trouble in El Paso, Sergeant Gillett and three enlisted men were left in Ysleta. Since there were only two pack mules available, Baylor had to leave with rations for only ten days. The trail was cold, but the Ranger was in no hurry. This was classic tracking, the kind of job the army did not do. The marauders had evidently headed southwest, so Baylor scouted down the bank of the Rio Grande in hopes of finding a trail. About twenty-five miles downstream they found tracks and a glove, which they thought might have belonged to Crenshaw.

The tracks crossed into Mexico and the Rangers followed them. During the next two days they found Indian camps with the remains of animals butchered Apache-fashion. The location of the camps on high ground further indicated they were following Apache Indians rather than white outlaws. In one camp they found a boot top identified as belonging to the missing stage driver. The trail turned back into Texas where they found another, fresh camp site.

They followed the trail along the riverbank, then north to where they could see the Eagle Mountains on the horizon. Although cut by numerous ravines and gullies, the country was generally open and the Rangers could be seen for miles if the Indians were up in the mountains. The trail now seemed to be possibly several days old, and the Rangers camped in a sheltered spot for the night. At daylight they advance cautiously into a major canyon's cutting into the mountains where they found an abandoned camp. Signs indicated the Apaches had fled just hours before, probably after having seen the Rangers.

The Indians had abandoned many of their possessions, as well as papers and cards from the looted stage. The Rangers found some clothing, evidently belonging to the missing Crenshaw, and the other boot of the driver. Mescal and plenty of food had also been abandoned. The Rangers' good fortune was overshadowed by a change in the weather; it became bitter cold with an ice sheet's covering the ground.

Baylor had long since been convinced Apaches had attacked the stage. He first mentions his three Pueblo Indian scouts, Bernado Olgin, Domingo Olgin and Anaseta Duran, during the search in the Eagle Mountains; for some time the Rangers and the Indians searched the area, but could find no tracks in the frozen ground.

Baylor gave up for lack of a trail and rode around to the west of the mountains, hoping to find tracks in better ground. His rations were almost exhausted, but rather than quit he sent a courier to Fort Davis asking Lieutenant Nevill to join him, or to send supplies. Unknown to Baylor, Nevill had already heard about the Apaches and started out on his own with nine men and supplies. By good luck, Baylor's courier found Nevill at Eagle Springs. Nevill had already discovered two Indian trails, one old with possibly thirty people and the other more recently made by ten to fifteen Indians. When the two Ranger forces joined, Nevill shared his rations with Baylor, giving them enough food for another five days, and on January 25 the combined force started across the open country on the fresh trail.[3]

This part of West Texas is about three-thousand feet above sea level. Scattered mountains reaching five-six thousand feet with some peaks above seven thousand force travel into corridors between the mountain ranges. The Apaches had circled around the Eagle Mountains and moved northwest towards the Sierra Diablo, the Devil Mountains, which run generally north, then northwest. The west face is sheer, cut by two large canyons; the east slope is more gradual but also difficult climbing. The Apaches were heading for several springs on the level ground close to the eastern side of the Diablos.

The Rangers and the Pueblo Indian scouts trailed the Apaches around the south and up the eastern side of the Diablos. They camped briefly on the plains below the mountains to melt snow from the mountainside for water and to kill and eat part of a horse then, not wanting the Indians to scatter and hide in the mountains, cautiously trailed the Apaches.

Baylor's account mentions the names used in the 1880s for the several springs, which can be located on maps of the period and which, under different names, are still water sources for ranchers today. He also mentions a canyon near one of the springs, an area that can be identified, where the Indians slept for the first time since leaving the Eagle Mountains. The Rangers, fearing the Apaches would escape into the canyon and vanish, did not move on the camp, and on January 28 they discovered another camp in the Diablos indicating the Indians were finally relaxing somewhat. Nevill states they found this last Indian camp in the "extreme north west part of the Sierra Diablo."

From the tracks, it was clear most of the Apaches were on foot, having eaten their horses as the animals played out. A few doves flew over the Rangers, suggesting the location of water ahead where the Indians might possibly stop. The trail led over a crest which would expose the Rangers to the view of anyone on the far slope or the higher ground ahead. The possibility of exposure was too great a risk; the Rangers and their Pueblo scouts made a dry camp in a sheltered spot and passed the rest of the day and the night under cover.

While there was still light, Baylor, Nevill and the scouts had checked the ground as carefully as they could without showing themselves. Before dawn, the Rangers and the scouts were up and mounted and riding slowly forward. It was difficult to follow the trail in the half light, but the scouts led the Rangers along the crest of a mountain from which they could see a campfire a half-mile ahead.

Preparations were made for the fight. Five disgusted Rangers were selected to guard the horses while the remaining nineteen and the three Pueblo Indian scouts began moving towards the fire. Baylor sent Sergeant Caruthers of Company E and six men to maneuver to the left of the camp while the rest spread out and crawled through the rocks and dagger plants. Without being seen the two groups were able to maneuver to within a hundred yards of the camp, where the Apaches were beginning to crawl out of their blankets, wrapped against the freezing cold.

It was daylight by the time the Rangers were in position and opened fire. Some of the Texans had crept to within twenty-five yards of the startled Indians, and the attack was a complete surprise. The Rangers shot at everything that moved or was covered in a blanket. One Apache put up a fight, standing in place to fire, but was immediately shot in the head. Sergeant Caruthers and his detail shot three braves huddled before the fire, but the other Apaches made no effort to fight and instead ran, chased by the yelling Rangers. One huge brave, dubbed Big Foot by the Rangers, bolted up the side of the mountain; Caruthers and several men chased him on foot for over a mile but finally gave up. The big Indian left blood in the snow and along the rocks, and the Rangers did not worry too much about a wounded man, even an Apache, on foot in the bitter cold.

As the Rangers ran through the camp, they saw a little girl. One of the men motioned her to lie down, and the child ducked down in the rocks. When the Rangers swept through the area and began chasing men up the mountain, an Apache left for dead managed to get up and run. Wounded, he made his escape to whatever fate awaited him in the mountains. Most of the Indians who escaped left bloody prints in the snow. Without food, weapons, water or horses, it is doubtful if any survived the cold.

It was still early morning of January 29 as the Rangers and the scouts began to give up any further chases on foot and returned to the scene of the fight. In the official adjutant general report, six Indians are listed as killed,[4] but there is some variation in other reports of how many Indians were in the party and how many killed. Nevill thought there were about fifteen Apaches in the group, six of them killed and, from the blood on the ground, four wounded. He believed more might have been killed and lost in the exceedingly rough country. Baylor estimated there were sixteen to eighteen Apaches; like Nevill he noted most of the fleeing braves left blood trails. In addition to the three braves Caruthers' men had killed and the one who had stood and fought, Baylor also lists two squaws killed and one mortally wounded as well as two children killed and one wounded.

Baylor explained in his report that it was cold and windy and all the Indians were wearing blankets; it was impossible—nor was it necessary—to distinguish men from women.[5] Gillett, although not in the fight, heard about it from participants and stated three squaws and three children were killed. The child that had been told to hide was shot in the foot; she, two other children, and a squaw were captured.[6]

The Rangers rounded up seven mules, nine horses, some weapons, and a number of U.S. cavalry saddles. There was plenty of food, both venison and horse meat, and the hungry Rangers ate a hearty breakfast. They took two Winchesters, a Remington carbine, two Colt pistols and other items easy to carry, and set fire to the rest. As the Rangers started back to their horses, the smoke's rising into the cold mountain air signaled the last Indian fight in Texas. Somewhere in the Diablos there is a crest with remnants of burned saddles, several hundred corroded cartridge cases, possibly skeletal remains and, according to Baylor, a magnificent view of the countryside for many miles. Is was a fitting site for an historic event, as Baylor said, "marred by man's inhumanity to man, the ghastly forms of the dead lying about."

The Rangers wasted no time in searching for additional dead Indians in the bitter cold. Both commanders mentioned the fatigued condition of their men, who had not eaten or had adequate water in many hours. They were especially concerned about their horses, which had not had proper water in over thirty hours, and the nearest water was thirty miles away. Because the Rangers had no hospital facilities, Nevill took the Indian woman and children to the doctors in Fort Bliss; Baylor and his men returned to Ysleta.

Both commanders filed reports of the scout, Baylor on February 9 and Nevill on February 6.[7] Nevill also sent Neal Coldwell a letter, when he forwarded his monthly return and ration return for January 1881, in which he included a shorter account of the chase and fight, much as in his official report. It was his belief that the fight had been a heavy blow, "We know of only one trail not bloody...." Nevill then launched into a personal and highly critical appraisal of Baylor, "I thought many times of the remark you made last summer that Capt Baylors Co was like a cow outfit. I think it is worse....I have never seen men disobey orders and get away with it...." Nevill went on at length about the deplorable lack of control and discipline and stated flatly that he did not want to work again with Baylor unless conditions improved. He closed on a happier note, telling Coldwell that "the people here are more than ever pleased with the Rangers. It is the remark of all that we have killed more Indians in a short time than the 10th Cavalry did all last summer...." He noted that one of his men had lost his horse on the scout, and the citizens around Fort Davis had raised sixty dollars for a new mount.

Nevill's letter, placed in the regular adjutant general files by Coldwell for anyone to read, is very interesting. Nevill must have felt strongly about the matter; he had taken his case to Jones in a letter, dated February 8, which was considerably more diplomatic than his personal letter to Coldwell.[8] He mentioned that he had twice had difficulties with personnel in Company A, who acted like the recruits of 1874 before Jones straightened them out. He tactfully suggested some rules of conduct might be in order, but he did not say to Jones that he would not serve with Baylor again. Nevill closed by saying if Jones would authorize fifty men between the two companies, he and Baylor could handle any Indian trouble no matter how many left the reservation. As far as the records show, Jones took no action on Nevill's complaints.

Gillett also mentioned that Baylor did not maintain the same kind of control that his previous company commanders had demanded; he thought the former regimental commander may not have been used to commanding a small outfit and didn't care much about such trivia.[9] Gillett had served under some of the best Ranger captains, and he gave Baylor high marks for courage, marksmanship and knowledge of Indian fighting, but he did not approve of the way his captain enlisted anyone who applied for a position in the Rangers. Baylor had a poor choice of recruits in his area, but he undoubtedly was too trusting and believed any hard-luck story told him. His monthly reports show considerable personnel changes with men's signing on, being dropped, deserting. A few of the men he signed on were wanted felons and had to be arrested.[10]

Whatever his faults in judging men, Baylor was a highly successful Indian fighter. Nevill had also done good work on the scout; his letter to Coldwell and another to a friend in Fort Davis suggested he had done most of the job himself. Neither commander realized at the time that the days of chasing Indians were over; there was never again to be another real fight with Apache, Kiowa or Comanche. Up on the Plains, Arrington followed a trail for ten days in March, again in May and lastly in July, but all were without incident. Nevill was active but without results the rest of the year, following small trails and even sighting an Indian or two along the Rio Grande in the Big Bend. Although Indians stole a few animals, there were no more fights.[11] The frontier was not only changing, it was vanishing.

Bryan Marsh and his Company B were the next Ranger unit to make headlines. Like most army posts, a settlement had grown up around Fort Concho, and the gathering of widely diverse groups, plus plenty of whiskey and women, often provided work for the Rangers. The new town, San Angelo, had plenty of saloons, and in one of them ranchman Tom McCarty had an argument with a black trooper from the fort. The soldier was shot and killed, and McCarty was taken in by the local officials. The soldiers were unhappy about the incident and began making wild threats. A number of the men in San Angelo began quietly moving their families to other locations.[12]

Aware of the feeling in the fort, the court held an immediate examining trial for McCarty and bound him over to the sheriff for trial without bond, decreasing the tension among the troops. Shortly thereafter, however, McCarty's brother, who resembled him, rode into town and rumors spread that McCarty was free and riding about town. It was just the spark needed to ignite a riot. The soldiers left the fort and shot up the town; their officers lost control of both the men and the situation, and for a time it seemed the town would be burned and pillaged.

Frantic town officials sent a courier to the Ranger camp at Hackberry Springs in Mitchell County and a message to the governor requesting help to preserve civil order. Marsh, commanding Company B, received the plea from the town officials on February 4 and did not wait for permission from Austin. Leaving the company cook, Jim Werner, to load the rations and follow, Marsh mounted his entire company and started for San Angelo.

The Rangers entered San Angelo early the next morning, finding a seemingly calm town. Marsh, basically a soldier in a military operation rather than a peace officer, took no chances. He took over a wagon yard for his camp, posted sentries about the town to alert him to any troop movement, placed a strong guard on the jail, then took several men and went to see the post commander, Colonel Grierson.

As commander of the 10th Cavalry, Grierson moved between forts Concho, Stockton and Davis where the elements of his regiment were stationed. A capable and skilled commander who had just worked with the Rangers in chasing Victorio, he now had the opportunity to meet another Ranger captain. On the post, Marsh posted one of his Rangers on a roof to watch for anyone approaching the area, then directed Jeff Milton to chamber a round in his Winchester and kill anyone who bothered his captain.

The meeting was private, and neither Grierson nor Marsh reported what they said to each other. Much later Jeff Milton, probably basing his account on talks with Marsh, said the Ranger told the colonel that he would kill any man, black or white, who crossed the river and tried to enter the town. Grierson, amazed by the threat, suggested the Rangers might not have enough men to make the boast good; Marsh assured him that he had enough men to kill any man who did not obey his order. Grierson may have contemplated what twenty Rangers with repeating Winchesters could do to his men while trying to cross the shallow water. There were no more attacks on the town; the officers regained control of their troops and maintained order.

Marsh probably did threaten Grierson; it is in keeping with his general mode of operation and very much in character. He never, however, made any reference to the incident in any official report. After reaching San Angelo he had reported only "Arrived here Saturday with Company. All quiet. Citizens telegraphed Govr,"[13] and in his only account of events after he arrived, his monthly return, Marsh was rather noncommittal and diplomatic, saying he and his men had arrived at the town and cooperated with Grierson in keeping the peace.[14] Sergeant John Hoffar transported McCarty to the jail in Junction, where he was held until tried for shooting the soldier. It was probably no great surprise when he was eventually acquitted.

Adjutant General Jones continued to have administrative and fiscal problems, which undoubtedly caused him more concern than rumors about one of his Ranger captains'

cussing out army colonels and drinking now and again. At
the end of February 1881 he had a Frontier Battalion of five
small companies with only one officer each, four captains
and one lieutenant. There were eleven sergeants and nine
corporals, eighty-seven privates and three teamsters. The
Special Company had one captain, one lieutenant, two
sergeants, two corporals and twenty privates with two teamsters. The entire Ranger force mustered one hundred and
forty-three men of all grades.

Small as it was, even this force could not be maintained
when the legislature reduced the appropriation for frontier
defense from $100,000 to $80,000 and included no funds
for the Special Company in South Texas. To alleviate the
situation, Jones assigned the Special Company to the Frontier Battalion and changed its designation to Company F,
which had been disbanded since March 1879. The move was
completed in March 1881.[15] The shuffle brought the battalion's strength back to six companies, but its total strength
was reduced to one hundred and twenty, a loss of twenty-
three men.

When the Frontier Battalion was organized in 1874 there
was general agreement on the location of the "frontier" line
or region. Thanks to the military campaigns of 1874, much
of the Indian threat that had prevented civilian expansion
westward was eliminated, and the continuous presence of
Rangers from the Frontier Battalion rapidly opened new
land to settlement by chasing down and blocking small
Indian raids. Even more important, elimination by the
Rangers of outlaw gangs from entire counties allowed peaceful settlers to enter the area and establish farms. The final
elimination of a definable frontier, however, occurred when
the railroads were completed across Texas from east to west.

Long a dream, engineers had surveyed routes many
years before the dream became reality. The early 1880s saw
the railroad line from the west coast reach Franklin and
continue on to meet tracks being laid west from San Antonio. The meeting of these crews near Langtry in 1881 opened
a complete railroad across southern Texas. As the construction crews had moved east and west, their end-of-the-tracks
rail camps often became small settlements as the tent
camps developed into towns like Van Horn, Marfa, Alpine,
Marathon and Sanderson. In these settlements, cattlemen

Del Rio, Texas. This photograph shows a frontier town in the early 1880s. Del Rio was one of several settlements that grew up along the railroad between El Paso and San Antonio.

and farmers had a place to buy supplies and began extending into the countryside away from the rail line. The railway constructed a crossing of the Pecos River near its junction with the Rio Grande. During this period, work was also underway on a more northerly rail line to connect El Paso with Dallas. Although stage lines continued to operate through the end of the century, and although wagon trains would continue to haul many a load to out-of-the-way ranches and settlements, the completion of the railroads across Texas nevertheless marked the end of the frontier.

Nothing indicates the Rangers noted any such historic events. All they noted was more work; the railhead camps and settlements attracted gamblers and prostitutes, gunmen, and men looking for easy money. The rail camps replaced the isolated army posts as the primary trouble spots to which the cowhands and farmers rode for weekends of gaming, drink and ladies.

Colorado City was a booming tent city by the end of 1880, but it had no civil law; Rangers from Company B, the nearest unit, visited the place from time to time to keep the peace.[16] Unlike many of the end-of-the-track camps, Colorado City survived and became a town when the rails moved west. It swapped tents for permanent buildings, and a considerable number of the drifters settled down to become citizens who organized a county in January 1881 and elected the necessary public officials. Even though still a Ranger, Sergeant Dick Ware was nominated for sheriff. His fame was widespread and his election assured, but his opponent's supporters did not accept Ware's election with grace. Ware accepted the position and resigned from the Rangers to become the first sheriff of Mitchell County.

The defeated candidate, W.P. Patterson, did not retire from politics quietly and instead engaged in frequent shooting sprees in Colorado City. Patterson was finally arrested and chained by the Rangers to a big mesquite tree since the young settlement had not yet built a jail. In those simpler days, shooting up the town was not considered much of a crime and Patterson was soon released. Evidently, however, he still believed he had the right to celebrate in any manner he wished, including shooting in a saloon. One night while on duty, Corporal J.M. Sedberry, Jeff Milton, and a recruit, L.B. Wells, heard gunfire, went to investigate, and found Patterson outside a saloon. When they asked to check his revolver, he refused and fired at Sedberry. Milton shot him, and in the confusion the new Ranger also shot Patterson after he was down.[17]

It was no different from a hundred other gunfights, except for the consequences for the Ranger force. The three Rangers surrendered to now-Sheriff Ware. They were surprisingly indicted for murder and bound over for trial but released on bond,[18] the beginning of a lengthy legal battle.

During the time he was in Colorado City, Marsh evidently drank more than usual because a number of complaints were made to Austin. The killing of Patterson, justified or not, caused a considerable furor and his friends raised the usual allegations about Ranger brutality and spread the story that the three Rangers murdered him in cold blood. Jones sent Coldwell to investigate, and the quartermaster reported that Marsh was guilty of excessive drinking and that company morale and discipline were not up to battalion standards.[19] Jones also sent Dan Roberts to check on the shooting of Patterson. In his memoirs, Roberts described going to Colorado City and talking to various people about the shooting, including Marsh who seemed relieved to have him in town "as it relieved him of embarrassment." He found Patterson was a respected cattleman when sober but had a habit of shooting anything in sight when drunk. According to Roberts, Patterson and Marsh had engaged in a fist fight on one occasion.[20] Jones had been in poor health and became quite ill at this time, and for the time being nothing more was done about Marsh and Company B.

Adjutant General John B. Jones died on July 19, 1881, and was buried in Oakwood Cemetery in Austin;[21] his death ended one of the eras of Ranger history. It would be difficult to overstate Jones' importance in the development of the Rangers. He organized the Frontier Battalion after the long, lawless years of the Civil War and Reconstruction, and as battalion commander he occupied a position no other Ranger had filled in peacetime. Jones put his brand on the form and style of discipline, morale and conduct. He set the standard for administration, something no earlier Ranger command had been much required to consider. Jones developed a business-like fighting force which he personally supervised, riding up and down the frontier each year. When necessary, the slight major led them in battle or on major scouts.

As adjutant general, Jones was forced to spend most of his time in Austin, but he never lost his love for his men and continued to visit the companies from time to time; he knew each officer and noncommissioned officer and many of the privates. In recurring times of financial crisis, he kept the battalion together, reduced perhaps but still viable. Without him the Rangers would probably have been dissolved, and it is a tribute to him that in his day he was known, admired and respected as *the* Texas Ranger. Only with the passing of years and the emergence of more colorful captains has his fame diminished.

Anyone following Jones would be walking in very big footprints; there was certain to be comparisons and prejudgments, particularly since the new adjutant general fell heir to the problem of Marsh and Company B and the situation in Colorado City. Wilburn Hill King's record for supporting the Rangers as a member of the Texas House of Representatives from 1878 to 1881 had not been outstanding. He admitted as much in his first Report of the Adjutant General.[22] King, however, had been a soldier of some distinction in the Confederate army, knew the military, and was a man of honor and duty. He entered into his new duties determined to do his best. Of the men who became adjutant general in the last quarter of the nineteenth century, King served the longest, almost ten years, and became a worthy successor to the legendary Jones.

King wisely did not attempt to run the Frontier Battalion. The position of battalion commander had ceased to exist when Jones became adjutant general; although Jones had directed that copies of all Ranger reports be sent to him, he soon found the other duties of the adjutant general required most of his time. King, as will be seen, relied heavily on Captain Coldwell and gave his company commanders full authority.

King was confronted with the situation in Colorado City as soon as he took office. Based on the Coldwell report and citizen complaints, he decided to reorganize the company and remove Marsh from command. To avoid a court martial, for which there was no precedent in either legislation or custom, he simply disbanded Company B. He then selected the best men from the disbanded unit, enlisted new Rangers, and formed them into a new unit which became a new Company B, preserving the current organization of the Frontier Battalion. Lieutenant S.A. McMurry was transferred from Company F, promoted to captain, and given the command of the new unit.[23] McMurry took command of Company B on September 1, 1881, in Colorado City.[24]

During the reorganization period, Milton, Wells and Sedbury, still under arrest for the death of Patterson, were transferred to Company E to protect their rights and defuse some of the tension in Colorado City. Before their first trial, King commented on the dilemma facing all police officers, that

> it is easy to see that the energy, efficiency and zeal of the individual ranger may, and probably will, be greatly impaired in a large class of cases in which he is called upon to act with vigor and resolution, by the conviction fastened in his mind that if his eye and hand fail him at the right moment his life will pay the penalty, and yet, if they do not fail him, he places himself in the position to be indicted for one of the highest crimes known to law. . . .[25]

Written over a century ago, King's comments could be a lament from any contemporary police department. King

went on to note that the state had made no provision for
defending Rangers in civil or criminal cases. The strange
case of the three indicted men went on for several years;
they attended trial after trial, only to have the case continued without explanation. Their expenses became severe,
and the battalion took up a collection at one time to defray
costs. The Rangers raised $177, of which Neal Coldwell
contributed $10.[26]

Milton's attorney, searching for a suitable defense, referred back to the Act of 1874 that had created the Frontier
Battalion. He noted the act said that "officers" could make
arrests and argued this was intended to cover *all* Rangers
who acted as officers of the law. King noted this interpretation and that subsequent acts governing the special companies had authorized all Rangers to make arrests. He
strongly urged the current legislature to amend the Act of
1874, but when the three Rangers were finally acquitted in
1883 it must have seemed no other action was necessary.
The Act of 1874 remained as written, and the legal question
of whether enlisted Rangers or only commissioned officers
could make arrests remained unanswered. This legal tech-
nicality would eventually destroy the Frontier Battalion.

At the time Marsh was removed, there were several other
changes within the officer ranks. On the same day that
McMurry was promoted to captain, Nevill won a deserved
advance to that rank. The other major change was the
retirement of Dan Roberts, who had been worried about his
wife's health for some time. Roberts, the senior company
commander in the battalion, had been with the unit since
1874. It was characteristic of the force to be able to find
suitable replacements; Orderly Sergeant L.P. Sieker, one of
the two brothers who had served so outstandingly in Company D, was promoted to lieutenant and placed in command
of the company.[27]

By the time he published his first report, Adjutant
General King was honest enough to admit his earlier views
of the Rangers did not fit conditions in the still sparsely
populated half of the state, where he found the people still
wanted Rangers.[28] To his report he attached a list of appeals
made directly to the adjutant general from private citizens,
judges and peace officers; there was one call for help in
January and six in February.

During the eleven-month period between January-November 1881, the Rangers made 295 arrests, including eleven army deserters. They made 349 scouts and traveled 63,317 miles. Sixty times during the period they escorted local officials who were afraid to travel alone, and they guarded twenty court trials and twenty-three jails. Eighty-five times they provided assistance of other kinds to civil officials. Rangers recovered 595 animals of various types. There were only three fights, resulting in two outlaws' being killed and another two wounded.[29]

Buried among the figures totaling the accomplishments for the period were two arrests in the classic Ranger tradition, one with international complications. Sergeant Gillett had made a commendable name as a Ranger before he went to El Paso County, where he became famous for his role in capturing the Baca brothers.

The case originated during the Christmas season of 1880, in Socorro, New Mexico. A.M. Conklin and his family were attending services in a local church when Abran and Enofre Baca walked in and began creating a disturbance. The men were drunk, and Conklin walked over and tried to calm them. He invited them to stay but please to be quiet. The men left, after trying unsuccessfully to persuade Conklin to come outside and fight. After the services were over, Conklin and his wife walked outside to find the two men still near the church. Abran Baca grabbed Mrs. Conklin and pulled her away from her husband; Enofre Baca drew a pistol and killed Conklin. Several posses pursued them, but the brothers managed to escape into Mexico.[30]

Conklin was a popular citizen, editor of the local paper, and the senseless murder created a demand for justice. The citizens of the town posted a $500 reward for the Bacas, dead or alive, and the governor of the Territory of New Mexico offered a like sum. Posters were sent all over New Mexico and into West Texas. The Rangers in Company A soon received the wanted circulars in Ysleta.

The reward was considerable. An uncle of the fugitives, Jose Baca, was both a local merchant living in Ysleta and the county judge of El Paso County. Without being obvious, the Rangers maintained a watch on the uncle's store for some time without result. Gillett finally decided the Bacas would not risk coming across into Texas.

In March 1881, Ranger Jim Fitch rode into the Ranger camp and told Gillett he had noticed two strangers on the porch of Judge Baca's home and thought they might be the wanted men. Gillett took four of his men and arrested the two men, who seemed to be the killers.

Gillett took the prisoners and started up the road to El Paso and Socorro. Before long he was overtaken by Judge Baca, with an interpreter, who offered Gillett $700 to look the other way for a moment and allow Abran to slip into the brush. When the Ranger declined, Baca offered him a thousand dollars. Gillett said he told the judge there was not enough money in El Paso County to buy him off. He was fair enough to note the elder Baca, who rode back to Ysleta, was hesitant about making his bribe offer.

The rest of the trip to Socorro was without incident, and the jubilant citizens paid him $250 as their part of the reward money for Abran Baca. The second man was a cousin with no connection to the murder of Conklin. Local officials sent word to New Mexico's governor, who promptly mailed the Ranger a check for another $250 and a letter of thanks. Official accounts of this arrest are terse, saying only, "Feb 3, Gillett & three men arrested Abram & Messias [sic] Baca—turned over to proper authorities—$500 reward."[31]

The reward was almost as much as Gillett made in a full year, but he had not done the job for cash; he could have had twice the amount for just turning his head for a moment. It was the chase that he enjoyed, and the other brother was still somewhere. Gillett kept on with his normal duties, but he had his scouts on watch. About a month later, Santiago Cooper came back from Mexico and told the Ranger he had seen a man in Saragosa who looked like Enofre Baca.

Gillett gave Cooper $25 and sent him back to obtain a good description of the suspected man, where he stayed and where he worked. When Cooper returned, Gillett was certain the man was Baca because the killer had red hair and a florid complexion. He was working as a clerk in the main store in the little town. Gillett had no illusions about extraditing the man out of Mexico, even with wanted posters and warrants. In mid-1880, he and another Ranger had arrested two Mexican herders, who had murdered several men and fled into Mexico, and turned them over to local officers. The Mexicans promised to hold the killers until Gillett could acquire proper warrants, but instead the prisoners were released.[32] Cooperation while fighting Apaches was one thing, but cooperation in turning over Mexican nationals for killings in Texas was quite another matter.

The Ranger had no illusions about what he faced. There was no possibility Mexican authorities would extradite Baca, particularly since he had rich and influential relatives. He knew simply going over and taking the man would present legal problems and would never be authorized by Baylor. Gillett kept the location of Baca a secret for a week and finally took Ranger George Lloyd into his confidence. He sent Cooper back to Saragosa once again, and the scout reported the man was still working in the store.

It looked fairly simple. Saragosa was on the road from Ysleta. The road crossed the Rio Grande at an easy ford, and the little settlement of about five-hundred people was only a few miles from the river. The biggest danger in cutting across the countryside was the wet earth, soggy enough in many places to trap a horse. Travel was limited to the narrow road, twisting and turning through the irrigated fields.

Gillett said nothing to his captain, and none of the Ranger guards saw anything strange about their sergeant and another Ranger riding towards the river. The two Rangers rode slowly along the river, crossed into Mexico and followed the road towards Saragosa for several miles. When they reached firm ground, they left the road and circled the town on the west before entering unnoticed. Lloyd waited in front of the store with the horses, while Gillett walked inside and saw Baca waiting on a woman customer. The sergeant drew his pistol and told Baca he was under arrest. The woman promptly fainted; others ran screaming out the front door. Baca asked Gillett where they were going, and the Ranger told him while pointing his pistol muzzle against the man's head. He rushed the prisoner outside and had him mount behind Lloyd. He hastily mounted his own horse and they started through the town at a gallop.

For a few moments the Rangers had surprise on their side; people stared at them in amazement, too startled to shoot or form a barrier. They reached the edge of town and were well down the road before there was any pursuit, although they could hear the church bell's ringing, the traditional signal of alarm and danger. The Rangers kept their mounts at a run for two miles, following the twisting road, but were still a considerable distance from the river when Lloyd's horse, carrying double, began to slow. Gillett halted briefly to take up Baca on his own horse. They could see a fast-moving dust cloud behind them, and their lead began to shrink. At six-hundred yards the Mexicans began firing but did no damage; Gillett believed the Mexicans were trying to scare them into stopping.

They reached the ford and were able to cross the hundred yards of low water before the pursuers reached the river. Gillett turned and waved; the Mexicans made no effort to follow or shoot at the vanishing men, and the Rangers rode safely with their prisoner into their camp and into an international incident.

All the Rangers in camp crowded about the men and their prisoner, making such a commotion that Captain Baylor came over from his house. He examined the wet and spent horses and the frightened prisoner and asked where he had been captured. Gillett said they had taken him down the river, and Baylor began quizzing him for details. Finally the story came out. Baylor was rightly afraid that Governor Roberts would disband the company for such a violation of international law and began berating Gillett; Gillett replied he had worked for six years and advanced to orderly sergeant making fifty dollars a month, with no chance to advance because the captains were frozen on their jobs.

Baylor, more understanding than he probably should have been, told Gillett to take his prisoner and leave before he had to answer any questions. The sergeant took Baca and bought stage tickets to Mesilla, New Mexico. Gillett had no papers for the man and was taking him to an area outside his legal jurisdiction; bringing in the first Baca brother had been relatively simple because no one knew he had been captured until too late to react, but this second brother was a different matter.

Lloyd rode the stage with him to El Paso, then Gillett and Baca continued to Mesilla. The Ranger was afraid to incarcerate Baca in the jail, fearing the local authorities might refuse to release him and claim the reward, so he took Baca to a hotel and spent the night manacled to his prisoner. Gillett had wired the Socorro officials from El Paso that he was bringing his prisoner to Socorro, but Baca's friends convinced the governor to bring the prisoner to Santa Fe. At San Marcial, Gillett received a telegram from the governor instructing him not to stop in Socorro.

Gillett boarded the train to Santa Fe at Rincon without

trouble and arrived at Socorro late at night. When the train stopped, a mob led by the deputy sheriff boarded the coach and forced Gillett and Baca to get off. Gillett protested as much as he could, showing the telegram from the governor instructing him to bring Baca to Santa Fe. When he mentioned that the reward for Baca would be paid for delivery of the murderer inside the Socorro jail, the mob agreed and locked Baca in jail, then the deputy sheriff wrote out a receipt for Baca and gave it to the Ranger.

Several of the men in the mob suggested they go to the community hall and discuss the matter further and, relieved, Gillett agreed, but as they neared the hall most of the men turned and ran back for the jail. There was nothing Gillett could do except watch; the mob took Baca to a nearby corral and hung him from the crossbeam of the gateposts.

Later in the morning some of Baca's relatives asked a mortified Gillett for the key to the leg shackles. Before he left town, a delegation of citizens gave Gillett $250 cash as their share of the reward and thanked him for capturing the two murderers. They promised to help him in any way if he landed in trouble for riding into Mexico.

Gillett did not have any personal problems because of his version of law enforcement, but his actions generated paper difficulties for various officers in Mexico and the United States. The U.S. Secretary of State wrote Governor Roberts, who sent Captain Baylor a letter demanding details; Gillett remembered kindly that his captain defended his actions. The Mexican government dropped the matter, but Roberts wrote each Ranger commander, warning them not to repeat the incident. Captain Dan Roberts recalled his dressing down from the governor, the "Old Alcalde," even though he had nothing to do with the incident and even though Gillett had long since been transferred from his company.[33] The official record of the second Baca capture is accurate but quite brief and omits more than it states, "Enferio [sic] Baca was captured on March 28th & turned over to the Sheriff in Socorro on March 31st. A reward of $250 was paid."[34]

The Baca affair made Gillett famous. The division superintendent of the Santa Fe Railroad offered the Ranger a job as captain of guards at a salary of $150 a month, three times his Ranger pay. After some thought, Gillett accepted the position. There were few enlisted men remaining in Company A who had been there when they arrived at Ysleta, but he did hate to leave his captain. On December 22, 1881, Gillett sat down and ate the noon meal with his company, shook hands with everyone and rode out of camp and Ranger life.[35] Like many former Rangers, he managed to return to law enforcement. After working for the railroad, he became town marshal of El Paso during the wild railroad boom days, then became partners with Nevill in a ranch. Much later, in 1921, he wrote one of the most fascinating of the Ranger memoirs.

During the ten-month interval between Adjutant General King's first two reports in February and December of 1882, he traveled widely in West Texas and came to appreciate the vastness of the region and the potential for growth and settlement. In his second report, King mentioned the relocation of the Ranger companies necessitated by the rapid construction of the new railroads and by the population increases in the Panhandle. Company D, so long in Kimble, was shifted south to a camp near Uvalde where it could guard the final construction of the Sunset Railway into San Antonio. A detachment of Company F was also in Uvalde. Company C was sent from its old station in Blanco Canyon to the far north of the Panhandle at Mobeetie. Lastly, Company F was transferred to Cotulla.[36]

Dick Ware was the first famous Ranger to move directly from the Rangers to a position as a county sheriff, but others followed him during this period. Arrington was elected sheriff of Wheeler County and Nevill became sheriff of Presidio County. Not as well known, Captain Oglesby of Company F was elected sheriff of Maverick County. While these were serious losses to the Rangers, they did strengthen local enforcement of the law. Had county officials been able to preserve the peace, there would have been little need for the Rangers, and every trained man on the force who entered a local police force was a further bulwark against crime. Being a Ranger, however, was not an automatic guarantee of being elected; Captain Baylor and Sergeant C.B. McKinney also ran for sheriff, in El Paso and La Salle counties, but both lost their elections.[37]

Because there was only one officer to a company, senior sergeants were promoted and assigned command of the three units which had lost their commanders. On a strong recommendation by Arrington, John Hoffar took over Company C. McKinney received some consolation for losing his race for sheriff by being promoted to lieutenant and becoming commander of Company F. Sergeant J.T. Gillespie assumed command of Company E. Hoffar was promoted on September 1; the others on December 1, 1882.[38]

In his official reports, King made a strong case for retaining the force. He admitted there was no longer a danger of serious Indian attacks, but he cautioned that the presence of the Rangers prevented the occasional horse thief's slipping away from the reservation or coming up from Mexico. The real danger was bad whites.

> Rapid progress in population and in wealth has been made and is being made at many points on our frontier, and the groundwork for peaceful and prosperous communities appears to be well laid, and yet in many of these young centers of life and trade their stability depends upon feelings of security given to person and property by the presence of, or occasional scouts in their vicinity by, Rangers.[39]

King could well afford to be proud of the Ranger force and praise the men for efficiency, usefulness and discipline. He had maintained the force as large as the appropriation permitted, but towards the close of 1882 he was again faced with the financial dilemma that had plagued Jones for so many years. Despite saving $10,000 from the previous allocation, the rising costs of supplies and a reduced appropriation forced the adjutant general to cut personnel. On November 18, 1882, General Order No.8 reduced each company to fifteen men, leaving the Frontier Battalion with a strength of only ninety enlisted men and officers. The order was effective from December 1, 1882 through the fiscal year ending February 28, 1883. Coldwell was not included in the battalion strength, but the position of quartermaster was retained and Coldwell highly praised for his performance of duty. In a search to save every possible dollar, however, King recommended the travel allowance of the quartermaster be reduced from fifteen-hundred dollars to three-hundred dollars, citing the greatly reduced need for travel and the improved conditions of 1882 as opposed to the mid-1870s.[40]

— 9 —

Much Work—Little Glory
1883-1885

When L.P. Sieker sent in his January 1883 monthly report for Company D of the Frontier Battalion, his cover letter provided a good description of how the next few years would develop.

> Sir: I enclose monthly report for Co "D" for the month ending Jan 31st 1883. I have nothing unusual to report, this section is very quiet and peaceable at present. I shall in the course of the next month make a scout to big devils river and that section to look out for the stock interests. Have not enlisted a man in place of Davis, have not found one to suit me, Did Davis return his gun. We are all anxiously waiting the proceedings of the Legislature, Would you please send me a copy of your report.
>
> Respectfully your
Obdt servt
L.P. Sieker[1]

Sieker's comment concerning the legislature reveals the keen interest the Rangers took in legislative matters—their very existence depended on how much money was allocated for the Ranger units. Sieker was also, very naturally, concerned about what the adjutant general had to report about his company and took the simplest way to find out; he asked. The letter also demonstrates how careful Sieker was about enlisting men; he was more willing to be a man short than to sign on someone he did not think could do the job.

In contrast, George Baylor of Company A near El Paso

continued to sign on almost anyone who applied. In Baylor's defense, he still had little choice in many cases, but he never performed a thorough screening of his applicants. Some weeks after Sieker's letter, Baylor reported that a Ranger named William Stapleton had deserted on the last payday, owing money both to his fellow Rangers and to local citizens. Stapleton had also stolen some jewelry and weapons. Baylor asked for money to go down into Mexico and bring the man, who had given the entire company a bad name, back to Texas.

Baylor also forwarded a letter from authorities in New Mexico and several newspaper clippings. The Rangers had just assisted in capturing several men wanted in the Territory of New Mexico, and Major Fontaine of the New Mexico Volunteer Militia expressed the thanks of the governor and sent his own offer of assistance to the Rangers. Baylor explained to the adjutant general that the offer did not mean much without correct paperwork because any man arrested would be immediately released on writs of *habeas corpus*, but he could nevertheless arrest and send back citizens of New Mexico with little trouble, as he had done with the men mentioned by Fontaine. He concluded his report by stating the company had been active and would show up better than the preceding month.[2]

A major change in officers early in the year showed the passing of time. The battalion quartermaster, Neal Coldwell, retired on February 15, 1883, and was replaced by John O. Johnson with the rank of captain. Coldwell, the last of the original officers of the Frontier Battalion, had served as a company commander, chased both Indians and outlaws, marched thousands of miles, and explored unknown country. As quartermaster he had performed equally well, acting both as an administrator and as an inspector for the adjutant general on many sensitive matters. His retirement was another indication of changing times; the Rangers were accomplishing their usual hard work, but there was little of the sensational in what they were doing. Their work was made easier when the Eighteenth Legislature added $10,000 to the Frontier Battalion's allocation for the two years ending February 28, 1884 and 1885, enough to increase the battalion to 120 officers and men. The extra funds enabled additional officers to be assigned to Company F, in which Sergeant W.L. Rudd was promoted first lieutenant, and another to Company D to which George H. Schmitt was assigned after being commissioned a first lieutenant.[3]

A digest of the Scout Report of one company shows typical Ranger activity during 1883:[4]

August 1. Sergeant Shaw and a private went to a roundup on North Fork to arrest one Alf Beard for theft but could not find him. At the urgent request of the deputy U.S. marshal, Lieutenant Hoffar, the Company C commander, left camp with four men from Company B to go to Vernon. They arrived the next day and arrested one man for selling liquor to Indians and another on a theft charge.

August 2. Corporal Grimes and five men rode to Doan's Store on the Red River and arrested Alf Phillips for selling liquor to Indians. The scout went another twenty-five miles after a cattle thief; failing to locate him, they returned to camp. The Company C patrol turned the prisoner over to Company B Rangers and the deputy marshal on August 4.

August 8. Lieutenant Hoffar arrested a man in Vernon and left for Stephensville, in Erath County, where he took a prisoner from the sheriff and transported him by rail to Wichita Falls, arriving on August 12. There he was joined by Private Hensley, who had brought in a cattle thief, and they left Wichita Falls in a hack with the two prisoners. During the night, one of the men managed to free himself from his irons and escaped. They brought the other fugitive to Vernon and turned him over to local authorities.

August 15. Lieutenant Hoffar and four men left Vernon and returned to camp on the 19. The day they left, Private Gillock arrested Lew Childress at Doan's Store on a cattle-theft warrant and brought him in to Vernon, riding on to join Hoffar for the return to camp. Corporal Grimes and his detachment remained in Vernon at the urgent request of local officials and citizens.

August 18. Corporal Grimes arrested men in Vernon and again on the 20, both times for cattle theft. The prisoners were turned over to Company B. The corporal sent Private Hensley to escort the prisoners to Wichita Falls before rejoining his company.

August 21. Lieutenant Hoffar and seven men left camp to select a location for winter quarters and begin construction of the new camp. Hoffar supervised the work until August 28 when he rode back to the old location.

August 23. Sergeant Shaw went into Mobeetie and made four arrests for minor charges, returning to camp on August 26.

August 24. While traveling by train from Henrietta to Wichita Falls, Private Hensley recognized a wanted man, arrested him on a cattle-theft warrant, and turned him over to the U.S. marshal. During the months of July and August, Hensley had traveled 310 miles by horse and rail.

During this month of August 1883, Company C did not engage in any dramatic incident of chase; they merely performed the standard Ranger patrols, backed local law-enforcement agencies, and arrested outlaws. If an occasional prisoner escaped, many more were held and delivered to trial. There was little glory in any of their efforts to enforce law and order and make the laws work.

As late as 1883 there were still occasional reports of Indian raids into Texas. Both companies A and E followed suspected trails leading into Mexico, but it became fairly certain they were tracking outlaws or rustlers rather than Indians.[5] In his report for the year ending December 1883, Adjutant General King commented concerning the end of Indian attacks, which had significantly changed the nature of the force,

> and has made it that of an armed, mounted and active police force, with the same authority as sheriffs, *and no more*, but not limited to county lines in the exercise of authority, as sheriffs ordinarily are. This essential modification of duty has necessitated a different management and character for this force, and has placed it more directly

under the control of the restrictions and limitations required by civil law, and made regular military measures or orders inapplicable and useless.

As a police force this body has no power to act, except as directed by civil law, and are liable, as all other officials, for any unauthorized or illegal proceedings which they may carry out under the pretense of public duty. This limitation of power in this force is constitutionally proper and wise, and conforms strictly to the genius and spirit of our government and laws, and yet it has recently given rise to some complaint in certain quarters of inefficiency in this service, because unlawful and impossible things were not done and are not done or attempted by this force. This misconception as to the legal power of the Rangers has possibly had a place in the minds of many persons for a long time, but peculiar circumstances have lately made it active.

The regular scouting, attending district and other courts, when needed, arresting criminals, and other lawful duties of a police force, have been actively and zealously performed by the Rangers during the year, and the results in these particulars have been beneficial to the communities in which their services have been rendered, and satisfactory to this department.[6]

In King's report for the year 1883, fence cutting and sheep killing appear for the first time as real trouble areas, both outgrowths of the rapid spread of ranching and farming in unsettled areas as well as the vast increase in the grazing of public lands. The invention of barbed wire had made the fencing of huge tracts of land easy and relatively cheap; large landholders could fence out "nesters" and small farmers who considered all of the land's as being available for grazing. The introduction of large sheep herds also conflicted with the cattleman's idea of what the range should be; it was believed sheep destroyed cattle range.

The sheepherders cut the fences, and the cattlemen killed the sheep. Ranger detachments went into Hamilton County to stop sheep killing, and other units were active in

Clay, Jack and Coleman counties attempting to catch fence cutters. The Rangers in Hamilton County finally arrested two men for killing sheep, but resentful county officers asked them to leave.[7] The Rangers did not succeed in catching any fence cutters in the other counties, but they did preserve order. Eventually they were asked to leave Jack County because some of the prominent people believed their presence might be troublesome.[8] These Ranger attempts to curtail fence cutting and sheep killing were their introduction to what would be a major Ranger mission in the years ahead; no other Ranger duty was as vexing and frustrating as chasing fence cutters. The average Texan of the time had little sympathy for the large landowners who fenced off huge pastures that others considered to be open range; the fences often blocked roads and waterways, cut off travel through natural gaps, and destroyed the character of the countryside. It was a battle of the little man against the big and rich, and public support was for the little man.

King understood the conflicting philosophies, but he was also able to put the problem into realistic perspective; the growing number of large ranches and farms benefited the state's economy in numerous ways, and for the most part the ranch owners were operating legally. Nevertheless, some landowners did fence land that was not legally owned, often cutting off access to free water, and refused to install gates in the fences, thus restricting cross-country travel. King recommended legislative action on the problem.

Although the Ranger mission had changed from defending the frontier against Indian attack to chasing outlaws, the life of the individual Ranger had remained pretty much the same. On January 1, 1883, J. Willis Holston applied for a position with Company C. Although some recruits joined up in Austin, most enlisted directly into one of the companies, and Holston described how Hoffar questioned him at length before accepting him into the force.[9] In addition to being of good character and in fine physical condition, each recruit still had to own a horse which met Ranger standards, saddle, bridle, bedding, a Colt revolver and a Winchester.

Camp routine in Company C was not too different from earlier days, except that each day two men were assigned duty as cooks for the company mess. One man was assigned duty with the horses and another with the camp proper, twenty-four hours of every day.

Certainly the weather in the Panhandle had not changed. Holston went on his first scout of the year in the middle of January. The weather was mild for the time of year, and six Company C Rangers started out on a scout after some rustlers that had been hitting the Goodnight Ranch. Along the way the weather changed to a few rain drops, then to light snow, then to sleet, and soon they were caught in one of the worst blizzards of the season. Unable to continue to Clarendon, they made camp for the night; when they awoke, the ground was covered with snow and the temperature was continuing to fall. They rode past Clarendon and were half frozen when they finally reached the shelter of the ranch, their ears and feet frostbitten. Holston remembered his ears were "black as a black cat. I thought they were going to come off."

The patrol stayed two days at Goodnight's waiting for the weather to clear enough to travel, then rode up Palo Duro Canyon to check cow camps for the wanted men. They found nothing and, believing runners had already warned the rustlers, returned to camp. Many scouts ended this way, with no definitive accomplishments other than establishing a Ranger presence as a warning to rustlers.

Often, however, their attempts were more successful. Holston had not been long in service when they started out to catch a man wanted in Mobeetie. Hoffar, who knew the man, led the scout. The Rangers, who had ridden all night and needed to rest their horses and eat breakfast, appeared to be only another cow outfit as the camped near a fence line which they believed the fugitive to be riding. Even while at a halt, however, they had men scanning the area through field glasses, and one of the sentries spotted a man riding towards them.

Hoffar and another Ranger hastily saddled and rode towards the distant rider. leaving the rest eating. The two Rangers rode slowly, and the approaching man did not suspect anything until Hoffar grabbed the fugitive's gun. The prisoner began raving and cursing, but Hoffar kept him under guard and sent him to Mobeetie with two of his men. The remainder of the patrol rode to Vernon, then scouted as far east as Wichita Falls before returning to camp.

The tough little town of Vernon was a trouble spot for the Rangers, and telegrams from officials requesting help were continually arriving in the Ranger camp. Hoffar and his men were no sooner back than another call for help arrived; the town officials said twenty armed men were camped in the Round Timbers and had decided to take Vernon.

Although he did not know if the town was in danger of a major raid or was merely being threatened by some cowhands threatening to shoot up signs, Hoffar took every man he could spare and rode into Vernon. Rangers placed at each corner of the town disarmed riders as they entered Vernon, and Ranger patrols moved through the town disarming any man they found in the hotels, saloons and stores. All was done in a polite manner, and the men were returned their weapons when they left town. The Rangers took over a vacant building for their headquarters and remained in Vernon for several weeks, during which there was no trouble. The region's cowhands drifted in and had their fun, often loud and profane, but neither they nor the town citizens were in danger. The Rangers' peacekeeping missions such as this did not make headlines or foster legends.

Holston recalled one not-so-happy experience during this period when his horse and that of another Ranger contracted pinkeye. A Ranger was only as good as his horse, and the two men drew camp guard for the three weeks their horses were unable to travel. It was the only easy time Holston had in the Rangers, and he said he almost died of boredom.

When his horse was fit for duty, Holston again joined the scouting parties. After receiving reports that liquor was being sold to Indians at Doan's Store, he and two other Rangers rode over to bring in the saloonkeeper. One man held the horses while Holston went in the front door and the third Ranger through the back. The saloonkeeper argued that he could not leave his business, but the Rangers merely closed up the place and started back to Vernon, the nearest town. On the way the saloonkeeper offered them a drink. They refused but allowed him to sample his stock; he had prepared for jail by stuffing several bottles under his coat. When they reached Vernon, the prisoner was roaring drunk and quite happy considering his situation. They piled him in with several other prisoners in the log house that served as a jail.

We would keep them there until the sheriffs or
the U.S. Marshals would come and get them. They
would take them to where they were wanted. And
they [the marshals] get the credit in most of the
places for the capture of the outlaws.

We Rangers would do most of the work but the
other authorities would get most of the credit for
getting their men.[10]

Young Holston did not stay with the Rangers for long; like
many others in the service he had signed on for the adventure and moved on to another job after a few months or a
year or so. He took advantage of the yearly reorganization
in August to request a discharge.

There were several officer changes in 1883. As mentioned, Sergeant W.L. Rudd, one of the old "McNelly Boys,"
was promoted to lieutenant and assigned to Company F.
During late 1882 and early 1883, Mexican bandit raids
along the lower Rio Grande valley brought repeated calls for
police help from citizens and legislators from the region;
Lieutenant Rudd and a large detachment from Company F
were sent to the Rio Grande and remained there during
much of 1883. Late in the year these Rangers, with a part
of the detachment from Rio Grande City in Starr County,
were moved to San Diego in Duval County. In another
Company F change, Lieutenant McKinney resigned to become a county sheriff and was replaced by Joe Shely, who
was promoted to first lieutenant and commander of the
company. Captain Hoffar resigned on November 10, and
Lieutenant George H. Schmitt was moved from Company D
and promoted to captain to become commander of Company
C. Lieutenant J.T. Gillespie, having served twelve months in
command of a company and "having manifested capacity,
good sense and zeal...was promoted to the rank of Captain,
his commission dating December 1, 1883." He remained in
command of Company E.[11]

The completion of the railways across Texas led to some
changes in company locations. Company A was split; a
detachment remained in Ysleta, a larger unit was sent to
Toyah in the newly created Reeves County, and the rest
about one hundred miles east of Ysleta to the north of the
Texas and Pacific Railway line. Company B had its main
camp near Colorado City, with detachments at Vernon and

Wichita Falls. Company C was transferred from Mobeetie to the boundary between Greer and Collingsworth counties. Company D had been moved the year before to the Uvalde area and remained in place. Company E moved south from Musquez Canyon to the new town of Murphysville, the present-day Alpine, where it shared with Company A the responsibility for the entire Trans Pecos area. Company F was shifted twice during the year as trouble threatened, but returned to Cotulla.[12]

These assignments had nothing to do with a frontier, for there was no longer any defined line or region that could be considered a frontier. Instead, the Ranger companies were sited where they could move and cover large areas that seemed most likely to require help. Men and detachments could now be shifted by rail to most areas of the state. Despite the gain in funding from the Eighteenth Legislature which enabled the force to increase from ninety to one hundred and twenty Rangers, the relative handful of men was still scattered over half of Texas. Although the Rangers had only two shooting engagements during 1883, killing one man and wounding four others, they nevertheless traveled a total of 69,335 miles, largely by horseback, and arrested 302 wanted men.[13]

Any review of the various scouts during 1883-1885 would be tedious because most of the operations were very similar. The reports of the adjutant general give a satisfactory overview; King had become an astute observer and saw conditions in the state in a clearer light than most of his contemporaries. He continued to be worried by the widespread increase in fence cutting across Texas as well as the growing number of thefts of cattle and horses. He deplored the publicity given to the fence cutters by newspapers.[14]

Local officials continued to look to Austin and the Rangers for assistance that was not constitutionally allowable, and King described how the efficiency of the Rangers had actually created some problems.

> This influence arises from the services of the Frontier Battalion, and the very efficiency of this force, while highly creditable to its members, only increases the trustfulness of the people in the power of the State rather than in themselves and the ordinary means for their safety and protection.

While this is the indirect and, to an extent, the certain and unavoidable results of the services of this military force, the organization is not responsible for it, and their services in many ways, and at all times and places, since they were put into the field under control of the law, have been of such incalculable advantage, and have produced results so striking and beneficial, as to far outweigh the possible harm to the public in the manner indicated.[15]

The "manner" to which King referred was the natural tendency to call upon the Rangers for almost anything, even to arresting persons suspected of fence cutting, a minor crime, instead of handling the problem locally with local peace officers. The Rangers were intended only to support and reinforce local law, and King rightly saw their role as peace officers reinforcing town marshals or county sheriffs but capable of moving anywhere in Texas unfettered by political boundaries.

The Rangers received a measure of assistance from a special session of the Eighteenth Legislature, which addressed many of the problems created by lawless and wildcat fencing. The legislators made it illegal to fence public lands and sharply restricted the blocking of roads, natural passages, and access to riverbanks and water holes. Long fence lines had to be provided with gates at regular intervals. When these provisions went into effect, much of the public support for fence cutting ceased, and the job of the Rangers became easier although they would still become involved in some severe cases during the years ahead.

During 1884, although there was nothing of the high drama of the Sam Bass chase or the cleaning up of Kimble County, the Rangers nevertheless killed seven outlaws in a variety of fights and had two men wounded. On July 29 four Rangers from Company D, led by Corporal P.C. Baird, ran onto four men who had just cut a fence. There was a gunfight in which one of the Rangers was wounded, but one of the fence cutters was killed and the others captured. All the Rangers were cleared of any wrongdoing at an inquest, but friends of the men filed a suit against Captain Baylor, as the senior Ranger, and all of the Rangers involved in the fight.

Another of their fights was purely accidental. Sergeant

W.F. DeJarnette of Company A was traveling to San Angelo in February when a gang of robbers had the bad luck to try stopping the stage; DeJarnette wounded one of the men and prevented the robbery. In another incident, Captain Schmitt of Company C killed a bank robber in Wichita Falls on March 27. Several other men were killed or wounded in various fights listed merely as resisting arrest or trying to escape.[16]

In an earlier incident on the first day of 1884, Lieutenant W.L. Rudd of Company F attempted to arrest a man named Chris Salinas who resisted and was shot and wounded. In a complete reversal of conduct the next day, Rudd refused to arrest drunks he encountered in Gonzales. According to an investigation by Captain Johnson, the battalion quartermaster, Rudd was told by one of the drunken men to return to his hotel room, and complied! On January 26, a battalion circular was published stating Rudd would cease to be an officer on the last day of the month and would be discharged from the force.[17]

There was no disputing the facts, and Rudd evidently made no defense to the charge. He may have balked at shooting some drunks having a good time, or he might have finally had enough of killing although he had been a Ranger for years and served with honor in many hard fights. The incident was another example of the narrow line walked by the Rangers.

The restraints under which the Rangers operated are shown by the publication of General Order No.13 on January 7, 1884, in which Adjutant General King called attention to an earlier order, General Order No.25 dated February 28, 1878, still in effect, which specified Rangers would lay aside their weapons when in cities or towns unless on specific duties. They were not to enter saloons, circuses or other places of amusement with their arms unless on duty. The new order reminded the Rangers they were in service to assist civil authorities and citizens to maintain the peace and to act so as to gain confidence and respect. To guard against persons making false claims about being Rangers, each Ranger was to carry a descriptive list which would show his name, rank, age, height, color of eyes and hair, and when, where and by whom enlisted. Since the Rangers did not have any form of badge, this paper served as identification and authority.[18]

General Order No.13 was not published merely as a

public relations gesture; everyone from the adjutant general to the most junior private was serious about the standards for Ranger conduct. Captain Gillespie discharged a man from Company E for not following the provisions of the order.[19] Later Gillespie again reminded his men about good conduct; they could wear arms while on duty but not when drinking, gambling or visiting houses of prostitution. He reminded his men there had been some complaints that members of the company "have rudely displayed their pistols to the annoyance of all present."[20] The quieter Texas became, the more the Rangers came under scrutiny. People wanted them posted on every street corner, but they also expected more and more in the way of deportment.

During much of 1884, with enough money to keep a decently sized force active, the Frontier Battalion had a higher numerical strength than usual; during the last nine months of the year there were 136 officers and men in the field.[21] Some of the allocated money would have been carried over to the next year except that the increase in both fence-cutting duties and in medical costs added to expenses. The state did what it could, or at least made an effort, to pay Rangers' medical bills, but in many cases there simply was no extra money for such expenses. The sad case of McNelly's doctor bills is the best known example, but many a lesser-known Ranger found his medical bills causing financial problems.

The situation became serious in 1884 with an inordinate amount of sickness, and King felt called upon to address the problem in his annual review.[22] Detachments had been required to relocate near expected danger areas in unhealthy sites, and measles had taken a toll in several companies. Medical bills sent to the quartermaster for payment had been checked and double checked, and had frequently been returned for reduction by the submitting doctor.

One example from Company E is typical. Captain Gillespie explained that he was doing all he could to obtain a reduction on a bill sent back by Captain Johnson. He sent in the bills and wanted to know if, after additional review, he should give the doctor a voucher for $215.65. Gillespie mentioned the doctor was prepared to go to the adjutant general and contest the matter, and he complained that the bills and letters back and forth were so mixed by now that "it is hard to tell which is which."

Undoubtedly Gillespie would have preferred chasing outlaws to company administration, but he knew he had to keep Austin satisfied and felt compelled to explain all the background of how his man had become ill.

> He was taken on the road here. . . we camped on the Bayou [and,] not having time nor fearing rain[,] did not stretch any tents and about three oclock at night it commenced to rain and contin- ued on next morning, and Freuthann being very sick and spitting blood and suffering a great deal I hurried him off to town....

Sergeant Sedberry was also ill, and both Rangers were sent into the nearest town and placed in a boarding house until they could recover. The state received a considerable bill from the landlady, who claimed the two Rangers moaned so much she could not rent her front rooms for a decent price.

Gillespie wanted King to know he was not idle. He had come to this area in search of horse thieves, and the company was actively looking for the thieves and chasing a man who answered the description of a fugitive on the adjutant general's list. The captain was also keeping an eye on local conditions because both a town citizen and a prisoner in jail had died with small pox. Gillespie's long report ended with a postscript, "I write this explanation in order that everything may be clearly seen."[23]

Gillespie had the longest account of medical expenses, but he was not alone. King explained in his report that mounting medical expenses had cut into funds to such an extent that he would have to make personnel cuts in the third quarter ending February 28, 1885.[24]

King's hopes for only minor strength adjustments were dashed when the Nineteenth Legislature reduced the Ranger appropriation from $75,000 to $60,000, a cut that meant considerable personnel adjustments. In view of past experience, King decided to disband a company rather than to reduce all the units to a level that would make them ineffective. The selection was made solely on the basis of which unit could be spared with the least danger to the state, and Company F was selected with a February 1885 mustering out date. Company F was responsible for the lower Rio Grande, a section that had recently enjoyed a rather uncharacteristic period of peace.

The meandering river area, however, had little consideration for the plans of men in Austin; while the reorganization was being developed, fighting broke out again in South Texas. In early February, the sheriff of Dimmit County led a small posse into Mexico in hot pursuit of stolen horses, following a clear trail about a mile across the border. They came upon a large encampment which they later estimated contained close to one hundred men. The sheriff rode up to a man who appeared to be the leader while several of the posse checked on horses with recognizable Texas brands. They never had the opportunity to ask for the return of the stolen animals; the rustlers opened fire as soon as they saw the few Texans were not being followed by a larger force. The members of the posse ran for their lives, pursued by the Mexicans, and were able to return across the river alive with the loss of only one horse.[25]

Encouraged by their "victory," the band of Mexicans began a series of raids into Texas, claiming to be looking for cattle stolen by the Texans. The rustlers became careless, a number of them were killed by local citizens, and most of the others lost interest when a detachment of volunteer cavalry and other civilians arrived in the area. Nevertheless, Governor John Ireland received several appeals for help and directed King to go to the border and take control using what state forces he thought necessary to restore order. Ireland did not want any raids into Mexico, but he did want the guilty rustlers punished. The governor directed King to shift Captain Sieker and Company D south from Uvalde and to hold up on disbanding Company F until the area was quiet.[26]

In compliance with the governor's orders, King started south on the I.& G.N. railway to Encinal, then moved by private conveyance to the southwest corner of Dimmit County. On the way he met Captain Joe Shely and Lieutenant William Scott, who were trying to get to the scene of the trouble, and the three went to the home of William Votaws about nine miles from the Rio Grande. The day King and the two Rangers arrived, a "truce" had been arranged; three men from Mexico and three from Texas had met on a sandbar in the river and agreed to stop the raiding back and forth.

About fifty armed Mexicans, and a mixed force of thirty Rangers and citizens, had watched the proceedings. Although entirely unofficial, the agreement held; when he felt satisfied the truce would hold, King returned to Austin. By the time he left, Sieker and companies D and F had reached the scene and remained near Votaw's place until all signs of danger had vanished. Company F soon had to be shifted to yet another danger spot and again escaped mustering out. Company D remained in extreme South Texas until it was certain there would be no major raiding.[27]

In the first part of 1885, Company E Rangers were faced with one of the mysteries of Ranger history. In early February Lieutenant Sedberry was on a scout when Ranger B.G. Warren became sick. The nearby town of Sweetwater offered shelter for the sick Ranger, who coincidentally had to appear in court in Sweetwater to answer a charge of killing a cow and who was acquitted after a brief court appearance. Feeling better, he was sitting in a chair in the hotel office about 8:30 in the evening of February 10 when someone killed him. No one saw anything and the crime was never solved. The following month Captain Gillespie visited Warren's widow to ask about some papers found in the dead Ranger's pocket, hoping they might be a clue to his killer, but she was as baffled as the Rangers.[28]

Although trouble along the lower Rio Grande had stopped, the Rangers' financial situation was as severe as ever and a company still had to be disbanded. Company F could not now be spared, and the only other unit located in a somewhat quiet zone was Baylor's Company A, whose good performance in pacifying its territory now made it a candidate for dismissal. Another contributing factor was the company's low strength; in January, five men had been dropped and five others discharged for various reasons, reducing the company to nine men. The last major service of Company A occurred in March when Lieutenant L.S. Turnbo and seven men hurried to preserve order at Fort Davis, where there had been an announcement of a troop transfer. Some of the disgruntled soldiers had threatened to burn the town as they left, but the arrival of the Rangers prevented any disorder.[29]

General Order No.21 dated March 31, 1885, directed the mustering out of Company A to take effect April 15. Initially,

Captain Johnson was designated to go to Murphysville to handle the disposition of public property, but the order was changed the same day and Captain Gillespie was sent to close out the accounts of Company A, dispose of company property, and pay the men.[30] The company passed into history, never to be reorganized; Adjutant General King saluted them.

> This company was commanded by Capt. George W. Baylor, an officer of long and valuable experience and rare courage, and through the increase of population and growth of power and pluck in the courts on some portions of the frontier, and particularly in the region covered by this company, made it possible, it was thought, to disband it without serious harm, yet it was with regret that any portion had to be 'mustered out' of the gallant band of Rangers which had driven back the Indians forever and had helped to carry peace and protection to so many portions of our widely extended border.[31]

Baylor did not serve again as a Ranger. He had made his one of the famous names in the battalion, a man almost too brave and a skilled Indian fighter. Despite some claims he was mainly interested in chasing hostile Indians, the arrest records of Company A attest to the fact that he was also a keen hunter of outlaws. He continued an active life, serving in the Texas legislature and later as a court clerk. He always got along well with his Mexican neighbors, a trait not shared by all Rangers, and lived in Mexico from 1898 until 1913, returning to San Antonio where he died in 1916. Baylor, Colonel, CSA, was buried in the Confederate Cemetery in that city.[32]

There were no major problems along the Rio Grande during the remainder of 1885. Company D, still in Dimmit County, had a relatively easy time during the spring of the year, but the quiet was deceptive and the company would figure in the last shootout of the year. In late May 1885, Captain Sieker received a report about escaped convicts, Mexicans, heading south and sent Sergeant B.D. Lindsey on a scout to see if they could intercept the felons. The scout left May 31 and included Frank Sieker, a younger brother of the company commander. Also along was Ranger Ira Aten, who had enlisted in Austin and been assigned to Company D when the unit was still near Uvalde. Aten was one of the several Rangers who later wrote detailed memoirs.

Because they were expecting to be out several days, the Rangers had a pack mule with extra supplies; as the newest members of the company, Sieker and Ranger Ben Riley shared the duty of leading the mule. The scout was riding near the river, about eighty miles above Laredo, when the Rangers spotted two men on horseback and leading a third horse. The Rangers started in pursuit when the two men, apparently Mexicans as were the escaped convicts, began running.

The Mexicans abandoned the extra horse and galloped up a nearby slope. Aten and Sieker, on duty with the mule, were to the rear of the patrol. Lindsey and the others, well in advance, chased after the fleeing men but had to cross and then recross a creek. In their haste, the Rangers did not notice how slippery and boggy the banks were until the animals began to slip and fall. Ranger C.W. Griffin broke his collar bone when his horse threw him, and in short order only Aten, Sieker and Riley were mounted. The two with the pack animal avoided the creek by riding directly towards a slight hill where they were joined by Sieker.

Riley had the fastest horse and rode up the hill ahead of the other two Rangers, confronting the two Mexicans atop the rise. Riley, probably inexperienced, never drew his weapon as he approached the two suspects; he merely told them he was a Ranger and they were under arrest. Both men opened fire as soon as Riley started talking and knocked him from the saddle, but he managed to fire back as he was falling.

Aten opened fire with his Winchester while Sieker rode closer and fired with his pistol. One of the Mexicans, wounded, dropped his rifle, fell forward to grab the neck of his horse, and galloped away. The two Rangers exchanged shots with the remaining man. Just before Aten hit the Mexican in the hand, shattering his rifle stock, Aten heard Sieker cry out. The wounded man abandoned the fight and galloped down the slope after his companion.

Lindsey and the three other Rangers finally made their way through the muddy banks of the creek and rode up to discover Private Sieker had been killed, hit once in the heart.

Company D. Frontier Batallion, Texas Rangers, 1885. Left to right, unknown, Pete Edwards, Capt. Joe Sheely, George Farrer, unknown, Charlie Norris, Link Sheely, Tom Mabrey, unknown, Cecilio Charo. Courtesy of the Dudley Dobie Collection.

Riley had several wounds, and Griffin was out of action with a broken collar bone. Gathering up his patrol, Lindsey rode down the hill towards a small settlement of adobe buildings on the riverbank, where the deputy sheriff said he would arrest the wanted men. He was as good as his word.

Sergeant Lindsey made arrangements to have Sieker's body taken to Eagle Pass. Griffin, although in pain, was able to accompany the corpse. Riley, in more serious condition, was sent to a nearby ranch where a doctor could see him. His wounded cared for and his prisoners secured, the sergeant and the rest of the Rangers started for Laredo, a two-day ride away, accompanied by the deputy.

In Laredo the Rangers turned the prisoners over to Sheriff Darrio Gonzales, who put the men in jail. A short time later, while the Rangers were outside the jail, they were surrounded by a large gang claiming to be deputies. The amazed Rangers were told they were under arrest for assault, and rather than cause more killings they went to jail.

Lindsey demanded the sheriff come to the jail, where the Ranger insisted they be allowed to leave to acquire bail. The Rangers wandered about town trying to find someone who would vouch for them and put up bail but found only one store sign in English—Grants Feed Store. They went inside and talked to the owner, who went to the sheriff and told him to let the Rangers go. Even after the passing of many years, Aten still had kind memories of Grant.

The sheriff also let the other two prisoners loose, a father and son named Gonzales who crossed back into Mexico. Why they had fled at the approach of the Rangers was never explained; their possible relationship to the sheriff was also cause for some speculation. Aten believed one of them may have subsequently died from his wounds.

At the time, Laredo was divided into two political factions with the sheriff leading one party and the town marshal the other. The marshal sided with the Rangers, but they had problems with Sheriff Gonzales as long as they remained in the area. Politics along the Rio Grande was a serious business, and the differences in Laredo would eventually lead to battles in the streets and a return of the Rangers.

The incident created a commotion in Austin, and Governor Ireland sent the attorney general to Laredo to investigate. The ridiculous charges against Lindsey and his men were later dropped, but the matter created considerable ill will. To avoid further conflict, Company D was moved back to their former camp near Uvalde.[33]

The company operated from this location for some time with no major changes until October. The resignation of Captain John O. Johnson as quartermaster on October 15, 1885, led to the appointment of Captain L.P. Sieker as his replacement. Lieutenant Frank Jones became commander of Company D when Sieker went to Austin.[34]

There were no outstanding actions during the remainder of 1885. Lack of money and resulting personnel problems continued, despite the mustering out of Company A. Company B was reduced to eighteen officers and men, and the other four companies were cut to seventeen.[35] It was the beginning of a cutback that, this time, would never be reversed.

— 10 —

Fence Cutters and Troubleshooters
1886-1889

History often refuses to be broken into distinct chapters, but some organization must be attempted. The Ranger story, luckily, does divide somewhat into loose chapters. The year 1886 began a long period, lasting until 1900, when the Frontier Battalion no longer had a frontier to defend and when it actually was no longer a true battalion but a slowly shrinking group of small detachments which continued to be called companies. Rather than being the defenders of the frontier, the Rangers had become peace officers who went wherever there were too many problems for local officials. They had become troubleshooters.

Some writers have suggested the Frontier Battalion should have been disbanded after Major Jones died; since there was no longer a frontier, why continue to support a frontier battalion? By 1885 the Rangers and advancing settlement had erased any real frontier line, but lawlessness had not yet been chased from the state, particularly along the Rio Grande and in the Trans Pecos. More and more, however, the Rangers would be faced with problems in the settled counties. In one of those ironies that occasionally dot Ranger history, the Rangers made possible the settlement of the frontier then had to turn away from the old frontier to restore law in many of the interior counties.

By the end of 1885, Company C had been moved from the Panhandle to Pearsall, a small town south of San Antonio on the Laredo Road. Fearing the outbreak of another feud, the citizens of Cotulla sent urgent pleas for Ranger help in early January 1886. Company C was only thirty-two miles away, and Captain Schmitt was ordered to move his camp to Cotulla. He went at once, arriving just

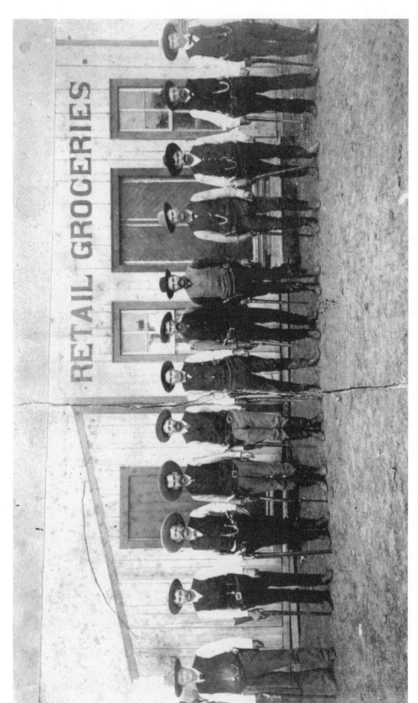

Company C at Cotulla, Texas. February 16, 1887.

after a man had been killed in what was evidently a widening of the trouble. Schmitt described conditions in a letter forwarding his December 1885 monthly report.

> ....after receiving the orders to move to Cotulla I ordered all my men in and had the Corn, Provisions & the other heavy things shipped to this place so that there was not much load on the Wagon to go quick, I went ahead on the train to attend some business at the Laredo District Court and went to Cotulla to select a good camping place I arrived on the 30th and found things in a bad state of affairs there is no grass in this County and the water scarce and the Citizens requested me to stay right in town to give them Protection I rented a Store house and a yard near the depot and the Artesian Well as I had to get a place to store my Corn & Provisions....The Citizens are very much Excited here and are afraid to go about their business and no one risk it to come out at night I had the town guarded for two nights and requested the Saloon men to close their business afterdark, which they all done willingly I also notified all parties to lay aside their arms as I have been notified by the Co. Clk. that there was not a single person in the county duly authorised to carry arms, or had lawfull appointments as deputy Sheriff & Co the Sheriff was absent and I was the only lawfull Officer in the place, and the people looked on me for protection, I am satisfied if I had not been here the day George Hill was killed, there would be a generly killing and you never seen Rangers more welcome and wanted for protection....

Schmitt went on to describe what he was doing to catch the murderers, known in the community, who had killed Hill. He finished with a plea for hay and corn because there was no grass and he was worried about his animals.[1]

Schmitt and Company C remained in South Texas during most of 1886, moving from one trouble spot to another. In the fall, Schmitt sent another report to Sieker.

I suceeded in having Juan Coy the Karnes Co.
Murderer Captured and Extradited. I took Sheriff
Sanchez from here with me as he talk the language and have a great deal influence on the
Mexican side, we worked for the last 10 days &
night, and had Coy to us delivered last night, he
is now in the Laredo Jail he give the other Mexicans where abouts away and we have the Mexican
Police after him now....[2]

Company C remained in Laredo for a time, evidently
cooperating with local officials and a new sheriff, until
someone in Austin finally reacted to petitions that had been
sent from Rio Grande City when there was another rumor
of a revolution in Mexico. Schmitt and his Rangers were
shifted downriver, and once again he reported.

I arrived here yesterday evening and found
this to be a hell of a hole, nothing but Mexicans,
everybody was surprised that Rangers are to be
stationed here there is nothing going on here, and
the Sheriff himself says there is nothing to do for
us here he says that he signed a petition about
three Months ago for Rangers to be stationed here,
that time there was a Revolution in Mexico and
they were afraid....this is no place for us to be, I
cant do no work here whatever....I think Pena is
the proper place for us to be stationed there we
have at least grass for our horses and wood and
water, I can from there operate in all directions in
quick time and the cost would be about one half
then of what it would cost here....[3]

Schmitt's writing skill may have been marginal, but he
was a good Ranger and knew what was best for his company
and the force. He was moved to and remained for some time
in Pena, which was on a narrow-gauge railway which enabled the unit to move quickly in several directions.

While Company C was operating in traditional Ranger
country, the Rangers in Company F were beginning to move
towards the eastern counties where a gang had caused
considerable damage and alarm in Sabine and adjacent
counties. Company F was now commanded by Captain

William Scott, who had been promoted to his new rank on May 1, 1886.[4] It was the first time a large Ranger force had worked the piney woods, although detectives and small detachments had tried to locate and capture the men responsible for extensive stealing and some murders. It was not pleasant duty for Scott.

> Enclosed I send you [Sieker] voucher for incidental expenses for month ending July 31st. I have gone through fifteen days of the "toughest Ranging" that you ever saw. I had rather be a pack mule out west than be a million heir in this brush. We have been going out every day and each man brings back Ticks, Enough to keep him scratching and "Kussing" all night. Yes it is a sure rough country on man and beast. My stock have been fed on rotton corn and they will barely make it back to Marshall. I could only get corn in the ear and of course there was a considerable waste et. I have made quite a great failure on this scout but can stand it if I can only get back to the prairie alive. I will return to Vernon on or about Aug 6th.[5]

Despite Scott's grumbling about conditions in East Texas and his belief the scout was a failure, the adjutant general reported at the end of the year that the Rangers had captured two brothers named Connor believed to be the leaders of the gang that had terrorized the area.[6] Just what happened to the two men is not known, but they evidently did not spend any time in jail because Scott and his Rangers were back in Sabine County in March 1887, once again after the Connor's gang. On March 31 Scott and three Rangers were scouting through heavy brush, just after daybreak when the light was still poor, and Ranger J.H. Moore was killed by a volley of shots from a distance of only twenty to thirty feet. Although they never saw the men who fired, Captain Scott, Sergeant J.A. Brooks and Private J.H. Rogers opened fire. There was a brief, heavy exchange of shots at close range, the powder smoke further reduced visibility, and every man in the fight became a casualty. Scott was shot through the lungs, Brooks lost three fingers, and Rogers had a ball pass through his right arm and enter his side. Despite their carefully planned ambush, the Connor brothers were finally finished, Bill Connor dead, his brother seriously wounded. The outlaws' pack horse and four of their dogs were dead; in the poor light, the Rangers had fired at anything that moved. This fight finally broke up the gang and the trouble in Sabine County.[7]

The strict accounting procedures for battalion funds is shown by the paperwork generated by this fight. In explaining his bill of $495 the attending physician, Doctor J.W. Smith of Hemphill, described his services and the care given the three injured Rangers. Smith was called to help several badly injured Rangers and a dead man, evidently Bill Connor, early the morning of March 31. It was a ten-mile trip into the woods where the doctor found Scott in extremely serious condition, shot through the chest. About noon Doctor Smith was able to extract the ball, which enabled Scott to breathe somewhat easier. During the day he also dressed the wounds in Moore's side and arm. Sergeant Brooks had been hit in both hands, and Smith had to amputate three fingers on one hand and remove a ball from the other hand. He remained with the wounded men, providing treatment until the following evening when they were transported to Hemphill.

One can admire this doctor of the 1880s for his skill and devotion to his patients. Doctor Smith went on to describe how he spent the following ten days with the injured Rangers, neglecting his regular practice. He called in two other physicians and included their fees in his bill. In all, Smith billed the state for twenty-two days, at five dollars a day, although he said he spent more time on the case. He concluded:

> Now I leave the case with you. I have made out my voucher for what I think my services worth, if you think not [,] allow me what your judgement may seem right for like surgical works and I am satisfied.[8]

Somewhere in the quartermaster files there may be a voucher for what Doctor Smith was finally paid. It was not that the state was stingy or ungrateful; there simply was not enough money allocated to the battalion to enable it to meet all charges. King specifically mentioned that medical expenses for wiping out the Connor gang were a drain on the budget.[9] Fortunately, in time Scott, Rogers and Brooks recovered and returned to duty. The enlisted men would eventually become officers and company commanders.

Gunfire and fatalities attract more attention, but the other companies were also busy during this period. In mid-May 1886, J.T. Gillespie advised the adjutant general he was again moving Company E back to Murphysville because water and grass had played out near his old camp. There was some trouble between the "Mexicans" and the "Anglos" in the town, another reason to move closer. He thought a few Rangers in the vicinity would "have a tendency to keep the rowdy class quiet.[10] Captain McMurry of Company B also reported on some of his activities.

> I have been down in Archer & Clay [counties] among the fence cutting warriors for the past week things looked pretty serious a while, there were about two hundred men in arms, One party wanted to turn about 3,000 drift cattle on a portion of the country, and the other swore they would have their blood before it should be done, The trouble is about over now I think the "drifters" have come to the conclusion to take their...cattle & hunt water and grass for them.[11]

These were old and familiar problems, but Texas and the Rangers were also thrust into new and unsettling conditions in 1886. The shift by enterprising outlaws from holding up stage coaches to robbing trains was merely a variation of old practices, but now for the first time the state was faced with large-scale labor strikes, primarily among the large number of people employed by the railroads. On a lesser scale, the opening of several mines led to the organization of even more workers and an increased potential for labor violence.

The organization of labor was a new threat that struck officials and most citizens as something foreign and as attacks on property rights, due process and the very law itself. Adjutant General King expressed this view of this new danger.

> A gigantic organization has been created with many thousands of men bound by secret oaths and obligations; its ramifications extending into

every State and Territory and beyond; its leaders invested with unknown and immeasurable powers; its mandates promptly and implicitly obeyed; even when opposed to the laws of the country, and dangerous to the peace and security of society....

This is a strange and startling condition of affairs in a country and government where the ballot is the privilege of every full grown, honest man....This dangerous and destructive spirit is of foreign birth and parentage, but among the multitudes of our own country, both native and foreign born, who have grown discontented under selfish and sectional laws, and the power and greed of capital and corporations, it has found lodgement, support and increased strength. Under the mad and murderous teachings of Communists and Socialists, these oath bound organizations have many strikes, have openly defied the law, have beaten and abused and sometimes killed people who only desired to honestly earn a living....[12]

King, like many others, could not understand how men would join something called the Knights of Labor and accept orders from leaders they did not know, even to seizing property or killing their fellow workers. He was honest enough to admit that the newly risen corporations had sometimes managed the law to suit their interests, but none of this justified doing away with the law, or the necessity for following due process in seeking redress from financial wrongs.

The Rangers had figured in railway strikes the preceding year when part of Company E took an unofficial hand in calming disagreements at Big Spring between striking railway workers and their fellows who refused to stop work. By valiant diplomacy, a few Rangers had calmed a potentially violent mob and dispersed the two sides without incident.[13]

Subsequent incidents, however, were more violent. Galveston and Houston were involved in a strike by the Gulf, Colorado and Santa Fe Railway, and it became necessary to call out militia units to maintain the peace. No large employer was exempt; when the Mallory Steamship Line was struck, King fulfilled the task of peacemaker and avoided open fighting, but nothing was accomplished to alleviate the causes of the troubles.

Actual fighting broke out early in 1886 when a strike by the Knights of Labor against the Texas and Pacific spread through the entire Missouri Pacific system. Trains were tied up from Marshall in East Texas, over to Mineola, on to Denison, Sherman, Palestine, Waco, and up to Alvarado and Fort Worth. The strike continued for three weeks without official notice because the railway made no call for help until the strikers had crippled it. In the Palestine yard, for example, there were close to six hundred loaded cars unable to move in any direction. Thirty-seven engines blocked the rails, twenty-seven of them "killed" and unable to operate because of stolen parts. Hundreds of couplings and links had been taken from cars and tracks, further blocking movement; cargoes on the cars began to spoil, and there was a growing danger of fire and explosions. The strikers declared there would be no movement until the leaders of the Knights of Labor said the strike was over.

On March 23 the railway asked the governor to issue a proclamation ordering the strikers to cease their illegal acts. A second request a few days later reported the mob was most dangerous at Palestine, Denison and Alvarado and asked King to go to those points and act to quell the mobs.

King was in poor health and did not reach Palestine until March 27. He found that the railway had decided to try moving some of the cars the following day, even if the attempt caused trouble. The district judge's order to the sheriff of Anderson County to appear with two-hundred armed citizens and unblock the mess in the Palestine railyard was promptly obeyed, and the massive posse was able to take control of the grounds without opposition. Slowly the cars began to move, but the well-planned sabotage took time to repair. The sheriff of Houston County arrived by rail with a strong reinforcement and the work continued; the strike leaders were arrested and further opposition collapsed. When King returned to Austin, the rails were clear and traffic was moving through Palestine. King then went to Denison and talked with railway officials, but the local officials there had the situation in hand; the Grayson County sheriff, with elements of the local militia and armed civilians, had taken command of the situation, faced down the strikers, and opened the line.

On April 2, however, a train moving south from Fort Worth was attacked by an armed group of strikers, one of the train guards was killed, and several were wounded. Later it was learned the ambush had been set on orders from a labor leader in Missouri, specifically to show the power of the union. It was a tactical blunder.

King heard of the attack on the train and arrived at Fort Worth on April 4, a Sunday. He found twenty deputy U.S. marshals' guarding the railyard because the railway line was in receivership and controlled by the federal court. With the potential for violence, local authorities had called for state aid even before King arrived, and in short order militia companies began arriving in town. Challenged, the state responded with three hundred militia troops, and the governor himself traveled to Fort Worth. Large groups of local citizens armed themselves and supported the militia.

Rangers officially became involved in the strike when companies B and C and part of F were moved to Fort Worth. The prompt intrusion of a considerable number of armed Rangers and the state's evident willingness to meet force with even greater force brought an abrupt end to the strike and to the threat of more attacks on trains or railway equipment. Captain Schmitt and Company C were sent back to their post near Laredo on April 6 because King did not want to leave the Rio Grande area unprotected. He was not willing, however, to take a chance on trouble's arising again when the militia units went home, and he kept McMurry's Company B and part of Company F in Fort Worth and Alvarado for several weeks.[14] According to King, the comparative handful of Rangers evidently had no difficulty in maintaining order.

> Quiet and orderly and without uniform of any kind, the sturdy and determined manner and appearance of the rangers, and their well established character for the fearless observance of orders made a powerful impression on the minds of the strikers, and had due weight in bringing about a condition of peace.[15]

This would not be the last strike duty for the Rangers; in the changing world of the years ahead, the Rangers would find this unwelcome job a necessary part of their service.

After Fort Worth, however, for a time they returned to more familiar duties. As mentioned earlier, Scott was sent to East Texas, and Company C became involved in a political war in Laredo.

The possibility for violence in Laredo had been recognized a year earlier when Sergeant Lindsey and his men had been "arrested" by the sheriff of Webb County, in which the "Bota" faction supported the sheriff and the "Guaraches" supported the town marshal. The Botas won the April 1886 election and sent circulars for their victory celebration to their defeated foes, which the Guaraches took as an insult. Snipers opened fire on the victory parade, but Bota snipers also posted atop several rooftops returned fire and did most of the damage according to later examinations of the dead and wounded.

Governor Ireland sent Brigadier General A.S. Roberts to Laredo with several detachments of state troops. When Roberts reached town, soon joined by Captain Schmitt and nine Rangers, the fighting had ceased but the danger level was still high. Roberts held interviews with both sides in the dispute and came to the conclusion they were equally guilty; the sheriff and county judge and most other county officials had actually participated in the fight. Although the town marshal was the admitted leader of the opposition, he had not taken part in the shooting.

With everyone guilty, Roberts made no arrests, left the matter with a grand jury to make indictments, and returned home with his troops. Schmitt and his Rangers remained in Laredo to preserve order until feelings had cooled, then returned to their camp.[16] The Laredo incident was yet another example of border politics in which the law enforcement officials, with whom the Rangers were supposed to cooperate, were part of the problem.

During much of this time, fence cutting remained a major cause for requests for Ranger assistance. In numerous cases, county officials simply did not try to arrest friends, relatives or supporters, and consequently many Rangers were assigned duties as detectives, their actions suggested but not described in the reports of the adjutant general. The only way a conviction could be obtained was to catch a fence cutter at work, and this undercover work became another drain on funds, unpopular but necessary.

One of the men who made a reputation catching fence cutters was Ira Aten, who not only wrote lengthy reports but later recounted his adventures in his memoirs. Aten began his detective work in the summer of 1886 in Lampasas County with a relatively simple assignment in which he apprehended two young men who had been cutting wire as a joke. Aten took his work seriously and soon had them before a judge, but to his surprise the young jokesters had a clever attorney who instead accused Aten of being the culprit! The Ranger did not appreciate or understand this legal trick and slugged the lawyer. He was promptly fined by the presiding judge.[17]

Hitting an attorney was not considered a bar to continued beneficial service as a detective, and Aten earned a reputation for his work in Lampasas. Towards the end of the year, a serious outbreak of fence cutting took place in Brown County and King sent Aten to investigate. Because of the extensive nature of the fence destruction, the adjutant general also sent Captain Scott and a detachment to Brownwood as a backup force.[18]

Aten was still young but he knew his job. He took the railroad to Coleman, some thirty miles west of Brownwood, where he bought a pony then rode into the area where some of the fence cutting had taken place. Aten had a talent necessary in any detective work—patience—and never rushed or tried to force anything. Posing as an orphan looking for work, for a week he did odd jobs, made friends and played the part of a young man trying to make a living. He did odd jobs for a family which felt sorry for him and helped him with food and shelter.

After some time, the head of the family trusted him enough to send Aten with some stolen horses to Belton. Aten hid the horses on a ranch until they could be returned to their owners, then rejoined his new friends after staying at the ranch long enough to have ridden to Belton and back.

After overhearing plans for the next fence cutting and horse stealing raid, Aten managed to slip away and joined Captain Scott for the arrest. Scott had five of his Company F Rangers and Aten when he accosted the fence cutters on November 9, 1886. The Rangers' demand for the men to surrender was answered by gunfire; in the brief fight two of the fence cutters were mortally wounded and died within a short time. Aten recognized one of them as a local constable![19] Although some of the gang escaped, the killings stopped further fence cutting in Brown County and added to Aten's reputation as a detective.

Scott's participation received mention in the adjutant general's report and considerable newspaper coverage, but Captain Schmitt saw the matter in a different light and was pointedly critical.

> I dont want to say anything officially, as their management is not my business, but it might be brought to the proper light and corrected, as all money drawn from the Appropriation of the F[rontier] B[attalion] all officers and men are interested and have to suffer by it when run short....myself and Capt. Jones are the only Officers who obey Gen. Kings orders, and run the companies as Economical as possible....there is Capt McMurray, Capt Scott told me that he was nothing but a fraud, he never stay with the company and batting about Fort Worth & Dallas all his time....

Schmitt complained that his fellow captains traveled about for nothing and submitted vouchers not justified by actual service. He also criticized Scott's performance in the killing of the two fence cutters; it was his opinion that if Scott had taken enough men, the other miscreants would have been captured. He was evidently irked about the newspaper publicity given Scott and told Sieker that he had spoken to a man named Copeland who had done all the undercover work while Scott received the credit. In closing, he suggested the quartermaster look into the matter and make some changes.[20]

Schmitt would not let the matter rest and wrote again to Sieker after reading more newspaper accounts of the fight, again faulting Scott for not taking more men. Most of his rather short letter concerned conditions in the country. Whether or not Schmitt's letters had any effect in Austin is unknown, but no official action was taken on his complaints. It is highly unlikely any Ranger succeeded in padding his expense accounts; the quartermaster checked and rechecked each voucher and expenditure and returned any that seemed inflated or improper in any respect. Schmitt was correct, however, in his statements that any unneces-

Ira Aten, a Texas Ranger. 1887.

sary expense hurt the entire battalion.

Not long after the second letter, funds for the Rangers fell below the money required to maintain the current size of the Frontier Battalion. In another critical economy move, the legislature cut funding from $60,000 to $30,000, too severe a cut to be balanced by minor personnel reductions. The decision was made to disband Company E, and Sieker traveled to Murphysville to muster out the men and sell the state's property. On April 6, 1887, Company E joined Company A in the history books.[21]

Ira Aten's Ranger service had many similarities to James Gillett's career. Both served in Company D, each served during periods of great action, and each was more than equal to the task. Both men served with distinction but never became officers due to circumstances beyond their control. Fortunately, both Rangers later wrote of their experiences, although Aten's work never achieved the fame of Gillett's classic account of Ranger life.

Aten's memoirs contain a little-known event that involved someone who was to have great impact on the Ranger force. Sometime in 1885, four men remained at liberty for some time after killing an old German near Fredericksburg. The cold-blooded murder incensed Governor Ireland, who sent Company D to track the killers. After a long hunt by the company with no sign of the wanted men, Ireland had Aten come to Austin and told him he wanted the men, dead or alive.[22]

The killers had relatives or friends willing to hide them, but Aten remained on their trail and managed to wound one of the murderers. The man managed to escape and went into hiding. The Ranger knew he would stay hidden until he healed or died, so Aten patiently went about other business. Several months later he received a tip that the wounded man was recovered but still in hiding. Aten rode out to the farm of the informant, but the man refused to cooperate further and said he would be happier if the Ranger left his place. He did offer the name of a man who might guide Aten to the fugitive.

Aten then rode to the ranch of John Hughes, who was more than willing to help and offered suggestions for capturing the murderer. The two men captured the fugitive without trouble. Aten suggested the rancher might want to join the Rangers, and after some thought Hughes enlisted in 1887 to begin a twenty-eight-year career in the Ranger service. Though older and a private, Hughes became good friends with Sergeant Aten and they served together on several scouts.[23]

Company D was probably the first Ranger unit to move all of its men, horses, mules, wagon, supplies and camp gear entirely by rail, after trouble between cattlemen and rustlers became so bad in McCulloch County that the adjutant general hurriedly ordered Captain Jones and his company to the area. It would have been impossible to march overland and reach McCulloch in time to be of use, so the Rangers moved into Uvalde, from their camp near the town, where the railroad had placed several boxcars at their disposal. They traveled east to San Antonio, switched to a new line, rode north through Austin and on to Fort Worth where they changed again to travel west to Cisco. While unloading, they received an urgent message to proceed to Brady City where trouble was expected.

Jones, leaving the wagon and equipment and supplies, formed most of his company and started for Brady City. On the way a man told them there was a big roundup ahead and plenty of trouble; not knowing they were Rangers he said if they hurried they might get in on the shooting! Their informant was not exaggerating; ahead they soon saw about forty men's facing each other in two lines and ready for battle. Captain Jones walked his company between the two opposing ranks of men and told them to put up their weapons, "Any shooting to be done, men, we will do it!"

It was obvious the Rangers were not taking sides, and the cattlemen decided to let them be the arbiters for questionable cattle brands. Peace of sorts was restored and the roundup continued. Ranger patrols accompanied each part of the county-wide drive, examining brands and taking possession of disputed cattle. When the drive was over the Rangers had more than five hundred unidentified cattle with burned or altered brands, most of which were sold and the money placed in the county fund. Aten and the rest of the company remained on this duty for four weeks, arresting a number of suspected rustlers and brand changers. Like fence cutters, the men believed to be altering brands had to be caught in the act, and there were few convictions.

With the tensions eased in McCulloch, the company was moved down to Menard County, where Company D had served before, and worked in various troubleshooting capacities. One of the odd jobs with which the Rangers would be increasingly tasked, that of tax collector, came up in Menard. In the more settled and civilized areas, citizens did not resist paying taxes other than their normal reluctance to part with hard-earned money, but out west, particularly along the Devils and Pecos rivers, many men refused to pay taxes on land which they considered belonged to God and whomever had guts enough to live on it. The preceding year they had run off the collector; he refused to return or risk his life for a few tax dollars.

Soon several of the Rangers were riding with the tax collectors in Menard, but not everyone capitulated gracefully. There some near fights but, as Aten recalled, "this year the collector had two Rangers with him who did not have any more sense than to shoot it out with the ranchmen when it came to that." It was probably the best tax year they had ever had in Menard.

Company D had brought all their gear with them but was not prepared for winter this far north; their tents were inadequate protection against the cold and Jones asked the adjutant general for permission to return to the warmer climate at Uvalde. Aten was all in favor of the move—half the men had girls in Uvalde—but the state was not wasting train fare on a non-emergency move. Company D marched home, down to Junction City then across to the headwaters of the Nueces River, downstream through the canyon to Uvalde.[24] With no road, the distance is much more than the 160-mile, straight-line distance, but the men of Company D did not mind; they were home near their girls.

Sheriff McKinney of La Salle County was murdered late in 1886. His death would have been a cause for Ranger concern in any event, but he had also been a Ranger captain. The chase for the murderers is another interesting example of the adjutant general's official reports' failing to present a complete account of what actually took place; the official version states only that Captain Schmitt and five men watched a water hole and ordered the murderers of Sheriff McKinney to surrender when they appeared. In the fight that followed one man was killed and one surrendered but later escaped.[25] Schmitt's report to Sieker does give some detail.

> I suppose you seen from the News Papers allready that I succeeded in Capturing the Murderers of Sheriff McKinney I have been out since I am here to find out the whereabouts of them and Employed men to try and locate them last Friday I received news that the party were some where near Twohig Station and that night about two OClock I took five of my best men and started out with a guide layed conceiled in the bushes in day time and got at once to work with my spotters to locate the camping place but we failed to find that Saturday and Sunday, but I got information on Monday that one of the Parties would come to a Well for Water & Co so I waylaid the trail in the Pasture going to the Well and on Monday evening after dark two men on horse back came along the trail and we recognized them at once, and let them

come right close up where I had my men posted, and when he came up within about 6 feet to Sergt. Grimes we all raised with leveled guns and demanded the surrender, one Timkins held up his hands up at once but Crenshaw drew his Pistol quick as lightning and drawed on Sergt Grimes who was the nearest to him and the men fired & shot him off his horse during the Excitement Timpkins [sic] got away as every one attention was on Crenshaw who showed fight Crenshaw fired two Shots at us while down deadly wounded laying on his back and I ordered him again to drop his pistol and hold up his [hands] or my men would kill him, he lay the Pistol down on his side and when one of my men stepped up and came within two feet he quickly raised the Pistol at my man again and had it cocked when my man Kicked it out of his hand, he wanted to kill a man before he die this was just after dark I had him carried to the well....he died at 2 Oclock that night....

Schmitt continued with an account of efforts to catch another member of the gang, a man named McCoy. The Rangers had an idea of who would be willing to shelter the fugitive and maintained a close watch on possible hiding places. They constantly searched for McCoy, chasing him from one place to another until he lost his blankets and supplies, was exhausted from the running and hiding, and finally agreed to surrender if they would protect him. McCoy was as good as his word, riding in and giving up. The Ranger also told of an attempted murder of another citizen and how he posted a guard on the house. Schmitt's letter was a long one ending with a postscript, "Please excuse bad writing, I am tired & worn out."[26]

For Ranger incidents to be mentioned in the printed reports, the Rangers had to have engaged either in a gunfight involving casualties or some other incident of major importance. The hard, tiring chases after the McCoys were lumped under the topic of criminals captured for the year, without names or credit for the companies involved. Yet it was the many scouts and the arrests of outlaws, rather than the infrequent killings, that helped to maintain order in Texas.

Aten made a name for himself as an undercover detective with a flair for catching fence cutters, but his most famous case was officially described as follows:

> Nov. 4. Sergt Aten returned to camp after being on detached duty in Navarro County after fence cutters assisted by Pvt King, accomplished nothing, out 104 days, marched 1500 miles.[27]

This terse summary does no justice to what actually happened. Fence cutters were active in Navarro County in July 1888, operating close to the home of the new governor, L.S. Ross, and Aten said the governor called him in one day and told him to "get" the fence cutters. He took the new assignment on the condition he could have some help, not out of fear but for company. Undercover work was lonely, and Aten needed someone to talk to during the long periods in enemy country. A young Ranger, Jim King, was assigned to Aten, and the two began a lengthy adventure on July 25.[28]

Aten and King, roughly dressed with some tools and their weapons, reached the general area of trouble in a rickety farm wagon looking like young men trying to find work. They drove to Mexia, where they knew the sheriff had caught some fence cutters, and Aten left King and the wagon hidden in brush country while he took the train to Corsicana. In town he talked to the local judge and learned the men already arrested were believed to be small-time crooks rather than the criminals behind the fence cutting. The two Rangers evidently spent considerable time riding about the area, because Aten sent in a preliminary report from Corsicana that said in part:

> I will ask it as a special favor of the Adjutant General's office never to ask me to work after fence-cutters again under any and all circumstances for it is the most disagreable work in the world and i think I have already done my share of it for the State of Texas and her people.[29]

The Rangers retrieved their wagon and set out for Richland, where they inquired about the way to Kaufman County. With people's in Richland believing they were on the way to Kaufman, Aten and King had a stroke of luck when a wagon

wheel came off and broke about a mile outside Richmond—
Aten reported he was up at four in the morning pounding
off the tire and breaking the wheel with an ax. They had no
money to repair the damage and found out that the black-
smith in town had gone to Corsicana and would not be back
for a week; Aten said "we could not get our wagon wheel fixt
if we wanted to but we didnt want to very bad." The two
Rangers managed to move the now completely disabled
wagon back to Richland, where "a large crowd of the fence
cutters all seen us and I dont think any of them suspicioned
us being detectives for a moment."

By now, the Rangers were somewhat known in the
community. King's ability as a fiddle player—the Ranger
performed at local dances and was always ready to saw a
few tunes whatever the occasion—helped their cover. The
local men never suspected a Ranger would also be a musi-
cian.[30]

Aten and King soon knew most of the fence cutters in
the county, none of whom, as they boasted of what they had
done and were planning, suspected the two apparent farm-
hands were memorizing names and faces. Talking, however,
was not a crime; the Rangers had to catch the men in the
act, and Aten and King bided their time. The two men
worked at any job that came along; Aten picked cotton and
found King a job. They worked for a time building a rock
furnace around a gin boiler, hard work but they acted as if
they had been raised to it. Aten reported the fence cutters
were ranchers or farmers who objected to anyone's fencing
the land; many of the people who suffered the most were
small farmers who had spent money for wire to fence in
small plots to grow corn and cotton only to have their fences
shredded by the cutters.

The two Rangers had some anxious moments when the
local sheriff boasted that the governor had sent some detectives to help him catch the fence cutters. As the only
newcomers in the region, Aten and King came under suspicion and were forced to quit work and move out of the
immediate area to take employment with a rancher who
knew of their mission. They began to watch a three-mile
stretch of fence that had been talked about as a target, each
night hiding at likely places to wait for the fence cutters.

Aten, becoming disgusted with the project and discouraged about ever catching anyone, had a brilliant idea in

September. Suppose there was some device located along the wire that exploded when the cutters began their work....

> I dont want to lay on a fence two or three years just to catch a few villians while dinamite booms would always be there ready for them whenever they took a notion to cut. But I havent got the dinamite in the right shape and dont know how i could get it unless i go to chicago and join the anarchist and get them to fix it for me.[31]

There was a considerable time lapse before he again reported to Sieker on October 8.

> So I have come to the conclusion if it was not against the law to guard a fence with a shot-gun to protect the property, it certainly would not be 'against the law to use dynamite for the same purpose.

He went on to explain how he had developed his boom, making it safe against the accidental rubbing of the wire by cattle but exploding if the fence was cut or torn down. If the people in Austin did not approve, all they had to do was tell him to stop; they had sent him down to stop the fence cutters, this was how he proposed to do it, and he had even spent some of his own money buying the explosives.

On October 15 Aten wrote acknowledging his orders to stop work on the dynamite booms and return to his company. Aten said he was following orders to the letter; he would not use his dynamite, but nothing in the orders prevented his showing the ranchers how to make the devices. He had done this, and the word was all over the county.[32] In his memoirs, Aten merely said he detonated a few sticks of dynamite and made sure the word reached everyone. Although they did not actually catch any fence cutters, Aten and King greatly hindered fence cutting activities in Navarro County, but there would be occasional outbreaks for a number of years.

Despite King's strict financial controls and the disbanding of two companies, it again became necessary to reduce the Ranger force as the end of 1888 approached. In a rather

Report of Sergeant Ira Aten. As a rule, Ranger reports, especially those by enlisted men, did not go into extensive detail. In this one-page account of his actions, Aten covers an entire month of scouting back and forth trying to find witnesses and transporting prisoners. Courtesy of the Texas State Library.

ironic turn of events, Captain Schmitt's Company C was the unlucky unit to be selected; like other reductions, the choice was based on which company could be spared with the least loss of protection, an indirect tribute to Schmitt for cleaning up his territory. On November 30, 1888, the end of the reporting year, Company C was disbanded,[33] and the Frontier Battalion was reduced to three companies. It would be impossible for the less-than-fifty remaining Rangers to constitute a state-wide police force, but they did not realize it. As they had always done, the Rangers remaining on duty did the best they could. King reported:

> Their services have been necessarily arduous, and have proved of great value despite the small number of men now employed. Our frontier is an extensive one, and many of the border communities are largely dependent on the rangers for security to life and property, protection to courts and people, and the execution of the law....largely by the efforts of this organization fence cutting has ceased to be "epidemic," and appears to be entirely broken up in many of the border communities, and finds its few supporters mainly in old sections where the rangers are not expected ordinarily to be seen....

King recognized the value of the Rangers as a calming influence, even when they were not engaged in battle or arresting criminals. Even a few were of value.

> A simple "scout" by the rangers through any county infested by lawless men purifies the whole moral atmosphere, so to speak, and the criminal element disappears for the time being.[34]

The three remaining companies ended the year with Company B, commanded by Captain S.A. McMurry, at Quanah in North Texas where it could cover that section of the state and the Panhandle. Captain Frank Jones and Company D remained near Uvalde with responsibility for all of Central Texas and the far west. Captain William Scott had resigned on April 20, 1888, and Sergeant J.A. Brooks, despite the loss of three fingers in the Connor fight, was the logical choice for commander. With his promotion to lieutenant, Brooks headed Company F in Rio Grande City to maintain order in the lower border and interior counties. This handful of Rangers traveled 47,781 miles during fiscal year 1888. With no Ranger losses they arrested 249 men, killed one and wounded another who resisted arrest. They made 230 scouts and guarded thirteen jails, attended fifteen court sessions to preserve the peace, and provided escorts to civil officials on thirty-five occasions.[35] All and all, not a bad showing for the handful of men remaining.

The last years of the decade of the 1880s provided the Rangers many of the old problems that had faced them since 1874, but Texas changed dramatically during the decade with resultant challenges to all peace officers. Population grew over forty percent, creating new counties. In 1879 Wheeler was the only organized county in the Panhandle; by 1889 there were twelve new counties and an additional five were organized in 1890.[36] As late as 1880 there were no real towns west of Uvalde except distant El Paso; within three years Marfa, Murphysville, Sanderson, Dryden, Comstock and Del Rio were settled. Further north, Colorado City, Big Spring, Midland, Odessa and Abilene grew out of railheads or proximity to the rails.

This population increase and the growth of towns changed the political organization of the Plains, the Trans Pecos and the Panhandle. By 1885, Marfa on the railway had enough population to become a county seat; Alpine, the old Murphysville, became county seat of Brewster County in 1887.[37] During this period the Mexican city of El Paso del Norte was renamed Juarez to honor their great patriot, and Franklin became El Paso which grew into a major town of 10,000 within the decade with all the attractions of a booming city—saloons, brothels, hotels of all categories and stores of every description supporting decent, hard working men and women as well as gamblers, gunfighters and sharpies. The "Paris of the West" would require much help from the Rangers.

Another development in the Big Bend would also call for Ranger assistance; the old trail from Fort Davis to Presidio on the Rio Grande took on new importance with the discovery of silver north of Presidio in 1880. The site developed into a full-scale mining operation by 1884 when a settlement named Shafter was founded.[38] The trail north from Shafter to Marfa was pounded into a road of sorts. Hundreds of Mexicans crossed the river to work the mine while Shafter boomed with saloons, gambling halls, stores and rooming houses. Hundreds of miles away in Erath County, coal was

Company D., Texas Rangers, 1888.
Photo courtesy of the Texas Ranger Hall of Fame and Museum, Waco, Texas.

discovered in commercial quantities and mining began in that area. This industrial activity, new to Texas, added jobs and created wealth but would also require much from the small Ranger force.

Any increase in people and wealth attracted criminals. In late February 1889, Sheriff Pat Dolan of newly created Jeff Davis County asked for Ranger help after a store robbery in Toyah on February 21. Dolan, a former Ranger captain, had trouble finding deputies and was not too proud to call on his old comrades for support. A detachment from Company D commanded by Corporal C.H. Fusselman was sent to help[39] in the beginning of a gradual movement that would eventually find Company D transferred to the Trans Pecos.

The rest of Company D was scattered across Central Texas. Sergeant Aten's draft report for one month gives some idea of Ranger activities.

> Sergt. Aten left camp March 22nd 1889 to go to San Saba co. after the Duncan boys & H.W. Landers wanted for the murder of the Williamson family in Maverick co. Texas. The Duncans were arrested by the Shff the day Aten arrived there, & were turned over to Aten at Goldthwaite [sic] by Shff Howard of san Saba Co. Lawers for the duncans swore out a writ of Habaes corpus before Judge Blackburn & the trial was et [?] for April 11th to take place at Burnet. Aten met Sheff Cook of maverick Co. at temple & sent him back to rustle witnesses for the habaes corpus and tell other Sheffs to do likewise.
>
> Aten then went to San saba Co to look up witnesses for the State in the Duncans case hunt for Landers who was reported still in San Saba Co. but not finding him by the time to go to Burnet a witness in the Duncan case left & went to Burnet & reported back to Camp April 23rd.[40]

Aten had spent a month and traveled hundreds of miles on a single case, none of which received any official notice other than being lumped with other similar scouts under topics such as the number of men arrested or the number of courts guarded. The Rangers' scant numbers were not equal to the

Texas Ranger W.L. Sullivan on right.

demands for help during the reporting period 1889-1890; fifty-two requests for help were received in Austin of which fifteen could not be supported because no Rangers were available.[41]

During the 1888-1889 period, the Ranger companies remained in one place and sent men to other locales as requested.[42] Sending individual Rangers on assignment became common, and seldom was an entire company able to go on a scout. One of the few exceptions was the use of Company B to stop troubles in the Erath County coal mines. A detachment of B had been sent to the mines in 1887 when the first strike troubles developed, but during 1888-1889 the problem became so severe that King retained most of the company in Erath and Palo Pinto counties for almost a year. What had started as an economic boon to the area and the state seemed likely to turn into financial ruin in the face of labor violence, and at one point King himself went to the area to act as a peacemaker.

King found a confused situation in the mines, where a force of several hundred strikers were abusing and threatening other miners who tried to work. There had been a recent change in the ownership of the mine, and the strikers were mostly Knights of Labor who had been employed by the previous owners but who had not been hired by the new management; technically speaking they could not be called strikers because they were no longer employees. Initially, they received some support from the Knights of Labor in keeping the situation disturbed.

Company officials had no objection to hiring union members and employed hundreds of miners belonging to the Knights of Labor, but they absolutely refused to deal in any way with the troublemakers who had set up camp near the mine. King talked to both sides and spent considerable time in the striker's settlement, but he believed the men were interested only in violence and brought in Captain McMurry and most of Company B before he left to return to Austin. King told the Rangers they were not to take sides in the labor dispute but were to meet force with force if there was any more violence or threats or intimidation by either side. The Rangers were kept on site for months, the situation gradually calmed, and after a time the union leadership saw the company was paying top wages and hiring anyone but the malcontents. It quietly withdrew its support from the wildcat strikers, most of whom went to work in other areas.[43]

Some interesting sidelights on the mine troubles were recounted by Ranger W.J.L. Sullivan when he wrote his memoirs. According to Sullivan, the mine operator, Colonel R.D. Hunter, was looking for a special agent to ferret out troublemakers. Captain McMurry asked Sullivan if he wanted the job; the sergeant agreed and worked for the coal company for eight months for $100 a month.

Sullivan had little to say about his tour as an agent, but he did recount an incident when he and a few associates trailed some "anarchists" and listened while the leader told of his plan to dynamite one of the mines that night; Sullivan and his men arrested and jailed thirteen would-be saboteurs.[44] He also acted as a general guard, as did all the Rangers, and one night arrested a saloonkeeper known as Tom Lawson who tried to draw a pistol. Sullivan knocked the man down, arrested him, and saw him jailed and fined. Lawson later complained to Captain McMurry about his harsh treatment; McMurry told Sullivan that he should have broken Lawson's neck.[45]

While other Ranger units were soothing labor disputes, Corporal Fusselman and his detachment from Company D were riding over most of the Big Bend looking for known fugitives, scouting to prevent raids up from Mexico or down from New Mexico, or trying to keep the courts protected and the few jails guarded. In April 1889 there was so much trouble in the region that King had to send a few more Company D men to support Fusselman; on April 25 Private Bass Outlaw and three other Rangers started for Alpine and arrived May 11 after a four-hundred-mile ride. Their departure left Captain Jones with only three Rangers in their camp near Uvalde for whatever emergency arose; all eleven of his other men were on detached service.[46]

In early June, Fusselman arrived back at Alpine after a scout to be met by ex-Ranger Gillespie, who had a telegram from one of the stations on the railway which stated that a "Mexican" had shot a man and was riding around firing at everything in sight. The little settlement was terrified and crying for help. Fusselman and Gillespie took the next train to the station, where they found the man had gone to a place called Maxan Springs. They borrowed a handcar and pumped down a spur to the springs but again missed the man, now identified as Donaciano Beslanga. Returning to the station, Fusselman borrowed a mule, rode to the man's home, and waited until a heavy storm during the night forced the man to seek shelter. As he neared his house, he and Fusselman both fired almost face-to-face through the driving rain. Visibility was only a few feet and neither man had a clear shot; they became separated in the dark and rain.

Next morning Fusselman borrowed a rifle and started out in clearing weather to look for a trail. About a mile from the station, the Ranger heard someone coughing and moved cautiously towards the sound until Beslanga suddenly stood up. Fusselman said, "I could see that there was no chance for his giving up as he had a bad expression on his face so I fired and he did."

Both men fired at close range and Beslanga was hit several times. Fusselman emptied his rifle and ran forward, grabbed the barrel of the man's rifle, drew his pistol and shot Beslanga again at close range before the man collapsed and surrendered, dying within a short time. The Ranger had hit the man eight times, five in vital spots. Fusselman reported to the adjutant general that several people had witnessed the final shootout, and the inquest had shown him justified in the killing.[47]

On June 28, 1889, citizens in Presidio County asked King for help, and he directed Fusselman and his detachment to investigate the problem.[48] The Rangers were scouting for stage robbers near Shafter by July 1 and were out ten days on this scout, covering 220 miles. The day he returned to camp, a message from King sent Fusselman back down to Presidio after more robbers. Gone for nine days, he covered another two hundred miles and arrested two men. On July 22 he made a quick two-day ride into Brewster County after stage robbers, covering fifty miles.[49] At the end of July there were more calls for assistance from Brewster County, but the adjutant general could not send help because Fusselman and his men were already in the field and there were no free Rangers anywhere in the state.[50]

One of the biggest challenges for Fusselman and his detachment occurred in October at the silver mines at Shafter. Most of the trouble this time was racial, with the large Mexican and Hispanic miner population's clashing with the growing number of Anglos. Fusselman and his men rode down and managed to keep the friction from developing into open war.[51]

Towards the end of 1889, the district attorney for San Saba County petitioned for Ranger assistance to guard witnesses in some twenty murder cases. Even though the Rangers were hopelessly extended, King believed the trials were critical and shifted most of Company B from duty near the coal mines to guard the witnesses and protect the county's court sessions. The cases were not settled,[52] but this was the beginning of Ranger involvement with what was to become a notorious murder gang in San Saba.

Company D also spent some time attempting to alleviate election troubles in Roma, where politics along the Rio Grande were not only intense but also likely to be violent,[53] but they soon became embroiled in another voting war in a much older and settled county far to the east. Fort Bend County was similar to what El Paso had been during Reconstruction days with all Republicans in office. There were other striking similarities; in both counties the party bosses depended on large blocs of votes from minority populations to remain in office. The Republican Party ran the county with a firm and not always gentle hand after the Civil War. The area's crops were sugar cane and cotton requiring large labor forces, and the labor was still black with white overseers.

By careful manipulation of the large black vote, the party bosses had maintained complete control of the county and town offices, wisely filling some of the political jobs with black office holders but retaining the critical positions of sheriff and county judge for whites. White Democrats, who had the wealth and the property and the white majority but not the votes, had been unable to wrest power from the Republicans during Reconstruction. The long-simmering feud had developed a number of personal as well as political conflicts, and the Democratic "Jaybirds" were on a collision course with the Republican "Woodpeckers."

During the 1888 election, J.M. Shamblin, a Jaybird leader, was killed. Other Jaybirds were warned about trying to influence black voters, but a month later another Jaybird, Henry Frost, was shot and seriously wounded. Rangers were sent to the county and the election of 1888 was held without further violence, but the Republicans won again. The trouble had gone so far that no election could solve the basic rift in the community, and both sides made threats. On June 21, 1889, Kyle Terry, the Republican tax assessor, shot and killed L.E. Gibson in Wharton. A few days later Terry was killed by a Gibson's brother.[54] Captain Jones and seven Rangers went back to Fort Bend County on June 28 and stayed until July 10 when they returned to camp. Aten and three Rangers were left to preserve order.[55]

Once again it seemed a Ranger presence had brought peace, but it was only for a time and the Ranger presence did not eliminate the root causes of the trouble in Fort Bend. Aten and his men moved to Richmond, the county seat and the center of the trouble, where they were in another impossible situation. In most cases, the local sheriff and his deputies would have worked to maintain order, but in Fort Bend the sheriff, J.T. Garvey, was again part of the problem as the leader of the Woodpecker faction. Garvey told Aten he had not asked for Ranger help and refused to cooperate in any manner. The local judge, J.W. Parker, also a Woodpecker leader, stood squarely behind the sheriff, whose deputies were staunch Woodpecker partisans.[56]

The Rangers made a good try at keeping the peace. Aten and his men patrolled the streets of Richmond day and night. They refused to take sides, acted impartially to disperse crowds, and discouraged the open display of weapons. It was a troubled peace, and Aten probably had no illusions about the four Rangers' ability to maintain order for any extended period, but he kept on even after one of his men became too sick to walk.

On August 16 Aten rode out to their camp to check on a sick Ranger, who was despondent and wanted to return to their main camp near Uvalde. Aten promised he would try to get a replacement and sat and talked for a time until they heard a shot from the center of town. Aten hurriedly mounted and galloped to the courthouse where he believed the trouble would probably start. He was right. As the Ranger hurried towards the building, Sheriff Garvey and a number of armed men walked outside and waved him away, yelling to him to stay clear because this was none of his business.

Down the street a block or so away, the Ranger saw a crowd forming and rode towards them. Trying to quiet the threats, Aten rode between the two rapidly growing mobs. The other two Rangers joined him, but the three were caught between the growing scores of determined, angry men, now resolved to settle the Fort Bend political situation with gunfire. Someone from the crowd advancing on the courthouse fired a shot, and firing began all along the street. Within a few moments fighting spread across the town.

Aten yelled for his men to get clear; there was no way to stop the battle and no reason to be slaughtered in a senseless fight. He and one of the other Rangers managed to jump their horses across a barrier and escape, but then Aten saw Ranger Frank Schmidt lying out in the street. Despite the constant shooting from both sides, Aten managed to get Schmidt to relative safety and carry him inside a building. At first all he found was a severe bruise where a spent ball had hit the Ranger in the chest, but then he noticed a leg wound.

Outside, the battle in the streets continued for another twenty minutes in front of the courthouse and around the National Hotel and the McFarlane house. As word of the fighting spread, numbers of Democratic Jaybird supporters rode into Richmond, and the surviving Woodpeckers retreated. Sheriff Garvey and one of his deputies were dead; Judge Parker and another deputy were seriously wounded. On the Jaybird side, Aten reported that Henry Frost was killed and another man seriously wounded, but there were undoubtedly other injured whom Aten did not know about.

By sunset most of the civil officials were dead or wounded and the two uninjured Rangers were the only law in Richmond. Aten took over, telegraphed the governor, and requested the militia. At the time he had no way of knowing if any of the Woodpeckers would rally forces and return for another fight. On his own, he wired Houston for the Houston Light Guard and made arrangements with the railway to have a special train bring them to Richmond. This done, he and the other Ranger patrolled the dark streets of the town to prevent crowds from forming. About midnight, the militia company from Houston arrived and relieved the two Rangers.

At daybreak the following morning, the Brenham Light Guard reached Richmond, completely outnumbering the citizens, and the combined militia companies prevented any revenge being taken by the victors. Several of the Woodpeckers' black leaders had slipped away during the night, and the exodus of both black and white continued during the day. Governor Lawrence S. Ross and the assistant attorney general arrived by special train and conducted interviews with whomever could be found on both sides. The first priority was to find a new sheriff, and for once both sides agreed that another election was not wise.

Governor Ross suggested appointing Sergeant Ira Aten of Company D, the only man both factions would accept. Aten thus ended his Ranger service, resigning to become the appointed sheriff of Fort Bend County. When the governor boarded the train to return to Austin, he came close to an apology to the young Ranger for what had been done to him.

Corporal Robinson and four Rangers from Company D reached Richmond on August 16 to reinforce the acting sheriff, and Aten resigned on August 20 to become the official sheriff of the county. He did a fine job, with some help from Captain Jones who arrived on August 26 and assisted Aten in arresting twenty-three men on various assault and murder charges' growing out of the battle.[57] Aten did not remain in Fort Bend to run for sheriff after his appointed term was up. He married and went into ranching, but he again became a sheriff in 1893 in Castro County then worked for many years as manager of the ranch division of the famous XIT Ranch in the Panhandle.

Ranger Frank Schmidt was not so fortunate as Aten; his wound never healed. The state made a commendable attempt to defray his medical expenses, even sending him to St. Louis for special treatment, and Dr. Ferdinand Herff of San Antonio treated the Ranger for many months without submitting a bill. He was reported nearly ready to return to duty in 1890 and was retained on the Company D roll at full pay, but none of the measures was enough to keep Schmidt alive more than a few years.[58]

— 11 —

End of an Era
1890-1900

The Rangers began the last decade of the century just
as they had begun the previous decade of the eighteen-eight-
ies, by going where they were sent and doing what they were
told to do. No seer came forward to forecast a radical change
in Texas or to announce the end of an era and the final days
of the Frontier Battalion. Shrunken to three small companies, the force may have seemed on the road to oblivion, but
the cries for assistance from the Rangers were as numerous
as ever during the ten-year period, and with increasing
frequency requests came from the settled, interior counties,
forcing the small companies to send men on widely scattered
missions. Most operations would be by small detachments,
and increasingly involved only one or two Rangers.

The first shift in units was in March 1890 when Adjutant
General King moved Company D to Cotulla in La Salle
County. Company D, as noted earlier, had been in Uvalde
County with responsibility for La Salle, Uvalde, Edwards
and contiguous areas. It was little more than a transfer of
the headquarters and the camp because Captain Jones still
had only three men with him; the other eleven men were out
on assignments, the largest element with Sergeant Fusselman in the Trans Pecos.[1]

Sergeant Fusselman was the first Company D Ranger to
be killed in the far West. During April 1890 while in El Paso
in connection with a court appearance, Fusselman heard
about a theft of cattle outside town. The local sheriff was
tied up in the trial, so Fusselman decided to go after the
thieves and started out on the trail with one of the city's
policemen and several volunteers. The posse soon located
the tracks of cattle and horses near Franklin Mountain on

a trail heading towards New Mexico. Fusselman followed at
a fast pace, hoping to intercept the herd before the rustlers
crossed the state line, and broke into a gallop, the posse
close behind, when he spotted dust on the horizon.

As usual, the well-fed Ranger horse outdistanced the
others, and Fusselman was far ahead when he closed with
the six riders, pushing the cattle, who turned and opened
fire. Fusselman drew his rifle and returned fire, probably
believing his few supporters were nearby, but was struck in
the face and killed instantly. The small posse rode closer,
saw they were outnumbered, and returned to El Paso from
where some braver men went out to bring Fusselman's back
to town. Corporal John Hughes, the closest Ranger, rode to
El Paso when notified of the killing. Hughes learned the
name of the man believed to have fired the fatal shot and
began a search for the suspected killer but was called back
to the company by Captain Jones, who needed him for more
pressing work.[2]

For a time Fusselman's position of company sergeant
remained vacant, and corporals John Hughes and Bass
Outlaw shared the duties of attempting to maintain law and
order within a vast territory. The two were complete oppo-
sites; Hughes was the classic Ranger of popular legend,
large, impressive, fearless and a fine leader, Outlaw was
smaller than the average Ranger and rather dapper in dress
but completely fearless. Outlaw, however, could not drink;
when sober he was a perfect gentleman,

> but several drinks made a beast of him. When
> word got out that Bass was drinking, doors were
> locked, children brought in off the street and all
> of us kept silence and hoped for the best.[3]

It was a tragic flaw that would cost him his job and later his
life.

Continued trouble and the potential for violence caused
King to shift all of Company D to the Trans Pecos, and on
May 30 Captain Jones broke camp in La Salle and started
for Presidio County. The adjutant general left the choice of
location in the new area to Jones, depending on conditions
in the region.[4] Most of the company reached Marfa on June
1 but did not even get settled into their camp because there
was another call for help from Shafter. Jones hurried down

to the mine and stayed until he was satisfied there would be no more trouble for the time being.[5]

Moving Company D to Presidio County left a wide gap in the overextended Ranger forces. LaSalle remained a troubled area and was also a convenient location for dispatching detachments in all directions, so Captain Brooks and Company F were moved from the lower Rio Grande to La Salle where, as King reported, they had plenty to do.

> Large bodies of organized, well-armed and desperate characters were raiding the ranches and driving away stock in droves, and bidding defiance to the citizens and peace officers, or so arranging their wholesale thefts as to defeat all attempts at arrest and punishment. A special Ranger force had been organized....but this was not sufficient, and it required the presence of regular Rangers to afford any substantial relief.[6]

Company F still had the thirteen men with which it had begun the year when Brooks moved to Cotulla and set up his new camp as directed by King.[7] J.H. Rogers, now a sergeant, brought up the wagons and camp gear plus the remainder of the men. They began the usual unspectacular but effective scouting, sweeping the country to keep rustlers off guard. Late in May there were requests for help from Duval, and on June 18 Captain Brooks and four men began a forced march to Hidalgo where there were rumors the town was surrounded by invading Mexicans.[8] Fortunately the rumor was nothing more than talk, but the Ranger reaction demonstrates both the territory the companies were expected to protect and their willingness to take on any mission. At the end of 1890 King noted,

> Wholesale stealing has been stopped, but the thieves are still there, and the permanent or even temporary withdrawal of the Rangers will be the signal for renewed activity in lawless stock driving and stealing.[9]

During the year, Company B remained on duty insuring legal elections in January and February. In March, Company B Rangers were pulled from duty near the coal mines to protect court sessions in San Saba. In May, three Company B men were sent temporarily to Erath County to protect witnesses in litigation arising from previous strikes. September saw Company B Rangers working with New Mexico authorities to stop cattle thefts across the state border.[10] In October some of them were sent into East Texas to help the sheriff in Marshall recapture escaped prisoners; in the future more and more Rangers would be sent into the eastern counties.

Company D again occupied center stage in 1890 after a fight broke out in the Shafter settlement on August 4. Accounts of this riot are confusing—an army report drew sharp comment from King[11]—but details not in dispute describe a big dance at an Hispanic home in or near Shafter. The event attracted a mixed crowd, mostly Hispanic but with a sprinkling of Anglos. Ranger J.F. Gravis was at the dance, although it was never known if he was there in an official capacity. A fight broke out during the course of the evening, ending in a wild gun fight in which several people were killed. During or shortly after this fight, Gravis was shot and killed.

An army detachment reached the scene first, and the report of the lieutenant in command suggested that the Ranger had been at fault. Captain Jones heatedly denied Gravis' culpability and later filed his own report with King. Jones and a Ranger detachment arrived in Shafter and began rounding up suspects in the killings. He returned to Marfa on August 7 with seven men charged with murder. While he was gone, some of his men and a civilian posse had brought in another dozen suspects from the Marfa area, and the few Rangers guarding Marfa had arrested three men who were fleeing north from Shafter. It was believed a number of the people at the dance had come across from Mexico and had probably fled back across the river.[12]

The loss of Gravis was a severe blow; he had been a good Ranger and the small company could ill afford another fatality so soon after the death of Fusselman. With the company assembled in one location, Bass Outlaw was promoted to sergeant. On September 19 Outlaw and three other Rangers were sent to Fort Stockton to protect the court session, one duty led to another, and the new sergeant had to arrest the county sheriff who was roaring drunk and trying to murder one of the town citizens in a saloon.[13]

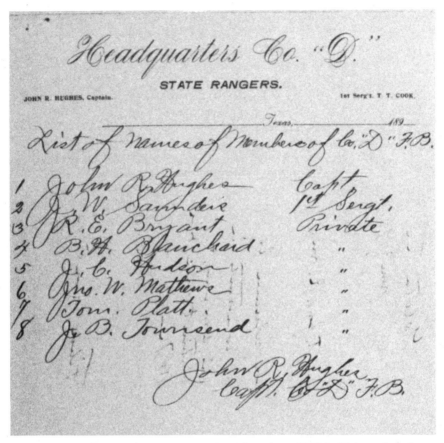

Roster of Company D, Frontier Battalion, late 1890s. This undated list of the members of Company D was evidently written by Captain Hughes and sent to Austin as an update. It is interesting, as it shows the letterhead adopted by Company D. There was nothing standard about the company stationery—each captain printed up whatever took his fancy. The memo shows how far the Ranger force had dwindled as the century drew to a close. Courtesy of the Texas State Library.

During the rest of 1890, Company D kept busy though without loss of life. A detachment was back in Shafter again in October and remained all month.[14]

Adjutant General King retired January 23, 1891, although he knew earlier that he would be leaving and mentioned it in his last report for 1889-1890, after serving almost ten years.[15] If he is not widely known or appreciated, it is not because he lacked skill or dedication to duty. King had a keen understanding of the legal requirements of the Ranger service, of the delicate balance required between the use of force and the letter of the law, and of the severe demands this balance often placed on the Rangers. His vision and understanding of what the Rangers were accomplishing, and the relationship of these accomplishments to the development of the state, was matched by few commanders and probably no elected official. He had begun his tour as adjutant general as a skeptic and ended as the Rangers' strongest supporter, backing them with his official power and personal loyalty. King was largely responsible for the development of the Special Rangers, civilians with what amounted to deputy sheriff powers formed to combat the outbreak of train robberies and assist the Rangers in scout duties, to augment the ever-smaller regular Ranger forces. King's detailed reports are a treasure trove for historians.[16] A line from his last report summarizes his career, ". . . I have worked earnestly and singly for what I believed to be the best interests of the State, its good people and its citizen soldiery, both Militia and Rangers.[17]

Woodford Haywood Mabry became the adjutant general on January 22, 1891, and was to serve with distinction although he had a different approach to the office. Ranger work during the rest of the decade did not change, but ascertaining their activities is more difficult during his administration because of a change in the way the adjutant general submitted his reports. Mabry abandoned the custom of detailed reports, the listing of special actions, and the summaries of arrests, scouts, *etc.* Instead, separate scout reports were sent to the adjutant general, and the monthly returns seldom contain much data other than strength figures. Interestingly, the Ranger companies began using printed letterhead paper during this period, although there was no standard format and each unit used whatever local printers could provide. The stationery is a considerable contrast to the reports of earlier days when company commanders wrote to Austin on whatever paper could be obtained, cheap notepaper or stationery obtained from a local business or county official.

Captain McMurry resigned as commander of Company B on the last day of January 1891,[18] and Governor James S. Hogg went outside the Ranger ranks to select a new commander. Hogg's choice was sound; William J. McDonald

Captain Bill McDonald. Photo courtesy of the Texas Ranger Hall of Fame and Museum, Waco, Texas.

had been both a Special Ranger and a peace officer, and he had made a considerable reputation as a deputy U.S. marshal.[19] A number of men actively campaigned for the position, including McDonald who traveled to Austin for a talk with the governor. There is a story that Hogg picked the ex-deputy marshal because of the numerous complaints he had received about McDonald while Hogg was attorney general of Texas; Hogg evidently figured any man who caused such outcry from criminal lawyers would be a good commander for a Ranger company.[20] Hogg sent McDonald up to join Company B in the Panhandle.

The new captain became one of the best known Rangers, a fortunate combination of skill and bravery who began as a captain and served throughout the rest of the decade and after. Many of his cases were high profile ones which attracted publicity; McDonald had a talent for phrase making and received good press coverage from the state's newspapers. As much as any Ranger, he was responsible for the fabled "one mob—one Ranger!"

McDonald's introduction to Ranger life occurred on his first night in Amarillo. Tired after a long train ride, he was sound asleep in his hotel room when a messenger delivered a telegram saying there was an Indian attack in Hall County. The startling news seemed unlikely to the new Ranger; it had been ten years since there had been serious Indian trouble in the Panhandle. Believing his men were playing a joke on their new commander, he went back to sleep until a second message arrived from a railway official whom McDonald knew and who was not one to play practical jokes. The Ranger dressed and went to the telegraph office and had the operator "talk" to the operator in Salisbury, the supposed site of the raid. The news seemed real enough; the operator in Salisbury was shutting down before the Indians reached town.

McDonald was not completely convinced, but he hurried what men he had in town onto a special train. When they arrived at Salisbury after daybreak they found the place deserted, its inhabitants' hiding in the fields and outlying farms. They began carefully questioning everyone they could and eventually decided the alarm had been given by a newcomer to the area. Riding alone the night before, the man had seen a group of "savages" dancing about a campfire and shooting guns into the darkness. Further investigation disclosed a group of cowhands, sobering up after a drunken party, who dimly remembered killing a cow and having a great feast around a campfire, with much shooting of guns.[21]

In the far southwest the Rangers of Company D were more successful than those of Company B's abortive chase after imaginary Indians. Scattered documents suggest an interesting story after Ranger J.M. Putnam filed a claim for his horse which he had been required to kill after the animal was injured in a fight the Ranger had with "Fine Gilliland, a fugitive from justice," on January 31, 1891. The same day Captain Jones signed an affidavit to the effect that he had instructed Putnam to kill the injured horse as an act of mercy, and the Ranger was entitled to "pay for same,"[22] but the claims for a lost horse fall short of telling what happened. Rangers Putman and Thalis T. Cook were out looking for Gilliland, wanted for the murder of H.H. Poe, a respected rancher, and found the wanted man northwest of Marathon, one of the new settlements along the railway. Gilliland saw the two riders and turned his horse slightly to pass them on the left, thus keeping his gun hand nearest the approaching strangers. Cook noticed he had drawn a pistol, concealed under a jacket piled atop his saddle horn.

The Ranger yelled a warning to Putman, and all three

men began shooting. Gilleland's horse was killed and he used the dead animal as a shelter. Cook suffered a bad leg wound, but both he and Putman maintained their fire until there was no return of fire from Gilliland. Putman approached cautiously with Cook's hobbling after using his rifle as a crutch, and they found they had killed the man.[23] Apparently, however, Putman's horse was wounded and had to be put out of its misery.

Company D remained busy throughout 1891 but did not engage in any major actions until autumn when Jones and a few of his men became involved in a major scout after train robbers who stopped the GH & SA on the great horseshoe curve near Sanderson, threatened and terrorized the passengers, and stole $50,000, one of the major thefts of the period. When Captain Jones received word of the robbery, he again had to react with whatever Rangers were on hand; a considerable detachment of his men under John Hughes was down in Shafter where the always volatile mine situation was again in need of Ranger peacekeepers. Jones went to the scene of the train robbery with what men he could spare. The trail was cold, but they did find tracks leading towards the Rio Grande about twenty miles to the south. Jones with five of his Rangers and five civilian volunteers had more than enough men to handle the robbers who had made the five sets of tracks they were trailing. For five days they crossed and recrossed the river following the trail; the country was uninhabited and the Rangers could enter Mexico without causing another international incident. On the sixth day they spotted a lone rider who was evidently a sentry because he turned and galloped towards the dense cane break that bordered the river.

Jones and his group ran after the man to the edge of the cane, but his lead was too great and he vanished into a tunnel cut through the dense thicket. The Rangers were too sensible to ride into an ambush; Jones spread them along the edge of the cane and set the thicket on fire.

As the fire destroyed the cane, steadily decreasing the cover and concealment, the officers closed in and found the camp, but the robbers had changed horses and escaped down the river. Jones' horses were too exhausted after the long, dry chase to make any effective pursuit. The Rangers found several saddles and other camp gear in the hastily abandoned camp; scattered about were documents and letters' identifying the gang leader as John Flint. Jones rode slowly back to camp and reported on the unsuccessful chase, careful to note that there were no settlements where he had entered Mexico.[24]

Jones was patient, kept his agents busy, and in time received word while in El Paso concerning a possible location for John Flint and his gang. He again had only a few Rangers, but they boarded a freight train and headed for Del Rio. Seven volunteers joined the Rangers at a train stop for water in Comstock, and from Del Rio the posse rode north into Crockett County and caught up with the gang in a ravine near the present town of Ozona. In a brief battle, two of the robbers were killed and another three wounded and captured. Another man was shot but managed to mount a horse and make a run for safety. The Ranger horses were fresh this time, and they ran him down after a seven or eight-mile chase. Seeing he was cornered, the man halted and shot himself. The Rangers buried him as best they could and rode back to the others.[25] The dead man turned out to be John Flint, who had just made out a will, before the fight, in which he said nothing about the loot from the train robbery. None of the money was found in any of the camps abandoned by the robbers—they evidently buried the money somewhere along the way—and men have been searching for it to this day.

Life in Company D during the early 1890s was not always this exciting. Alonso Van Oden joined the Rangers in early 1891 and began keeping a journal, one of the few Rangers to record his actions and thoughts on a daily basis. Early in his service he wrote that Ranger life was boring rather than the wild adventure he had thought. Chasing and arresting a twenty-year-old boy for making love to a girl, for example, was not his idea of real rangering.[26] In another incident a girl ran to his quarters in Ysleta requesting help for a woman who was being beaten by her husband. Van Oden sent her for the sheriff, who should have been taking the necessary actions, but went to the nearby house and found a German man severely beating a woman, evidently his wife. The poor woman's clothing was torn, her face swollen and bloody. The Ranger pulled the man away from the victim and knocked him down, but the woman jumped at her erstwhile rescuer, cursing and scratching and kicking. The husband rushed over and tugged the woman away from Van Oden, but she began to scream at the Ranger that he should never interfere with a man's beating his wife—it was his right. When the shaken Ranger left the house, outside he found half the population of Ysleta all laughing at his plight.[27]

In the continued fluctuations that marked Ranger funding, additional money became available during the summer of 1891 and a fourth company was reactivated as Company E in San Antonio on June 15, 1891. Again the governor selected an outsider for company commander, J.S. McNeel who had been a deputy U.S. marshal and a Special Ranger of some reputation. McNeel worked quickly, recruited fourteen men, and started for his new station west of Corpus Christi near Alice on June 20. They selected a suitable site and named their new station Camp Mabry in honor of the adjutant general.[28]

In short order they were required to react to troubles near the small settlement of Realitos, southwest of Alice where, although most of the ranchers and townsfolk welcomed the Rangers, the operations of a small number of smugglers were endangered by the lawmen. Smuggling had been a way of life and a profitable business in the area, where there was nothing between Realitos and the Rio Grande except open, sunburnt brush country. McNeel kept a detachment busy around Realitos during September, the smugglers and their confederates scattered, and most of the Rangers moved back to their camp near Alice.[29]

McNeel left two Rangers in Realitos to support the local lawman, Constable Evans. Believing the town free of lawmen other than the constable, a group of smugglers rode into Realitos and began shooting up the place, yelling "Send out the God Dam Rangers!" One group rode to within fifteen feet of the two Rangers and Constable Evans, who ordered them to surrender. The startled smugglers tried to fight, two of them were killed instantly, and the others fled. A telegram wire brought McNeel and the rest of the company, but the danger was over at least for the time. Although he may have been a new captain, McNeel handled the situation in Ranger fashion.

> I made the Mexicans a talk up there and told
> them that this had to stop or some good Mexicans
> would visit the other world. They all promised me

to behave and to give us information should anything turn up.[30]

McNeel cooperated with his nearest Ranger companions, Captain Brooks and Company F, for the next few
months. In December, both companies became involved in
what has become known as the Garza Trouble, instigated
by a man of considerable talent. Catarino Erasmo Garza was
a native of Matamoros who had moved to Texas at an early
age and returned to Mexico for schooling. Garza worked as
a clerk and sold Singer sewing machines for a time, but his
real skills were in writing and politics. By 1884, when
Porfirio Diaz had been in power in Mexico long enough to
make enemies, Garza had returned to Texas and began
working for a newspaper, writing a series of articles attacking the dictatorial president.

Garza had his own paper in Eagle Pass a year later. In
1890 he married the daughter of a wealthy rancher and
moved to his father-in-law's ranch and started a new publication. By now he had attracted wide attention as a
champion of everyone with a grievance against any level of
the Mexican government. An able speaker, Garza advanced
beyond the level of a newspaperman with a cause, changing
from newspaper crusader to active revolutionary. By the
summer of 1891 he was plotting with liberals in northern
Mexico, and it was a short step to raising an army in Texas.
Very likely, many of the people who joined him were moti-
vated by revolutionary zeal, but a goodly number were
border ruffians out for whatever plunder might be available.
Adjutant General Mabry tended to class all of the Garza
partisans in the latter category.

> From the apparent profit which smuggling
> offers, it seems to be a fruitful source of crime
> against the Mexican government. These smug-
> glers are citizens of Mexico who know the de-
> mands of, and the methods to reach customers
> in, the interior. They are outlawed by the Mexican
> government, and fights are frequent between
> them and the Mexican soldiers. From hatred of
> these troops, and the fact that they are shown but
> little quarter in battle, they are always ready to
> join issues under the banner of any revolutionary

leader who promises to create trouble on the border. They are material for ready draft to any movement of the Garza character.[31]

Garza easily attracted about two hundred men to his call for revolt. There were no state laws against such recruiting, and although the army watched his actions with interest, he had not violated any federal statutes. Moving southward, Garza collected his troops in Starr County and began an invasion of Mexico. He was a wonderful orator and a skilled writer, but he had no concept of military operations. Crossing the Rio Grande near Camargo, the mob advanced sixty miles into Mexico in complete disorder, and no one paid any attention to it. Garza, or someone in his motley crew, finally realized the danger of their situation, and they fled back into Texas.[32]

Garza had initiated a series of events that he could not control. Still the visionary, he made two more futile river crossings, but his "revolution" degenerated into a series of bandit raids. Diaz sealed the border, and his soldiers killed any revolutionaries they captured. Garza's little army turned bandit with a series of horse thefts for which, as early as December 18, McNeel's Rangers were after them. They were also scouting for Garza, now classed as a common criminal. A Company E scout chased two of the thieves a hundred miles and captured them.[33]

On December 22 an army patrol had a fight with some of the bandits and a Corporal Edstrom was killed; the bandits were scattered but most escaped into the brush. This action brought the army into the fight, and most of the 3rd Cavalry was thrown into the chase. On January 5, 1892, a considerable force from Fort Ringgold collided with the main bandit gang near the little settlement of La Joya on the banks of the Rio Grande, but most of the bandit-revolutionaries were again able to scatter through the brush and escape across the river or into the thick cover. Garza was in the fight, escaped, and was never seen again in Texas.

Just before the army's fight, McNeel was moving south; the killing of Edstrom had brought back the Rangers to join the army in the chase. The Ranger had been in San Antonio in late December, but Mabry wired him to return and start for the border. McNeel instructed Corporal Dowe to collect his detachment in Cameron County and meet him in Rio

Grande City.[34] By December 27, Company E was moving south to "arrest murderers of Capt [sic] Edstrom." They rested at Concepcion before continuing towards Ringgold, had a brief skirmish with some of the outlaws on December 29, and reached Fort Ringgold the next day.[35]

Company F was also alerted, reached El Penia on January 1, 1892, then moved to the vicinity of Roma. Captain Brooks took Sergeant Rogers and went into town to confer with Sheriff Shely, with whom the Rangers would work closely during the next few weeks.[36]

The Rangers, and often the army, tried to check out each rumor of bandit raids and Garza's hiding place. One seemingly authentic report had a large bandit force at Havana Ranch, so Troop C of the 3rd Cavalry and Company E, joined by Captain Brooks and Sergeant Rogers of Company F and Sheriff Shely, went to check the place. The combined force scouted for two days in the heavy brush and found an abandoned camp, but their slow movement through the dense undergrowth had alerted the bandit sentries, and the outlaws escaped, many on foot, but with the loss of twenty horses, ten saddles, an army mount and much camp equipment.[37]

This was the beginning of a close working arrangement between the Rangers and the army. Although the army had broken up the main body of the bandits, the job of tracking down the scattered bands fell to the Rangers, a mission well suited to the Ranger organization. In this work they received valuable logistical support and intelligence from the army. Diaz had sent large forces to close the Mexican border, forcing the Garza partisans to flee to Texas, and there is little doubt the refugees would have pillaged the southern counties of Texas had not the Rangers maintained a relentless search along the river.

The threat was enough to bring Adjutant General Mabry from Austin, where he "visited the field in person, and for two weeks assumed immediate command of the two Ranger companies."[38] Mabry makes considerably more out of his presence than the facts support. Scout reports of the two companies show McNeel and Brooks met Mabry in San Diego and accompanied him to Corpus Christi, arriving on January 21. Neither captain mentioned what was discussed during the time they were with the adjutant general, but their men continued to work together. Brooks went with

Mabry to Laredo, while McNeel returned to his unit. On January 30 Brooks and Mabry sent Private Musgrave and another Ranger to Nueces County to check out a possible lead.[39] If he did not have the impact his reports suggests, Mabry did understand the difficulties facing his Rangers.

> The situation was a peculiar one, and the obstacles to a successful raid at one dash were nearly insurmountable. The resident population of the interior was composed entirely of Mexicans who claimed citizenship in Texas, but were with singular unanimity in sympathy with the Garza movement....they would, at first, harbor them secretly, act as spies, and notify the revolutionists of any approach of rangers or United States troops....[40]

Not all Texans of Mexican descent sided with the bandits. Although they may have had initial sympathy for the idea of ousting Diaz, the ardor of many cooled when the revolution changed to bandit operations of horse thefts and forced food requisitions. A number of Hispanics served as scouts for the Rangers and some joined the companies, especially Company E. Both units increased their strengths during the emergency. J.S. McNeel, Jr., visited his father's camp during the start of the trouble, while Mabry was there, and the adjutant general suggested that the young man be signed up. McNeel mentioned the companies were expanded at this time.[41]

During his visit to the camp Mabry was saluted by the Rangers, who had borrowed an old cannon from the King Ranch. They loaded the piece with loose powder and stuffed a mesquite chunk down the barrel. When the charge was set off, there was a terrible roar and the chunk sailed through the air, scaring some passersby half to death. McNeel recalled Mabry was quite pleased with the salute.[42]

February 1892 was quiet as far as contacts went, but the Rangers never ceased scouting through the brush. Company E logged 1,488 miles in the saddle and reported "the cooking & camping utensils are all wore out."[43]

March was an even more active month for both companies and saw the complete collapse of the bandit movement. Unlike the army, the Rangers never quit and there was no time when detachments were not out searching the brush, checking on rumors and visiting known or suspected sympathizers. Even a hint of an outlaw camp or gathering would bring a large Ranger force, and they began arresting known supporters and suppliers of the outlaws.

During early March Sergeant Rogers and seven other Rangers from Company F worked with Company E on a four-day scout trying to find the main bandit camp, but there was no longer a main force to find, only bandit groups because the fugitives were afraid to assemble in large numbers. At the end of March, McNeel's men found seven large camps, recently abandoned, in which there had been an effort to settle, with wells dug and some huts erected.[44] Although the army left the scouting in the brush to the Rangers, they did continue to cooperate, furnishing supplies and shifting troops to form blocking units in attempts to catch the bandits in pincer movements.

The Garza Trouble attracted national attention, and a number of famous men came to the area to report on the fighting and scouting; Richard Harding Davis and Frederic Remington were two who visited the "front." It was not always a front-page war, and some of the reporters undoubtedly embellished their copy; McNeel told Mabry to read everything with caution, because he had not talked with any of the writers.[45]

On March 20 Company E arrested a man for aiding Garza, and the following day they caught others and shot one who refused to surrender. It was not all one-sided; on March 22 Ranger E.E. Doaty was killed in a skirmish with some fleeing outlaws. On the same day another sympathizer was arrested. Captain McNeel and a Ranger detachment arrested five men on suspicion of aiding the bandits on March 24. They had the prisoners in tow and were sweeping the brush and checking isolated houses and ranches when they received word an outlaw band was trying to slip into Mexico. Unable to keep the prisoners on a forced march, McNeel turned them loose and made a run for the river, but it was another false alarm.[46]

Captain Brooks also kept his company busy. On March 26 one of his Company F Rangers had a fight with two bandits and managed to break free and return to camp. The following day Sergeant Rogers located the trail and tracked the two men until March 30. He and Lee Hall, who had joined the chase as a volunteer, caught up with the two fugitives, brothers Jose and Pancho Ramirez, who had been charged with killing Corporal Edstrom. Tough border *bravos*, they refused to surrender and Jose was slain; Pancho managed to escape on foot into the brush. At the end of the month, Mabry directed Brooks to join forces with McNeel to search for a reported bandit camp in Duval County.[47]

There was no camp, and the Garza Trouble was about over. The constant Ranger scouts had prevented the bands from reforming, their arresting or watching known supporters had eliminated any support, and most people eventually made the distinction between a revolution of patriots and victimization by bandits. As Mabry claimed in his report, the Rangers, though few in numbers, had prevented major looting and killing without a large outlay of special funds. Mabry estimated a quarter of a million dollars would have been spent if the militia or regular troops had been engaged during the entire period.[48] Both companies returned to their stations and continued routine duties until the end of the year.

Sergeant Bass Outlaw, mentioned earlier by Van Oden as a fine Ranger when sober but dangerous and unreliable when drunk, evidently was drunk on numerous occasions in 1892. The final straw was a big drunk in Alpine late in the year, and Jones decided it was time to stop Outlaw before he hurt or killed someone. Because of his often-excellent record, Jones allowed Outlaw to resign on September 18, 1892, without any punitive action, and John Hughes was promoted to fill the sergeant's vacancy.

In December 1891 Captain McNeel was discharged. The Ranger had done fine work, and his replacement by Sergeant J.H. Rogers has never been satisfactorily explained. In some of his reports to Mabry, McNeel seemed to be concerned that his conduct might not meet with favor, and he asked the adjutant general to advise him if necessary. It seems he was worried about conversations he had held with reporters. Whatever the cause, it was not a normal change of command.

McNeel's son mentioned the discharge in his memoirs, with the notation that the entire company resigned in protest,[49] but the monthly return merely states NcNeel was replaced by Sergeant J.H. Rogers of Company F.[50] The muster and pay roll however, indicates the entire member-

Company E. Front row (l-r): McMurry, Judge Dubose, Frank McMahon.
Middle row (l-r): John Nix, Capt. J.H. Rogers, Tupper Harris, unknown.
Back row (l-r): Augie Old, C.L. Rogers, Kingsberry, Townsend.

ship of Company E was discharged at their own request on December 31, 1892.[51] Rogers had been an outstanding enlisted Ranger and was probably known to many of the Company E Rangers, but they nevertheless evidently believed their captain had been slighted and quit. The resignation of an entire company and its replacement within a month was a unique event in Ranger history.

When newly promoted Lieutenant Rogers assumed command of Company E on January 1, 1893, he was the lone member of the unit. The next day he enlisted Tupper Harris as sergeant, on January 5 he signed on six more, and by the end of the month he had the full fourteen authorized strength for duty. Only one man from the old company reenlisted, and he remained less than a month.[52]

The chase after Garza had received most of the publicity, and the Rangers of Company D were functioning less conspicuously and without newspaper headlines. Sergeant Hughes had been sent to the silver mine at Shafter to learn who was stealing ore. Cooperating with the mine officials, he began a careful investigation and, early in his mission, saw a miner he recognized as possibly being a former Ranger. The man was Ernest St.Leon, nicknamed Diamond Dick by his fellow miners. Although Spanish-speaking and married to a Mexican woman, St.Leon's sympathies and duty were to Texas. Hughes met secretly with him and devised a scheme, involving considerable hardship for St.Leon and possible danger, to discover who was robbing the mine. Hughes managed to have the man fired from the mine, using the pretense that St.Leon was discharged because he was married to a Mexican and, pretending outrage, St.Leon and his wife left Texas and went to live in Mexico.

Over a period of time St.Leon became friendly with the actual robbers and learned that mine workers in the gang selected choice silver ore and hid it in an abandoned tunnel. When enough ore was collected, members of the gang in Mexico came up at night with burros and hauled the ore across the river. St.Leon was able to warn Hughes when the next raid was planned.

Hughes managed to have Ranger Lon Oden join him on the night the raid was scheduled. The two Rangers waited outside the abandoned shaft in bitter weather before they heard the sound of approaching animals. St.Leon was with the robbers but managed to stay well back. Ordered to halt, the approaching men opened fire; in the confusing gunfight in the dark, St.Leon was able to join the Rangers and the three of them killed the would-be robbers. No one came to claim the bodies, and Hughes buried them atop a slight hill. It was probably assumed that St.Leon was also killed; Hughes had a place already selected for him far from Shafter and the man simply vanished for the time being.[53]

Captain Jones and a few men were stationed in Langtry, but the rest of Company D was scattered all over the Trans Pecos. The little settlement of Langtry would not seem to have been large enough to cause trouble, but April and May of 1893 were busy months for Jones, and he had serious doubts about the order he received to move to El Paso County.

Ysleta and San Elizario again required watching. Jones must have been in contact with someone in El Paso because he was well aware of the tense situation in the county where some of the old Salt War participants were active again.

Since he was married to George Baylor's daughter, his father-in-law could have been the source of his information. Jones was afraid the few men he could take with him would not be able to accomplish anything and expressed this opinion in a letter to the adjutant general, saying only four men would probably be murdered by the fifty or more outlaws who were causing trouble,[54] but the decision to move the company, such as it was, to El Paso County remained in effect. Sergeant Hughes had a detachment in the Alpine district and could not be moved, and some men had to remain in Langtry, so when Jones left Langtry on June 14, 1893, he had only eight men with him. It was a permanent shift of camp, and he took his wife and daughter with him.

The Rangers wasted no time after reaching their new station. Corporal Carl Kirchner and three men made a reconnaissance scout to an area called Pirate Island looking for any of the Olguin family known to live in the region but found no one.[55] The so-called island was a piece of land cut off a half-century earlier by a flood of the river, leaving a strip of land six miles deep and several miles long north of the river. By international treaty the area was a part of Mexico, but Mexican authorities hesitated to cross the river to patrol the place and Texas officers had no legal jurisdiction. As a result, several hundred lawless people had a secure base for whatever criminal activity they chose.

The leading family on the island was headed by Clato Olguin, too old to do much riding but with three sons to carry on the family business. One of the sons, under indictment and on the Rangers' list, was the object of Kirchner's first scout. Two days later the Rangers were back again with Captain Jones in command. With him were Corporal Kirchner, privates Tucker, Aten and Saunders, and Deputy Sheriff R.E. Bryant, probably as a guide. They camped during the night below San Elizario and, at first light, entered the Olguin quarters where the old man was home alone. He was very old, almost blind and not on any wanted list, so they left the settlement and started downriver to see if they could locate any of the others. The patrol crossed and recrossed the old river bed several times. Even Sheriff Bryant, who knew the country, was not exactly certain about the national boundaries.

Later in the morning the Rangers saw two riders who

started to run when they saw the lawmen. The area was covered with heavy brush and cactus, hiding several low adobe buildings where the two riders dismounted and took shelter. Kirchner galloped up, leading the chase, and a shot hit the magazine of his rifle, jamming the weapon. The two men had plenty of help in the houses; shots were fired from every building. As they galloped up to the buildings, Saunders was behind Kirchner with Aten next in line firing his revolver. Jones was next, firing his rifle.

The first three Rangers ran between the four buildings and out into the brush, then turned and galloped back, seeing Deputy Bryant to one side. Jones followed, but opposite one of the buildings he was hit in the thigh. The shot broke his leg and knocked him from his horse, but somehow he managed to straighten out his leg and keep firing while lying in the dirt. Tucker was near and asked if he was hurt.

"Yes, shot all to pieces," Jones muttered just as he was hit again near his heart. "Boys I am killed." He was dead, sprawled on the ground as firing continued all about him.[56]

The fight stopped when the bandits were able to slip away into the cover of the brush. Two of the Olguins may have been hit, probably others in the houses were wounded, and there must have been considerable confusion among the bandits to cause them to leave the heavily outnumbered Rangers and run. Deputy Bryant, who had time to check his bearings and possibly talk to someone who remained in the settlement, was beginning to worry; they were clearly in Mexico and close to other settlements.

In his report, Kirchner said his first thought and duty was to remain with his dead captain and kill or capture the men who killed him, but this was clearly impossible. They did remain for almost an hour but recognized they could be cut off and surrounded if they hesitated any longer. Tucker had lost his horse in the fighting, probably when he dismounted to check on Jones, and they had to carry him double on another horse. There was no way to remove Jones' body. A dispirited and angry group of Rangers returned to San Elizario but could not obtain a single man to join a posse to go back for Jones or follow the outlaws.

Kirchner wired Hughes in Alpine, and the sergeant came down as quickly as possible to assume command of the company. A considerable amount of international wrangling and diplomacy took place before Mexican authorities in Juarez returned Jones' body, his personal effects, and Tucker's horse and saddle on July 1.[57]

Ranger Van Oden's journal contains an entry concerning the death of his captain. Although he was not in the fight, he evidently talked to those who were because his account agrees with the official reports. Van Oden, however, has some details that are not mentioned elsewhere. The prompt return of Jones' body and effects was due to unusual cooperation by the authorities in Juarez; the Mexicans had suffered as much trouble with the Olguins as had the Texans. Colonel Martinez, the commander in Juarez, had been awakened at midnight by the El Paso sheriff and told of the fight, and by seven the next morning a strong Mexican force had surrounded the Olguin settlement and captured all the family.

Van Oden noted the extensive newspaper coverage of the fight and of the death of the Ranger captain. Jones was universally praised, and for the most part reporters and editorial writers castigated the legislature for the economy moves that had reduced the force to such low levels, blaming them for the loss of Jones. There is little doubt the small size of the companies played some part in Jones' death, a fate he had foreseen.[58]

Officially at least, that was the end of the tragic story. In his biography of Hughes, Jack Martin has an interesting summary of the actions taken by Company D to avenge the death of Jones. Martin states that Hughes brought St.Leon back from cover and had him operate along the river, disguised as a Mexican. St.Leon located the Olguin brothers and killed two of them; the third fled into Mexico. Having located eighteen men who had taken part in the ambush that killed Jones, Hughes then began systematically hunting them down and captured or killed all of the wanted men within six weeks. None of this, however, can be officially documented, but as a reward for his services, Hughes did enlist St.Leon as a Ranger.[59]

Sergeant Hughes signed Company D's monthly report for June which had been started by Jones. By the following month he was signing as captain of the company.[60]

Matching reports with events that may or may not have happened is not always easy. Early adjutant general reports generally showed at least the numbers and often the names of men killed or wounded by the Rangers, but Mabry stopped this practice and only occasionally included tabulated information in his rather brief reports. Neither were actions always listed in the company scout reports or in the monthly returns, and there were undoubtedly actions that never received any mention. Even a diary is not always a reliable reference; Van Oden's was not a day-by-day journal with entries by specific date. Only when he mentions a Ranger by name, or describes an event that can be documented, can specific times be placed on many of his entries. His indefinite date-keeping in no way detracts from the value and interest of his diary, in which the descriptions of the countless hours spent crawling about in the brush, the waiting, the inaction, and the scouts that caught no one, interspersed with bits of violent conflict, give a rounded look at all aspects of Ranger life.

In one of his entries Van Oden describes a scout after a wanted man in a place on the river known as the San Antonio colony. It was a simple enough job, the man was caught without any trouble, and before they started the long ride back to Marfa the Rangers stopped at a store for some refreshments and watched as several men tried to load a drunk on his horse. Someone said the man was Florencio Carrasco, a man on the wanted list for murder, horse theft and other lesser crimes. The Rangers went outside and started towards the men, who abandoned Carrasco and ran for the Rio Grande. Not as drunk as he seemed, the wanted man dismounted and opened fire, killing Van Oden's horse, but he was shot and killed in the return fire. The incident occurred on the riverbank, and a crowd began to gather on the opposite shore. The Rangers obtained another horse, took their prisoner, and started for Marfa at a deliberate pace, initially keeping to the trail. Well outside of sight they left the road, such as it was, and cut across country to avoid a possible ambush.[61]

Other entries in Van Oden's diary show he was based in Ysleta, El Paso, Shafter and Marfa; he mentions scouts down to the Rio Grande and as far east as Emigrant Crossing on the Pecos near old Fort Lancaster and 240 air miles from El Paso. He makes no mention of rail travel. Although not all of his entries can be specifically documented elsewhere, they do illustrate how much territory the small company of Rangers patrolled on horseback.

The decade of the 1890s was primarily a time of individual actions and scouts by small detachments rather than the larger company sweeps of earlier days. It was the only way the small units could even begin to handle all the requests for help, and most of the time each company had men scattered all over the state with few left in camp for major emergencies. A random check of monthly returns shows one company with six men in camp and five detached; another company had only five in camp and ten men out on various missions. The fact that privates could go out and handle their missions without supervision was a tribute to the Rangers.

The single Ranger, however, was very vulnerable, especially if acting undercover. In the summer of 1893 Private J.W. Woods, who had enlisted in Company E on January 31, was sent on a secret assignment to Menard County to work with the sheriff on cattle theft cases. In July he simply vanished, his body was never found, and the three months pay due him was never claimed.[62]

The transfer of Company D to El Paso County had left a wide gap along the Rio Grande that had to be filled by the men in Company F. Langtry, little more than a train stop but on the river with a customs house and a deputy collector, continued to be a trouble spot for the Rangers. The only settlement's passing for civilization for many miles, it attracted cowhands looking for a drink, passing riders, and a great many smugglers. It was also the home of Roy Bean and his combination of saloon and courthouse.

On July 5 Mabry ordered Captain Brooks to send a detachment to reinforce the Customs Service at Langtry, and Sergeant Musgrave and two Rangers left by rail. There was plenty to do; by July 11 they had arrested Charles Small for smuggling and hauled him to jail in Del Rio, and a number of other men were caught for stealing cattle and turned over to the U.S. marshal.[63] Small did not spend much time in jail and was soon back in Langtry.

There was talk that a gang of rustlers led by Charles Small would soon raid the nearby Simmonds and McCormich ranches; instead, Small attacked the Rangers. F.A. Cunningham, the deputy collector in Langtry, believed the fight with the officers was an attempt to instigate a bloody conflict between the three Rangers and ten to fifteen armed men to destroy the peace officer detachment and open the

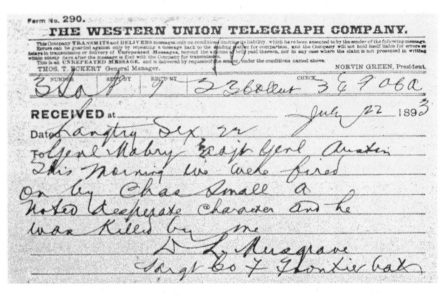

Form No. 290.
THE WESTERN UNION TELEGRAPH COMPANY.

THOS. T. ECKERT General Manager.   NORVIN GREEN, President.

RECEIVED at _____ July 22 1893

Dated Langtry Tex 22

To Genl Mabry Adjt Genl Austin

This morning we were fired

on by Chas Small a

noted desperate character and he

was killed by me

D L Musgrave

Sargt Co 7 Frontier Bat

Report of Sergeant D.L. Musgrave. This is one of the classic Ranger reports. Musgrave wanted to keep the Adjutant General informed of events—but saw no need to bother him with unnecessary details. It also illustrates the use the Rangers made of the telegraph, first the Army system between posts, and later the commercial Western Union. Courtesy of the Texas State Library.

way for large-scale rustling. If so, it failed. All versions of the fight agree Small had been drinking during much of the previous night. He made an attempt to take a revolver from Lewis, one of the Rangers, and was shoved away. Evidently the Rangers believed he was a harmless drunk, and he managed to enter the Ranger quarters, find a rifle, and fire a shot at Lewis and Sergeant Musgrave who had walked over to see what was happening.

Small started running, and both Rangers fired at him with their revolvers but missed the moving target. Small stopped and tried to fire, but the Winchester was empty so he ran back inside to look for another weapon. Lewis stayed by a water tank while Musgrave ran to get his rifle. Small soon returned with a second rifle and saw Lewis at the water tank trying to reload his revolver. He ran towards the tank, but Musgrave returned with his own rifle and fired quickly, wounding Small who wheeled about and managed to get off a wild shot. Musgrave shot him again, but the badly injured Small still struggled to lift the rifle and shoot. Musgrave took careful aim and shot the man through the heart.[64] The sergeant's report was brief, "This morning we were fired on by Chas Small a noted desperate character and he was killed by me."[65]

Musgrave must also have wired his company commander, because Captain Brooks telegraphed Mabry to report the shooting and saying he could go to Langtry with one man if necessary.[66] Customs collector Cunningham sent a copy of a newspaper clipping to Mabry and explained the part he and his men had played, a factor that may have cooled the spirits of the waiting rustlers, "all credit is due to those rangers here but do believe that the force should be augmented by at least two or three others[;] it would doubtless have a tendency to over awe those outlaws."[67] There were not enough Rangers to augment the force, however, and Mabry was hardpressed to keep the three men in Langtry and had to recall them in September.

The Trans Pecos region continued to be a primary source of trouble for the Rangers. Company D lost another man in April 1894 in a strange grouping of men, Rangers, ex-Rangers and men with Ranger connections who met in an encounter in the always dangerous alleys of El Paso.

John Selman had been the object of Ranger searches and attention earlier in Fort Davis but was no longer on the wanted lists; he was now serving as a constable in El Paso. By all accounts he did a commendable job. Bass Outlaw, discharged as a Ranger for uncontrolled drinking but who had cleared his name, was now employed as a deputy U.S. marshal and was also in El Paso, with his boss and former Ranger Dick Ware now the U.S. marshal for the Western District of Texas. Also in town in connection with court appearances were Ranger Joe McKidrict and Ranger McMahan from Hughes' Company D.

During the morning of April 6 McKidrict gave testimony before the grand jury, was dismissed, but was instructed by the jury foreman to remain close by because they might wish to ask additional questions. The Ranger walked to a nearby printing shop where he had friends; while there he heard a police whistle and ran outside thinking an officer needed help. In the street he heard shots and went towards the sound.

McKidrict saw Outlaw on the back steps of the leading brothel in El Paso, drunk and belligerent, holding his pistol, threatening everyone and trying to go back inside. The whistle had been blown by one of the establishment's ladies, who used it to bring police help when patrons became drunk or too angry to listen to reason. From inside the house Constable Selman heard the whistle and ran to the back to investigate; he approached the back steps at about the same time McKidrict came in sight.

Ranger McKidrict evidently recognized both Selman and Outlaw and must have assumed Outlaw was just having some drunken fun. He began to talk to Outlaw, trying to calm him down, and walked between the men but for some reason turned his back on Outlaw. It was a fatal mistake; the drunken little deputy marshal raised his pistol and shot the Ranger over the left ear, killing him instantly. Outlaw shot him again as McKidrict fell face down. Selman rushed up and Outlaw snapped a shot at him, missing but powder-burning Selman's face. The former outlaw did not make the same mistake as had the trusting Ranger; he shot Outlaw above the heart. Despite his wound, Outlaw was again able to shoot at Selman, this time hitting him in the leg and putting him out of the fight.

Outlaw managed to climb down the stairs and walk a block up Utah Street where he met Ranger McMahan. The Ranger ordered him to surrender, which Outlaw did, then McMahan and a passerby helped him into a nearby saloon where he was placed on a bed in a back room. Despite the location of the wound, Outlaw lived for another four hours. Captain Hughes rushed to El Paso, conducted a full investigation, and arranged for the burial of McKidrict. Outlaw, for all his faults, had enough friends to see he was given a decent burial.[68]

Selman, who recovered from his wound and remained as a peace officer in El Paso, would figure once again in Ranger-related matters; on August 19, 1895, he murdered John Wesley Hardin in the Acme Saloon in a quarrel over one of the local ladies for hire. He was himself killed on April 5, 1896, by Deputy U.S. Marshal George Scarborough in a dispute over a card game.

The year 1895 was such a quiet period in Ranger history that it is not even mentioned in the adjutant general's report. Van Oden has an interesting entry, which must have been from this time because it appears shortly after his account of the death of McKidrict and Outlaw, which illustrates that the Ranger legend, and the misconceptions of Ranger life, were already well established in Texas' historical lore. Van Oden, a literate man who attended plays and read a great deal, wrote of his displeasure incurred by a play, evidently in El Paso, depicting Ranger life. In the play all the Rangers were big men who swaggered about with revolvers offering solace to every young girl they met; Oden had been in service long enough to know a Ranger's life was a hard one with few comic moments.

Shortly before he attended the play, he had returned from a scout trying to find Mexican raiders who had been active along the border. The outlaws made no national distinction, killing and robbing on both sides of the Rio Grande. One day a dozen of the raiders rode onto an isolated ranch and demanded food. The owner of the ranch and his young son were in the main house; a Mexican ranchhand was working in another building. After cooking for the men, the ranch owner tried to explain he did not have any money, but most of the outlaws were drunk and kept demanding money. The ranchhand walked over to look through a window and almost fainted as he watched the bandit leader hack off one of the rancher's arms to make his demand clear. There was no money, but it did not save the poor man's other arm. They smashed the unconscious man's head and then cut the boy's throat. The ranchhand managed to slip away for a horse and rode for help. The Rangers were too late to catch the raiders and could only trail them to insure they had fled into Mexico.

Van Oden, fresh from this chase, had trouble matching the romance of the play with the reality of life in West Texas. He feared the image, not the reality, would remain and wrote, "In years to come, these atrocities will be forgotten, and people will think of us as dull-witted hypocrites."[69]

During the early 1890s, the Rangers in Company B were generally overshadowed by the more dramatic actions of the other three companies; McDonald and the men of his small company kept busy, but they did not become involved in the major cases that would later make McDonald a household name in Texas. The company was stationed in Amarillo with responsibility for the Panhandle, which contained roughly twenty-five thousand square miles. For several years McDonald and his men moved from one part of this vast land to the other, generally on scouts after cattle thieves of which there are few mentions in the records.

One common feature of many of these chases, however, was the almost total lack of cooperation by elected peace officers; prisoners they had captured were released before the Rangers were out of town, and few of the men they caught ever came to trial. In disgust McDonald even bent the law; on several occasions he defied the local sheriff and kept prisoners in confinement or moved them to places where a fair trial was possible.[70]

Although not mentioned in the adjutant general's reports, there was a major shooting incident in 1895 that almost cost McDonald his life. According to his biographer, the Ranger prevented John Pierce Matthews from joining a secret society of which McDonald was a member, beginning a series of events that progressively convinced Matthews the only way to restore his pride and honor was to kill McDonald. He was an accomplished marksman and began sending word to his foe that he was coming to Quanah to kill him, but his plan to unnerve the Ranger was not successful and McDonald kept on about his work.

In December 1895 Matthews felt confident enough to enter Quanah with several friends. After drinking through most of a dreary winter day, Matthews sent word that he wanted to make peace with McDonald. The Ranger walked out to the designated place, where he saw Matthews walking slightly behind the sheriff and several other men. Matthews fired at the Ranger over the sheriff's shoulder; McDonald stepped to one side and shot Matthews twice above the heart but hit a notebook and a plug of tobacco under the man's coat. Realizing something was wrong, McDonald shifted his aim and fired again.

The duped sheriff had dropped to the ground, and both McDonald and Matthews fired again. McDonald leaned over and was hit in the left shoulder, the bullet driving down through his body, but was able to fire again, this time dropping Matthews. The other two men with Matthews fired several rounds, one disabling McDonald's arm and lodging in his neck. He lifted the single-action revolver, trying to cock the weapon with his teeth, but the other two assassins turned and fled.

The first help on the scene believed the Ranger had a mortal wound, but when a doctor arrived McDonald instructed him to remove the slug in his body and let the neck

Company D, Frontier Battalion, 1894. The photographer is unknown. This small group shows how the Ranger companies had shrunk in the mid 1890s. Captain John Hughes is seated on the stool. On his right is Sergeant Carl Kirchner. A Mexican prisoner is seated on the extreme left, front row.

Texas Rangers, El Paso, 1896. These are the Rangers gathered in El Paso to stop a boxing match. Most of the Frontier Battalion is posed on the steps of the Court House. By 1896, financial problems had reduced the "Battalion" to the size of an earlier company. Note the "town" dress of the Rangers. Front row, left to right: Adjutant General Mabry, Captain Hughes, Captain Rogers, Captain McDonald, Captain Brooks.

wound alone for the time being. This was done, to please a dying man, but McDonald refused to die although he remained in a hospital bed for two months before continuing his recuperation in a sanatorium. Matthews was not so lucky and died within a few days.[71]

McDonald was on his feet, though far from well, when the Rangers were called to perform one of the strangest duties in their long service. Men who had served as irregular cavalry in the U.S. Army, invaded Mexico after rustlers, fought Indians and entire counties of troublesome whites, faced down gunfighters and acted as undercover detectives chasing fencecutters, suddenly found almost their entire battalion called to El Paso to stop a boxing match.

In early February 1896 Dan Stuart, a sports promoter and gambling hall owner in El Paso, attempted to stage a boxing match for the championship of the world and brought Bob Fitzsimmons, the champion, and Pete Maher to the Texas city to stage a bout. Today it is hard to understand the furor this promotion caused. Prize fighting had not been illegal in Texas until the governor persuaded the legislature to pass an act outlawing boxing in the state. There was considerable opposition to holding the fight in El Paso, mostly from church groups, but a substantial number of the gambling fraternity was just as determined to see the fight was held.

The upcoming bout became the subject of widespread newspaper coverage in which Stuart milked the event for every possible angle. He offered free tickets for reporters who promoted the fight in their stories and refused tickets to those who wrote unfavorably of his efforts.[72] There were reports that Bat Masterson, the celebrated buffalo hunter and gunfighter, was on the way to town with up to 150 gunmen to see that the fight took place. Masterson did show up, alone, but large numbers of gamblers, gunmen and sharpies of every description flocked to El Paso looking for victims or out of curiosity.

For a time there was considerable movement of the ring equipment and the fighters, from place to place as Stuart ostensibly attempted to stage the fight, but this activity was probably nothing more than an attempt to build interest. Adjutant General Mabry, however, was worried the fight might be held and ordered Captain Rogers to send some of his Company E Rangers to El Paso to ascertain the situation;

he feared the Company D men would be known to the sporting fraternity. On February 3 Rogers sent Sergeant Harris and Private Ross to El Paso to see if the fight location was known. They were not to identify themselves to anyone other than Captain Hughes. Four days later, on orders from Mabry, Rogers enlisted three new men and started them toward El Paso, where they arrived on February 9.[73]

The governor also ordered the other three companies to go to El Paso, and Mabry personally went to the scene to take command of the operation.[74] Thus, practically the entire Ranger force was deployed for several weeks to stop a prize fight, almost the strength used to halt the Garza Trouble, leaving the rest of the state to fend for itself. During this time, the average company had seven or eight men.[75] An interesting photograph taken on the court house steps shows Adjutant General Mabry, the four captains and the enlisted men of the battalion, thirty-one officers and men in the only picture ever taken of the entire unit.

Mabry had a Ranger team's watching each fighter and his camp, not bothering anyone but shadowing every move and making it impossible to sneak away and hold the fight. Stuart declared he would not hold the fight in Texas because there was no neutral ground, but fighting in Mexico was impossible because the governor of Chihuahua had refused permission, and holding the bout in nearby New Mexico had also been ruled out by the U.S. government. Stuart was in a tight fix; the city of El Paso, largely the gambling community with some of the business leaders, had raised $10,000 to have the fight in or near the city, and Stuart and others had considerable money invested, largely in bets. It was absolutely necessary to stage the fight.

In the meantime, everywhere the fighters or any of the promoters went, the vigilant Rangers accompanied them to much complaining about infringement of liberties and freedom of action. Rangers not assigned to follow the fighters helped the local police to maintain order; Sergeant Sullivan, who had come out with Company B, patrolled the streets with Constable Selman and considered the populace to be the toughest crowd he had ever seen.[76]

Even the officers were busy; Captain Hughes arrested a man suspected of swindling but the man was soon released on a bond signed by a notorious, red-light district figure. The constant patrols by the Rangers maintained order in El

Paso without being overly intimidating, and their presence was appreciated by that portion of the business community alarmed by the influx of potential troublemakers. On February 18 Rogers and one of his men, working with two deputies, arrested and jailed four men for robbery.[77]

The fight was finally scheduled for February 13, but neither the fighters nor the ring attendants could escape their Ranger shadows and Mabry continued the close monitoring until February 20. At one point it was announced that Pete Maher had an eye problem, delaying the fight, but the physician in attendance said he had not even seen Maher.

Suddenly, on February 20, Stuart loaded a special train with the fighters, attendants, officials and as many fight fans as had been able to obtain tickets, and headed east accompanied by about twenty Rangers. When business leaders learned the fight would be held outside El Paso, they petitioned Mabry to keep some of the Rangers in town, fearing the three banks would be susceptible targets if all the Rangers departed. Mabry, well aware of the volatile situation, retained eleven Rangers in El Paso, a wise precaution which kept El Paso quiet.

The train ride was calm enough, the large Ranger force a considerable inducement for orderly deportment. The train traveled east to Sanderson where there was a stop for food since the special did not have dining facilities. Many of the passengers were eating in a small cafe where Bat Masterson became irritated at the slow service and threw a "table-castor" at a Chinese waiter. McDonald, at another table, cautioned him, and Masterson asked him if he wanted to "take it up." The Ranger quietly replied, "I done took it up!," and that was the end of the altercation.[78]

In the 1890s before the construction of the high bridge over the Pecos, the train tracks passed right by Langtry, and here the train stopped and the passengers dismounted to wait while the ring was unloaded and set up on Mexican soil. Bean's saloon undoubtedly did a thriving business during this pause. The ring was set up on a small island in the Rio Grande; the river bed has shifted but the hump of this island can still be seen north of the present channel. The Rangers remained well back on Texas soil, despite the stories that they were present at ringside during the fight. Fitzsimmons' win by a knockout surprised few at the fight.

With the fight finally held, spectators and Rangers scattered. It was probably the largest crowd ever assembled in Langtry, and many of the men were unable to return to their homes until after other trains arrived from east or west. Company E boarded a train and arrived on February 22 in San Antonio, where Rogers left a sick man in the hospital before again scattering his company throughout South Texas in an attempt to catch up on long-overdue business. He took five Rangers and rode to Alice; two men went to Karnes City; Sergeant Harris traveled to Sinton to appear in court and then returned to Karnes City. Private Rogers had to go to Beeville to stand trial for killing two Mexicans in a chase after stolen cattle in 1893, but he and another Ranger were acquitted. Captain Rogers learned his man in San Antonio was seriously ill and returned to the hospital to care for the Ranger personally and insure he did not lack for medical attention. All this activity was accomplished during a week's time.[79]

Companies D and F returned to somewhat similar conditions and duties, but Company B became involved in a major scout, before they had reached their home camp, while riding the train towards Wichita Falls where a bank robbery had taken place; an old Ranger antagonist named Kid Lewis had decided to rob the City National Bank at noon. With a helper known only as Crawford, he entered the bank and demanded money from Frank Dorsey, the teller, who refused to hand out any money and was murdered. The two robbers then began shooting at the other men in the bank, wounding the bookkeeper and hitting the vice president whose life was saved by a small case of surgical instruments inside his coat which deflected the bullet. Afraid the shots had alarmed the town, Lewis grabbed a small bag with about six hundred dollars in currency and ran out the door.

The robbers were barely on their horses and heading for the edge of town before shots were being fired at them by a disorganized group of mounted men in pursuit. In the running fight Lewis' horse was killed, but he stole another and the two robbers managed to escape. When their horses gave out, they stole two big Clydesdales from a farmer plowing a field and lumbered towards the Wichita River. For some unknown reason, the pursuing citizens stopped to organize a formal posse; by the time they had done so Lewis and Crawford had disappeared in the brushy area along the river.

Someone in the town was aware that Rangers were on the train presently nearing Wichita Falls and wired news of the robbery to the station below. When the train stopped and Captain McDonald read the message, he wired for horses to be waiting at the station. The Rangers arrived at the town at about two in the afternoon and in short order McDonald and five Rangers were galloping down the road taken by the robbers and the posse. McDonald's horse slipped and fell at a muddy creek crossing, covering the captain with mud and some degree of embarrassment, but they continued on and met the returning posse. The civilians told the Rangers where they had lost the trail and continued towards town, but they shortly turned about and followed the Rangers. In a river bend, the lawmen found the abandoned farm animals and believed the robbers must be near.

At this point, the two main accounts of this chase[80] begin to differ in some of the details. Paine's account, written from talks with McDonald, states that Sergeant Sullivan broke a stirrup while riding up to the horses, fell, broke a rib and had to leave the chase. Sullivan, who has an extended version in his memoirs, does not mention that he was injured.

The day, however, was ending and the light failing as the Rangers tracked the robbers through the brush. The trail led back to the riverbank, where it was clear the men had waded across to the opposite side, and twice more the trail crossed the river and forced the Rangers to wade through the icy water. The tracks indicated the men were trying to reach the border between Texas and the Indian Territory, and McDonald called for one of his men to obtain what help he could and block a road that led north to the border. Unknown to the Rangers, the robbers were close enough to hear his instructions and turned back, heading for a creek that ran parallel to the river.

By this time it was dark but with a bright moon. Some of the posse members saw the fugitives crossing an open field, fired, and were fired upon in return. McDonald, in a farm house drinking coffee, heard the shooting and borrowed a horse to ride towards the firing. The posse members told him what had happened and that the robbers were still near, but none of the men would go with him for a closer look. McDonald's nephew, Ranger McCauley, and Ranger McClure joined McDonald and the three Rangers moved cautiously through the brush and trees.

By good tracking and some luck, the three soon noticed two men beneath a large tree. McDonald motioned the two Rangers to spread to either side and started edging towards the resting men. He called for them to surrender, and the robbers dropped their cocked pistols into their laps and raised their hands. When McDonald approached he saw they had a row of cartridges atop a log, prepared for a battle. The other two Rangers closed in from either side, and the chase was over.

Sullivan has a less-dramatic account in his book; he said the Rangers all came upon the robbers at about the same time and cornered them. He agrees Lewis and Crawford were holding cocked revolvers but suggests they were not awed by McDonald, merely too smart to take on three Rangers. Both storytellers agree the prisoners were returned to Wichita Falls and placed in jail. McDonald, rightly suspecting there would be a mob out to avenge the death of the popular bankteller, did not want to take the men back to Wichita Falls but said he was talked into doing so. The Rangers had trouble forcing their way through the big crowd and placing the prisoners in jail.

From here on, there is considerable dispute about the actions of the Rangers. McDonald had faced down an angry mob to put the men in jail and had every reasonable expectation that the deputy sheriff who was the jailer could protect them, but he still believed it wise to move the prisoners to a safer location. The district judge, however, notified him not to do so because the move might cause more trouble. Sullivan said the Rangers actually guarded the jail all night and the next day before departing for Amarillo after the town seemed quiet with no crowds or demonstrators.

The judge asked McDonald to remain, but McDonald had witnessed the swearing-in of twenty-five men as jail guards and had every reason to believe they could protect the jail so he decided to leave. The night they departed, a mob broke into the jail and hanged Lewis and Crawford from telephone poles near the scene of the robbery and murder. There was an outcry about the Rangers' having left the men to be lynched, and the adjutant general asked McDonald for a full report. The Ranger's version, which included some comments about the judge, was the official end of the matter.[81]

There was a final note; the Wichita Falls banks paid a $2,000 reward for the capture of Lewis and Crawford, and the gallant members of the posse divided the reward into thirty shares and generously allowed the Rangers a portion.

In the final months of 1896, Company B became involved in a major case in San Saba County where, for a number of years, the Rangers had attempted to prevent and solve a series of over forty murders. The breaking up of the gang that dominated the area was a notable Ranger achievement, but it was also another example of the thinly disguised rivalry between McDonald and Sergeant Sullivan that resulted in differences in their reports of the events.

Sullivan opens his story by stating, "In 1896 I was ordered by Governor Culberson to go to San Saba and put down the mob that had existed there for sixteen years." He mentions that he had been in the county before and knew many of the people involved. On this trip, he took Dud Barker from Company B. The various companies were so short of manpower that no one unit could handle the assignments, and Captain Rogers sent Allen Maddox and Edgar T. Neal from Company E, all to be under Sullivan's command. The four Rangers had a wagon and team supplied by the county, and Sullivan wrote that the state furnished him a cook. The detachment, after covering many miles to reach their destination, camped outside town at Hanah's Crossing on the Colorado River.[82]

In his account, Sullivan never mentions his captain but does provide keen observations on how the killer gang developed. He believed the mob started many years earlier as a vigilante force to preserve the peace and slowly changed into a force that dominated the entire region. After a time, the leaders of the gang found they could obtain almost anything they wanted by the simple process of killing those who opposed them. They gained ownership of much valuable property by making low offers and then murdering the owners if they refused to sell; some people fled the county and abandoned their homes and farms. By the time Sullivan arrived, the gang controlled the sheriff, the local judge and all other elected officials. Honest people were too frightened and too unorganized to stand up to the mob, but some were not too afraid to write secretly for help from the Rangers. Sullivan stops his account at this point; although he has a few brief accounts of other events in later chapters, he relates nothing more concerning actions that finally broke the gang.

In McDonald's account of the events, soon after arriving Sullivan almost participated in a gunfight with the sheriff for rearresting a man the sheriff had turned loose. The district judge stopped the shootout before it started and sent the Ranger to locate some witnesses who could help make a case against the gang. The men did not exist, and the wild goose chase kept Sullivan away for an extended period of time.[83]

In early 1897 McDonald arrived to take charge of the investigation. He spent some time becoming familiar with the situation and arranged to have Sullivan come back to town. The sheriff, when he heard the sergeant was returning, said he could not remain in the same town with Sullivan, so McDonald suggested the sheriff leave.

McDonald still had to become familiar with the players and was in his hotel checking mail when he heard gunshots. He rightly suspected the gang members were making a show for his benefit and traced the shooting to a saloon. The Ranger entered the saloon and disarmed the crowd inside, telling them to appear the next day for examination. They complied and were duly discharged, their weapons returned. On the surface it seemed the gang still controlled the law, such as it was, but it was the first time anyone or any group had faced down a sizable part of the gang. This event was a critical break in gang dominance and undoubtedly led to secret cooperation from those honest citizens who still remained in the community.

Sullivan's detachment had gained an idea of how the gang operated, and McDonald built on this knowledge. The gang held monthly meetings at an isolated spot called the Buzzard's Water Hole, and the Rangers hid in the vicinity and learned passwords and future plans and identified gang members. They also managed to learn about a former gang member who might be willing to testify against the gang. McDonald began a campaign of psychological warfare mixed with force when required. Rangers rode to the homes of gang members at night and yelled out the passwords, then disappeared before the gang member came outside expecting to find friends.

One of the major players in the gang, Bill Ogle, wanted for the murder of a man named Jim Brown, was selected for special treatment. When Ogle was with several friends, McDonald walked him out into the middle of a street and told him the Rangers knew all about his part in the gang and in the recent killing. Ogle's friends remained back while McDonald told the now-frightened Ogle that he was going to be tried for murder. In a final act of humiliation, Ogle became so frightened he could not stand and slumped down in the dirt. The message was clear. Later when Ogle tried to escape from his house, watching Rangers arrested him.

A final effort to show gang dominance occurred when Ranger Barker was outside the court room while McDonald was talking with the district judge, who had been making every effort to discredit all witnesses against the gang. A man armed with a rifle came up and attempted to kill the Ranger, but Barker shot him five times before he could fire. Barker was promptly cleared.

Despite legal maneuverings by the district judge, Ogle was finally brought to an examining trial. The legal fighting continued for some time, but a number of people were now willing to testify and the man was held over for trial without bond. The case was moved to another county, where an unbiased court and jury found him guilty and sent him to prison for life.

The actions against the San Saba murder gang were the highlight of Ranger activities from late 1896 to the outbreak of the Spanish American War in 1898. The length of time the Company B and Company F Rangers were in the area is indicated by the number of them who fell in love with San Saba girls and returned to marry them; eight ex-Rangers who had served in the county came back and married and settled down. When honest elections were held, a slate of good men assumed office. Edgar Neal of Company F was elected sheriff and served for eight years. With a capable, honest sheriff backed by seven other ex-Rangers, San Saba became another law-abiding Texas county.[84]

By any standard, W.H. Mabry made a good adjutant general. Only the historian's lamenting Mabry's sparse reports would fault him; despite his praise for the force, Mabry seldom entered specifics into his reports, other than brief summaries of arrests and the like, and his only detailed accounts are of actions he supervised such as the Garza Trouble and the El Paso boxing match. As had King before him, Mabry grew in the job and came to have a deep respect and understanding for what the Rangers were accomplishing. Although his chief concern was with the extensive militia force, he continued to support the small Frontier Battalion in every possible way. It was, after all, the Rangers who faced some form of trouble every day wherever they were located; militia units could exist for years facing nothing more arduous than summer encampment. Nevertheless, the majority of the adjutant general's funds went to the militias, and the ranging peace officers had to make do which what could be spared.

Mabry often mentioned the difficulties of funding and made a good case for the Rangers' more-than-paying their own way through the taxes generated in areas they protected.[85]

> The amount of taxes paid to the state for the last fiscal year in those unorganized counties and other counties along the border line, which is almost exclusively policed by frontier forces, is $302,928, without including taxes paid to the counties....it is not believed that the above sources or revenue would remain intact if the frontier force and the protection it offers was abolished.
>
> The organization of the ranger force, with the duties they perform, acts as a restraint against any such condition above named. They are circumscribed by no county limits, can easily and rapidly move from one section to another, and criminals do not care to invite their pursuit. Specially equipped for continued rapid movement, they take up the trail and follow it with the persistency of the sleuth hound, until the criminal is either run out of the country, captured or killed.

In what was almost a review of events that would take place in San Saba, Mabry continued,

> Again, in the sparsely settled but organized counties it is frequently the case that a lawless

element hold the balance of voting power, and
officers are elected who are friendly to them and
collude at their depredations. Factions are created, and it is only the rangers that preserve the
peace, restore order, and offer the necessary protection. They represent the majesty of the State,
and belong to no faction, and merely their presence often prevents bloodshed, and peace and
quiet are restored.[86]

Unfortunately, a Ranger presence was not an automatic
prevention of bloodshed. On August 16, 1896, a detachment
of Company F led by Sergeant Cartwright investigated a
town disturbance after reports of someone's shooting a
pistol while under the influence of alcohol. The Rangers
trailed the unknown celebrant to a saloon and found the
wanted man was J.M. Morris, sheriff of Reeves County. The
Rangers, unaware the man was in a drunken stupor, walked
up behind him believing he was merely enjoying some
innocent, if loud, fun. When Sergeant Cartwright approached, Sheriff Morris wheeled about and started firing.
Cartwright drew his pistol and killed the sheriff, but when
he turned around to calm the crowd Cartwright discovered
Ranger T.P. Nigh had been killed by Morris' gunfire.[87]

The following month, Company D Rangers were the ones
to be involved in a gunfight. On September 24, J.B. Gillett,
who was ranching and serving as sheriff in part of his old
territory, informed the GH & SA Railroad that there were
some suspicious men camping in the Glass Mountains and
possibly waiting for a chance to rob the trains. The line
superintendent asked Captain Hughes, who did not have to
worry about county boundaries or possible motives, for
help. Hughes loaded Rangers Thalis T. Cook and R.E.
Bryant, with horses and a pack mule and supplies, onto the
next train and headed for Alpine. In town the Rangers were
joined by Deputy Sheriff Jim Pool and two civilian volunteers, one of whom had lost a prize stallion to unknown
thieves.

They rode to the Glass Mountains, east of Alpine, and
on September 27 cut a trail, leading northwest out of the
hills, which they followed towards the distant Davis Mountains, dimly seen through a heavy rain. According to the
monthly return, they rode for some eighty miles on this trail,

well into the Davis Mountains, and reached the McCutchen Ranch in a valley, now the route of Texas Highway 17, on September 28. Hughes, afraid his party of armed men and the tell-tale pack mule would identify them as Rangers, assigned each of his Rangers to one of the ranchhands and had them check the countryside in pairs that would cause no alarm.

In one of the side canyons Ranger Cook and his ranch-hand companion rode up to two armed men who told them to go back or they would be killed. Cook acted as if he thought the men were joking and asked if they were serious. The men began cursing him and said there were seven guns aimed at them; Cook pretended to be frightened and hurried to a sheltered spot and halted. He informed his companion they were going back to confront the two men; the cowboy, however, had merely come along for the ride and all Cook could obtain was a promise to ride for help while he stayed to watch the canyon in case the men tried to run.

Cook waited for what seemed a long time then started back but ran into Hughes and several men's galloping to his support. The two Rangers discussed what to do as they rode back towards the canyon. Suddenly, shots were fired from the top of a small hill to one side.

The two Rangers and the several civilians started up the incline, exchanging fire with three men atop the hill, and were able to ride up the gentle slope to the crest. One young man named McMaster was not even armed, but he kept up with the others, dismounting at the top. Two of the despera-dos were killed during a stubborn fight on top of the hill; the third managed to hide in some boulders, slide down the reverse slope, reach some hidden horses and escape.

A bullet hole through the hat of a civilian named Coombs was the extent of damage among the posse. Young McMas-ter, a guest at the ranch, picked up a pistol, cartridge belt and holster's belonging to one of the dead outlaws; he probably had some tall tales to tell when he returned home to a quieter life. Hughes sent back to the ranch for a buckboard and had the bodies taken to Fort Davis for an inquest and proper burial. Hidden nearby were a number of stolen horses, including the lost stallion.[88]

Adjutant General Mabry resigned May 5, 1898, to serve in the Spanish American War. He was followed by A.P. Wozencraft, basically an interim administrator but one who returned to the previous system of reporting, compiling tables showing battalion activities and providing considerable detail on events during the reporting period.

The first weeks of the war were filled with rumors of imminent raids across the border resulting in heavy demands for militia units and Rangers from every section along the Rio Grande. Although there was no increase in funding, the companies were shifted nearer the river and each captain was authorized to bring his company up to twelve men.[89]

It has become popular to castigate Porfirio Diaz for being a dictator, but he could keep peace along the border when it was in his interest. Wozencraft credits the Mexican president with aborting any planned raids into Texas, and the border became so quiet that the Ranger companies were returned to their regular stations. On June 15 each unit was again reduced to eight men.[90] The cost of the movements and the pay of the additional men had cut into the always-limited Ranger funds, and strict economies were necessary to fund the battalion through the rest of the year. Nevertheless, the Rangers made 951 arrests during the two-year reporting period 1897-1898 and traveled 135,833 miles.[91]

During 1897-1898 there was only one incident involving a Ranger fatality when Ernest St.Leon, once again a member of Company D, was in Socorro on August 20, 1898. In company with a deputized civilian, Dr. Breaux, he investigated a drunken disturbance in a saloon and arrested three cowboys for disturbing the peace. It must not have been a serious situation, because St.Leon decided to release the men. Just what happened is unclear, but the two lawmen and the three cowhands evidently got drunk together. Without warning the three men opened fire, killing Dr. Breaux and seriously wounding St.Leon. St.Leon was moved to the Ranger camp in Ysleta on August 29 and to El Paso the next day. Despite the better medical care in the city, he died on August 31. What happened to the three cowboys is unknown.[92]

The Rangers were involved in two disparate actions during March 1899 involving different sections of the state. In one case, McDonald exemplified the motto "one mob, one Ranger"; the other incident was a classic shootout in Laredo.

For several years the Reece and Townsend families had engaged in an old-fashioned feud in Colorado County; the streets of Columbus had seen gun duels on occasion. The death of an innocent boy during one of the senseless fights was too much for the townspeople; a call went out for Rangers, and Company B was ordered to send three men to the scene. McDonald alerted two of his men and ordered them to meet him in Columbus, then he boarded a train and traveled to the scene alone. After arriving, he reported to the district judge, noting several groups of armed men in the streets.

The judge could not believe McDonald had come by himself; he thought at least twenty-five Rangers would be needed. McDonald assured him he would have two more men by the next day, but he wanted to stop the fighting before it developed and suggested they go back to the courthouse. When they entered the courthouse square, McDonald saw the Reece faction to one side and what he presumed to be the Townsends on the far side. The two groups were disorganized but clearly preparing for a fight.

McDonald and the judge went inside and climbed the stairs to the top floor. It came as no great shock to learn Sheriff J.C. Burford was a member of the Townsend gang and was now out in the street helping his faction prepare for battle. The Ranger walked over to a window and yelled, "J.C.Burford!" three times until the surprised man left the square and came inside. McDonald introduced himself and suggested the sheriff stop the needless killing about to take place, but Burford said none of the men would listen to him. McDonald replied that he himself would disarm the mob, and the sheriff yelled for his friends to join him.

Obeying the sheriff's call, the Townsend men came inside and climbed to the top floor. Without anger, fear or haste, McDonald talked to them calmly, without threats, and suggested they store their weapons in a wardrobe in the room while he disarmed the Reece group. The men thought about it and placed the guns inside the wardrobe, which McDonald locked before he left to confront the Reece gang.

As he had with the others, McDonald calmly explained there was no need for guns; the governor had sent him down to preserve the peace, and he wanted to secure their arms just as he had with the Townsend weapons. One dissenter's refusal earned him the Ranger's rifle muzzle in his neck and a threat of jail. The leader of the faction suddenly called it all off and told his people to surrender their arms. McDonald walked them to a nearby store where their guns were locked in a secure place, and both groups dispersed quietly. Next morning, the other two Rangers arrived, and the three were rather conspicuous about town for some time and then returned to camp.[93] The account as reported by the adjutant general is quite undramatic.

> During the month of March, 1899, Captain McDonald and two men were ordered to Columbus, Colorado County, for the purpose of preventing trouble between the Townsend and Reece factions. Captain McDonald went alone, his men not being able to meet him in time, and his courage and cool behavior prevented a conflict between the two factions.[94]

McDonald had prevented trouble, at least for the moment, but he had not removed the cause of the trouble and Rangers would be back to prevent the two groups from resuming the feud.

Small pox was common along the Rio Grande—1899 was an especially bad year—and trying to vaccinate people brought on another of the odd jobs given the Rangers. The outbreak was so severe in Laredo that the state's health officer went to the city to supervise the vaccination program. He found the largely Hispanic population had never had the necessity for vaccination explained to them and held a widespread fear of the new technique and of the idea of quarantine. When Doctor Blunt decided to move a number of sick people from their homes to quarantine sites, there was armed resistance, doors were locked and barricaded, arms were collected and loaded. City police made no effort to help the doctor, and on March 19 a riot broke out when several hundred people fired on the police.

Doctor Blunt's call for Ranger assistance brought Captain Rogers and Ranger A.Y. Old to Laredo. The two Rangers worked with the county sheriff and managed to restore some semblance of order, but it was a temporary calm. It was clear there would be major difficulties in placing any number of people in quarantine, so Rogers wired Sergeant H.B. Dubose at Cotulla to obtain whatever men he could from Company E and join him in Laredo as soon as possible.

On March 20 Dubose and two Rangers arrived in town

*Company E. Left to right, H.B. Dubose, John Moore, Will Old,
J.H. Rogers, Bell, Augie Old, Frank McMahan*

and were sent by Rogers to a hotel to rest and await
developments. With his men settled, Rogers and Old joined
city officers in a search through the eastern part of town
where there had been reports that arms were being hidden.
At one location there was trouble when the owner, Agipito
Herrera, resisted while a number of other men attempted to
slip away down an alley. Ordered to halt by the Rangers,
two of the men surrendered. A third man opened fire and
was hit by the Rangers but managed to slip through the city
police and vanish. The police made no effort to help the two
Rangers.

Herrera managed to find a rifle, returned with several
armed friends, and shot Rogers in the shoulder. In the
ensuing confusion, the two Rangers shot Herrera in the
chest and head and a woman and another man were
wounded. The men with Herrera lost heart and fled, but the
neighborhood women were not afraid and began cursing the
two Rangers and throwing stones at them. It was an impossible situation, and the Rangers retreated. Somewhere in
the confusion, Old was separated from Rogers and took no

part in the following events.

Hearing the firing, Sergeant Dubose and his men left the hotel and began running towards the fight. He met Rogers, going for medical assistance, who waved them on and continued towards the hospital. Dubose and the two Rangers continued up the street and saw a crowd of a hundred men, many with rifles, standing around a body which the Rangers presumed to be Old's but which was probably Herrera's. Some of the men in the crowd opened fire on the Rangers, who never stopped, firing as they advanced towards the mob. The steady advance and the falling bodies completely unnerved the mob and there was a rush for shelter. The Rangers found four wounded men in the street and captured four more injured outside town. It was the end of the Small Pox War; Adjutant General Thomas Scurry, who had replaced Wozencraft after serving as adjutant general less than nine months, said in his report that, "After this the work of moving the small pox patients to the hospital was an easy task."[95]

One of the interesting features of the last years of the Frontier Battalion is the number of times they had to work in the old, settled counties. While McDonald was quieting the Reece-Townsend feud, a multiple murder took place near Athens in Henderson County, deep in the heart of East Texas, where three members of the respectable Humphrey family were lynched.

Athens was a law-abiding town with capable officials, but the lynching occurred in a wild section of land between the Trinity River and Cedar Creek where law was little more than a name and where moonshiners and petty criminals lived in complete immunity from peace officers. Decent people in the Bottoms were in the minority and survived only be keeping quiet; the Humphrey family had settled there because it was all they could afford.

After a group of unknown persons took Humphrey and his two sons to a massive tree and hanged them from a large limb, there were suspicions that the Wilkerson family, led by Joe Wilkerson, was responsible for the vicious lynchings, but those who had taken part kept silent. County authorities were incensed at the brutal slayings and asked for help from the governor, who wired McDonald to investigate. Barely home from Columbus, the Ranger headed for East Texas where he found all county officials willing to support his work fully. The governor also sent the assistant attorney general, N.B. Morris, to help with the case.

It was the kind of job McDonald, who later made a reputation as a man "who would charge hell with a bucket of water," did best; his greatest skill was in detective work. He had patience, a keen sense for tracing every lead, and the courage to crash head-on into any obstacle in his path, if that became necessary. The Ranger captain had arrived in Athens before the evidence around the lynching tree had been completely destroyed by time and weather, and he found five sets of tracks. One trail led to the Wilkersons' settlement, confirming suspicions but not definite proof.

McDonald had been joined by Ranger Old, and for two months they patiently questioned scores of people, gradually chipping away at alibis and promising protection to those willing to testify. The Rangers obtained a good idea about the composition of the lynch party, and many of the guilty men suspected they had been discovered but were afraid to run, since flight would be an admission of guilt. Instead, they waited for the Rangers to tire and leave the area as other lawmen had done. McDonald, however, never slackened; each day he held his interrogations under the shade of an old arbor.

In time three of the guilty men began to worry about their own safety and turned state's evidence upon the others. When the case finally came to trial after being moved to Palestine, eight men were convicted and given life sentences.[96] An official evaluation of the Ranger work on this case was made by Assistant Attorney General N.B. Morris.

> ...Captain McDonald and Private Old were sent there to assist them and myself in the investigation of that horrible murder which was then enshrouded in a mystery that it seemed impossible to uncover. Before the rangers reached us the people in the neighborhood of the murder seemed afraid to talk. They said they would be murdered, too, if they took any hand in working up the case....The work of the rangers in this one case is worth more to the state, in my opinion, than your department will cost during your administration.[97]

Company E also engaged in detective work within an older, established county when a two-man detachment was sent into Wharton County in April to check on organized cattle theft. The Rangers made a careful investigation and arrested the recognized gang leader and several of his companions. The thefts stopped.[98]

Captain Hughes and Company D occupied the most dangerous part of Texas, but they enjoyed an unusually peaceful time in early 1899. Their main camp was still in Ysleta, with a detachment at Marathon, and the company made numerous quiet arrests without being confronted by the big challenges that faced the other units. This changed in the spring when a well-organized gang began a novel operation in their territory. Some of this gang worked from a camp on the Rio Grande near Fort Hancock, an abandoned army post fifty-two miles downriver from El Paso. Another part of the group camped close to the New Mexico border near the base of the Guadalupe Mountains, roughly ninety miles north of Hancock. The country between the two camps was rough, arid, and without settlements or roads. One part of the gang stole cattle in Mexico, the other in New Mexico or in Texas near the border. They drove the stolen herds either north or south and exchanged them for cattle in the other location. If stopped, they always had cattle that had not been stolen in their area, and the warrants carried by peace officers were never for the herds they caught. Besides the regular cattle business, the men had a profitable sideline smuggling goods in and out of Mexico.

Company D was brought into the case to assist the Customs Service. Captain Hughes and three of his Rangers, with a customs inspector, started tracking this bewildering switch-and-swap gang in April 1899 and worked on the scout for twenty-seven days. They solved the puzzle and stayed after the rustlers until they captured four of the six men involved; the remaining two fled the state. The prisoners were placed in jail in El Paso, where they were indicted for cattle theft and smuggling.[99]

This scout was typical of Company D's work during the two years 1898-1899, during which they did not kill or wound anyone or suffer losses themselves. In 348 scouts they traveled over 57,000 miles and made 395 arrests, the largest number of any company in the battalion.[100]

Ranger operations for the remainder of the year were

Texas Rangers with Captain John H. Hughes seated at right.
ca. 1900. Courtesy of the Texas Ranger Hall of Fame and
Museum, Waco, Texas.

largely in the settled counties where they became troubleshooters, going wherever needed without regard to the
company location. In September 1899 a critical combination
of racial violence and old-fashioned criminal activity developed in Orange, where a gang of borderline criminals began
a campaign to run certain blacks out of the county. Warnings, unsigned but clear in intent, were sent to targeted
blacks; when they refused to move, additional threats were
made. Finally a mob gathered at night and opened fire on a
house, killing one black and wounding several others. Local
police hesitated to investigate, much less make any arrests,
but some of the officials were concerned enough to ask for
the Rangers.

Rogers and a detachment from his company went to
Orange County on the Louisiana border to investigate. There
was evidently little problem in identifying some of the guilty,
and the Rangers began making arrests. In one arrest, Rogers
was involved in a scuffle with a man who was part of a group
that did not take kindly to anyone's interfering in their right
to keep the peace as they saw it. The arrests were made, but

Rogers reopened the wound he had suffered earlier in Laredo. Although there was plenty of work remaining to be done in Orange, Rogers was unable to take the physical strain without the danger of serious injury to his arm and shoulder. The Company E Rangers were pulled out and replaced by McDonald and six men of his Company B, a sizable force for the time.

Company B had completed its mission in Athens before being moved south to the Gulf, a long way from their normal station in the Panhandle, where they picked up on Rogers' work and began making sweeps of their own. It was not easy. A considerable element in Orange sympathized with the mob, many in the gang were no more than criminals' trying to take over the area, and local police were of little help.

The troublemakers had no respect for the law, including the Rangers. When Ranger T.L. Fuller, a promising young Ranger who had completed his freshman year at the University of Texas and who was working for a time as a lawman to earn enough money to continue his studies, arrested a man causing trouble and was trying to get him to jail on December 21, 1899, he was jumped by another man. Either the prisoner, Denny Moore, was part of the gang, or Fuller's attacker just hated any authority; whatever the reason the Ranger was attacked with a knife and had to shoot his assailant in self-defense. The slain man was identified as Oscar Poole, one of the gang leaders.[101]

After the death of Poole, McDonald and his men maintained their pressure upon the rest of the gang and finally arrested twenty-one men with enough evidence against them for indictments. They turned the prisoners over to the local authorities and left town but were barely out of sight before the police released all the suspects.[102]

With the numerous and widespread demands for Ranger assistance, the companies were always split with detachments' serving in widely separated locations. When Captain Rogers had his Company E Rangers in Orange, three of his men were working with customs inspectors in the Del Rio region along the Rio Grande almost 450 miles away. Since the customs people were with the Rangers there were probably smuggling angles to the case, but Sergeant Dubose and Rangers Moore and Hutchissons were after three men wanted in Sutton County for murder and robbery. On November 8 they trailed at least some of the wanted men through the bush, following tracks to an isolated house. Sergeant Dubose's call for the occupants to surrender was answered by shots, and the Rangers returned fire, killing Mauricio Garza, one of the fugitives.[103]

Captain Brooks and Company F, equally scattered with detachments in Alice, Brownsville and Hebbronville with responsibility for the lower river country, were also busy during the last months of the year. In September 1899 part of the unit was sent to Columbus where the Reece-Townsend feud threatened to flare again. McDonald had prevented violence there but had not been able to eliminate the cause of the friction; Brooks followed McDonald's system of disarming both sides and maintained the peace, or at least prevented any killings during the remainder of the year.

At the beginning of 1900 Brooks was again called on to keep the peace between the two factions, this time in Bastrop where Jim Townsend was being tried for the murder of Dick Reece. Brooks had three men, not enough to cover every part of the county, and Walter Reece and some friends were able to ambush and kill Arthur Buford and wound Will Clemens, supporters of the Townsend clan. Within twenty minutes of the killing, Brooks left one of his Rangers to guard the prisoners at the jail, and to keep the Townsend men away, and began with his other two men to arrest and jail seventeen of the Reece faction.

When it was time for the *habeas corpus* hearing for the indicted Reece murderers, the adjutant general collected sixteen Rangers to disarm both sides and insure there was no fighting. The Rangers gathered up every weapon in sight. Working with the local freight and rail officials, they examined all baggage and boxes' entering the town and confiscated any weapon sent to either side. An innocent-looking trunk mailed to one of the Townsends was filled with guns; a large parcel mailed to a Reece friend was also found to contain weapons. Without arms, there were no more fights and the feud was ended.[104] This was the opening service for 1900, and the Rangers began the new century unaware it was to be the end of the old system and the last year of service for the Frontier Battalion.

When a scout from Company F left for Alice in March 1900, they saddled up and rode out just as Rangers had done a thousand times before. Sergeant Bates took Rangers Baker and Livingston and Special Ranger Dunn to look for

stolen cattle near Alice; on March 21 they caught three
Mexican rustlers' trying to cut cows from a local herd. The
Rangers yelled for the men to surrender, but the men opened
fire and scattered. There was not much to see in the
darkness, other than gun flashes, but the Rangers wounded
and captured one man and were certain they hit another
who managed to escape in the night. They saved the herd
and brought a doctor from Alice to treat the wounded rustler,
who was later moved to Corpus Christi for better care but
died from his wound. [105]

Despite the obvious need for the Rangers' service, there
were rumors of possible reductions early in 1900. Some of
the correspondence to Company D is of interest in this
respect. The manager of the Cibolo Creek Mill and Mining
Company in Shafter, still a hot spot, wrote Captain Hughes
on May 11 informing him that Rangers Matthews and Elliot
had arrived the week before and had a very hearty calming
effect "on our turbulent population and have already done
some good work." They had arrested and fined three of the
worst six-shooter offenders, making quite an impression on
other troublemakers. He was sorry the Rangers had to be
pulled out so suddenly and wanted to know if he could do
anything to influence the legislature. Much the same message was sent by the Presidio County sheriff.

> Dear Captain:—
> Replying to your favor of the 10th, inst will say
> I am extremely sorry to hear you have to cut the
> strength of your comp down, and I am also sorry
> very sorry you had to recall the boys from Shafter,
> but allow me to thank you for the way you helped
> me out down there, the boys did good work and I
> am sorry they could not stay for I had a good deal
> of work planned for them.
> I believe the people of Shafter are going to
> petition you to have one or two men stationed
> there permanently, and I hope you will be in a
> position to comply with their request, for as you
> well know a ranger seems to have a heap more
> influence over these unruly characters than a
> county peace officer. [106]

Unfortunately, the sheriff's hopes for Rangers at Shafter

never came about; during June all of the companies were reduced from nine to six men.[107]

A series of legal actions culminating in May 1900 effectively destroyed the old Ranger force and the Frontier Battalion. Asking the question first raised during the trials of Milton and his two companions years before, lawyers again queried whether a Ranger other than an officer could make a legal arrest. There is little doubt the original intent of the Act of 1874 was for any member of the Frontier Battalion to have arrest authority—there would have been no point in authorizing a company of men if only one or two officers could arrest felons—but it seems likely that the legal minds who again raised the question were interested in how to cripple the Rangers rather than original intent.

Governor J.D. Sayers asked the attorney general for an opinion on the matter, and on May 26, 1900, Attorney General Thomas S. Smith decided the language of the act was specific and allowed only officers to make arrests. Smith's was a very narrow ruling based on a definition of the term "officer" to mean only commissioned personnel as opposed to "police officer" or "peace officer." In effect, the ruling said that almost every arrest made since mid-1874 had been illegal.

The same day the attorney general delivered his opinion, Adjutant General Thomas Scurry issued General Order No.24 outlining his guidelines for Ranger operations and making arrests. Until the legislature could meet and draft new laws, the enlisted Rangers would be little more than a supporting force for the officers. Only a commissioned officer could make an arrest, but he could use enlisted men to help him.

The adjutant general began a desperate campaign to save the Rangers. Public opinion was a critical feature of his plan, and earlier orders governing Ranger conduct were dusted off and rewritten.

> Company commanders will instruct their men to keep within the bounds of discretion and the law under all circumstances, and should there be any men now in the service who make unreasonable display of authority or use abusive language to or unnecessarily harsh treatment of those with whom they come in contact in the line of duty, or

who are not courageous, discrete, honest or of
temperate habits, they will be promptly discharged....[108]

There had been changes in the public perception of the
Rangers; most agreed they had done a fine job, but many
now believed they were no longer needed. Lawyers and
families of arrested felons were quick to raise the issues of
every real or fictional abuse of power, however small.
Scurry's instructions, which had been in effect for decades,
were an obvious attempt to counter such adverse publicity.

In the meantime, Scurry had to deal with a situation in
which only four Ranger captains were able to make legal
arrests. He had enough money to pay the Rangers, so he
organized a new "battalion" by reducing each of the four
companies to an average strength of four men and organizing two new companies. Three officers were authorized in
each of the six units. On June 1, 1900, companies A and C
were reactivated; Sergeant Dubose and W.J. McCauley were
promoted to lieutenant and given command of the new
companies.[109] Scurry's stopgap solution added at least two
new officers in the four previous companies, and when all
the officer slots were filled, the "battalion" had eighteen men
who could make arrests.

It may seem today that the state's officials moved hastily
in reorganization attempts and could have waited until the
legislature changed the old law. At the time, however, it must
have seemed that there might be a major effort to have
numerous earlier cases retried. Only one case, as related
below, can be documented, although Adjutant General
Scurry mentioned that several criminal cases had been
brought against privates for earlier arrests. Balancing everything, it was a safer choice for Scurry to go the way he did.

The census of 1900 showed Texas had a population of
3,048,710, an increase of 36 percent over 1880 with little
land's remaining outside the organized counties. Few places
still had peace officers who allowed family, friends, or
political loyalties to influence their duties. Railroads criss-
crossed the state linking all big cities and most of the major
towns. The frontier army posts had long since been abandoned; only those along the Rio Grande were still in existence. A handful of Rangers could take much of the credit

for pushing a land of gunfighters and near-anarchy towards civilization.

Their reward was a campaign to discredit the force and abolish the battalion, but the new companies went to their assignments as though nothing was happening. There is nothing to suggest a conspiracy to bring about the end of the Rangers, but an incident in Orange shows that some people were able to take advantage of the change in status of the Rangers.

In October Captain McDonald and Private A.L. Saxon were in Orange as witnesses in a case involving T.L. Fuller. As described earlier, Fuller had been involved in an arrest in September 1899 and had killed one of the Poole brothers. Although now one of the new lieutenants, Fuller had been indicted for making an illegal arrest while an enlisted Ranger. McDonald protested that the charge was nothing more than a ploy to get the Ranger back in Orange, but he was overruled by superiors acutely concerned with maintaining good will. During a break in court, Lieutenant Fuller was in a barber shop with his back to the door and never saw the entrance of Tom Poole, brother of the man Fuller had killed. Poole shot the Ranger from behind, and Fuller was dead before he fell to the floor. Poole was never punished and even became a deputy sheriff but in time was killed by another peace officer who was in turn murdered by the Poole family.[110]

Rangers continued to perform any duty assigned. Following the disastrous hurricane that destroyed Galveston, two Rangers joined Adjutant General Scurry and helped patrol the littered mainland beach, on which much property and many bodies had been washed ashore, for looters. They apprehended two brothers stripping bodies, recovering several hundred dollars in cash, and arrested another man for robbery in Texas City and turned him over to the Galveston County sheriff.[111]

Occasionally they still participated in incidents that seemed like the old days. On the evening of October 24 Lieutenant W.L. Wright, one of the new officers in Company E, attempted to arrest a drunken man in a Cotulla saloon. The Rangers had run into J.R. Davenport before, wounding him in an earlier gunfight, and when Wright tried to take him into custody the drunk jerked away and fired a pistol at the Ranger. Wright shot and killed him.[112] October 1900 was thus a special month in battalion history; the death of Lieutenant Fuller was the last Ranger fatality in the Frontier Battalion, and Davenport's death was the final use of deadly force by a member of the unit.

The new, smaller companies continued in operation as best they could from June 1, 1900 until July 8, 1901, when legislation authorizing a new force laid to final rest the honored Frontier Battalion, which joined the Special Troops and Special Forces in history. The Rangers remained; a new command was created consisting of four companies each commanded by a captain with no more than twenty men. The Ranger still provided his own horse, weapons and equipment and had neither uniform nor badge.[113]

After a quarter century, the force most associated with the Texas Rangers had been disbanded. Much has been made about the Rangers being an out-of-date command, since there was no longer a frontier and no Indians to chase, but the need for the Rangers continued. They had worked themselves out of their original job, but there was still a need for a statewide police force, and the four new companies continued to serve for years. L.P. Sieker continued as quartermaster, the only remaining Ranger who had begun his service in the 1870s.

The company commanders gave continuity to the new force, now officially designated "Ranger." In 1935 a reorganization in state government moved the Rangers from the adjutant general and placed them under the jurisdiction of the newly created Department of Public Safety, where they serve today. Although they now use the most modern weapons and transportation and wear distinctive badges, they are still without uniforms.

And they are still Rangers.

— 12 —

Ranger Camp Life

When reading Ranger scout reports, reviewing the monthly returns, or examining laconic telegrams, it is easy to believe the Rangers were the stuff of legend and myth rather than very real men who possessed the foibles and faults of all men. Rangers had to eat and sleep, liked to have a drink and chased women on occasion, and a few were thrown out of the force for excessive fondness for some or all of these habits. Very little of the reality of daily Ranger life is revealed in official records; fortunately, most of the Rangers who wrote memoirs included descriptions of camp life which provide a portrait of the Ranger as a person rather than a manhunter.

Food and shelter are the basic requirements for life; eating and sleeping for themselves and their mounts had a great influence on most Ranger operations. During the early years of the Frontier Battalion, the battalion's quartermaster supplied each Ranger company with a set ration consisting of flour, bacon, beef, coffee, sugar, salt, soda, soap, vinegar, pepper, candles, potatoes, onions and rice.[1] A ration was the amount each of these items an individual Ranger would consume in one day, and the company orderly sergeant was required each month to write out a list of how much was on hand of each item. There was some variation in the rations issued the companies because the quartermaster could not always find every authorized item in each company location.

The ration system remained in effect during most of the period 1870-1900. In the 1880s a printed form was developed for use, but much the same staples were issued although beans were added and vinegar dropped. There were still problems with shortages in some areas; one form lists no beef available but corn sent as a substitute.[2]

McNelly's company was an exception to the ration issue. Because of their location and rapid and extensive movements, McNelly's Boys usually got along as best they could by buying their food and supplies as they went and using state warrants for payment. Durham mentions meals of beans and johnnycakes, with coffee for those who had their own cups. His company had a cook, not usual at this time.[3]

During the early years with larger companies, the Rangers were divided into "messes" responsible for keeping their own rations and cooking their meals. Each mess divided the chores and cooking responsibilities so that one man was not saddled with this duty all the time. A mess with men who were good cooks and who had decent cooking utensils lived better. Gillett recalled one mess with a man detailed as cook who boiled up the ten-day supply of rice at one time, filling up all the camp's utensils and finally having to pour the rice on the ground.[4]

Occasionally a unit would enlist a Ranger skilled in cooking or baking. Ranger Nick Donley of Company D, who had been a baker in civilian life, constructed a Dutch oven in his company's frontier camp and provided the unit with fresh bread each day. Unfortunately, in furnishing this unexpected treat he used up the entire supply of flour within a short time and Captain Roberts had to order the oven dismantled.[5]

Although the Rangers did not have a very varied diet, it was not bad for the time and probably better than most people's on the frontier, who ate what they could grow or hunt. Many of the staple items were hard to find away from the settlements, and the Rangers often swapped surplus flour, rice and sugar for fresh milk and eggs and butter.[6] Many accounts mention the ease of finding wild game and fish. At time the Rangers would camp near pecan groves or in an area where they could find wild honey. These natural supplements to their diet were always welcome and often vital on long scouts when supplies ran low.

During the 1890s the Rangers of a company were seldom together in camp for any length of time, and the detached individuals and smaller units began to operate on an "expense account" basis much of the time. Being on detached duty was an advantage; a Ranger could often eat in a cafe or hotel and sleep in a decent bed. Such expenditures required strict accounting; the state was no more generous than in earlier days.

A series of accounts for Company B illustrate some of the expenditures submitted for reimbursement, their costs at the time, and other factors in the changing life of Texas. During an extended scout, two Rangers submitted expenses covering railroad fare from Cotulla to Temple, lodging, meals, express costs for guns, and a stagecoach ride for two persons from San Angelo to Sonora. This set of records included charges on five different days for the use of the new telephones. Board and lodging for ten days for the two Rangers totaled $14.75.[7]

No matter how much the unit was dispersed on assignments, there was always a company camp or headquarters where, if nothing else, the horses were stabled and had to be fed and cared for, and the bills in the later years show feed for the animals as a major expense. The vouchers for purchases of supplies from local stores, when detachments were near settlements for an extended time, list about the same staples as earlier ration returns with the addition of matches.[8]

The canvas tents which the state furnished as the basic Ranger shelter worked well enough in warm months, but the bitter weather in North Texas required special winter quarters, generally log huts or cabins depending on how much timber was available. Gillett describes how Company D constructed log cabins when they were in winter quarters near the San Saba River. Each mess of five men built a cabin about sixteen to eighteen feet square with a fireplace and chimney.[9] Rangers also took advantage of any building available; Baylor's men were able to live in stone or adobe houses while in Ysleta, and Nevill's company found some old buildings below Fort Davis which the men occupied in a combination of adobe and tents.

In earlier days a favorite pastime of the Rangers was horse racing, and many units developed race tracks. Generally betting was not allowed because the danger of hard feelings over losing money was too great; Mrs. Roberts said the races were for amusement, but Company D did permit wagers.[10] The proscription of gambling also applied to card games; Durham describes a card game in which he cheated in an attempt to beat an old hand who was a master poker player. The deception almost ended in a gunfight.[11] Nevertheless, card playing remained a favorite way to kill time when off duty, and some companies even set the hours for play. When Company E petitioned for definite times, Lieutenant Gillespie published a company order to set the rules; men, when not on duty, could play cards between eight and eleven in the morning and one and five in the afternoon. If any man gambled for cartridges or after hours, he lost his priviledges.[12]

Mrs. Roberts wrote about a croquet set, among the possessions of Company D while she was with the unit, which the Rangers "enjoyed.". Music was also a great favorite, although not every company was lucky enough to have musicians. Mrs. Roberts mentioned the number of Company D's men who played some instrument; Captain Roberts was a talented violinist, and the men formed their own band and played concerts for people when they were near a settlement or army post.[13] Gillett mentions that the musicians in Company D were not the only ones; Company A also had a number of talented musicians. Major Jones enjoyed the concerts by the members of his escort company.[14]

When a company was near a town or army post, the Rangers took advantage of any social events' taking place. Mrs. Roberts mentions one combined dance and quilting bee, lasting day and night, which people traveled considerable distances to attend. The Company D dandies always attended such festivities but sometimes on a take-your-turn basis when they had to pool their decent clothing so that at least a few might attend. On one occasion, Company D Rangers when stationed near Menard put on a minstrel show and raised sixty dollars which they donated to a struggling new church.[15] After Ranger Jack Martin complained to Mrs. Roberts about the lack of society near the Ranger camps, he was known as "Society Jack" the rest of his life.[16]

Most men signed on as Rangers with little more than the clothing on their backs. Although a Ranger was obligated to have a horse, saddle and arms in order to enlist, even these requirements were not always followed to the letter of the law. Especially in the early years, the state frequently allowed a promising recruit to enlist without personal weapons, furnishing his arms and deducting the money from his first pay. In late December 1874, Captain Kenney, the battalion's quartermaster, wrote Lieutenant Wilson in Company A and gave him a list of men who owed money for clothing or horses. Most of the sums are modest, suggesting the purchase of clothing, but a sixty-five dollar debit indicates reimbursement for a horse.[17] Durham mentions arriving in Texas with only the clothing on his back and wearing the same outfit for over a year before he could save enough for a new outfit.[18]

Photography was popular during this era, and there are many pictures of the Rangers of the last quarter of the nineteenth century. The average Ranger of the late 1870s normally lived in his work clothes, which were also his dress clothes. He did not look like the movie cowboys; unlike the "cowboy" boots popular today, he wore boots almost knee high and cut square across the top with a high heel and somewhat pointed toes. Usually a Ranger's boots were the best item of clothing he owned. His spurs were heavy, with large rowels. A wide-brimmed hat was a necessity, and they were worn in almost every color and shape. The Ranger had long underwear, and his pants and shirt were generally of fairly heavy weight. He wore a vest, a handy place to keep a watch if he had one, coins, tobacco and any papers. In the colder portions of the state, or during winter, the Ranger wore a heavy coat manufactured of anything from thick cloth to buffalo hide.

Unlike the cowboys depicted on TV and in movie westerns, the Ranger carried his knife and pistol on a belt worn high on his waist; he needed his handgun ready at any time and could take no chances on a belt hung low on his hips. A number of contemporary photographs show Rangers wearing cross-draw holsters, a convenient way to draw a weapon when riding.

The pistol and belt were worn on a cartridge belt, the scout belt, with loops for shells. Most of the Rangers used a .45 caliber Colt and a .44 caliber Winchester. Both types of cartridges would fit in a belt, but they did not fit in each weapon and the wise Ranger carried his rifle rounds in a pouch or pocket. Some men used a .44 Colt which fired the same round as the Winchester, adding loops to the belt and carrying the ammunition where it was easily available. Whatever the ammunition, the scout belt was wide enough to distribute the weight of knife, pistol and holsters.

After most Rangers switched to the '73 Winchester and adopted the new .45 Colt, in general they retained these arms until the end of the Frontier Battalion. Most photographs show these weapons in use well into the 1900s, but there were exceptions. In the celebrated photograph of the entire battalion in El Paso in 1896, Captain McDonald is holding a '94 Winchester, and other men hold '76's. There is a photograph of Captain Brooks, posed with his men, holding a new Mauser automatic complete with wooden holster-stock. The Rangers took advantage of new developments such as the telegraph, railroad and typewriter, but by and large they continued to use the two types of arms that had worked so well.

The grim, relentless manhunters were also practical jokers. Since Texas supplied the Rangers with little more than the opportunity to get shot, each recruit was eager to obtain anything free, and a favorite trick was telling new Rangers that the state furnished them with free socks. Naturally, the man issuing the free socks was the company commander, and the old hands would watch from cover as the new man approached the captain to ask for his socks. Captain Roberts of Company D always went along with the gag.[19]

Some of the pranks were more physical in nature. During winter, when the Rangers lived in log cabins, a great favorite was blocking the chimney with rags. When the smoke forced the occupants to flee, other Rangers would rush up screaming "fire!" then dash inside to throw outside all the possessions of the victims.[20]

Jeff Milton, besides being a good man with a gun, was a champion jokester. One of his friends could never understand why his girl friend had dropped him and refused even to talk to him; he never knew Milton had confided to her in strictest confidence that her boyfriend was an escaped convict.

The classic Milton joke involved Major Jones. One day, when the major was visiting camp, a number of the Rangers were fishing using some hooks purchased in Austin. A rancher riding by and noticing the great luck the Rangers were having, asked where he could buy some of the hooks. Milton told him they were being sold by the little peddler in the tent up the road; the unsuspecting rancher rode up to the tent and tried to buy some of the items from the commander of the Frontier Battalion. The major was a leader of men, brave and a great organizer, but he did not

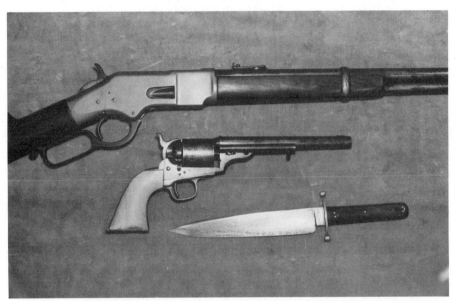

Ranger weapons, 1870. Top to bottom: Winchester '66, Colt Navy, converted to fire cartridges, typical belt knife. These arms were those used by the Rangers formed in 1870.
Courtesy of the Texas Ranger Hall of Fame and Museum, Waco, Texas.

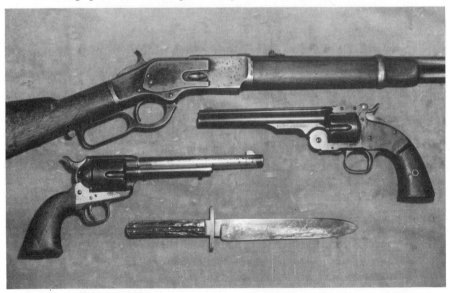

Ranger weapons, 1875. Top to bottom: Winchester '73, Smith and Wesson, Colt .45, the "Peacemaker," the favorite revolver of the West from 1873 down to the present. Courtesy of the Texas Ranger Hall of Fame and Museum, Waco, Texas.

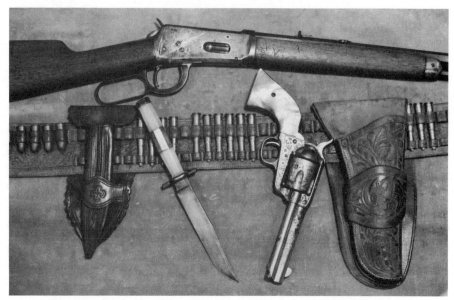

*Ranger weapons, 1890s. top, Winchester '92, belt knife and Colt
revolver. The Colt is the familiar model with a short barrel. By the
1890s, Ranger—and popular—taste accepted ivory or bone grips
and knife handles and some decoration on holsters and saddles.
Courtesy of the Texas Ranger Hall of Fame and Museum,
Waco, Texas*

have a sense of humor. The rancher, who did, recognized
they had been the victim of a master joker, so when Jones
demanded to know who had told him the preposterous tale,
the man said he heard it from a rider down the road. Not
satisfied, Jones had the company fall in and made the
rancher go down the line to identify the guilty party, but the
cowman claimed to recognize no one and Jones finally had
to let the matter drop.[21]

One day when alone in camp, Mrs. Roberts received
some letters addressed to her husband, who was away on
business. One of the letters was from Austin, and usually
any message from the capitol was bad news; the Rangers
asked her about the contents, certain it was news about
cutting the company strength. She finally told them they
were right; the legislature was on another economy move
and all men under five feet ten inches would be discharged.
For some time the company was in turmoil as men meas-

ured each other trying to estimate heights to see if they had made the cutoff, until Captain Roberts returned and told them it was all a joke. Mrs. Roberts said the Rangers thought it was a good joke and "did not hold it against me."[22]

Not every Ranger spent his time in playing cards or thinking up practical jokes. When off duty, especially during the long winter evenings, some of them studied and eventually became lawyers, doctors, or other professionals.[23] Probably about the same number of men, however, were unable to read or write, although some of these learned the rudiments during their enlistment. A number of the older men saved their money and purchased cattle and land; others not interested in being tied down to a ranch purchased a few head and had nearby farmers or ranchers keep their stock with the larger herds. The Sieker brothers did well financially with this type of investment. A number of Rangers became big landholders when they left the service; Nevill, Gillett and Dolan all had large ranches in the Trans Pecos, and Armstrong became a major landholder in South Texas. Many Rangers went to work as ranch foremen or ranch managers. R.R. Russell saved his money, became a banker and one of the few Ranger millionaires. Perhaps the majority of the Rangers, however, had a good time and spent their wages about as fast as they were paid.

The Rangers changed as Texas changed. Living conditions improved dramatically from 1874 to 1890, and to some degree the Rangers reflected these improvements. The men were still young and looking for adventure, but they were somewhat better educated and dressed better. In 1875 Gillett wrote about the necessity for gathering up all the good clothing in Company D to obtain a few complete and decent outfits for the local dances; a photograph of Company D in the mid-1880s shows every man in a coat and tie. The battalion picture of 1896 portrays each Ranger in a good "Sunday" suit, something almost unknown in the 1870s. Ranger Van Oden describes very matter of factly how he spent a month's pay for a new suit and a pair of boots, a commonplace expenditure by the 1890s.[24]

A few things remained constant during the quarter century, and one of the features of camp life has received little mention over the years. Much has been written about the celebrated Ranger horses, but each company also had a few mules for hauling the company wagon or for use as pack animals on long scouts. A tribute to the Ranger mules is overdue.

The mules, carefully selected and smaller than most of their breed, had impressive endurance and made possible the long scouts that became a Ranger trademark. They kept up with the horses and charged along with the unit in a fight. The Rangers swore the animals knew what was happening and enjoyed the battle. At least one was killed in action, and many others were cut free and lost.

Brave as they were, the feature that most impressed those who wrote about the mules was their sense of the ludicrous. They were animal comedians which, unless confined, wandered through the camps taking food from the Rangers. They delighted in frightening wagon trains by spooking other mules or horses hauling freight. Once in Austin, a Ranger mule got loose and wandered about the streets until it ran into one of the new, mule-drawn trolley cars; the Ranger mule charged the other mule, which bolted and jerked the trolley from the tracks.

On scouts, the little mules were laden with everything from Dutch ovens to ammunition boxes, frying pans, coffee pots, canned food, and forage, most of which made a terrific racket startling to other animals. The mules seemed to be aware of their ability to instill fear and would charge other animals to cause confusion. Orders finally had to be issued to keep the mules out of settlements and towns and away from road traffic. The mules' antics and abilities didn't change over the years; Gillett wrote about their antics in the 1870s, Aten told the same wild tales in the 1880s, and even in the late 1890s Paine described McDonald's mules and the wild charges.[25]

So, after all their years of service, a belated tribute is hereby extended to the Ranger mules, essential features of camp and field who knew little of the law but understood duty.

Appendix A

Frontier Forces Organized Under Law
Approved June 13, 1870

CO.	STATION	CAPTAINS	MUSTERED IN	MUSTERED OUT
A	Mason	F. Jones	Aug 25,1870	Nov 12, 1870
B	Erath	A.H. Cox	Sep 8, 1870	May 15, 1871
C	Kerr	J.W. Sansom	Aug 25,1870	May 31, 1871
D	Uvalde	J.R. Kelso	Sep 10,1870	Jan 20, 1871
E	Fort Inge	H.J. Richarz	Sep 9, 1870	Jun 15, 1871
F	Wise	D.P. Baker	Nov 5, 1870	Jun 15, 1871
G	Starr	C.G. Falcon	Oct 8, 1870	Apr 30, 1871
H	Zapata	B. Chamberlain	Nov 15,1870	Feb 28, 1871
I	Mason	J.M. Hunter	Sep 12,1870	Jan 24, 1871
K	Lampasas	J.M. Harrell	Sep 16,1870	Feb 16, 1871
L	Gillespie	H. Beberstin	Oct 10,1870	May 31, 1871
N	El Paso	G. Garcia	Aug 21,1870	Jun 15, 1871
O	Kimble	P. Kleid	Aug 29,1870	May 31, 1871
P	Coleman	J.P. Swisher	Aug 29,1870	May 31, 1871

Source: Adjutant General's Report, September 30, 1875, 2.

Appendix B

Minute Companies Organized Under Law
Approved November 25, 1871

CO	STATION	COMMANDED BY	ORGANIZED
A	Blanco	James Ingram	Jan 4, 1872
B	Wise	G.W. Stevens	Mar 2, 1872
C	Kendall	C.A. Patton	Feb 4, 1872
D	Comanche	J.A. Wright	May 25,1872
E	Kerr	H. Schwethelm	Apr 6, 1872
F	Gillespie	B.F. Casey	Apr 18,1872
G	Brown	G.H. Adams	Jun 5, 1872
I	Cooke	J.M. Waide	Apr 24,1872
K	Bandera	R. Ballantyne	Jul 2, 1872
L	Coleman	J.M. Elkins	Volunteer without pay
M	Lampasas	G.E. Haynie	Aug 10,1872
N	San Saba	W.H. Ledbetter	Aug 13,1872
O	Burnet	J. Alexander	Aug 19,1872
P	Parker	J.C. Gilleland	Aug 19,1872
Q	Llano	F.C. Stewart	Aug 21,1872
R	Mason	D. Herster	Aug 26,1872
S	Jack	N. Atkinson	Aug 23,1872
T	Palo Pinto	D.H. McClure	Aug 22,1872
U	Mantague	J.M. Willingham	Apr 20,1872
V	Medina	Geo. Haley	Sep 6, 1872
W	Webb	J.D. Martinez	Oct 2, 1872
X	Maverick	Ma'n. Barr	Oct 8, 1872
Y	Uvalde	D.A. Bates	Oct 12,1872
Z	Erath	C.M. O'Neal	Oct 12,1872

Source: Adjutant General's Report, September 30, 1875, 4.

Appendix C

Minute Companies Reorganized Under Law
Approved November 25, 1871

CO	STATION	COMMANDED BY	REORGANIZED
A	Blanco	S.B. Gray	Apr 1, 1873
B	Wise	G.W. Stevens	Aug 7, 1873
C	Kendall	J.C. Nowlin	Mar 1, '73
			Jan 3, '74
D	Comanche	W.C. Watkins	Sep 18,1873
E	Kerr	H. Schwethelm	Apr 7, 1872
F	Gillespie	B.F. Casey	Nov 21,1873
G	Brown	G.H Adams	Aug 12,1873
I	Cooke	J.M. Waide	Apr 24,1873
L	Coleman	J.M. Elkins	Nov 7, 1873
M	Lampasas	E.W. Greenwood	Sep 12,1873
N	San Saba	W.H. Ledbetter	Sep 19,1873
P	Parker	J.C. Gilleland	Oct 29,1873
Q	Llano	J.M. Smith	Sep 29,1873
R	Mason	C.C. Smith	Dec 9, 1873
T	Palo Pinto	J.H. Carothers	Oct 1, 1873
U	Montague	J.M. Willingham	May 31,1873
Z	Erath	N. Keith	Mar 29,1873
No.1	Kerr	S.R. Merritt	Sep 7, '73 without pay
No.2	Gillespie	Geo. Laremore	Nov 21,'73 without pay
No.3	Kinney	J.H. Kennedy	Jan 6, '73 without pay
No.4	Callahan	J.W. Jones	Oct 6, '73 without pay
No.5	Menard	P.J. Mires	Aug 25,'73 without pay

Source: Adjutant General's Report, September 30, 1875, 6.

Appendix D

Ranging Companies called out by Governor E.J. Davis November 1, 1873 for four months

STATION	COMMANDED BY	ORGANIZED
Wise	G.W. Stevens	Nov 26,1873
Jack	S.W. Eastin	Dec 3, 1873
Palo Pinto	W.C. McAdams	Dec 13,1873
Parker	W.L. Hunter	Dec 24,1873
Erath		Apparently never organized
Comanche	M.R. Green	Jan 17,1874
Montague	G.W. Campbell	Dec 13,1873
Young	A.C. Tackett	Jan 6, 1874
Brown		Apparently never organized
McCullough	J.G. Connell	Jan 6, 1874
San Saba		Apparently never organized

Source: Adjutant General's Report, September 30, 1875, 8.

Endnotes

CHAPTER 1
RECONSTRUCTION IN TEXAS 1865-1873

1. John Salmon Ford, *Rip Ford's Texas* (Austin: University of Texas Press, 1963), 388-97, contains Ford's version of this engagement.

2. Walter Prescott Webb, ed., *The Handbook of Texas* (Austin: The Texas State Historical Association, 1952), hereafter *HBT*, I:370.

3. John Wesley Hardin, *The Life of John Wesley Hardin* (Seguin, Texas: Smith & Moore, 1896), 13.

4. Ibid., 62-63.

5. Hardin saw the fight from his Taylor family's viewpoint, and almost all accounts of this "feud" were written by partisans of the Taylor side. As will be seen later, this so-called feud was an attempt to control the region and had little to do with a struggle between families.

6. Ford, *Texas*, 415-16.

7. *HBT*, II:446-47.

8. Chapters One through Five of Allen Lee Hamilton's *Sentinel of the Southern Plains* (Fort Worth: Texas Christian University Press, 1988) cover in detail the Quaker influence upon Indian reservation policy and the results on communities such as Jacksboro.

9. *Journal of the House of Representatives of the Twelfth Legislature, State of Texas*, First Session, 26-27.

10. H.P.N. Gammel, ed., *The Laws of Texas*, VI:5-8. This act actually created a "Frontier Force." Although the members of the Frontier Force were not specifically named as Rangers, this term is used in this book. The units were based on earlier Ranger companies and were considered Rangers by people of the day. Governor Davis so designated them in his January 10, 1871, message on the State of Texas: "...strength of Rangers authorized for frontier defense...." (*Journal of the House of Representatives of the Twelfth Legislature, State of Texas*, Part First, 57).

11. *Adjutant General Records*, hereafter *AGR*. John R. Kelso to Col. Davidson, July 28, 1870.

12. *AGR*. H.R. Biberstin to Colonel Davidson, August 10, 1870. While this spelling, and Beberstin, is used in official documents, family members say the proper spelling is Bieberstein.

13. *AGR*. J.P. Swisher to Col Jas. Davidson, August 15, 1870.

14. *AGR*. John R. Kelso to James Davidson, August 11, 1870.

15. *Adjutant General's Report, State of Texas, September 30, 1875*, 2. This report is an unbound document, pp 1-15, which does not follow the numbering sequence in the 1875 report and which was probably issued as a fold-in with the bound 1875 report. The report is largely devoted to the companies of 1870-1873.

16. *AGR*. Franklin Jones to James Davidson, Adjutant General, Aug

8, 1870.

17. *Adjutant General's Report, September 30, 1875*, 2.

18. *Frontier Forces Muster Rolls.* Muster rolls, Co. N, Co. G, Co. H.

19. *AGR.* Captain Jones to Gen James Davidson, September 15, 1870.

20. *Frontier Forces Correspondence,* hereafter *FFC.* Capt. A.C. Cox to Col James Davidson, November 13, 1870.

21. *Report of the Adjutant-General of the State of Texas, from June 24, 1870, to December 31, 1870,* hereafter *RAG,* 6.

22. *Frontier Forces Muster Rolls,* Co. C, 1 May, 1871-31 May, 1871. Also *FFC,* Cox to Davidson, November 25, 1870.

23. Typical examples are Captain H.J. Richarz's complaint to the adjutant general on November 4, 1870, and Captain Cox's requirement for medical supplies, Cox to Davidson, November 22, 1870. *RAG,* 64, supports the complaints of the various commanders about the adverse effect of not having access to army supplies.

24. *Adjutant General's Report, State of Texas, September 30, 1875,* 2.

25. Ibid.

26. A.J. Sowell, *Early Settlers and Indian Fighters of Southwest Texas* (Austin: State House Press, 1991; reprint of 1884), 202-205.

27. H.J. Richarz to Colonel James Davidson, December 29, 1870. Printed in *RAG,* 65-67.

28. *AGR.* Report of Captain H.R. Biberstin of a patrol by Lieutenant Louis Von Hagen, December 30, 1870 to January 13, 1871. Report dated January 17, 1871.

29. A.J. Sowell, *Rangers and Pioneers of Texas,* 233-327.

30. Harold F. Williamson, *Winchester - The Gun that Won the West* (New York: A.S. Barnes and Company, Inc., 1952), 49.

31. *Adjutant General's Report, State of Texas, September 30, 1875,* 2-3.

32. *AGR.* Citizens of Uvalde County to Adjutant General, January 23, 1871.

33. See Appendix A for dates.

34. *Adjutant General's Report, State of Texas, September 30, 1875,* 4-5.

35. Ibid., 6-7.

36. Ibid., 8.

37. Ibid.

38. See *HBT,* II:663, for a brief sketch of the State Police.

39. *Message of Gov. Edmund J. Davis on the State of Texas, Austin, January 10, 1871.* Printed in the *Journal of the House of Representatives of the Twelfth Legislature, State of Texas,* Part First, 12-13.

40. Henry W. Strong, *My Frontier Days & Indian Fights on the Plains of Texas* (privately printed, undated), 6-7.

41. *Waco Examiner,* quoted in *Texas State Gazette,* January 25, 1871.

42. Walter Prescott Webb, *The Texas Rangers,* 225-26.

43. Otis Singletary, "The Texas Militia During Reconstruction," *Southwestern Historical Quarterly* LX, 23-35.

44. Webb, *The Texas Rangers* (New York: Houghton Mifflin Company, 1935), 224.

45. *Daily State Journal,* March 17, 1871. Quoted in Webb, *The Texas Rangers,* 225.

46. Hardin, *Hardin,* 80.

47. See Robert C. Sutton, *The Sutton-Taylor Feud* (Quanah, Texas: Nortex Press, 1974). This is one of the few books not written from the viewpoint of the Taylor side. It is a largely factual account that clears away much of the myth and legend that clouds most versions of the fighting.

48. Hardin, *Hardin*, 81-82.

49. Ibid., 86.

50. Ibid., 89-94.

51. James B. Gillett, *Six Years with the Texas Rangers 1875 to 1881* (Lincoln and London: University of Nebraska Press, 1976; reprint of 1921), 73-76. Other versions of the saloon fight, having seven state troopers, differ from Gillett's account. All agree on the general outcome with four men killed.

52. *HBT*, I:469-70.

53. Ford, *Texas*, 415-35.

CHAPTER 2
THE FRONTIER BATTALION 1874

1. Gammel, *Laws of Texas* VIII: 86-89

2. *AGR*. General Order No.2, May 6, 1874. As indicated by the numbers, No.1 and No.2 were the initial General Orders of the Adjutant General in the new Democratic administration in Texas. GO No.1 established a permanent battalion, to be called the Frontier Battalion. GO No.2 announced the battalion commander and the company commanders and their two lieutenants. Companies were designated A through F, with a county headquarters, or main base, and their patrol areas.

3. *Weekly State Gazette*, Austin, Texas, August 8, 1874. In a letter to the editor, C.M. Winkler praised Jones although he offered little more than a recounting of Jones' service with the governor during the Civil War.

4. W.J. Maltby, *Captain Jeff or Frontier Life in Texas with the Texas Rangers* (Colorado, Texas: Whipkey Printing Co., 1906), 65-66.

5. Maltby, *Captain Jeff*, 68.

6. *AGR*, General Orders No. 1, 2, May 6, 1874.

7. There are various spellings of Coldwell, both in handwritten documents and printed reports. It appears that the spelling with an "o" was his preference.

8. Maltby, *Captain Jeff*, 68-71.

9. Frontier Battalion, *Monthly Returns*, hereafter FB, *MR*, Company E, June 1874.

10. *Supplemental Report of the Adjutant General of the State of Texas, for the year 1874*, 8.

11. There are differences between the organizational dates shown on company monthly returns and on the printed accounts.

12. *RAG*, 1874, 11.

13. Ranger Reminiscences Files, J.H. Taylor. Taylor's manuscript has been quoted as he wrote it. He was proud of teaching himself to read and write in later years and knew his work needed correction. He mentioned to the State Librarian that she might want to edit his work, but she wisely refused.

14. FB, *MR*. Monthly Return, Company A, June, 1874. The Battalion Monthly Return was a large printed sheet containing the names and rank of company members, with any personnel changes since the

previous report. The form had spaces for an inventory of company animals and property, wagons, harness, tools, *etc.* There was a blank section for major events during the month such as scouts, fights, casualties. There was a section for listing arrests made during the month. The monthly return was used as a basis for payment and gave a comprehensive report of the condition of the company. In this early example for Company A, Captain Waller made his main action reports on the return, resulting in considerably cramped handwriting! As time passed and actions increased, company commanders resorted more and more to individual, more detailed scout reports, leaving the monthly return for personnel and equipment data.

15. Ranger Reminiscences Files, J.H. Taylor.

16. *RAG*, 1874, 12.

17. Ranger Reminiscences Files, J.H. Taylor.

18. Hardin, *Hardin*, 94-98.

19. Ibid., 106.

20. Ibid., 106-107. Note this is Hardin's version.

21. Ranger Reminiscences Files, J.H. Taylor.

22. FB, *MR*. Monthly Return, June 1874.

23. Dan W. Roberts, *Rangers and Sovereignty*, 34.

24. FB, *MR*. Monthly Return, June 1874. Note this date for Company F is a week later than most accounts for that unit's organization.

25. FB, *MR*. Monthly Return, Company F, July 1874.

26. FB, *MR*. Monthly Return, Company E, June 1874.

27. FB, *MR*. Monthly Return, Company D, June 1874.

28. FB, *MR*. Monthly Return, Company C, July 1874.

29. FB, *Correspondence Files*, Petition from Company E, July 31, 1874.

30. Charles T. Haven & Frank A. Belden, *A History of the Colt Revolver* (New York: Bonanza Books, 1940), 145-46.

31. Williamson, *Winchester*, 50-51.

32. Ibid., 66-68.

33. *Supplemental Report of the Adjutant General of the State of Texas, for the year 1874*, 3-4.

34. FB, *Correspondence Files*, Certificate of Value, June 8, 1874.

35. Mrs. Dan Roberts, *A Woman's Reminiscences of Six Years in Camp With the Texas Rangers* (Austin: State House Press, 1987; reprint of 1914), 21-22.

36. Gillett, *Six Years*, 62.

37. Dorman H. Winfrey and James M. Day, editors, *The Indian Papers of Texas and the Southwest, 1825 to 1916* (Austin: Pemberton Press, 1966; reprint of 1959-1961, hereafter *Texas Indian Papers*, 4: 383.

38. *Supplemental Report of the Adjutant General of the State of Texas, for the year 1874*, 9. This is Jones' estimate, based on information gathered after the fight.

39. FB, *Correspondence Files*, Jones to Steele, July 14, 1874. There are several versions of this fight. A newspaper clipping in the Ranger Papers, with no city noted but a date of August 22, has a detailed account, making a point that the Rangers were never surrounded, as sometimes believed. Roberts, *Rangers and Sovereignty*, 41-44, has a version probably based on talking to participants. *The Supplemental Report for 1874*, 9, has a brief account. Hamilton, *Sentinal*, 147-51, has a modern description of the battle.

40. See Hamilton, *Sentinal*, 211-12 for a full list of citations on this

subject, covering military and political aspects of a different problem.

41. Newspaper article, August 22, cited in endnote #39 above. Wattles wrote the article. He was listed on a certificate establishing the value of his horse, as was Major Jones. Other records show him as part of the major's escort, and he obviously was writing from personal experience.

42. FB, *Correspondence Files*, Jones to Steele, July 23, 1874.

43. Maltby, *Captain Jeff*, 78-79.

44. Ibid., 81-83.

45. Ibid., 87-91.

46. Ibid., 91-101.

47. Ibid., 102-6.

48. FB, *Correspondence Files*, Jones to Steele, July 23 and August 9, 1874.

49. Maltby, *Captain Jeff*, 118.

50. FB, *Correspondence Files*, Jones to Steele, September 14, 1874.

51. Ibid.

52. FB, *Correspondence Files*, Battalion General Order No.5, October 27, 1874.

53. *Supplemental Report of the Adjutant General of the State of Texas, for the year 1874*, 11.

54. Roberts, *Rangers and Sovereignty*, 45-51.

55. *Supplemental Report of the Adjutant General of the State of Texas, for the year 1874*, 11.

56. *RAG*, 1874, 12.

57. *Supplemental Report of the Adjutant General of the State of Texas, for the year 1874*, 9.

58. FB, *Correspondence Files*, Jones to Steele, October 24, 1874.

59. *Supplemental Report of the Adjutant General of the State of Texas, for the year 1874*, 8.

60. Ibid., 11.

61. Ibid., 4.

62. Ibid., 10.

63. FB, *MR*. Monthly Returns, all companies, December 1874, January 1875.

64. Maltby, *Captain Jeff*, 108.

65. Roberts, *Rangers and Sovereignty*, 17.

66. *Supplemental Report of the Adjutant General of the State of Texas, for the year 1874*, 5.

67. L.H. McNelly Papers, The Center for American History, University of Texas at Austin. References to McNelly's Civil War service is from this collection of his papers.

68. *Supplemental Report of the Adjutant General of the State of Texas for the year 1874*, 4.

69. McNelly Papers, McNelly to Genl. Wm. Steele, November 30, 1874. This report was received in the Adjutant General's Office, according to the log of incoming messages. The original has been lost, but there is a typescript in McNelly's papers in The Center for American History.

70. Special State Troops, *Monthly Returns*, Washington County Volunteers, October-December 1874. McNelly sent reports to the Adjutant General July-September, but muster rolls for these earlier months are missing.

71. Special State Troops, *Correspondence Files*, McNelly to Steele, November 30, 1874.

CHAPTER 3
A SMALLER FRONTIER BATTALION   1875-1876

1. FB, *Correspondence Files*, Jones to Steele, January 3, 1875.
2. Ibid., Company A, Special Orders Nos. 1, 2, 3, February 1, 8, 11, 1875.
3. FB, *MR*. Monthly Return, Company F, February 1875.
4. Ibid., Company F, March, April 1875.
5. Ibid., Company F, May 1875.
6. *AGR*. Special Order No.13, March 17, 1875. Usually the title is spelled "Quarter Master" in orders and correspondence.
7. *AGR*. General Order No.14, March 17, 1875; FB, *MR*, Monthly Returns all companies, March, April 1875.
8. *Report of Maj. J.B. Jones, commanding the Frontier Battalion, Texas State Troops. March, 1876*, printed in pamphlet format by the State Printer and issued as an insert to *RAG*, 1876.
9. FB, *Correspondence Files*, Jones to Steele, April 20, 1875.
10. Gillett, *Six Years*, 23-26.
11. The following account is based on the recollections of Roberts, *Rangers and Sovereignty*, 67-75, and Gillett, *Six Years*, 33-45. The two accounts agree to a remarkable degree, except for the number of Rangers involved. Gillett remembered that Roberts had fifteen men detailed for the scout and listed them by name. In his account, Roberts merely stated he headed out with eight men.
12. FB, *Correspondence Files*, Roberts to Jones, August 26, 1875. Roberts may have been so tired he confused dates and times; according to other accounts, the scout took longer than six days.
13. A.C. Greene, *The Last Captive* (Austin: The Encino Press, 1972), 68-76.
14. Ibid., 69.
15. Roberts, *Rangers and Sovereignty*, 77-79, covers this scout. Gillett, *Six Years*, contains a brief mention on 44-45.
16. Gillett, *Six Years*, 27-28.
17. Roberts, *Rangers and Sovereignty*, 81.
18. Ibid., 82.
19. FB, *Correspondence Files*, Special Order No.5, August 5, 1875.
20. *AGR*. Special Order No.22, August 14, 1875.
21. FB, *Correspondence Files*, Jones to Roberts, August 27, 1875.
22. FB, *MR*. Monthly Returns, Companies A and B, September 1875.
23. *RAG*, 1876, 6-7.
24. Roberts, *Rangers and Sovereignty*, 87-94, and Gillett, *Six Years*, 46-52, both left accounts of this trouble that follows. Roberts was in Mason part of the time, making arrangements to bring his wife to camp. Gillett had the opportunity to talk with the men from Company D who were in Major Jones' escort and had a good secondhand view of the trouble. See also FB, *Correspondence Files*, Jones to Steele, September 28, 1875, reprinted in RAG, 1876, and Jones to Steele, September 30, 1875.
25. Roberts, *A Woman's Reminiscences*, 8-10.
26. Gillett, *Six Years*, 50.
27. Ibid., 51.
28. *RAG*, 1876, 5.
29. Roberts, *Rangers and Sovereignty*, 93.
30. FB, *Correspondence Files*, Jones to Steele, October 28, 1875.

31. *RAG*, 1876, 6.

32. FB, *MR*. Monthly Return, Company A, October 1875.

33. FB, *Correspondence Files*, Special Order No.6, October 25, 1875.

34. FB, *MR*. Monthly Returns, Companies A, D, E, F, October-December 1875.

35. *AGR*. General Order No.24, December 9, 1875.

36. Gillett, *Six Years*, 56.

37. The name should have been Monroe Hughes.

38. This and the following letters to Roberts are found in FB, *Correspondence Files*, Jones to Roberts, October 16-25, 1875. A needle gun was a German, single-shot, breech loading infantry rifle used in the Franco-Prussian War, so-called because of its long needle-like firing pin. Lord only knows why Roberts wanted it; Jones apparently didn't either and sent a Sharps.

39. Ibid., Jones to Mr. C. Nauwald, October 26, 1875.

40. Ibid., Sgt. C.H. Hamilton to Jones, December 18, 1875.

41. *AGR*. General Order No.9, March 1, 1876.

42. Ibid., General Order No.28, March 15, 1876.

43. The following account is based on Gillett, *Six Years*, 58-60, and the official report of Major Jones printed in RAG, 1876.

44. *RAG*, 1876, 8.

45. FB, *MR*. Monthly Returns, Company E, July and August 1876.

46. *RAG*, 1876, 6.

47. FB, *Correspondence Files*. Special Order No.54, discharged Corporal J.D. Nelson because he could not provide a suitable horse.

48. Ibid., Special Order No.64, August 15, 1876.

49. *AGR*. Special Order No.10, August 25, 1876.

50. *RAG*, 1876, 8.

51. Gillett, *Six Years*, 61-62.

52. Ibid., 67.

53. Roberts, *Rangers and Sovereignty*, 95. Roberts mistakenly set the date in 1878 rather than 1876.

54. Gillett, *Six Years*, 67; AGR, General Orders No.36, 37, December 8, 1876.

CHAPTER FOUR
MCNELLY'S BOYS 1875-1876

1. *RAG*, 1876, 4. The earliest enlistments for this new company were on April 1, 1875. It was evidently considered a reorganization of McNelly's 1874 company; for example, service records for R.P. Orrell, who was in the 1874 unit, show him *reenlisting* on April 1, 1875.

2. FB, *Correspondence Files*, John McClure to Steele, April 18, 1875.

3. George Durham, *Taming the Nueces Strip: The Story of McNelly's Rangers* (Austin: University of Texas Press, 1962), 4-5, 8-13.

4. Ibid., 15-16.

5. Ibid., 17-21.

6. Special State Troops/Special Forces, *Correspondence Files, 1876-1880*, hereafter SST/SF *Correspondence Files*, McNelly to Steele, April 29, 1875.

7. *RAG*, 1875, 8-13.

8. Durham, *Nueces Strip*, 8-33.

9. Ibid., 35-39.

10. Ibid., 42-46.

11. SST/SF *Correspondence Files*, G.A. Hall to McNelly, June 7, 1875.

12. Durham, *Nueces Strip*, 50-55.

13. SST/SF *Correspondence Files*, McNelly to Steele, June 1875.

14. Ibid.

15. Callicott's story, told in letters he wrote Walter Prescott Webb, is printed in Webb, *The Texas Rangers*, 241-51. The following account of the fight on the Palo Alto prairie is a composite of Callicott's letters to Webb, McNelly's report printed in SST/SF *Correspondence Files*, McNelly to Steele, undated but in June 1875 after McNelly was in Brownsville, and Durham, *Nueces Strip*, 57-62. The several versions agree on most major details except that, naturally, McNelly did not include details of how the prisoners were treated. It should be remembered that each Ranger saw the events from his own vantage point and told what he observed. Complete agreement of every account would be suspicious.

16. Durham, *Nueces Strip*, 63-64.

17. The statements of these three men were written on June 16 and June 17, 1875. They are reprinted in *RAG*, 1875.

18. Durham, *Nueces Strip*, 66-67.

19. SST/SF *Correspondence Files*, McNelly to Steele, June 14, 1875.

20. Durham, *Nueces Strip*, 66, 71..

21. Ibid., 67-68. This account does not agree with the company's monthly return. Later, in August, one man was discharged for cause. Two were allowed to resign on August 8 and August 11, six more on August 31. Whether Durham's memory played him false or the discharges were not reported until later is of no great importance. What is important is that McNelly refused to have any man with him who was not willing to obey any order he issued.

22. Ibid., 68-69. Durham mistakenly wrote Major "Anderson," but it was Major A.J. Alexander.

23. Ibid., 70-73.

24. Ibid., 73-76. Durham was referring to the *List of Fugitives*, first issued in the early 1870s by the adjutant general, which consisted in large part of Democrats and ex-Confederates. After 1874, with the Democrats in power, it was revised to list current fugitives and reissued as a guide for each Ranger company. It is easy to understand Browne's interest in who was wanted in his county.

25. SST/SF *Correspondence Files*, McNelly to Steele, July 7, 1875.

26. Ibid., McNelly to Steele, August 13, 1875.

27. Durham, *Nueces Strip*, 75-78.

28. SST/SF *Monthly Returns*, Washington County Volunteer Militia, August-October 1875.

29. Durham, *Nueces Strip*, 87-94.

30. Ibid., 97-100.

31. Ibid., 101-102.

32. SST/SF *Correspondence Files*, McNelly to Steele, October 31 and November 4, 1875. See also footnote #49.

33. Durham, *Nueces Strip*, 104-105, and Webb, *The Texas Rangers*, 261.

34. Durham, *Nueces Strip*, 104-105.

35. SST/SF *Correspondence Files*, McNelly to Steele, November 18, 1875. How McNelly was able to use a telegraph in what was little better than wilderness country may be of interest. The Ranger obviously tapped into the army's telegraph system running between the army posts along the Rio Grande. The telegraph placed the developing fight

only minutes away from Fort Brown, Austin, and even Washington. This convenient and speedy method of communication would be a mixed blessing to McNelly.

36. Based on after-action reports by Clendenin and McNelly, December 5 and November 22, 1875. *AGR*, D.R. Clendenin to A.A.A.G., U.S. Forces at Fort Brown, December 5, 1875. Copies of the army messages were sent by McNelly, or later furnished, to the adjutant general and are still in the archives. McNelly to Steele, November 22, 1875, was sent as shown by the log of messages received but is no longer in the archives. The original was still available in the 1930s when Webb was writing his book. I am indebted to him for the references in this chapter.

37. Durham, *Nueces Strip*, 106, and Callicott as printed in Webb, *The Texas Rangers*, 261-262.

38. SST/SF *Monthly Returns* Washington County Volunteer Militia, November 1875.

39. The above and following is based on Durham, *Nueces Strip*, 106-28, and Callicott as quoted in Webb, *The Texas Rangers*, 260-79. The action in the preceding paragraph is described by Durham only; throughout there are minor and major differences between the official reports and the recollections of Callicott and Durham.

40. *AGR*, James F. Randlett to the A.A. Adjutant General, District of the Rio Grande, December 1, 1875. This is a lengthy report and covers the early actions of the cattle thefts, as well as the fighting on the river.

41. SST/SF *Correspondence Files*, McNelly to Steele, November 20, 1875.

42. Ibid., McNelly to Diego Garcia, Garcia to McNelly (1st and 2nd), all November 21, 1875.

43. AGR, A.J. Alexander to A.A.A.G. Dist. of the Rio Grande, November 29, 1875. Alexander's report is so brief as to prevent any differences with other reports. Callicott did not describe any physical assault or death of a Mexican, and he noted that Sullivan was the interpreter, but Sullivan was not one of the ten men who crossed the river.

44. Durham wrote that a young lieutenant, Guy Carleton, had reported the destruction of the Rangers, another Alamo!, over the army telegraph. If so, it has not survived, nor has any later correction by Carleton.

45. Durham, *Nueces Strip*, 129-33.

46. SST/SF *Monthly Return* Washington County Volunteer Militia, December 1875.

47. Ibid., January, February 1876.

48. Durham, *Nueces Strip*, 133-34.

49. SST/SF *Correspondence Files*. In two letters to Steele, October 31 and November 4, 1875, McNelly indicated he had seen Kells' instructions and considered them grounds for starting a war. For further discussion on this subject see Michael G. Webster, "Intrigue on the Rio Grande: The Rio Bravo Affair, 1875." *Southwestern Historical Quarterly* LXXIV, 149-64.

50. SST/SF *Correspondence Files*, Robinson to Steele, January 3 and March 1, 1876.

51. Ibid., McNelly to Steele, March 8, 1876.

52. Durham, *Nueces Strip*, 132, has a brief mention of the beginnings of the Diaz revolution. The initial confusion provided some work for the Rangers, but Diaz eventually brought considerable stability to

the border regions.

53. Ibid., 134.

54. *RAG*, 1876, 9. McNelly to Steele, May 19, 1876.

55. SST/SF *Correspondence Files*, McNelly to Steele, May 31, 1876.

56. Durham, *Nueces Strip*, 138-50.

57. *RAG*, 1876, 9.

58. Durham, *Nueces Strip*, 148.

59. SST/SF *Monthly Returns*, Captain McNelly's Company of Texas State Troops, July 26, 1876.

60. *Texas Frontier Troubles*. House of Representatives. Report No.343. 44th Congress, 1st Session, 83-84.

61. Durham, *Nueces Strip*, 136.

62. Ibid., 154-57.

63. Dora Raymond, *Lee Hall of Texas*, 1-39.

64. SST/SF *Correspondence Files*, Hall to Steele, October 4, 1876.

65. Ibid., Charles Roberts to Governor Coke, October 22, 1876, and E.R. Lane to Governor Coke, October 22, 1876.

66. Durham, *Nueces Strip*, 157-58.

67. SST/SF *Correspondence Files*, Armstrong to McNelly, October 1, 1876, and Durham, *Nueces Strip*, 159-60. These accounts generally agree, but there are some differences in numbers slain. Time could have dimmed Durham's recollection. Further complicating the number of men killed is Jennings' claim that he again met McAllister in 1892!

68. SST/SF *Monthly Return*, McNelly's Company, Special State Troops, September 30, 1876.

69. Ibid., McNelly's Company, Special State Troops, November 30, 1876.

70. Durham, *Nueces Strip*, 164-74, and SST/SF *Correspondence Files*, Hall to Steele, October 10, 1876. Evidently the Winchesters donated by King had been considered personal property and were taken with them by the Rangers as they quit the service.

71. The account of this action is largely based on Durham, *Nueces Strip*, 164-72. During the 1920s and 1930s a number of elderly ex-Rangers wrote their stories for magazine and newspaper articles, with both general agreement on events and expected variations. N.A. Jennings, *A Texas Ranger* (Dallas: Southwest Press 1930; reprint of 1899), 277-90, contains a more dramatic version of this confrontation in which Hall disarms the wanted men and their friends. Other accounts, however, agree that only two men were personally armed, although there were weapons of all types throughout the house. The Rangers were heavily outnumbered—and within seconds a score or more of Sitterlee's friends could have been firing—but the Sutton-Taylor fight had altered since its beginnings. No Suttons or Taylors were participants in this incident; long since the feud had become little more than outlaws *vs.* the law.

72. SST/SF *Monthly Return*, Special State Troops, December 1876. Durham had a keen memory for details, but he was mistaken when he said the arrest took place on Christmas Eve.

73. Durham, *Nueces Strip*, 173.

74. *Galveston News*, January 6, 1877.

CHAPTER 5
CHANGING MISSIONS 1877

1. FB, *Correspondence Files*, Coldwell to Jones, January 15, 1877. This correspondence indicates that the winter camp for the company

had been moved from its previous location above San Antonio, and that Major Jones was no longer with the company. From Coldwell's plans, as outlined to Jones, it is difficult to tell just where the company was now encamped.

2. For the early life of Arrington see Jerry Sinise, *George Washington Arrington: Civil War Spy, Texas Ranger, Sheriff and Rancher, A Biography* (Burnet, Texas: Eakin Press, 1979).

3. FB, *MR.* Monthly Return, Company A, January-February 1877.

4. Ibid., Company B, January 1877.

5. Ibid., all companies, February 1877.

6. FB, *Correspondence Files*, Kisinger to Jones, March 11, 1877.

7. Ibid., Campbell to Jones, March 29, 1877.

8. Ibid., Coldwell to Jones, March 30, 1877.

9. FB, Special Order No.15, March 20, 1877.

10. FB, *Correspondence Files*, Jones to Col. H.C. King, April 12, 1877.

11. See O.C. Fisher, *It Occurred in Kimble* (Houston: The Anson Jones Press, 1938) for an account of the origins of Kimble County.

12. FB, *Correspondence Files*, Felix Burton to Jones, February 22, 1877.

13. Ibid., Waddill to Jones, February 27, 1877.

14. Ibid., Judge W.A. Blackburn to Jones, March 30, April 2, April 6, 1877.

15. Ibid., Jones to Blackburn, April 2, 1877.

16. Ibid., Jones to Steele, April 12, 1877.

17. Ibid., Jones to Lt. F.M. Moore, April 11, 1877; Jones to Lt. Pat. Dolan, April 11, 1877. Jones' reference to "Paint Rock" may be confusing but, since he specifically places Paint Rock on the South Llano, he was obviously talking about a local landmark rather than the present town of Paint Rock located near the Indian pictographs along the Concho River.

18. Ibid., Jones to Mers. Faltin & Schreiner, April 11, 1877.

19. Ibid., Jones to Steele, April 12, 1877.

20. Ibid., Jones to Steele (telegram), April 19, 1877.

21. Ibid., Jones to Steele (telegram), April 22, 1877.

22. Ibid., Jones to Judge Blackburn, April 23, 1877.

23. Ibid.

24. Ibid., Jones to Sheriff, Lavaca County, April 25, 1877.

25. Ibid., Jones to Steele, May 6, 1877.

26. Gillett, *Six Years*, 69-70.

27. FB, *Correspondence Files*, Jones to Steele, June 14, 1877.

28. Gillett, *Six Years*, 76-78.

29. Jerry Sinise, *Pink Higgins, The Reluctant Gunfighter And Other Tales of the Panhandle* (Quanah, Texas: Nortex Press, 1973), 34. Sinise has the following undated extract, probably from early June, from *The Lampasas Dispatch*, "we are all civil now ... nobody having been killed in a week or more."

30. Sinise, *Reluctant Gunfighter*, 35.

31. FB, *Correspondence Files*, Jones to Blackburn, July 16, 1877.

32. Ibid., Jones to Steele, June 14, July 16, 1877.

33. Gillett, *Six Years*, 78-79. Gillett had a sick horse and did not take part in this action. He probably talked to companions who were present, but his version differs in many details from Reynolds' story. Of interest, Gillett refers to Jones as "General" long before he became Adjutant General of Texas.

34. FB, *Correspondence Files*, Jones to Steele, July 28, 1877.

35. Written on August 4 and published August 9, 1877, Reynolds' account has considerably more detail than Gillett or the sparse official records. Sinise, *Reluctant Gunfighter*, has an excellent version of this action, including a reprint of the newspaper article.

36. FB, *Correspondence Files*, Jones to Steele, July 31, 1877.

37. Ibid., July 30, 1877.

38. Ibid., August 2, 1877.

39. Sinise, *Reluctant Gunfighter*, 23. Gillett says the two Horrell brothers were arrested rather than surrendering voluntarily.

40. *Lampasas Dispatch*, April 4, 1878.

41. FB, *Correspondence Files*, Coldwell to Jones, June 21, July 10, 1877.

42. Ibid., Moore to Steele, April 15, 1877.

43. FB, *MR*. Monthly Return, Company F, June 1877.

44. FB, *Correspondence Files*, Arrington to Steele, July 11, 1877.

45. *AGR*, AG General Order No.20, August 29, 1877.

46. *HBT*, II: 549.

47. *HBT*, I: 561-62.

48. Portions of this account are from Gillett, *Six Years*, 136-40. The full story of the power struggle in El Paso County, with pertinent documents, personal statements and reports from all sides of the bitter fight, may be found in "El Paso Troubles in Texas," *House Executive Document No.93, Forty-Fifth Congress, Second Session, Serial No. 1809.* Some of this material was reproduced in *RAG*, 1878.

49. *AGR*, A. Blacker to Governor Hubbard, October 9, 1877.

50. Ibid., Charles Kerber to Governor Hubbard, October 10, 1877. This does not mean that every Mexican American in the area was against Howard. Two signed his bond, and a number were in favor of settling the salt question by peaceful means. Other Hispanics served in the local militia company and stood for law and order. Most, however, were afraid to take an open stand for fear of violence.

51. Webb, *Texas Rangers*, 352.

52. FB, *Correspondence Files*, Jones to Steele, November 7, 1877.

53. FB, Special Order No.109, Frontier Battalion, November 12, 1877.

54. FB, Special Order No.110, Frontier Battalion, November 12, 1877.

55. FB, *Correspondence Files*, Steele to Jones, November 17, 1877.

56. Ibid., Jones to Steele, November 18, 1877.

57. Ibid., Jones to Steele, November 20, 1877.

58. Ibid., Howard to Jones, November 23, 1877.

59. FB, *MR*. Monthly Return, Detachment of Company C, November 1877. Tays' report was written the end of November and apparently referred to Howard's earlier return to El Paso from Mesilla, to make bond, while Jones was still there.

60. FB, *Correspondence Files*. This telegram is filed under correspondence for December 15, 1877. It was probably intended for Adjutant General Steele.

61. This version is based on Lieutenant Tay's official report in "El Paso Troubles in Texas" as reprinted in *RAG*, 1878.

62. Gillett, *Six Years*, 138-39. Gillett was not in San Elizario at this time, but he later served with several men from the Detachment of Company C and probably obtained this version from one or more of them.

63. Testimony of Juan Nep. Garcia, "El Paso Troubles in Texas," *RAG*, 1878, 96-98.

64. Based upon a story in the *Mesilla Valley News* by an unnamed eyewitness. It agrees exactly, even to phrasing, with the testimony given by Juan N. Garcia in "El Paso Troubles in Texas," reprinted in *RAG*, 1878, 96-98.

65. FB, *MR*, Monthly Return, Detachment of Company C, December 1877.

66. Gillett, *Six Years*, 140.

67. SST/SF *Correspondence Files*, Armstrong to Steele, February 22, 1877.

68. SST/SF *Correspondence Files*, Hall to Steele, May 16, 1877.

69. FB, *MR*. Monthly Return, Company A, April 1877.

70. Proceedings of the West Texas Stock Association, June 11, 1877, *Galveston Daily News, August 2, 1877.*

71. SST/SF *Correspondence Files*, Hall to Steele, August 6, 1877.

72. Hardin, *Hardin*, 112-14.

73. The capture of Hardin is one of the least-documented events of the period. Armstrong never made a formal report nor wrote about his exploits, but he did describe the capture of Hardin to his sons, who told the story as recounted to them to Webb, *Texas Rangers*, 298-301. In the 1960s John B. Armstrong III retold the story to Diane Solether Smith, who used it in *The Armstrong Chronicle*, 99-104. This version is essentially the same as in Webb. Hardin, *Hardin*, 114-21, contains a detailed description. The two accounts agree in at least the broad outlines, but differ in their descriptions of the actual capture of Hardin.

74. *AGR*, AG Letter Ledgers, Armstrong to Steele, August 23, 1877. This and several following telegrams are the only official documents relating to the capture of Hardin. The ledger of incoming messages fortunately has a digest of each message or letter, because some of the original documents are now lost. The ledger clearly shows the date as August 23, although Hardin, writing years later, said it was July 23.

75. *AGR*, AG Ledger File, Armstrong to Steele, August 24, 1877.

76. Smith, *Armstrong Chronicle*, 109.

77. Gillett, *Six Years*, 81-85.

78. Donley Brice of the Archives Division of the Texas State Library has done extensive research on Reynolds, for a proposed biography, and kindly shared some of his findings with the author.

79. Gillett, *Six Years*, 84.

80. Hardin, *Hardin*, 121-24.

81. Ibid., 134-44.

82. FB, *Correspondence Files*, Jones to Coldwell, December 12, 1877.

83. Ibid., Coldwell to Jones, December 26, 1877.

84. *San Antonio Express*, January 1, 1878.

CHAPTER 6
SAM BASS AND OTHER BAD MEN 1878

1. FB, *Correspondence Files*, Jones to Arrington, January 8, 1878.

2. FB, *MR*. Monthly Return, Company C, February 1878.

3. Ibid., Company C, March and May 1878.

4. Gillett, *Six Years*, 139-40, 148-49.

5. FB, *MR*. Monthly Return, Detachment, Company C, March, July, August 1878.

6. FB, *Correspondence Files*, Jones to Campbell, March 18, 1878.

7. Ibid., Campbell to Jones, April 3, 1878.

8. Ibid., Fleming to Jones, May 16, 1878.

9. Unless otherwise cited, material on Sam Bass is based on Anonymous, By a Citizen of Denton County, Texas, *Authentic History of Sam Bass and His Gang* (Denton, Texas: Monitor Job Office, 1878). The unknown writer either had good sources or knew Bass and members of his gang. He also made use of contemporary newspaper accounts. While not used, another unknown writer wrote his version of the outlaw: Anonymous, *Life and Adventures of Sam Bass, The Notorious Union Pacific and Texas Train Robber*, also published in 1878. The first had Bass in Denton in 1872, the latter in 1870, but they agree on major details. A more available source is Gillett, *Six Years*, 108-28. Gillett, obviously, knew nothing of Bass' early life, and he or his editor evidently used the second book as a reference. Gillett is nonetheless of value because he took part in the final events of Bass' life.

10. FB, *Correspondence Files*, M.F. Leech to Jones, July 27, 1878.

11. In recent years there has been some effort to make Hall a major player in the Bass chase, making more of Hall's endeavors than actual events warrant. Dora Raymond, *Lee Hall of Texas* (Norman: University of Oklahoma Press, 1940), devotes a chapter to Hall's activities in the Bass chase. From time to time Hall and some of his men did search for Bass, but they were never close.

12. Raymond, *Lee Hall*, 154.

13. FB, *Correspondence Files*, Steele to Jones, April 12, 1878.

14. Gillett, *Six Years*, 115-16. Gillett overstated the fact when he referred to Peak's new company by writing, "the bandit leader played with it as a child plays with toys."

15. *AGR*, Steele to Jones, April 22, 1878.

16. FB, *Correspondence Files*, B.J. Jacobs to Governor Hubbard, May 7, 1878.

17. Ibid., Peak to Jones, May 1, 1878.

18. Ibid., Peak to Jones, May 14, 1878. The telegram was sent after the Rangers returned to Decatur. Peak reported the fight took occurred on May 13.

19. Ibid., Jones to Campbell, May 1, 1878.

20. Ibid., Jones to Campbell, May 18, 1878, and Special Order No.131, Frontier Battalion, May 18, 1878.

21. FB, *MR*. Fifteen Day Report, Company B, June 15, 1878.

22. FB, *Correspondence Files*, Peak to Bower, May 11, 1878.

23. Ibid., Jones to Steele, May 17, 1878.

24. Ibid., Jones to Steele, May 28, 1878.

25. Ibid. Details of this portion of the Bass Story are based on two statements made by Murphy on July 23 and July 26, 1878. The two documents agree in main details. The latter was probably written by Murphy to prove he had kept his part of the bargain.

26. Ibid., Floyd to Peak, July 12, 13, 1878. It might be helpful to review the several references to Company B. Peak's unit was organized originally as a detachment of Company B and, technically speaking, was still in that category. Sergeant Riper, at least on paper, commanded the few men still in the original Company B. Now a captain, Peak continued the chase after Bass, without regard for the niceties of protocol, and left the reorganization of Company B for the future.

27. Ibid., Peak to Jones, July 16, 1878.

28. Gillett, *Six Years*, 123-27, has an account of the fight in Round Rock and Bass' capture. As he was a member of Nevill's patrol, his

version is of interest. He states, however, that "Harold" [Harrell] was not the one who killed Bass, asserting that it was Dick Ware who fired the shot that "struck Bass's belt, cutting two cartridges in pieces and entering his back just above the right hip bone." Whoever fired the fatal shot, it hit Bass as he was running away.

29. FB, *Correspondence Files*, Peak to Jones, July 21, 26, 1878.

30. Ibid., Peak to Jones, August 2, 1878.

31. *Galveston News*, July 21, 1878.

32. FB, *Correspondence Files*, Murphy to Jones, August 27, 1878.

33. Ibid., Jones to Peak, August 1, 1878.

34. Ibid., Jones to C.T. Campbell, August 20, 1878.

35. Ibid., Murphy to Jones, September 6, 1878.

36. Ibid., Jones to Reynolds, September 5, 1878.

37. Ibid., Reynolds to Jones, September 8, 1878.

38. Ibid., Reynolds to Jones, October 14, 1878.

39. Ibid., Jones to Arrington, October 7, 1878.

40. FB, *MR*. Monthly Return, Company C, November 1878.

41. *RAG* 1878, 30-31. This report includes Ranger losses during the Salt War.

42. Ibid., 31, 34, 35.

43. Ibid., 51-55.

CHAPTER 7

THE CHANGING FRONTIER 1879-1880

1. *HBT*, Vol I, 925.

2. Ibid., Vol II, 484-85.

3. FB, *Correspondence Files*, Jones to Peak, January 14, 1879.

4. FB, Special Order No.11, para III, May 9, 1879.

5. FB, *Correspondence Files*, Jones to Williamson, August 28, 1879, for one example.

6. Sinise, *George Washington Arrington*, 22-23, has a more complete account of these scouts.

7. An excellent discussion of the opening of the Panhandle is contained in *The Texas Panhandle Frontier* (Austin: University of Texas Press, 1973) by Frederick W. Rathjen.

8. Sinese, *George Washington Arrington*, 23-24.

9. Documenting the opposition of the sutlers and others to settlement is difficult because it was mostly verbal. Their fear of losing revenue is understandable, even if their opposition was unreasonable.

10. FB, *Correspondence Files*, Arrington to Jones, June 18, 1879.

11. Ibid., Arrington to Lieutenant-Colonel Davidson, June 18, 1879; *AGR*, statement by John Donnelly, June 18, 1879, and Lieutenant-Colonel J.W. Davidson to Governor Roberts, June 25, 1879.

12. Ibid., Peak to Jones, July 5, 1879.

13. Ibid., telegram, Peak to Jones, August 23, 1879.

14. Ibid., Corporal Taylor to Peak, September 13, 1879.

15. FB, *MR*. Monthly Return, Company C, September 1879.

16. W. Curtiss Nunn, "Eighty-six Hours Without Water on the Texas Plains." *Southwestern Historical Quarterly*, XLIII no. 3, 356-64.

17. There is one official report on this scout: FB, *Correspondence Files*, Arrington to Jones, February 9, 1880. Arrington's field report January 20, 1880, was only a partial report covering events to that date. The version of the expedition outlined here is based on the field

report, the official report, and a long reconstruction which Arrington wrote in later years, contained in "The Arrington Papers," edited by L.F. Sheffy, *The Panhandle Plains Historical Review*, vol.I, no.1, 54-66.

18. This and the earlier quote are from the Arrington Papers.

19. Rathjen, *Texas Panhandle Frontier*, 228-31.

20. FB, *Monthly Returns*, Company A, March, April, May 1879.

21. Gillett, *Six Years*, 132-33; FB, *MR*. Monthly Return, Company F, March 1879.

22. Based on research by Donley Brice, as cited earlier. Chuck Parsons, who worked with Brice, uncovered papers showing Reynolds began processing an application in 1912 for a federal pension based on his Civil War service in the Union Army! This undoubtedly accounted for Reynolds' reluctance to discuss his early years. Reynolds died in 1922, his past still a secret, but the revelation was published in the March 30, 1997, edition of the *Dallas Morning News*. Reynolds' letter of resignation was dated February 14, 1879, to take effect on February 28, 1879 (FB, *Correspondence*). Although not documented, he may have been offered a captaincy to return; if so, he did not accept.

23. O.L. Shipman, *Taming the Big Bend* (Austin: Von Boeckman-Jones Co., 1926), 109-12. Dolan came to Texas following the Civil War and was Uvalde County sheriff by 1873. He served as a lieutenant before being promoted to captain and company commander. One of the lesser-known officers, he nevertheless did a workmanlike job and was well respected.

24. This account is from Gillett, *Six Years*, 87-89.

25. Ibid., 92.

26. Ibid., 92-95, describes the scout after the Dublins. Gillett's letter, reprinted in *Texana*, Vol 2, 78, reveals that Gillett had an average education for an 1870s cowboy.

27. Roberts, *Rangers and Sovereignty*, 125-29.

28. Gillett, *Six Years*, 102-4.

29. FB, *Correspondence Files*, Roberts to Jones, August 1, 1879.

30. *RAG* 1880, 27, 34. Jones reported that Dick Dublin was killed by Company D Rangers in August 1879, but it was actually Dell Dublin. Dick Dublin had been shot by Gillett much earlier.

31. *RAG* 1880, 35.

32. Ibid., 27-28.

33. George Wythe Baylor, *Into the Far, Wild Country* (El Paso: Texas Western Press, 1916), 275. The following account of the journey from San Antonio to Ysleta is based on Baylor's later recollections, 275-76, and Gillett, *Six Years*, 140-48, a considerably more detailed version.

34. *RAG* 1880, 33.

35. FB, *MR*. Monthly Return, Detachment, Company C, August 1879.

36. Gillett, *Six Years*, 149-50.

37. Baylor, *Wild Country*, Introduction, 21.

38. The following incident is from Gillett, *Six Years*, 151-60, and Baylor, *Wild Country*, 276-81. Gillett referred to Gregorio Garcia as "Captain," probably having heard of his service as a company commander in 1870.

39. Robert M. Utley, *Fort Davis* (Washington, D.C.: National Park Service, 1965), 17-18. *HBT*, Vol I, 124.

40. FB, *MR*. Monthly Return, Detachment, Company C, October 1879.

41. FB, *Correspondence Files*, Baylor to Jones, October 10, 1879.

42. FB, *MR*. Monthly Return, Detachment, Company C, October 1879.

43. Gillett, *Six Years*, 161-64.

44. FB, *MR*. Monthly Return, Detachment, Company C, November 1879.

45. Gillett, *Six Years*, 165-69. FB, *Monthly Returns*, Detachment, Company C, November 1879; *Correspondence Files*, Baylor to Jones, December 3, 1879.

46. *RAG* 1880, 33.

47. FB, *Correspondence Files*, J.M. Dean to Governor Roberts, May 21, 1879.

48. Ibid., Frazer to Jones, June 3, 1880.

49. The telegram to Roberts has been lost, but Roberts mentioned it in *Rangers and Sovereignty*, 111. He thought the message was on June 23, 1889, but this is incorrect. Based on Frazer's other message to Jones and the departure of the Company D Rangers, it was probably May 25. Roberts summarized the telegram, mentioning that five outlaws had robbed merchants in Stockton and sacked the town. They then went to Fort Davis and repeated the performance, in addition arresting some county officials and holding them in jail. After the Stockton and Davis episodes, and before the arrest statements, Roberts added a few sentences that are confusing and could possibly be construed as saying the Rangers arrested the officials. This was obviously impossible, as there were no Rangers in the area at this time.

50. Sieker left May 30, 1880, according to the monthly return for Company D. He is shown with nine men, not seven as recalled by Roberts. It is possible Caruthers is included in the monthly return figure.

51. FB, *Correspondence Files*, Caruthers to Nevill, June 8, 1880.

52. FB, *MR*. Monthly Return, Company D, June 1880.

53. Roberts, *Rangers and Sovereignty*, 111-12.

54. FB, *Correspondence Files*, Sieker to Jones, June 15, 1880.

55. Ibid., Caruthers to Jones, June 14, 1880.

56. Ibid., Caruthers to Jones, June 28, 1880.

57. FB, *MR*. Monthly Return, Company D, July 1880.

58. FB, *Correspondence Files*, Sieker to Jones and Sieker to Roberts, July 12, 1880.

59. Roberts, *Rangers and Sovereignty*, 114-15.

60. *RAG* 1880, 33.

61. Gillett, *Six Years*, 180-89. Gillett refers to "General" Grierson, who had been a major general during the Civil War but been reduced to colonel in the regular army after the war. He was not again promoted to general until 1890.

62. The full details of this brief campaign by the U.S. Army are not recounted, but they do reveal the different methods the army used to mount a full-scale campaign, and their often-inept efforts at chasing small raiding parties. In this instance, Grierson conducted a skilled small war and bested one of the greatest Apache leaders.

63. FB, *MR*. Monthly Returns, Company A, September-October 1880.

64. FB, *Correspondence Files*, Baylor to Jones, October 28, 1880.

65. FB, *MR*. Monthly Return, Company A, September 1880, is the first to be signed by Baylor as captain, also the first with the "Company A" designation. What few men who remained from the old Company A were mustered into Lee Hall's company of Special Troops.

66. FB, *Correspondence Files*, Nevill to Jones, August 26, 1880.

67. Ibid., Nevill to Jones, September 1, 1880.

68. Ibid., Nevill to Coldwell, September 17, 1880. Nevill's reports refer to "Mauskes" Canyon.

69. Ibid., Nevill to Jones, December 20, 1880.

70. FB, *MR.* Monthly Returns, Company A, October-December 1880.

71. Ranger Reminiscences Files, Rush Kimbell.

72. Ibid. Kimbell was unsure about the time spent on the trail. Fort Lancaster had been abandoned by the army but was on the stage road, and his message was probably carried back to Company D by one of the stage drivers. Roberts, *Rangers and Sovereignty,* 117-20, also has a short account of this scout.

73. Kimbell's memoirs continue after his discharge from the Ranger service and provide an interesting account of frontier life.

74. *RAG* 1880, 28.

75. Ibid., 27.

76. FB, *Correspondence Files*, Resolution of Company B, April 10, 1880.

77. J. Evetts Haley, *Jeff Milton: A Good Man with a Gun* (Norman: University of Oklahoma Press, 1948), 23-24.

78. FB, *MR.* Monthly Return, Company B, July 1880.

79. FB, *Correspondence Files*, Long to Jones, July 10, 1880.

80. FB, *MR.* Monthly Return, Company B, July 1880.

81. Haley, *Jeff Milton*, 31-34.

82. Ibid., 35; *RAG* 1880, 27.

83. The monthly return for December 1880 is signed by Marsh.

84. Haley, *Jeff Milton*, 35.

85. *RAG* 1880, 29-30.

86. Ibid., 25-26.

CHAPTER 8
THE VANISHING FRONTIER 1881-1882

1. Gillett, *Six Years*, 200-203.

2. FB, *Correspondence Files*, Baylor to Jones, January 16 9, 1881.

3. Ibid., Nevill to Jones, February 6, 1881. This is Nevill's after-action report, much shorter than Baylor's account because Nevill joined the chase days after Baylor started and did not go into every detail of camps and routes in and around the Diablo Mountains. Both accounts agree on the main details of the actual fight. Nevill's ration return for January 1881 lists the actual supplies shared with Baylor's company. It also describes the January weather, "bitter cold with heavy snows."

4. *RAG* February 28, 1882, 36.

5. FB, *Correspondence Files*, Baylor to Jones, February 9, 1881. This is a long account with much detail, but the account of the chase in the Sierra Diablo region is almost impossible to follow. In later years, Baylor wrote a newspaper article covering the chase and fight, equally detailed and with additional details on the actual fight. In this account, he has the Rangers going generally along the east face of the mountain and lists the Indian scouts as Bernardo Olguin, Domingo Olguin and Aniceto Duran. See Baylor, *Into the Far, Wild Country*, 304-22.

6. Gillett, *Six Years*, 209. Gillett's version of this event is on pages 203-10. He had access to Baylor's report, and much of his account is based on his captain's story, even to exact wording.

7. The reports referenced in footnotes 3 and 5 are the sources for this narrative. Both commanders were unstinting in praising their men's conduct during the fighting. Each officer mentioned a feeling of elation when they surprised the Apaches and avenged the loss of military and civilian lives in just such ambush attacks.

8. FB, *Correspondence Files*, Nevill to Coldwell, February 9, 1881; Nevill to Jones, February 8, 1881.

9. Gillett, *Six Years*, 143.

10. Ibid., 190-99.

11. *RAG* February 28, 1882, 37-38.

12. The account of this incident is from Haley, *Jeff Milton*, 36-38.

13. FB, *Correspondence Files*, Marsh to Jones, February 7, 1881.

14. FB, *MR*. Monthly Return, Company B, February 1881.

15. *RAG*, February 28, 1882.

16. FB, *MR*. Monthly Return, Company B, November 1880.

17. The account of this incident is from Haley, *Jeff Milton*, 48-50.

18. FB, *Monthly Returns*, Company B, May 1881.

19. *RAG* February 28, 1882, 23.

20. Roberts, *Rangers and Sovereignty*, 63-65.

21. *HBT*, Vol I, 925.

22. King, like many legislators from eastern areas of Texas, did not understand the need for the Rangers. A fair man, however, he went out into the field and saw first-hand the condition of much of the state.

23. *RAG* February 28, 1882, 23.

24. FB, *MR*. Monthly Return, Company B, September 1881. McMurry is another name subject to various spellings and is also listed as McMurray.

25. *RAG* February 28, 1882.

26. Ibid., December 31, 1882, 26. Because of Jones' death, the new adjutant general, King, issued two reports in 1882, one in February and the other in December.

27. *RAG* February 28, 1882, 25-26.

28. In addition to finding a widespread need for the Rangers as peace officers, King suggested using them as guides and guards for scientific, economic and historical explorations of the largely unknown areas in the western part of Texas.

29. *RAG* December 31, 1882, 27.

30. Gillett, *Six Years*, 211-22, contains this account of his most famous case. Gillett says the murder of Conklin occurred at Christmas 1881, which is incorrect.

31. FB, *MR*. Monthly Return, Company A, February 1881. Not surprisingly, the spelling of names by Gillett does not always agree with company documents.

32. Gillett, *Six Years*, 176-79.

33. Roberts, *Rangers and Sovereignty*, 118.

34. FB, *MR*. Monthly Return, Company A, March 1881. Gillett uses the name "Enofre" although company documents use "Enferio."

35. Ibid., Company A, December 1881. In *Six Years*, 231, Gillett says he ate his final meal on December 26, but the company records indicate he departed on December 22.

36. *RAG*, December 31, 1882, 24-25.

37. Ibid.

38. Ibid.

39. Ibid., 27.

40. Ibid., 21, 28.

CHAPTER 9
MUCH WORK—LITTLE GLORY 1883-1885

1. FB, *Correspondence Files*, Sieker to King, January 31, 1883.

2. Ibid., Fontaine to Baylor, March 15, 1883, Baylor to King, March 18, 1883.

3. FB, Special Order No.33, February 16, 1883; *RAG* 1883, 19. The additional strength and officers were added following the end of the fiscal year ending February 28, 1883. As funds became available, additional officers were authorized in the next year.

4. FB, Scout Report, Company C, August 1883.

5. *RAG* 1883, 20.

6. Ibid., 20-21.

7. Ibid., 22.

8. Ibid., 23.

9. Ranger Reminiscences File, J.Willis Holston.

10. Ibid. Dan Roberts made a similar statement in his memoirs, *Rangers and Sovereignty*, 40.

11. *RAG* 1883, 19.

12. Ibid., 19-20.

13. Ibid., 33.

14. *RAG* 1884, 17.

15. Ibid.

16. Ibid., 28-29.

17. Ibid., 31.

18. Ibid.

19. FB, Special Order No.31, Company E, January 19, 1885.

20. Ibid., Special Order No.33, Company E, April 21. 1885.

21. *RAG* 1884, 21.

22. Ibid.

23. FB, *Correspondence Files*, Gillespie to Johnson, April 22, 1884. The Sergeant Sedberry mentioned by Gillespie was J.M. Sedberry, who last appeared as a member of Company B in the preceding chapter. Sedberry moved to Company E and became a sergeant in February 1884. He served as a sergeant until May 31, 1884, when he was promoted to lieutenant. Sedberry resigned from the Rangers on October 5, 1885.

24. *RAG* 1884, 21-22.

25. *RAG* 1886, 50-51; report of M.C. Kelly, County Clerk, Dimmit County, February 10, 1885, reprinted in *RAG* 1886, 63-64.

26. Ireland to King, February 7, 1885, reprinted in *RAG* 1886, 50.

27. *RAG* 1886, 52.

28. FB, *MR*. Monthly Returns, Company F, February and March 1885.

29. Ibid., Company A, January and March 1885. L.S. Turnbo served in Company C from October 1, 1876, to August 31, 1880. After a break in service, he joined Company A on February 18, 1882, where he advanced to the rank of lieutenant. His service was terminated April 15, 1885, when Company A was disbanded. He is typical of many Rangers who served honorably, well and long, yet were never in the right place for wide recognition.

30. FB, *Correspondence Files*, King to Gillespie, March 31, 1885.

31. *RAG* 1886, 50.

32. *HBT*, Vol. I, 123-24.

33. Ira Aten, *Six and One Half Years in the Ranger Service*, 2-4. Aten's account agrees closely with the scout report filed by Sergeant Lindsey, Lindsey to Sieker, July 10, 1885, reprinted in *RAG* 1886, 60-61.

34. FB, Special Order No.85, October 12, 1885; *RAG* 1886, 56.

35. *RAG* 1886, 50.

CHAPTER 10
FENCE CUTTERS AND TROUBLESHOOTERS 1886-1889

1. FB, *Correspondence Files*, Schmitt to Sieker, January 4, 1886. As with most Ranger correspondence, Schmitt's reports and letters are printed as they were written to present a rounded picture of Rangers and Ranger life. Many documents were written in the field, often under adverse conditions, and Ranger leaders were chosen for abilities that did not necessarily include grammatical expertise with the written word.

2. Ibid., Schmitt to Sieker, October 7, 1886.

3. Ibid., Schmitt to Sieker, November 13, 1886; *RAG* 1886, 56.

4. *RAG* 1886, 56. Lieutenant Frank Jones, commanding Company D, was also promoted to captain the same day.

5. FB, *Correspondence Files*, Scott to Sieker, July 31, 1886.

6. *RAG* 1886, 55.

7. Ibid., 47.

8. FB, *Correspondence Files*, Dr. Smith to Sieker, May 19, 1887.

9. *RAG* 1888, 44.

10. FB, *Correspondence Files*, Gillespie to Sieker, May 15, 1886.

11. Ibid., McMurry to Sieker, July 2, 1886. All of these reports indicate that company commanders reported to Sieker, the quartermaster, rather than to the adjutant general. Sieker was the *de facto* battalion commander; King was too busy with his varied duties to become involved in day-to-day Ranger operations, but this in no way implies that he did not do everything possible to support them.

12. *RAG* 1886, 4-5.

13. Ibid., 54.

14. Ibid., 8-12.

15. Ibid., 55.

16. A.S. Roberts to Governor Ireland, April 11, 1886, reprinted in *RAG* 1886, 48-49.

17. Aten, *Ranger Service*, 18.

18. This was after Scott and his men had returned from East Texas and before he returned in 1887.

19. Aten, *Ranger Service*, 17-20; *RAG* 1886, 66.

20. FB, *Correspondence Files*, Schmitt to Sieker, March 31, 1887.

21. *RAG* 1886, 41, 46.

22. Aten, *Ranger Service*, 15.

23. FB, *MR*. Monthly Returns, Company D, March and April 1887.

24. Aten, *Ranger Service*, 4-8.

25. *RAG* 1888, 46.

26. FB, *Correspondence Files*, Schmitt to Sieker, January 20, 1887.

27. FB, *MR*. Monthly Return, Company D, November 1888.

28. *RAG* 1888, 49.

29. FB, *Correspondence Files*, Aten to Sieker, August 20, 1888.

30. Ibid., Aten to Sieker, August 31, 1888. In his memoirs, Aten glosses over many details of this extended scout.

31. Ibid., Aten to Sieker, September 17, 1888.

32. Ibid., Aten to Sieker, October 8 and October 15, 1888; Aten, *Ranger Service*, 20-22. Aten devotes little space to his fence cutting scouts; he probably preferred forgetting those days.

33. *RAG* 1888, 46.

34. Ibid., 41-43.

35. Ibid., 46.

36. Frederick W. Rathjen, *Texas Panhandle Frontier* (Austin: University of Texas Press, 1973), 235.

37. *HBT*, vol. I, 214.

38. Ibid., 611.

39. *RAG* 1889-1890, 92.

40. FB, *Correspondence Files*, Draft Scout Report in files for 1889.

41. *RAG* 1889-1890, 92-94.

42. Ibid., 24.

43. Ibid., 26-28.

44. W.J.L. Sullivan, *Twelve Years in the Saddle for Law and Order on the Frontiers of Texas* (New York: Buffalo-Head Press, 1966), 33.

45. Ibid., 33-35; *RAG* 1889-1890, 29.

46. FB, *MR*. Monthly Returns, Company D, April-May 1889.

47. FB, *Correspondence Files*, Fusselman to King, June 5, 1889.

48. *RAG* 1889-1890, 92.

49. FB, *MR*. Monthly Return, Company D, July 1889.

50. *RAG* 1889-1890, 92.

51. Ibid., 93.

52. Ibid.

53. Aten's account of the Ranger peacekeeping effort reads like a comic opera. They prevented violence by allowing each party to vote at different locations and times, during which the party could vote as many people as they could get into the polling place. It may not have been legal, but it was better than a shooting war.

54. *HBT*, vol. I, 907-8; Aten, *Ranger Service*, 26.

55. FB, *MR*. Monthly Return, Company D, July 1889.

56. Aten, *Ranger Service*, 26-30. This account is largely based on Aten's memoirs.

57. FB, *MR*. Monthly Return, Company D, August 1889.

58. *RAG* 1889-1890, 29.

CHAPTER 11
END OF AN ERA 1890-1900

1. FB, *MR*. Monthly Return, Company D, March 1890.

2. Jack Martin, *Border Boss*, 88-96; *RAG* 1889-1890, 24. The chase after Fusselman's killer would continue over a nine-year period until Hughes was finally able to have the wanted man extradited from New Mexico to Texas to stand trial.

3. Alonzo Van Oden, *Texas Ranger's Diary & Scrapbook* (Dallas: The Kaleidograph Press, 1936), 10.

4. *RAG* 1889-1890, 25; FB, *MR*. Monthly Return, Company D, May 1890.

5. FB, *MR*. Monthly Return, Company D, June 1890.

6. *RAG* 1889-1890, 25-26. Special Rangers had been authorized in the late 1880s. They were carefully screened civilians who were permitted to bear arms and who served in emergency situations when

Rangers were not available. Generally, the concept worked well enough, but this case was an exception.

7. FB, *MR*. Monthly Return, Company F, May 1890.

8. *RAG* 1889-1890, 93-94.

9. Ibid., 26.

10. Ibid., 93-94.

11. Ibid., 25.

12. FB, *MR*. Monthly Return, Company D, August 1890.

13. Ibid., Company D, September 1890.

14. Ibid., Company D, October 1890.

15. *RAG* 1889-1890, 30.

16. King took an established format for the adjutant general's reports and expanded it to include his views of what the Rangers could and should accomplish in the future. Had the legislature acted on some of his suggestions, a great deal of trouble could have been avoided. In addition to his official reports, King wrote a history of the Rangers, the first such work, which was published as a part of a larger history of Texas by Dudley G. Wooten.

17. *RAG* 1889-1890, 30.

18. FB, *MR*. Monthly Return, Company B, January 1891.

19. Albert Bigelow Paine, *Captain Bill McDonald, Texas Ranger* (Austin: State House Press, 1986; reprint of 1909), contains the early career of McDonald.

20. Ibid., 140-41.

21. Ibid., 145-48.

22. FB, *Correspondence Files*, February 13, 1891.

23. Martin, *Border Boss*, 132-34, contains considerable detail on this incident.

24. FB, *Correspondence Files*, Jones to Mabry, September 11, 1891.

25. Ibid. Jones made a short wire report on this scout on October 22 and a longer, more formal account on October 24, 1891.

26. Van Oden, *Ranger's Diary*, 20.

27. Ibid., 75.

28. FB, *MR*. Monthly Return, Company E, June 1891.

29. FB, *Correspondence Files*, McNeel to Mabry, September 17, 1891. Mabry had evidently changed the previous practice of commanders' reporting to the quartermaster; during his tenure as adjutant general, all reports came to him.

30. Ibid., McNeel to Mabry, September 21, 1891.

31. *RAG* 1892, 10.

32. *HBT*, vol. III, 329. The details of Garza's life are based on the article in *HBT*.

33. FB, *Correspondence Files*, McNeel to Mabry, December 18, 1891.

34. Ibid., McNeel to Mabry, December 26, 1891.

35. FB, *MR*. Monthly Return, Company E, December 1891.

36. FB, *Scout Reports*, Company F, January 1892.

37. FB, *Correspondence Files*, telegram, McNeel to Mabry, January 5, 1892; McNeel to Mabry, January 7, 1892; FB. *MR*. Monthly Return, Company E, January 1892; *Scout Reports*, Company F, January 1892.

38. *RAG* 1892, 11.

39. FB, *Scout Reports*, Company F, January 1892.

40. *RAG* 1892, 11.

41. J.S. McNeel, Jr., *Memoirs* (unpublished manuscript provided by McNeel's grandson, Albert McNeel), 20; FB, *MR*. Monthly Return, Company E and Company F, February-April 1892.

42. McNeel, *Memoirs*, 21.

43. FB, *MR.* Monthly Return, Company E, February 1892.

44. FB, *MR.* Monthly Returns, Company E and Company F, March 1892; *Correspondence Files*, telegram, McNeel to Mabry, March 27, 1892.

45. FB, *Correspondence Files*, McNeel to Mabry, second page of undated letter, probably March 1892.

46. FB, *MR.* Monthly Return, Company E, March 1892.

47. Ibid., Company F, March 1892.

48. *RAG* 1892, 12.

49. McNeel, *Memoirs*, 23.

50. FB, *MR.* Monthly Return, Company E, December 1892.

51. FB, *Muster and Pay Rolls*, Company E, December 1-31, 1892.

52. Ibid., Company E, January 1-February 28, 1892.

53. Martin, *Border Boss*, 93-100. St.Leon's service record shows he *was* a Ranger, having enlisted in Company D on September 1, 1890. This puts a different light on the story and explains his cooperation. Whoever told the story to Martin evidently was not aware of his status.

54. FB, *Correspondence Files*, Jones to Mabry, April 16, 1893.

55. FB, *MR.* Monthly Return, Company D, June 1893.

56. Ibid., Company D, June 1893. Kirchner made an official report to Mabry on July 2, 1893. Both documents contain Jones' last words.

57. Ibid., Company D, June 1892. Some accounts say the body was returned on July 2, a892.

58. Van Oden, *Ranger's Diary*, 71-73, contains an account of Jones' death.

59. Martin, *Border Boss*, 125-28. These events are certainly in the Ranger romantic tradition. However, St.Leon's service record shows he was enlisted as a private on September 1, 1890, some two years earlier, with continuous service until he was killed in a saloon fight.

60. FB, *MR.* Monthly Return, Company D, June-July 1893. Hughes was the second Ranger promoted to captain in 1893; earlier on January 1, Jeff Rogers had been advanced to that rank and retained in command of Company E.

61. Van Oden, *Memoirs*, 58-59.

62. FB, *Muster and Pay Rolls*, Company E, September-November 1893. As late as 1899 the case was still open and the pay unclaimed.

63. FB, *MR.* Monthly Return, Company F, July 1893.

64. Based upon a newspaper clipping dated July 21, 1893, in FB, *Correspondence Files*.

65. Ibid., telegram, Musgrave to Mabry, July 22, 1893.

66. Ibid., telegram, Brooks to Mabry, July 22, 1893.

67. Ibid., Cunningham to Mabry, July 24, 1893.

68. Ibid., Hughes to Mabry, April 6, 1894, contains the official report of the incident. The *Memoirs* of Van Oden, 40-41, who was acquainted with both victims, also cover the shooting. He possessed the compassion to grieve for each man.

69. Van Oden, *Memoirs*, 67.

70. Paine, *McDonald*, 154-64, contains a good description of events and problems such as these.

71. Ibid., 165-75.

72. *RAG* 1895-96, 11.

73. FB, *Scout Reports*, Company E, February 1896.

74. *RAG* 1895-96, 10-12. Mabry's report in the *RAG* is the basis for most of this account. Being human, Mabry tended to emphasize

actions in which he played a role.

75. FB, *MR*. Monthly Returns, all companies, February 1896.

76. Sullivan, *Twelve Years*, 178-81.

77. FB, *Scout Reports*, Company E, February 1896.

78. Paine, *McDonald*, 194-98.

79. FB, *Scout Reports*, Company E, February 1896.

80. Paine, *McDonald*, 199-213; Sullivan, *Twelve Years*, 182-88. In many areas Sullivan agrees with Paine. At least he mentions McDonald in his account.

81. FB, *Correspondence Files*, McDonald to Mabry, April 4, 1896.

82. Sullivan, *Twelve Years*, 197-98.

83. Paine, *McDonald*, 224. Paine's account is on 221-42.

84. Both Sullivan and Paine mention the election of Neal and the settlement of other ex-Rangers in San Saba.

85. For example, see *RAG* 1895-96.

86. Ibid., 8-9.

87. FB, *MR*. Monthly Return, Company F, August 1896.

88. Ibid., Company D, September 1896; *Correspondence Files*, Hughes to Mabry, October 4, 1896.

89. *RAG* 1897-1898, 11.

90. Ibid.

91. Ibid., 13.

92. Ibid.

93. Paine, *McDonald*, 243-49.

94. *RAG* 1899-1900, 21.

95. Ibid., 22. Sergeant Dubose made a report of this incident to Adjutant General Scurry, March 28, 1899. This version is based on the *RAG* and the sergeant's report.

96. Paine, *McDonald*, 250-59.

97. *RAG* 1899-1900, 21-22.

98. Ibid., 22.

99. Ibid., 25.

100. Ibid., 32.

101. Ibid., 33.

102. Ibid., 22-23; Paine, *McDonald*, 260-62.

103. *RAG* 1899-1900, 23.

104. Ibid., 24.

105. Ibid., 24-25.

106. FB, *Correspondence Files*, G. Knight to Hughes, May 12, 1900.

107. FB, *MR*. Monthly Return, Company D, June 1900.

108. *RAG* 1899-1900, 26.

109. Ibid., 32.

110. Paine, *McDonald*, 261; *RAG* 1899-1900, 23.

111. *RAG* 1899-1900, 25.

112. Ibid., 23-24.

113. FB, General Order No.62, July 3, 1901.

CHAPTER 12
RANGER CAMP LIFE

1. FB, *Quarter Master Records*, Company D Ration Return, August 1874.

2. Ibid., Company E Ration Return, January 1881.

3. Durham, *Taming the Nueces Strip*, 13, 21.

4. Gillett, *Six Years*, 25-26.

5. Ibid., 55.

6. Roberts, *Woman's Reminiscences*, 26.

7. FB, *Correspondence Files*, Sergeant T. Harris to State of Texas, July 1898.

8. Ibid., Voucher of Sgt. Harris, Company B, August 1898.

9. Gillett, *Six Years*, 54.

10. Roberts, *Woman's Reminiscences*, 15.

11. Durham, *Taming the Nueces Strip*, 151-52.

12. FB, *Correspondence Files*, Special Order No.7, Company E, May 6, 1883.

13. Roberts, *Woman's Reminiscences*, 15.

14. Gillett, *Six Years*, 63.

15. Roberts, *Woman's Reminiscences*, 29.

16. Gillett, *Six Years*, 57.

17. FB, *Correspondence Files*, Kenney to Wilson, December 29, 1874.

18. Durham, *Taming the Nueces Strip*, 155.

19. Gillett, *Six Years*, 26-27.

20. Ibid., 54.

21. Haley, *Jeff Milton*, 39-40.

22. Roberts, *Woman's Reminiscences*, 29-30.

23. Gillett, *Six Years*, 54-55.

24. Van Oden, *Ranger's Diary*, 20.

25. Gillett, *Six Years*, 55-56; Aten, *Ranger Service*, 13-14; Paine, *McDonald*, 142-44.

Bibliography

Manuscript Sources

Texas State Library, Austin, Texas
 Ranger Papers are in the Archives and Information Services
 Division of the Texas State Library, Austin, Texas. These documents were originally part of the Adjutant General Office records, transferred to the State Library beginning in 1934,
 where they have undergone a lengthy period of conservation
 and refiling. Source materials used in this book were found in
 the following files:

 Adjutant General Records. This record group contains correspondence not found in specific files, listed below, as well as
 General Orders issued by the State Adjutant General.

  Frontier Forces:
   Frontier Forces Muster Rolls, 1870-1871
   Frontier Forces Correspondence, 1870-1871
   Frontier Battalion:
    Correspondence Files, 1874-1900
    Monthly Returns, 1874-1900
    Quarter Master Records, 1874-1900
    Muster and Pay Roll Records, 1874-1904.
  Special State Troops/Special Forces
    Correspondence Files, 1874-1880
    Monthly Returns, 1874-1880
    Muster and Pay Roll Records, 1874-1880
    Quarter Master Records, 1874-1880

 Ranger Reminiscences Files. Archives Division, Texas State Li-
 brary.
The L.H. McNelly Papers. The Center for American History, The
 University of Texas at Austin.
"Memoirs of J.S. McNeel, Jr." Typescript, unpublished, undated, pri-
 vate collection.

Printed Sources

"El Paso Troubles in Texas." *House Executive Document No. 93, Forty-
 Fifth Congress, Second Session, Serial No 1809.*

House Journal of the Twelfth Legislature, State of Texas, First Session. Austin: Tracy, Siemering & Co., State Journal Office, 1870.

Journal of the House of Representatives of the Twelfth Legislature. Part First. Austin: J.G. Tracy, State Printer, 1871.

Message of Gov. Edmund J. Davis on the State of Texas, Austin, January 10, 1871.

Report[s] of the Adjutant-General of the State of Texas, published by the State of Texas, 1870-1900.

Supplemental Report of the Adjutant General of the State of Texas, for the year 1874. Wm. Steele, Adjutant General. Houston: A.C. Gray, State Printer, 1874.

Adjutant General's Report, State of Texas, September 30, 1875.

Report of Maj. J.B. Jones, Commanding the Frontier Battalion, Texas State Troops, March, 1876. Houston: A.C. Gray, State Printer, 1876.

Special Report of the Adjutant-General of the State of Texas. September, 1884. Austin: E.W. Swindells, State Printer, 1884.

Texas Frontier Troubles. House of Representatives. Report No.343. 44th Congress, 1st Session.

Books and Articles

Anonymous, By a Citizen of Denton County, Texas, *Authentic History of Sam Bass and His Gang.* Denton, Texas: Monitor Job Office, 1878.

Anonymous, *Life and Adventures of Sam Bass, The Notorious Union Pacific and Texas Train Robber.* Dallas, Texas: Dallas Commercial Steam Print, 1878.

Aten, Ira. *Six and One Half Years in the Ranger Service.* Bandera, Texas: Frontier Times, 1945.

Baylor, George Wythe, edited by Jerry D. Thompson. *Into the Far, Wild Country.* El Paso: Texas Western Press, 1996.

Davis, Robert E., editor. *Texana* II (Spring 1964). Texian Press.

Day, Jack Hays. *The Sutton-Taylor Feud.* Privately printed, 1937.

Durham, George (as told to Clyde Wantland). *Taming the Nueces Strip: The Story of McNelly's Rangers.* Austin: University of Texas Press, 1962.

Fisher, O.C. *It Occurred in Kimble.* Houston, Texas: The Anson Jones Press, 1938.

Ford, John Salmon, edited by Stephen B. Oates. *Rip Ford's Texas.* Austin: University of Texas Press, 1963. Paperback 1987.

Gammell, H.P.N., ed. *The Laws of Texas,* VI, VIII. Austin: The Gammel Book Co., 1898.

Gillett, James B. *Six Years with the Texas Rangers 1875 to 1881.* 1921. Reprint. Lincoln and London: University of Nebraska Press, 1976.

Greene, A.C. *The Last Captive.* Austin: The Encino Press, 1972.

Haley, J. Evetts. *Jeff Milton: A Good Man with a Gun.* Norman: University of Oklahoma Press, 1948.

Hamilton, Allen Lee. *Sentinel of the Southern Plains.* Fort Worth: Texas Christian University Press, 1988.

Hardin, John Wesley. *The Life of John Wesley Hardin.* Seguin, Texas: Smith & Moore, 1896.

Haven, Charles T. and Frank A. Belden. *A History of the Colt Revolver.* New York: Bonanza Books, 1940.

Jennings, N.A. *A Texas Ranger.* 1899. Reprint. Dallas: Southwest Press, 1930.

Maltby, William Jeff. *Captain Jeff or Frontier Life in Texas with the Texas Rangers.* Colorado, Texas: Whipkey Printing Co., 1906.

Martin, Jack. *Border Boss: Captain John R. Hughes, Texas Ranger.* 1942. Reprint. Austin: State House Press, 1990.

McNeel, J.S. Jr., *Memoirs of J.S. McNeel, Jr.* Unpublished manuscript, typewritten, undated, provided by McNeel's grandson, Albert McNeel.

McNelly, Leander H. *Papers.* The Center for American History, The University of Texas at Austin.

Metz, Leon Claire. *John Selman, Texas Gunfighter.* New York: Hastings House, 1966.

Nunn, W.Curtiss. *Texas Under the Carpetbaggers.* Austin: University of Texas Press, 1962.

_____. "Eighty-Six Hours Without Water on the Texas Plains." *Southwestern Historical Quarterly* XLIII no.3 (January 1944).

Paine, Albert Bigelow. *Captain Bill McDonald, Texas Ranger.* 1909. Reprint. Austin: State House Press, 1986.

Rathjen, Frederick W. *The Texas Panhandle Frontier.* Austin: University of Texas Press, 1973.

Raymond, Dora. *Lee Hall of Texas.* Norman: University of Oklahoma Press, 1940.

Roberts, Dan W. *Rangers and Sovereignty* with Mrs. Dan W. Roberts, *A Woman's Reminiscences of Six Years in Camp with the Texas Rangers.* 1914. Reprint. Austin: State House Press, 1987.

Sheffy, L.F., editor. "The Arrington Papers." *Panhandle-Plains Historical Review,* vol.I, no.1 (1928). Canyon, Texas: Panhandle-Plains Historical Society.

Shipman, O.L. *Taming the Big Bend.* Privately printed, 1926. Austin, Texas: Von Boeckman-Jones Co., 1926.

Sinise, Jerry. *George Washington Arrington: Civil War Spy, Texas Ranger, Sheriff and Rancher, A Biography.* Burnet, Texas: Eakin Press, 1979.

_____. *Pink Higgins, The Reluctant Gunfighter and Other Tales of the Panhandle.* Quanah, Texas: Nortex Press, 1973.

Singletary, Otis. "The Texas Militia During Reconstruction." *Southwestern Historical Quarterly* LX No.1 (July 1956).

Smith, Diane Solether. *The Armstrong Chronicle.* San Antonio: Corona Publishing Co., 1986.

Sowell, A.J., *Early Settlers and Indian Fighters of Southwest Texas.* 1900. Reprint. Austin: State House Press, 1986.

_____, *Rangers and Pioneers of Texas.* 1884. Reprint. Austin: State House Press, 1991.

Strong, Henry W. *My Frontier Days & Indian Fights on the Plains of Texas.* Privately printed, undated.

Sullivan, W.J.L. *Twelve Years in the Saddle for Law and Order on the Frontiers of Texas.* 1909. Reprint. New York: Buffalo-Head Press, 1966.

Sutton, Robert C. *The Sutton-Taylor Feud.* Quanah, Texas: Nortex Press, 1974.

Utley, Robert M. *Fort Davis*. Washington, D.C.: National Park Service, 1965.

Van Oden, Alonzo, edited by Ann Jensen. *Texas Ranger's Diary & Scrapbook*. Dallas: The Kaleidograph Press, 1936.

Webb, Walter Prescott. *The Texas Rangers*. New York: Houghton Mifflin Company, 1935.

_____, editor in chief. *The Handbook of Texas*. Austin: The Texas State Historical Association, 1952.

Webster, Michael G. "Intrigue on the Rio Grande: The Rio Bravo Affair, 1875" *Southwestern Historical Quarterly* LXXIV no. 2 (October 1970).

Williamson, Harold F. *Winchester-The Gun that Won the West*. New York: A.S. Barnes and Company, Inc., 1952.

Winfrey, Dorman H. and James M. Day, editors. *The Indian Papers of Texas and the Southwest, 1825 to 1916*. Vol. IV. 1959-1961. Reprint. Austin: Pemberton Press, 1966.

Wister, Carl Coke. *Fort Griffin on the Texas Frontier*. Norman: University of Oklahoma Press, 1956.

Newspaper articles used as source materials for this book are cited individually in the notes.

Index